THE IROQUOIS IN THE WAR OF 1812

Until now, the story of Iroquois participation in the War of 1812 has not received detailed examination, and there have consequently been major gaps in our understanding of the Iroquois, their relations with Euroamerican society, and the course of the war itself. *The Iroquois in the War of 1812* proves that, in fact, the Six Nations' involvement was 'too significant to ignore.'

Carl Benn explores this involvement by focusing on Iroquois diplomatic, military, and cultural history during the conflict. He looks at the Iroquois's attempts to stay out of the war, their entry into hostilities, their modes of warfare, the roles they played in different campaigns, their relationships with their allies, and the effects that the war had on their society. He also details the military and diplomatic strength of the Iroquois during the conflict, despite the serious tensions that plagued their communities.

This account reveals how the British benefited more than the Americans from the contributions of their Iroquois allies, and underscores how important the Six Nations were to the successful defence of Canada. It will appeal to general readers in both Canada and the United States and will have relevance for students and scholars of military, colonial, and First Nations history.

CARL BENN is Curator of Military History at Heritage Toronto and author of *Historic Fort York, 1793–1993*.

The Iroquois
in the
War of 1812

CARL BENN

UNIVERSITY OF TORONTO PRESS
Toronto Buffalo London

970.3
17166
1998

© University of Toronto Press Incorporated 1998
Toronto Buffalo London
Printed in Canada

ISBN 0-8020-4321-6 (cloth)
ISBN 0-8020-8145-2 (paper)

Printed on acid-free paper

Canadian Cataloguing in Publication Data

Benn, Carl, 1953–
The Iroquois in the War of 1812

Includes bibliographical references and index.
ISBN 0-8020-4321-6 (bound)   ISBN 0-8020-8145-2 (pbk.)

1. Canada – History – War of 1812 – Participation,
Indian.*   2. Canada – History – War of 1812 – Indians.*
3. Iroquois Indians – Wars.*   4. Indians of North
America – Canada – Wars – 1763–1814.*   I. Title.

E99.I7B45 1998   971.03'4'0899755   C98-930484-1

This book has been published with the help of a grant from the Humanities and
Social Sciences Federation of Canada, using funds provided by the Social Sciences
and Humanities Research Council of Canada.

University of Toronto Press acknowledges the financial assistance to its publishing
program of the Canada Council for the Arts and the Ontario Arts Council.

To the memory of my grandmother
Effie Milloy Harvey Benn
Niagara 1899 – Toronto 1987

Contents

Illustrations follow page 82. Maps appear on pages xii and xiii.

Notes on Usage

As there is some debate on how First Nations people should be addressed these days, an explanation of my approach in *The Iroquois in the War of 1812* seems necessary. My main objective is to make this work as accessible as possible by employing terms that will be understood by the largest number of readers. Therefore, I refer to tribes by their common English-language designations (e.g., Seneca), and I use the European names of aboriginal people when they are more likely to be recognized than their native ones (e.g., Joseph Brant). I use the native designations for the Iroquois communities of Akwesasne, Kahnawake, and Kanesatake not only because they are better known in Canada today by their aboriginal titles, but also because these were the names their residents used in 1812, rather than the names St Regis, Caughnawaga, and Lac-des-Deux-Montagnes (or Oka) which dominate in the Euroamerican documents of the 1812 period. What now is the Six Nations Reserve near Brantford normally was called the Grand River Tract in 1812, and I have chosen to use that title as the more appropriate one for the time. Likewise, Tyendinaga near modern Belleville was known as a 'tract,' not a 'reserve.' The words 'nation' and 'tribe' are utilized interchangeably as was common among natives and non-natives in 1812, and phrasing such as 'the Iroquois in New York' is employed rather than 'the New York Iroquois' in recognition of aboriginal views of sovereignty.

I avoid the word 'Indian' except when quoting historical figures or when mentioning agencies such as the British Indian Department. Five centuries of ethnocentric use of this misnomer has twisted it to the point where it often conjures up inadequate sub- or super-human images of the 'drunken Indian' or 'noble ecologist' variety. Since aboriginal people are as diverse and complex as any other, I want to employ words that do not confine thought to stereotypes. However, the current substitutes – 'aboriginal' and 'native' – seem transitory and inadequate in the same way 'Amerindian' was a generation ago. To signify their limitations, I do not capitalize them, and I use them as parallels to two other problematic words, 'white' and 'black.' I do not use the term 'Native-Americans' because of its dissonance to Canadian ears and because its structure suggests that aboriginal people do not have an identity in North American history much different from immigrant groups such as Italian- or Irish-Americans. My preference has been to employ titles such as 'Onondagas' when historical records allow for definition, or to use names such as 'Six Nations' when the collective term is more appropriate. Sometimes my application of 'Iroquois' and 'Six Nations' is broader than normal because several communities in 1812 incorporated people who maintained distinct tribal identities outside of the Iroquois Confederacy. (An example would be the Delawares, who lived along the Grand River.) Historical records normally are too vague to distinguish these tribes from their neighbours, but my research suggests that their actions were substantially the same as those of the Iroquois in any given locality. Some people today feel uncomfortable with the word 'warrior,' but I use it because it was a term spoken with pride by natives in the colonial era and because it helps to signify the different social context in which aboriginal men served as combatants compared with their non-native contemporaries, whether regulars, volunteers, or militia. Likewise, the word 'chief' seems legitimate both for the period and to represent the distinct nature of aboriginal leadership in contrast to Euroamerican concepts of governance.

The word 'Euroamerican' in this book broadly encompasses the cultures and states of western Europe and the societies and polities that Europeans and their descendants created in North America. To assist readers in keeping track of opposing forces, I use Arabic numbers when referring to British regiments (e.g., 6th Foot) but write out the number when mentioning American units (e.g., Sixth Infantry). In most instances, it did not seem possible to be absolutely precise in such things as the size of the opposing forces or the numbers of casualties suffered because of temporary battle-induced desertions, poor records, and other problems. Therefore, I have usually rounded off figures from what I believe are the most credible statistics from the conflicting sources.

Acknowledgments

I would like to thank the people who helped me write *The Iroquois in the War of 1812*. My greatest debt is to the late Graeme Patterson of the Department of History at the University of Toronto, who introduced me to the historical study of native peoples, who encouraged me to undertake this project, and who helped me along in its earlier stages.

This work started out as a book-writing project in the 1980s, formulated as a military and material culture study inspired by my professional work as a museum curator. In 1990, while continuing to work full-time at my job, I enrolled as a part-time PhD student at York University, where the manuscript took a 'detour' to become a dissertation. This proved to be a most profitable diversion, because I benefited enormously from the advice of my supervisory team, consisting of three of Canada's most skilled historians, Ramsay Cook, John T. Saywell, and J.L. Granatstein. I am grateful to them and to the other faculty members in the Graduate Program in History who contributed to my development as a historian and who provided a problem-free, stimulating, and enjoyable educational experience. As well, I would like to thank Conrad Heidenreich and Ted Spence of York University, and Colin Read of the University of Western Ontario, who participated in my thesis defence and who raised questions and points that have helped improve this study.

Donald E. Graves, formerly of the Directorate of History at the Department of National Defence and now a historian in private practice, was particularly generous in commenting on the manuscript and in sharing his extensive research with me. I am also most grateful to the people who read different drafts and gave me the benefit of their critical thinking. They are: Gregory Evans Dowd of the University of Notre Dame, Brian Leigh Dunnigan of the William L. Clements Library at the University of

Michigan, Laurence M. Hauptman of the State University of New York at
New Paltz, Lieutenant-Colonel Joseph W.A. Whitehorne (U.S.A., retired),
Leo A. Johnson, Ann Joan Procyk, Stuart Sutherland, and the two anonymous reviewers associated with the progression of my work from manuscript to book at the University of Toronto Press.

Other people assisted me by sharing information and ideas, and I
would like to thank them sincerely. They are: José Brandão of the University of Western Michigan; Richard F. Cox of the United States National
Archives and Records Administration; Dennis Farmer of the Holland
Land Office Museum in Batavia, New York; Robert L. Fraser of the *Dictionary of Canadian Biography*; Dan Glenney of the Canadian War Museum;
Richard M. Gramly of the Buffalo Museum of Science and Technology;
Tom Hill and Sheila Staats of the Woodland Cultural Centre in Brant-
ford; J.C.H. King of the British Museum; Ken Lister and Trudy Nicks of
the Royal Ontario Museum; Bill Nesbitt of Dundurn Castle in Hamilton;
Donald B. Smith of the University of Calgary; Dean R. Snow of Pennsylva-
nia State University; Carolyn Strange and her staff at the Law Society of
Upper Canada Archives (she now is at the University of Toronto); Ron
Williamson of Archaeological Resources Incorporated; and Edward J.
Anderson, Chris Baker, James Elliott, Allan J. Ferguson, Adrian Foster,
Dennis Gannon, Richard Gerrard, Reg Good, Bill Gray, Fraser Harvey,
Lloyd Johnstone, Laurie Leclaire, Robert Malcomson, Robin May, Tom
Murison, Larry Ostola, Carolyn Podruchny, John Sugden, Wiley Sword,
Ian Vincent, the late Robert S. Allen, and the late Al Gamble. As well, I
would like to express my appreciation to the people who attend the
annual conference on Iroquois research in Rensselaerville, New York,
who, in papers and informal discussion, have helped me hone and
develop my understanding of Iroquois history.

Once the manuscript entered the production process, I incurred more
debts. The maps that grace this book are the creations of Byron Moldof-
sky. I would like to thank the staff of the University of Toronto Press, particularly Gerald Hallowell, Emily Andrew, Darlene Zeleney, and the
people behind the scenes at the Press for shepherding this work through
to publication. In addition, I would like to thank Henri Pilon for his ele-
gant and skilful copy-editing. Finally, I would like to acknowledge, with
gratitude, the Humanities and Social Sciences Federation of Canada,
which provided a publication grant through the Social Sciences and
Humanities Research Council of Canada.

THE IROQUOIS WORLD IN 1812

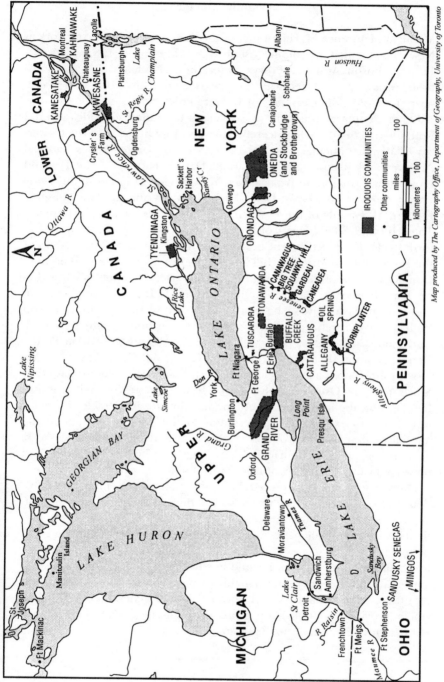

Map produced by The Cartography Office, Department of Geography, University of Toronto

IROQUOIS COMMUNITIES

• Other communities

100
miles
100
kilometres
0

CANADA

LOWER CANADA

KANESATAKE
Montreal
KAHNAWAKE
Chateauguay
Lacolle
AWESASNE
Plattsburgh
Lake Champlain
St Regis R
Ogdensburg
Crysler's Farm
St Lawrence R
Albany
Hudson R
Canajoharie
Schoharie

NEW YORK

ONEIDA (and Stockbridge and Brothertown)
ONONDAGA
Sackett's Harbor
Sandy Cr
Oswego
Kingston
TYENDINAGA
Rice Lake

CANADA

LAKE ONTARIO
Genesee R
CANAWAGUS
BIG TREE
SQUAWKY HILL
GARDEAU
CANEADEA
TONAWANDA
TUSCARORA
Buffalo
BUFFALO CREEK
OIL SPRING
Ft Niagara
Ft George
Ft Erie
CATTARAUGUS
ALLEGANY
CORNPLANTER

PENNSYLVANIA

Allegheny R

Lake Nipissing
Lake Simcoe
GEORGIAN BAY
Don R
York
Burlington
(Grand R) GRAND RIVER
Long Point
Presqu' Isle
Oxford
UPPER
Delaware
Moraviantown
Thames R

LAKE ERIE

LAKE HURON

St Joseph's
Ft Mackinac
Manitoulin Island
Lake St Clair
Detroit
Sandwich
Amherstburg
R Raisin
Frenchtown
Maume R
Ft Meigs
Ft Stephenson
Sandusky Bay
SANDUSKY SENECAS
↓ MINGOS

MICHIGAN

OHIO

Ottawa R

N

THE NIAGARA PENINSULA, 1812-1814

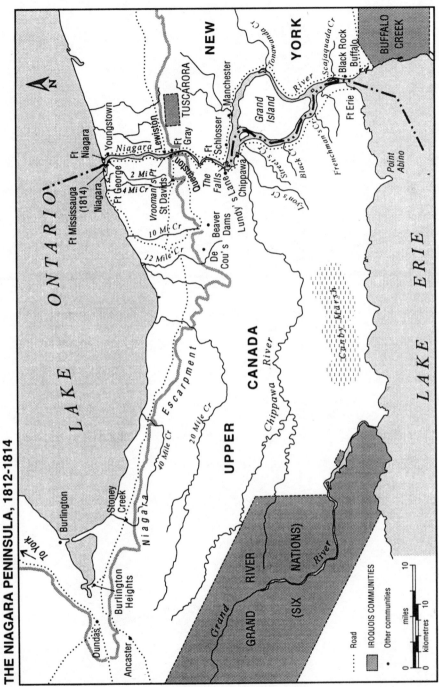

Map produced by The Cartography Office, Department of Geography, University of Toronto

LAKE ONTARIO

Burlington

Stoney Creek

Burlington Heights

Dundas

Ancaster

To York

N

Niagara

Ft Mississauga (1814)

Ft Niagara

Youngstown

Niagara

Ft George

2 Mi Pt

4 Mi Cr

Vrooman's
St Davids

Lewiston

Ft Gray

Queenston

The Falls

10 Mi Cr

Beaver Dams

Lundy's Lane

12 Mile Cr

De Cou's

Escarpment

40 Mile Cr

20 Mile Cr

UPPER CANADA

Chippawa River

GRAND RIVER

(SIX NATIONS)

Grand River

River

NEW

TUSCARORA

Manchester

Schlosser

Grand Island

Chippawa

Black

Street's Cr

Niagara River

Tonawanda Cr

Scajaquada Cr

Black Rock

Buffalo

Ft Erie

Frenchman's Cr

Lyon's Cr

Point Abino

YORK

BUFFALO CREEK

Cranby Marsh

LAKE ERIE

······· Road

IROQUOIS COMMUNITIES

• Other communities

miles   0   10
kilometres 0   10

THE IROQUOIS IN THE WAR OF 1812

Introduction

The main theatre of operations in the War of 1812 was the Great Lakes–St Lawrence border between the United States and British North America. The central point of confrontation within that region, geographically and militarily, was the Niagara Peninsula, which separates Lake Erie from Lake Ontario. It was here that the opposing armies shed the most blood, and it was here that Iroquois diplomats and warriors played their largest roles in the struggle that engulfed the United States, Great Britain, her colonies, and forty or more of the aboriginal nations in eastern North America. Despite the significance of Iroquois participation in the conflict, historians have not published detailed studies on the Six Nations story in the War of 1812. This contrasts markedly with the extensive efforts made to understand the conflict as it affected the western tribes, such as the Ottawas, Shawnees, and Potawatomis. This lack of attention does not come as a surprise, because historians who study aboriginal–white military strife tend to focus their efforts on contested 'frontier' regions. By about 1800 the 'sharp end' of the frontier had moved west, beyond the land where the vast majority of Iroquois lived. At the outbreak of hostilities their homes were the reservations, tracts, and missions that had been established through negotiations between whites and natives, beginning in the mid–seventeenth century but occurring mainly between 1784 and 1797, when the Six Nations reeled under the weight of the disasters of the American Revolution and the crises that beset them in its aftermath. Yet the War of 1812 was a critical event in Iroquois history. Furthermore, in the broader context of that conflict, the Six Nations still possessed enough power to make a meaningful impact on the course of the war. Thus, the lack of scholarly attention has left an important gap in the literature of both the Iroquois and the War of 1812. My objective is to help close this gap by presenting the Iroquois story between 1812 and 1815, based on an analysis of military, political, diplomatic, social, and material cultural sources.

Of course, my efforts are not completely without published precedents. While the Iroquois in the war have never received as detailed a study as this one, their involvement has been included to a limited degree in histories of the Six Nations, in biographies, and in general studies of the conflict itself. Yet there are only two article-length works, by George Stanley and Arthur C. Parker, in which scholars address the subject of Iroquois participation in the conflict as their primary focus. A paper I published drew on military history and material culture to examine Iroquois combat at a tactical level between 1812 and 1814. A fourth effort, by Charles M. Johnston, discussed the tensions between two important individuals associated with the Six Nations of the Grand River during the crisis of 1812–15, John Norton and William Claus. [1] In addition, there are four books of published primary documents on the Iroquois at the time of the war for which historians have written competent introductions. [2] I trust that the pages below will demonstrate that there is far more to the Iroquois story than the articles and introductions could have covered adequately.

I have concluded that the motivations behind Iroquois actions at the village and tribal levels between 1812 and 1815, the ways they addressed external and internal tensions within their communities, and the factors that played into individual decision making generally followed indigenous practices that had been modified, but not subdued, during the massive upheavals of two hundred years of contact with whites. In foreign relations, the Iroquois participated as allies, not subjects, of Great Britain and the United States. Naturally, their objectives often conflicted with those of their Euroamerican partners, thus engendering a troubled wariness between alliance members, as had been normal in the history of native–white coalitions. Within the world of the Iroquois, shared identities, needs, and a constant back-and-forth of personal interaction encouraged people from the different tracts, reservations, missions, and villages to consult, as in times past, with each other independently of their other alliances in order to maintain as much unity as possible and to mitigate the negative consequences of following opposing courses of action. As was traditional, however, individual communities ultimately were responsible for their own foreign affairs and frequently went their separate ways.

Within particular villages, the resolution of civil strife took place inside a functioning polity which incorporated a stunningly wide range of opinion and behaviour, as had been the case since at least the second quarter of the seventeenth century. To try to patch over potentially disastrous divisions and keep their communities together, the Iroquois employed a number of such ancient practices as reciprocal obligation, restraint (both personal and cultural, but rarely coercive), consensus (often expressed outwardly if not always accepted inwardly), and an inclusiveness in decision making, which incorporated a large percentage of the residents of any given village. While these practices generally succeeded, failures did sometimes occur. As in older times, the Iroquois typically addressed breakdowns through the exercise of individual freedom. This allowed people to move away or otherwise separate themselves from their rivals while they awaited some change in circumstances through which they could be reintegrated into the community or could advance their programs over those of their opponents. Because personal freedom was respected and because one group of Iroquois could not legitimately force compliance on another, reconciliation between opposing parties could take place relatively easily once conditions changed. The major exception in the twenty-one Iroquois territories in 1812 was Akwesasne on the St Lawrence River. There, the conflict's wounds did not heal and a state of near civil war endured for some years after the return of peace elsewhere in 1815. At the personal level, warriors carried a strong and longstanding legacy into the battlefield with them, as demonstrated by the differences between native and white modes of war and by the particular objectives warriors set for themselves in combat. Other individuals in Iroquois communities, such as the peace chiefs and the clan matrons, also fulfilled roles that plainly would have been recognizable to their ancestors two centuries earlier.

In terms of aboriginal–white relations, I believe this book will show that while both white powers benefited from diplomatic and military assistance from the Iroquois, the British profited from their native alliances more than the Americans did. This happened partly because King George III had far more aboriginal allies than President Madison, given that the British and most First Nations found common cause in defending themselves against an expanding United States. Yet beyond this obvious point, an important reason why the British derived greater benefit was that, contrary to popular mythology, the king's forces were more competent in light infantry and forest warfare than those of the American republic. As the 1813 Niagara campaign clearly demonstrated, this advantage allowed the British to cooperate with their native allies in the field more effectively and thereby achieve their combat objectives more frequently. Also, as revealed in the same campaign, British commanders felt less ambivalence towards employing aboriginal combatants than their American counterparts did, which allowed them to realize more of the potential inherent in having native warriors fight alongside their own troops. This was fortunate for the British, particularly at such pivotal actions as Queenston Heights, Beaver Dams, the blockade of Fort George, and Crysler's Farm, because Iroquois warriors from the Grand River, Tyendinaga, Akwesasne, Kanesatake, and Kahnawake proved to be formidable combatants who made substantial and meaningful contributions in thwarting American offensive efforts against Canada.

I also trust that my work will establish that the Iroquois still possessed enough diplomatic and military strength in 1812 to influence their British and American allies with some hope of securing their objectives of preserving their territory, culture, and independence despite the disasters of the previous two hundred years. Tragically, Iroquois influence in this last major conflict in the history of the Great Lakes region contrasts strikingly with the conditions of the post-1815 period. After the return of peace, massive white immigration and, in the United States, a large-scale eviction of natives to the west, saw most of the power the Iroquois possessed in 1812 evaporate as they dropped to a demographically fragile status in a sea of increasingly unsympathetic, self-confident, and land-hungry Euroamericans. This shift meant that white authorities no longer had to consider the objectives of the Iroquois when aboriginal needs conflicted with their own ambitions. Therefore, the participation and sacrifice of the Iroquois during the three years of hostilities ultimately only addressed internal issues and forged pride among many of their people. Their efforts proved to be of small benefit in the post-war years in stopping their former allies, who sought to exploit them for economic gain, deny them their independence, and assimilate them into the Euroamerican world on white terms. The chief exception to this sad story was that, as a result of the successful defence of Canada – a success achieved in part through Iroquois efforts – the Iroquois in British North America were not evicted to the west and were not excluded from the broader society's war-generated patriotism as much as were their relatives in the United States.

Archival records present problems for anyone attempting to understand the Iroquois in the early nineteenth century. There are only a few written records produced by literate natives, the voices of oral tradition are comparatively quiet for 1812, and material culture sources are limited by both the small quantity of surviving examples and the narrow range of questions that can be asked of such sources.[3] Euroamerican society produced the bulk of the surviving documents and imposed the gloss of an alien culture's priorities and prejudices. I have tried to mitigate the effects of Euroamerican bias, mainly by applying what other scholars have taught me about aboriginal societies and by trying to read through white documents for the Iroquois perspective. Nonetheless, I must assume that I have not been completely successful. Furthermore, the archival record is even limited in telling us about the white side of the Iroquois–Euroamerican relationship. To cite but one example of many outwardly promising archival collections that disappointed me, the correspondence of the American secretary of war on 'Indian Affairs' surprisingly preserved only a very small quantity of useful data on the Iroquois or on their associations with whites during the conflict.[4] The weakness of the archival record created a number of additional problems. While it is possible, for instance, to learn much about what happened among the Grand River Iroquois from the scattered historical sources, these records also raise frustrating questions that cannot be answered for want of information. Women, for example, played major roles in Iroquois politics but records about them for 1812 are very thin, especially in comparison with eighteenth-century sources. I tried to compensate for this by drawing on general ethnohistorical information and by recognizing that discussions over policy and other matters among the Six Nations included women. Therefore, my use of such terms as 'Onondagas' in these contexts obviously should be read to include women. In other cases, little exists to tell us what happened in some communities, such as among the Iroquois in Ohio, and they necessarily must figure lightly in this work. Fortunately, the Grand River Tract in Upper Canada, on the north shore of Lake Erie, which included people from all of the Iroquois nations and which was one of the communities most affected by the conflict, has the best documented history. Therefore, its story predominates in my attempt to understand the Iroquois presence in the war.

The most conspicuous exception to the dominance of Euroamerican records is the *Journal of Major John Norton*, a fascinating memoir written by a Mohawk over several years, between about 1810 and 1816, and perhaps the best memoir produced by a veteran of the war. Naturally, Norton's work features strongly in this book. While all autobiographical stories are subjective and all historical documents require close scrutiny, in his memoir John Norton fortunately was a comparatively reliable witness. I found few discrepancies of any substance whenever there were other eyewitness accounts to compare to his version of events. Like his biographer, Carl F. Klinck, I found Norton's manuscript to be 'carefully factual.'[5] Furthermore, Norton's descriptions of incidents in letters he wrote at the time the events occurred agree with those in the journal, which helps confirm the reliability of the manuscript.[6] Something else makes Norton's journal valuable: although he intended to publish it, he never completed the project. What survives, therefore, is particularly useful because neither he nor an editor cut out or massaged all of the problematic parts or compressed his detailed draft for the reading public. Thus the journal is more insightful than a polished publication would have been in telling us about Norton's thinking and about events in his orbit.[7] Of course, his work is not perfect. Norton sometimes left out details he did not like. He also struggled bitterly against his enemies in the British Indian Department and within the Grand River community, so researchers need to be especially careful when reading his version of those conflicts.

One might question how 'Mohawk' Norton's account really is, since he had spent his formative years in the United Kingdom and had Iroquoian Cherokee and Scottish parents. However, the Mohawks adopted him into their nation in the 1790s and his integration was so successful that he rose to become a diplomatic and war chief. Since at least the early eighteenth century, Iroquois society had a strong multiracial quality. Norton, as half white, fitted into that multiracial tradition, and, as half native, into the much older one whereby other aboriginal people were adopted as full members in Iroquois tribes.[8] By the Mohawk standards of the period, John Norton was a Mohawk. We would be arrogant if we did not accept their definition of who could be a member of their society. While some of his adversaries used his origins to defame him (in much the same way as Major-General Sir Roger Sheaffe's American birth was a target for his enemies in Upper Canada), that kind of prejudice does not detract from the legitimacy of Norton's 'citizenship' in the Mohawk nation.[9] (Another prominent Iroquois chief in the War of 1812 was Colonel Louis, or Atiatoharongwen, of Akwesasne, the son of a black man and an Abenaki woman. In addition, one of the most famous Mohawk chiefs of the eighteenth century, Hendrick or Theyanoguin, was an adopted Mahican.)[10] We should keep in mind, however, that individuals in Iroquois communities had greater or lesser contact with Euroamericans and felt different degrees of comfort in associating with whites and their ways. While John Norton is representative of a legitimate Mohawk perspective in the tradition of Joseph Brant, his place on the spectrum fell at the end of close contact and appreciation of Euroamerican society. Therefore, his views differed significantly from other, equally legitimate opinions within the Six Nations.

A second principal source of documentation that preserves aboriginal voices in this period is the council minutes from meetings among different native communities and between Iroquois and Euroamericans. However, people working for white agencies usually made the transcriptions and sometimes altered the words of the aboriginal speakers in translating speeches into English, frequently by accident but occasionally on purpose. Also, the surviving minutes obviously do not include all the speeches given at a particular council. Therefore, we must assume that important addresses did not make it into the archival record, especially as whites did not always know which Iroquois leaders best represented their communities and therefore which ones were to be taken most seriously. For their part, native orators chose their words carefully to achieve particular ends, and so their speeches, even when translated well, do not necessarily represent straightforward aboriginal opinion. Finally, as in any society, the real business of a council might take place privately, between formal sessions, and records rarely survive of what transpired during those discussions. At the Treaty of Big Tree in 1797, for instance, the Seneca orator Red Jacket denounced American attempts to purchase his people's territory in formal daytime council sessions, but by night sent messengers to tell the Americans to ignore his speeches because he only made them for show and in fact wanted to sell land. [11]

Despite all the limitations facing historians, the participation of the Six Nations in the War of 1812 is too significant to ignore. I hope this work will begin to do justice to the story of the Iroquois as well as open debate and create interest to encourage further study.

1

Survival:
The Iroquois to 1812

What has happened to us is calamitous! There is now no Long House where you and I can safely tell each other our fears ... You, who went away, should reconsider the policy of the Long House ... so that all our people will live again upon our former firesides and plantations, and smoke will rise again from our former cabins and all will enjoy the lordship of their lands again.

Little Abraham, a Mohawk, speaking to Iroquois refugees at Fort Niagara, 1780[1]

When French explorers began to penetrate the St Lawrence–Great Lakes region at the beginning of the seventeenth century, they met two aboriginal cultural groups, the Algonkians and the Iroquoians. Algonkians, such as the Nipissings and Ottawas, who lived in what is now central Ontario, were largely hunter-gatherers who moved through their territories in small groups on a seasonal cycle to exploit the hunting, fishing, wild rice, and other opportunities the environment provided for their subsistence. Iroquoians, such as the people of the Huron Confederacy near Georgian Bay, differed significantly from the northern Algonkians. They lived in semi-permanent, village-based societies where horticulture provided the bulk of their food. A typical Iroquoian village in the early 1600s had a number of large, bark-covered longhouses, each of which was home for several families. Palisades often protected the village, beyond which lay the community's cultivated fields. Several hundred people regularly lived in one settlement, and some housed as many as two thousand souls. The inhabitants of an Iroquoian village moved to a new location every generation or so after their fields became sterile, as convenient supplies of firewood became scarce, and as the longhouses deteriorated. Women grew the crops, gathered firewood, wild foods, and medicines, made pottery and other household items, fulfilled domestic duties, and raised the children. Men cleared the forest for planting, built longhouses and palisades, hunted and fished, traded, engaged in diplomacy, and made war. [2]

The Iroquois were a major sub-group of the Iroquoian peoples. Like the Huron tribes, they lived in a confederacy that had formed over a period of time. Theirs consisted of five nations, the Mohawk, Oneida, Onondaga, Cayuga, and Seneca. They likely had begun to construct their league in the fifteenth century, at about the same time these tribes had themselves formed when a number of closely related groups coalesced into nations within relatively small geographic areas. The twenty thousand or more people of the Five Nations at the time of European contact occupied 'Iroquoia' in what today is New York State, between Schoharie Creek on the east and the Genesee River on the west. According to tradition, they confederated to form the League of the Iroquois (or Houdenosaunee) primarily to end warfare among themselves following the mission of a prophet known as 'The Peacemaker.' This man had a dream in which he saw a huge tree connecting the earth to the realm of the Master of Life in the sky. In interpreting the dream, he proclaimed that the tree represented the sisterhood of the Iroquoian peoples, and that its roots were the five tribes who he said were destined to form a 'Great Peace' which ultimately would incorporate all peoples. [3]

Europeans who encountered the league in the early seventeenth century thought of the Five Nations as a united and powerful force. The Iroquois themselves cultivated this image of confederated strength in their diplomatic, trade, and military relations with whites and other natives. In reality, this unity was exaggerated, partly because the main function of the league was intertribal peace among its members based on spiritual (rather than political) values, not a unified foreign policy, and partly because nations did not give up sovereignty to the league. The consequence was that member tribes sometimes undermined fellow confederates in external relations or even fell into dangerous conflicts with one another, despite the efforts of the leaders of the Five Nations to maintain unanimity through consensus politics at the great league council in Onondaga, Iroquoia's geographic centre. Within tribes, distinct communities exercised so much independence that it was at the village rather than the national level that the Iroquois often made their most critical decisions concerning outsiders. Even there, important decision-making might drop to the sub-village plane because extended families (or lineages) regularly considered a problem first before an issue worked its way up to the clan, and then to the village before continuing on to national and confederacy councils. When the confederacy or national councils were the first to address an issue and arrive at a consensus, the agreement had to be ratified by the lower levels to take effect, thus preserving the independence of the confederacy's subunits. Decision-making typically stopped at the level where people could not arrive at a consensus, thus curtailing unity, and hence action, at the last point where agreement had been reached. For reasons of trade, geography, defence, and relations with neighbouring non-Iroquois groups, consensus-building often could not transcend village polities where the possibility of reaching an accord in foreign affairs was greatest.[4]

Iroquois people, living in a comparatively non-hierarchical society, shared power and decision-making widely. There was no head chief to impose policy. First lineages and then clans within a community typically discussed issues among themselves in an attempt to arrive at an agreement. At the village level, hereditary peace chiefs, who represented the clans' views and whose status was reinforced by their succession to a myth-ologically significant office, presided over local politics along with the community's elders, wise men, and other people who commanded a fol-lowing of some sort, but none of these people had much power beyond their consultative and persuasive skills to win others over to their leader-ship. The hereditary chiefs also served as national and confederacy chiefs. They were advised by elected pine tree chiefs who won their stand-ing in the community through their personal merits as politicians, ora-tors, and diplomats. Talented pine tree chiefs sometimes overshadowed the hereditary chiefs, particularly as time passed and the population losses and other upheavals of the colonial period weakened older social structures.

The hereditary and pine tree chiefs of a village often found themselves in conflict with another body of leaders, the war chiefs. The latter, who usually attained their positions through exemplary behaviour on the bat-tlefield, had objectives that frequently clashed with those of the peace chiefs, especially because decisions to go to war often came from within families and lineages to address family concerns rather than at the village, national, or confederacy level in response to larger challenges to the pol-ity. The leading women in the villages, as the heads of lineages, exerted their influence through a variety of means, from using their right to appoint, chastise, and dethrone (or 'dehorn') peace chiefs from among a group of eligible hereditary candidates, to demanding that war chiefs avenge the deaths of family members, and to pressing their views in councils, particularly at the lineage and village levels, either directly or through male representatives. Women with less power could subvert their rivals in other ways, such as by refusing to perform gender-based tasks that otherwise would support the efforts of those they opposed, or by lobbying during breaks in formal council sessions. Beyond these limits to centralized leadership, the clans, families, and independent individuals who made up Iroquois society acknowledged no higher human authority than that of their own will, although there were constraints that inhibited the unrestrained exercise of a self-determined decision. These included the various ways the Iroquois tried to counter dissent by uniting people through clan and other affiliations, by assessing what was possible in a given situation, by custom or religious belief, by the view that disunity endangered spiritual power, by the strong sense of reciprocal obligation, and by sensitivity to public opinion.[5]

An important consequence of this freedom and the integration of so many people in decision-making was that the Iroquois responded to external threats with tremendous diversity and fluidity as crises ebbed and flowed through their villages. Yet this fluidity could be a strength rather than a weakness since communities often divided into parties. The party 'in opposition' might assume the leadership in a situation where the policies of the side that had prevailed encountered serious difficulties, and party divisions allowed some leaders to continue negotiations with enemies, even in wartime, for both their own and their people's benefit. Encompassing a wide range of opinion within a framework of consensus was possible, partly because people could outwardly agree to a decision they did not like but limit their commitment to it and its consequences while they waited for a change which might favour their own views, and partly because those who decided to stand proudly by their opposition had the right to be respected as a result of the importance attached to personal freedom. Sometimes, however, communities split up during periods of intense disagreement. As well, some traditional spiritual practices allowed the Iroquois to step outside the normal bounds of restraint and reciprocal obligation in order to release the inevitable private stresses that built up within villages, thus helping to defuse potentially grave tensions.[6]

The two centuries that followed the league's first direct encounters with Europeans were marked by almost constant threats to its survival. The Iroquois confronted these challenges by exploiting divisions among neighbouring whites and natives skilfully, by warring, negotiating, and trading with vigour, by adopting large numbers of prisoners, refugees, and immigrants to replenish their population base, and by encouraging other hard-pressed native groups to resettle near them under their suzerainty. Their survival as a people marked their success, unlike most other Iroquoians, such as the Hurons to the north, the Kahkwas to the west, and the Susquehannocks to the south, who either disappeared or became ghostly shadows of their former glory, often as a consequence of hostility from the Five Nations. However, the ongoing integration of much of the confederacy's trade, diplomatic, and military endeavours into the Euroamerican world weakened its internal social order, increased its vulnerability to white manipulation, and restricted its opportunities to resist unwanted intrusions.[7]

For the Iroquois, like all native peoples facing the Euroamerican challenge, the most fundamental threat after population loss (largely caused by European disease) was the alienation of their land. Far to the south, in North Carolina, the Iroquoian Tuscaroras reeled under these twin assaults. In the second decade of the eighteenth century they fled north to Iroquoia as refugees. In the early 1720s they became the sixth nation of the confederacy. Within Iroquoia itself, land losses, though disturbing, were relatively small until the 1780s. Dutch and English settlers began to acquire Mohawk and Oneida lands in eastern Iroquoia during the seventeenth century, and in the 1720s the British and French established rival forts on the shores of Lake Ontario at Oswego and Niagara. After the fall of New France and the emergence of more severe settlement and other pressures from the British Atlantic seaboard colonies, many native people, especially to the west and south of Iroquoia, rose against the white population in the Pontiac War of 1763–6. Some Senecas and other people in Iroquoia supported the nativist cause while some Mohawks aided the British in suppressing the revolt. The British punished the Senecas for their hostility by taking away a strip of land along the Niagara River to secure communications to Detroit and the west.[8]

Yet the British made concessions that seemed to provide some security for the future of the Six Nations in the Royal Proclamation of 1763 and in the Treaty of Fort Stanwix of 1768. (Fort Stanwix was on the site of today's Rome, New York.) The proclamation and the treaty attempted to halt westward settlement (at a boundary that ran roughly southeast from Oneida Lake in New York to the Pennsylvania border and, after that, southwest to and then along the Ohio River), primarily by excluding everyone but the Crown from acquiring native lands north and west of these borders. Iroquois holdings east of this boundary also were protected. Thus, on paper at least, imperial authorities secured most of Iroquoia for the Six

Nations and shut out the old trinity of troublemakers, consisting of illegal squatters, greedy speculators, and corrupt colonial officials. Responsibility for this policy rested in part with Sir William Johnson, London's superintendent of the Iroquois and other northern aboriginal peoples, who himself had acquired large expanses of Mohawk land and who lived in baronial splendour at Johnstown, NY). Sir William thought the new boundary would last for decades and thereby bring peace to the frontier. He believed that secure borders would allow the white side of the treaty line to fill with so many people that the tribes would have no choice but to refrain from hostilities because war would be suicidal. As well, a controlled border would prevent whites from encroaching on aboriginal territory and thereby eliminate the need for natives to use violence to preserve their homelands in the first place. At the same time, Johnson assumed firm borders would give native societies the long period of time they would need to adapt to white ways so they could afford to give up most of their territories when future generations of settlers needed them. [9] This was about the most sympathy aboriginal people could expect from senior white officials in the mid–eighteenth century.

The population of Iroquoia at the time of the Treaty of Fort Stanwix stood at seventy-five hundred Iroquois and about eight hundred other people (mainly Nanticokes, Tutelos, and Delawares) who had sought refuge among the Six Nations from the struggles for control of their homes to the south and east. So large were Iroquois losses and so great was the adoption process over the period of contact that the adopted individuals (native, white, and black), their descendants, and the off-spring of mixed unions integrated within the Six Nations outnumbered the 'pure' Iroquois. [10]

Like other aboriginals, many Six Nations' people had left their home-lands to escape the conflicts of the seventeenth and eighteenth centuries. Some, especially Mohawks but also other Iroquois and some Algonkians, had allied themselves to the French and had begun moving to Roman Catholic missions near Montreal in the 1660s. By the 1750s there were four such settlements: Kahnawake, Kanesatake, Akwesasne, and Oswe-gatchie (now Ogdensburg, NY). Collectively, they, along with settlements located downriver of Montreal and dominated by Abenakis, Micmacs, and Hurons, formed the Seven Nations of Canada. In the mid–eighteenth century the Seven Nations numbered thirty-three hundred people, of whom about half were Iroquois. Another major migration began in the 1730s, when Iroquois and others in New York moved westward to Ohio. Emigrants from the Seven Nations and elsewhere joined them, and a new Iroquois nation, the Mingo, formed over subsequent decades. After the American Revolution, other people, mainly Cayugas, moved to Ohio to form another tribe, the Sandusky Senecas. Like the Seven Nations, the Mingos and Sandusky Senecas lived independently of the Iroquois Confederacy.[11]

While the people of Iroquoia had become reliant on trade with whites and had suffered from a significant population loss, they generally enjoyed a higher standard of living than their closest white neighbours in the years immediately following the 1768 Treaty of Fort Stanwix. Furthermore, they maintained most of their traditional values and enjoyed their freedom at the personal, village, national, and confederacy levels. Yet serious irritants continued to plague them, with colonists ignoring the restraints imposed by London and with ineffective and under-resourced British officials watching helplessly from the sidelines. George Washington was typical of large-scale colonial speculators in his dismissal of the imperial regulations that stood in the way of the fortune he was to make from seizing native lands.[12] To him, the Royal Proclamation was only a 'temporary expedient to quiet the minds of the Indians' until he, his business associates, and others could profit by accumulating aboriginal territory.[13] In 1774 Virginians, in an attempt to grab native land, invaded the territory to the south of Iroquoia in a brief campaign known as Lord Dunmore's War. Individual Iroquois, mainly Senecas and Cayugas, joined the Shawnees, Delawares, Mingos, and others against the Virginians. The Six Nations collectively considered a widespread strike on white settlements, but ultimately decided against war, primarily because of disputes between themselves and the Shawnees over the leadership of aboriginal affairs. (After the Iroquois had sold much of the Shawnee hunting ground in Kentucky in 1768, claiming suzerainty over them, the Shawnees attempted to organize an Ohio–region confederacy in opposition to the Iroquois Confederacy to undo the consequences of the actions of the Six Nations.)[14] Then, in 1775, far greater perils to Iroquois society emerged when British regulars and colonial militiamen opened fire on each other at Lexington and Concord.

The Six Nations initially tried to remain neutral at the outbreak of the American Revolution, although some people could not resist the opportunity to take up arms. Various Mohawk and Seven Nations warriors joined the loyalist cause while Oneida war parties sided with the revolutionaries in the early stages of the conflict. However, most of the generally pro-loyalist Mohawks felt constrained from acting because of the threat posed by their revolutionary neighbours, who both distrusted them and coveted their prosperous farms. For the majority of the other members of the Iroquois league, a white civil war seemed unrelated to their own interests so long as they could continue living unmolested and trading as they had before. Nonetheless, it became increasingly difficult to remain neutral as warriors wanted to prove themselves in combat, as loyalists and revolutionaries pressured the Six Nations to join their respective causes, and as Crown and rebel supporters contended for control of the territories immediately adjacent to Iroquoia. In January 1777, at the very time the league was struggling with how it should respond to the worsening conflict, an epidemic killed three important peace chiefs and dozens of other people at Onondaga. This crisis brought the already strained business of the confederacy to a halt as the Iroquois 'covered' their central symbol of unity, their great council fire, until new chiefs could be 'raised up' to replace those who had died. National and village councils filled the political void, and the arguments of the war chiefs attracted increased support. Some people with close connections to the rebel cause, including significant numbers of Oneidas and Tuscaroras, sided with the revolutionaries who might, however, represent a serious threat to native land holdings if they won their independence. More logically, the Mohawks, Cayugas, and Senecas generally allied themselves to the loyalists, who, if they triumphed, probably were more likely to affirm the 1768 border and the older forms of white–native relations, which, though far from perfect, were more attentive to aboriginal interests. The Onondagas split into pro-rebel, pro-loyalist, and neutralist parties. However, support for the opposing sides or for neutrality among the Six Nations as a whole varied considerably from one year to the next during the conflict. [15]

Within months of the breakdown of neutralist leadership, pro-loyalist Iroquois killed, and were killed by, pro-rebel Iroquois at the battle of Oriskany (near today's Rome, NY). In 1779 revolutionary armies, commanded by Major-General John Sullivan, invaded Iroquoia and burned most of the villages and rich farmlands, including those of neutral communities. The rebels hoped their campaign would knock the Crown-allied Iroquois out of the conflict and thereby relieve the serious disruptions that Six Nations raiders had been inflicting on the revolutionary war effort. While Sullivan's campaign was bleakly successful in destroying Iroquois property, the people themselves escaped in advance of the invaders. Those allied to the loyalists, though weakened, were not cowed into submission. Enraged by what had happened to their homes, they fought on, bringing death and destruction to their enemies until the end of hostilities. During these desperate years, a great many Iroquois fled to revolutionary or loyalist strongholds on the east and west fringes of Iroquoia to live miserably in squalid refugee camps. By 1783 the Six Nations population had declined sharply from what it had been before the war because of battle losses, disease, starvation, and the privations and social disintegration inherent in living in the environment of a gruesome and cruel civil war.[16]

In 1781 the loyalist cause suffered a fatal blow when Lord Charles Cornwallis surrendered his army at Yorktown in Virginia to an allied revolutionary and French force commanded by George Washington and the Comte de Rochambeau. In the 1783 Treaty of Paris a war-weary Britain recognized American independence and established a boundary – roughly today's Canadian–American border – between the new republic and the remnant of British North America. This border was an abomination for most natives. Despite the disasters of the conflict, the tribes and their Crown allies controlled most of the territory north of the 1768 treaty line at the end of hostilities. Therefore, the aboriginal peoples could not understand why Britain had transferred sovereignty over their lands to the Americans. They felt betrayed, knowing that the floodgates of hostile settlement had been opened as surely as George Washington's vision had replaced the somewhat more palatable one of Sir William Johnson.[17]

British authorities on the frontier tried to repair the harm done at the negotiating table to their native alliances by refusing to evacuate the American side of the Great Lakes frontier. To demonstrate the continuing strength of the Crown in the region, to preserve the Montreal-centred fur trade to the southwest, and to protect the refugee loyalist settlements in Canada from vengeful retribution by natives, the British violated the Treaty of Paris by keeping troops on American soil at such posts as Oswego, Niagara, and Detroit. British Indian Department officials operated out of these 'Western Posts' in an attempt to restore good relations with the tribes. As the 1780s passed they succeeded in improving their stature with the aboriginal peoples, partly because of shared interests but mainly because American behaviour towards the tribes proved to be so hostile that the natives had little choice but to turn to the British for whatever support they could get in their struggles with the United States.[18]

The British also offered land in Canada and financial compensation to their old allies, and many people in Iroquoia consequently crossed the border. John Deserontyon led one hundred Mohawks to the Bay of

Quinte in 1784. As the eighteenth century drew to a close the people of the new community of Tyendinaga (or Deseronto) separated from the league and went their own way under non-hereditary leaders. Another eighteen hundred people followed Mohawk peace chief Henry Tekariho-gen (or Dekarihoga) and war chief Joseph Brant to the Grand River on the north shore of Lake Erie. Although Mohawks and Cayugas were the most numerous, people from all of the Six Nations settled on the Grand River Tract, as did some of the Delawares, Nanticokes, Tutelos, Creeks, and Cherokees who had lived in Iroquoia before the revolution. Most settled in tribal villages along the river in a kind of abbreviated version of the old Iroquois Confederacy that once had spanned so much of New York.[19]

Crown officials purchased the Grand River lands from the Algonkian Mississaugas partly in response to a request made by Brant (who may have acted under instruction from Tekarihogen). Brant wanted the refugee Iroquois to settle close to the Senecas in western New York and to the tribes of the Ohio country so that the aboriginal peoples could unite in strength and secure their future in the unstable world of the late eighteenth century. However, Brant could not achieve his goals and this move seems to have been the last significant effort in the colonial era to rescue the confederacy's now-broken unity. For the British, the Grand River was a strategic site on which to settle the Six Nations. There, the Iroquois could serve as a barrier against American invasion from the west should hostilities with the new republic resume, as well as act as agents of British policy in the disputed territories to the south, serve as intermediaries in the fur trade to the southwest, and supply needed goods and services to the king's garrison at Niagara.[20]

The Iroquois of the Seven Nations posed less of a problem for Britain after the revolution because two of their communities, Kanesatake and Kahnawake, were well within British territory. The new border split Akwesasne, but its residents could move to the British side if they wished. Only Oswegatchie lay within the United States, and most residents of this predominantly Onondaga settlement emigrated to other Iroquois communities. In 1806 the state of New York forcibly removed those who remained.[21]

A significant number of Six Nations people did not relocate to British territory but chose instead to remain in Iroquoia. For these people and their Canadian relatives the instability of the frontier and the uncertainty over sovereignty, as exemplified by Britain's retention of the Western Posts, aroused hopes that they might be able to play the two white powers off each other in order to secure as much independence as possible, as they had done with the French and British during the first half of the eighteenth century. Unlike the earlier period, however, the Euroamerican menace was so much more powerful demographically and intrusive geographically that the Six Nations possessed only a limited chance of success. This began to be made clear when the Americans started to force the Iroquois in New York onto reservations following a new Treaty of Fort Stanwix in 1784. During the negotiations, American authorities insulted and physically abused people of the Six Nations before imposing harsh terms on them. As far as the victorious revolutionaries were concerned, the imperial restraint on westward migration was now a nullity. Instead, they saw Iroquoia fundamentally as conquered territory, even though Britain only had transferred political sovereignty over the land to the United States in the peace treaty, not ownership of the land itself, which continued to rest with the Iroquois. However, Americans soon realized that imposing the conditions of conquest might not be in the best interests of the United States. Such a policy likely would demand costly military action and drive the Iroquois in New York firmly into the orbit of the British and the still hostile Ohio nations. Instead, the Americans relented, asserting sovereignty over the tribes but not ownership of their territory. On the surface this stance was similar to the old imperial claim and represented a 'play-off' victory for the Six Nations. Nevertheless, Americans expected the Iroquois shortly to surrender most of their territory when the new republic, with its voracious desire for land, would need it. Once Iroquoia had been alienated, Americans assumed that Euroamerican agriculture would replace the incompatible aboriginal farming and forest way of life. Rather than large expanses of undivided aboriginal territory beyond a defined border in which the tribes could adjust to external pressures slowly, Americans wanted isolated reservations where the natives would be assimilated quickly by the surrounding white population as the traditional aboriginal economy became unviable. Ironically, the Oneidas and Tuscaroras who had fought on the revolutionary side were not able to use their alliance with the victors to preserve their lands. In fact, they were the first nations coerced to cede large amounts of territory. During this unhappy period, some Iroquois decided to leave their ancestral homes for Canada or Ohio rather than live under American domination.[22]

The revolution had created a situation in which there seemed to be no alternative to the loss of Iroquois lands. On one level, greedy land speculators, with excellent connections to the new, post-revolutionary powers, wanted to profit from the sale of aboriginal lands to settlers anxious to move onto what they considered to be uninhabited, virgin soil. On another, the experience of the revolution had hardened American attitudes towards native peoples. On a third, the costs of the revolution had to be paid for, and government saw aboriginal land as a core resource to liquidate its financial obligations and restore confidence in public finances.

Meanwhile, the Ohio tribes protected their lands as best they could through a protracted war. They hoped to establish an independent homeland in the 'Old Northwest' of today's Ohio, Michigan, Wisconsin, Indiana, and Illinois. Their resistance reached its zenith in 1790 and 1791, when they defeated two armies sent to subdue them. The Iroquois on both sides of the international border considered joining the western tribes, and one hundred individuals slipped away from their villages in New York and Canada to fight beside their western neighbours.[23] The Six Nations were also busy diplomatically in discussions between the western tribes, for whom they usually acted as moderate allies, the United States, and Great Britain. However, the Iroquois as a whole, especially after 1793, remained aloof from the military struggle and earned the contempt of the peoples in the west for not participating in what the latter considered to be the aboriginal war of survival. The Six Nations, despite some belligerent posturing, had different priorities: the Iroquois in New York might face destruction at the hands of the United States if they were not careful and took up arms in the Ohio conflict, which, fundamentally, was not their own.[24]

The tense frontier situation became more dangerous in 1793, when news arrived from Europe that America's old ally, France, had gone to war with Great Britain. The European contest (which would be waged almost continuously until 1815 and which would contribute to the outbreak in North America of the War of 1812) led to confrontations on the high seas between Great Britain and the United States. These clashes intensified already significant strains generated by Britain's retention of the Western Posts, her diplomatic support for the frontier tribes, and the American desire to annex the remaining British North American colonies. Fearing an American invasion of Upper Canada (now Ontario) in 1794, the British reconstructed an old post, Fort Miamis, at the centre of the western tribal confederacy, one hundred kilometres south of Detroit. Their objectives were to bolster native resolve and to guard the southwestern approach to Canada against the new American army sent to the west to replace the one lost in 1791. This measure, combined with bellicose speeches by the governor-in-chief of British North America and encouragement from local Crown officials in the war zone, led many natives to believe that Britain would go to war in support of the tribes. Yet in the summer of 1794 the British only provided a token force of Canadian militia to help their allies when the Americans and natives met in battle a very short distance from Fort Miamis at Fallen Timbers (near today's Perrysburg, Ohio). The natives suffered defeat. The contradictory British behaviour – showing some support for the aboriginal cause but not providing serious help – was driven by the simple fact that it was not in Britain's interests, just as it was not in those of the Iroquois, to provoke a war with the United States in defence of the western tribes. Yet, given the fear of invasion, it was in Britain's interests to have the assurance that the tribes would ally with King George III should the Americans continue their march into Canada.[25] In the longer term, had the tribes defeated the Americans again, it would have been to Britain's advantage to help negotiate the creation of a native homeland to maintain the southwestern fur trade, improve Canadian defensibility, and strengthen the British–native alliance. Thoughts of creating an inviolable aboriginal homeland out of American territory, however, probably were unrealistic given the weight of evidence from the territorial conflicts of the eighteenth and nineteenth centuries that Americans were simply unwilling to tolerate exclusive native occupation of significant expanses of productive land.

Later in 1794, Great Britain and the United States negotiated the Treaty of Amity, Commerce, and Navigation (or Jay's Treaty). The treaty resolved Anglo-American tensions on the frontier for the next decade and led to the British evacuation of the Western Posts in 1796 in return for some American concessions. Once again, as in 1783, the aboriginal peoples believed the British had deserted them. The Iroquois shared the same views of the western tribes, although they had not taken part in the 1794 campaign and had withdrawn their modest support for them during difficult diplomatic negotiations with the Americans in 1793. The aboriginal defeat in the west and the British agreement to evacuate the Western Posts created a situation in which the Six Nations in New York, for the first time in their history, lacked the power to fight back against Euroamerican encroachments with any remote hope of success. Now the challenge for them was to make the best of the situation by maintaining a friendly but dependent relationship with the United States. If they could achieve at least that, then they might survive the perils that would emerge once settlers began to pour into western New York.[26]

The western nations, defeated and without allies, negotiated the Treaty of Greeneville with the United States in 1795 in which they surrendered vast expanses of territory, encompassing most of Ohio, part of Indiana, and small parcels of land in strategic locations in Illinois and Michigan. American settlers ignored the new boundary almost as soon as it was established, while the government exploited divisions among the demoralized aboriginal peoples to purchase territory beyond the newly established border before the natives had begun to recover from their recent defeat. Towards the end of the first decade of the nineteenth century, intense American pressure led the western tribes to form a new defensive alliance around Tecumseh and his prophet brother, Tenskwatawa, one that most Iroquois refused to join. In 1811 war between the western tribes and the United States broke out again when American troops marched against the new confederacy at Tippecanoe (at today's Lafayette, Indiana).[27]

At the same time as the western nations fought American encroachments in the 1780s and 1790s, the morale of the Iroquois in New York collapsed. To the disgust of their people, chiefs frequently signed away land for little compensation in a desperate search for something of an income to help their communities as older subsistence patterns fell into decline, particularly among men. In their defence, Iroquois leaders hoped that the proceeds from these sales would provide at least some support for their people. Many of them also felt they had little choice, as the world around them was changing drastically and as even American federal laws designed to protect them from rapacious and illegal land sales went unenforced. By 1800 the Iroquois had been forced onto sixteen reservations in New York and a grant in Pennsylvania; and they would lose even some of these lands in the next decade. In the aftermath of the revolution the Iroquois found it impossible or impractical to rekindle the league council fire covered at Onondaga in 1777. Instead, they lit two fires, one at Grand River in Upper Canada, the other at Buffalo Creek in New York. In bitter contrast to the prosperity enjoyed on the eve of the American Revolution, Iroquois communities disintegrated into dismal forest slums where men found it was no longer possible to pursue their traditional roles as hunters, diplomats, and warriors as freely or as productively as they had before 1783. In their depression and desperation, in which some even began to doubt the worthiness of their native ways, many people turned to hard liquor and family violence in impotent, self-destructive defiance of the constraints of the new society of the reservations.[28]

After almost two centuries of contact with whites, the Iroquois looked back despondently at their gloomy condition, a condition brought on by the struggles between foreign empires for dominance of the Great Lakes basin. With this depressing heritage of white–native relations, there was little reason for the Iroquois to trust Euroamericans or to view their own future with anything but the most melancholy expectations. One Seneca, John Logan, expressed the prevailing belief in the 1790s when he reflected on the concurrent flow of settlers into Iroquoia and the march of the American army against the Ohio tribes: 'It appears to me that the Great Spirit is determined on our destruction – Perhaps it is to answer some great and now incomprehensible purpose.' [29] The Peacemaker's vision, which had inspired the Iroquois for so long, seemed to be dying.

Yet towards the end of the 1790s individuals arose within Six Nations communities who hoped to redeem their people through social reforms or by re-establishing a right relationship with the spiritual powers of the universe. The most famous was the Seneca prophet, Handsome Lake, who emerged in 1799 from the desolation of the Cornplanter Tract in northern Pennsylvania. Important features of his prophecy included demands that his followers renounce alcohol, witchcraft, promiscuity, quarrelling, and gambling, all of which he believed had contributed so much to his people's decline. Instead, he exhorted everyone to return to some of the ancestral rituals to rekindle lost spiritual powers. Nonetheless, he was not completely orthodox in his attempts to recover tradition. Rather, his objective was to address the needs of the developing reservation culture. He called his people to embrace a new program of confession and moral restraint in place of the older spiritual practices that they had used to release pent-up tensions. He advocated the use of the more productive farming practices of whites, which would eliminate the need to move villages and farms periodically on the now cramped reservations, and he encouraged lumbering and such crafts as spinning, weaving, milling, and coopering. Most radically of all, he preached that it was acceptable for men made idle by the new order to engage in the agricultural pursuits that previously had been the province of Iroquois women. Handsome Lake hoped that the adoption of white farming practices, including the replacement of lineages headed by females with nuclear families headed by males, would serve as the vehicles to restore his people materially, culturally, and spiritually. By freeing themselves from Euroamerican manipulation by means of agricultural prosperity, he thought the Iroquois could resist other forms of corrupting acculturation, retain what was left of their land, and avoid participation in the wars of the whites, which had proved to be so destructive for the Six Nations. [30]

Handsome Lake and other religious leaders found followers at Iroquois communities on both sides of the British–American border. Their efforts helped many suffering people regain their sense of self-worth, retrieve pride in their identity, rebuild their social structures, and accept a level of acculturation or accommodation made necessary by post-revolutionary conditions. In part, this was possible because many Iroquois, like natives elsewhere in the Great Lakes region, interpreted their woes not so much as a consequence of white power, but as something that stemmed from their own spiritual failures. If they could recapture the favour of the Great Spirit through a devout reformation and a renewal of ritual, then they might regain power and be healed. [31]

In addition to the spiritually inspired native leaders, other people worked to encourage the Iroquois to accept white agriculture and education, and to adjust in other ways to the changing world of the Great Lakes region. Congregationalist ministers in New York continued to run their long-standing mission to the Oneidas, Quaker missionaries worked with the Senecas along the New York–Pennsylvania border to improve farming practices, and Baptist evangelists proclaimed the gospel among the Iroquois of the Niagara frontier. Anglican divines visited Grand River and Tyendinaga to preach the word and administer the sacraments to the Mohawks as they had for a century, and Roman Catholic priests directed the affairs of the Seven Nations as much as the people in those settlements would let them. Within Iroquois communities, people such as the reformed drunkard Red Jacket among the Senecas in New York advocated social harmony through temperance, while in Upper Canada Mohawk leaders such at Henry Tekarihogen and Joseph Brant fostered white settlement along the Grand to provide model farms to help people adapt to new ways of cultivating their food. For some Six Nations reformers, the appropriation of some European ways, if embraced on Iroquois terms instead of the complete acculturation demanded by the paternalistic white society, and the sale of land, if controlled intelligently, could benefit their people and generate the means to replace the losses that came about as older ways of sustaining the population became less and less viable.[32]

The efforts of prophets, missionaries, and reformers were not universally accepted, and many Iroquois, loath to change, or unwilling to change in the ways others suggested they should, rejected innovation. Some Oneida men in New York were typical of opponents to the new order, declaring that the Great Spirit had given them bows and arrows, not white men's ploughs. They claimed, therefore, that they were 'made for war and hunting and holding "councils,"' while only 'squaws and hedgehogs' were 'made to scratch the ground.'[33] (Presumably Oneida women who wanted to preserve female-headed lineages and their dominance in farming rejected the new ways from a different perspective.) [34] Some Iroquois, such as the Mohawk chief John Norton, did not see farming as debilitating to Iroquois manhood. In 1808 he claimed that 'the most industrious at the plough, generally shew themselves the most persevering at the chase, when in Winter they throw aside the hoe and take up the gun.'[35]

The work of the prophets and others, combined with a measure of peace on the Great Lakes border after 1795, enabled the Iroquois to begin rebuilding their population and society towards the end of the first decade of the nineteenth century. By 1812 there likely were at least 3,800 Iroquois in New York and Pennsylvania exclusive of Akwesasne, 1,925 people along the Grand River, 240 at Tyendinaga, 3,375 or more at Kahnawake, Kanesatake, and Akwesasne, and 550 Mingos and Sandusky Senecas south of Lake Erie.[36] Outwardly, the frame- and log-house settlements of the vast majority resembled those of their white neighbours rather than the traditional palisaded, longhouse villages that had disappeared in the eighteenth century (with the exception of a few truncated longhouses which a small number of people still preferred to occupy). Some people, such as Joseph Brant, furnished their homes with the chairs, bedsteads, and cupboards of white society, while others followed older practices and lined their homes with a double row of bunks to meet their needs for seating, sleeping, and storage. In their fields they grew a mix of native and European crops: corn, squash, beans, tobacco, pumpkins, wheat, rye, oats, peas, potatoes, turnips, flax, and orchard fruits; and the variety of livestock they raised was similar to that found in white settlements. But there were differences too: their standard of material well-being was generally lower than that of their white neighbours, hunting and fishing were more important than they were to whites, and the cultural framework of Iroquois society, although modified by generations of Euroamerican contact and recent reforms, remained fundamentally aboriginal, especially at the village and lower levels of society. [37]

In the early nineteenth century, the descendants of the founders of the League of the Houdenosaunee were a badly bruised people. They lived on land located at the Euroamerican end of the white–aboriginal frontier, and they possessed fewer options and lower expectations of what they

could do to protect their lands, interests, and society from white en-
croachment and assimilation than did the native peoples farther to the
west. Nonetheless, most Iroquois at the beginning of the second decade
of the nineteenth century were very much their own people, living dis-
tinctly Iroquois lives, and they were determined to keep their society
strong despite the enormity of the challenges facing them.

Sadly, new war clouds began to form which would lead to calamity and
bloodshed. In 1812 Britain was in the middle of a desperate war with
Napoleonic France. Her strongest weapon was the Royal Navy, which had
won control over the Atlantic Ocean in numerous ship-to-ship actions
and at the Battle of Trafalgar in 1805. To win the European war the navy
had to blockade France and her allies in order to weaken their econo-
mies and prevent vital supplies from reaching Napoleon's huge armies.
To keep the blockading warships fully manned, the British rigorously
searched out deserters from the navy, including those who had joined the
crews of American vessels. Some of the deserters were United States citizens who had served in the Royal Navy, others were British subjects, and
some were innocent victims. A great many Americans strongly opposed
the blockade, although American shipping interests, on the whole, pros-
pered enormously because of new and expanded markets created by the
war in Europe. The Royal Navy's searches offended many Americans
because they represented an assault on national sovereignty, particularly
given that the United States government, for political advantage, exaggerated the number of sailors impressed. Largely because of the prosperity
the European war brought to them and of a relative lack of concern over
impressment, however, the Atlantic states of the American union generally opposed going to war with Great Britain.[38]

The main impetus for hostilities came from people whose interests lay
in the frontier regions of the United States. These people regarded British behaviour on the high seas as an affront to their country's dignity, but
supported war mainly because of strong local issues. Southerners wanted
to acquire Florida from Spain, then a British ally, and thought war with
Britain would lead to the acquisition of the Spanish colony. Westerners
coveted both native territory and the British colonies as natural areas for
American expansion. In the minds of many Americans, defeating the
aboriginal population and pushing the tribes off their lands would be easier if the ally of the natives, Britain, could be expelled from Canada.
Many others believed that the American Revolution was somehow incom-
plete because the British had not been expelled from North America in
1783. For his part, President James Madison saw significant value in con-

quering Canada. Before 1812 Madison had used economic pressure to try
to coerce Britain to change policies the Americans did not like. However,
these efforts failed because Britain could acquire most North American
products from her own colonies or from American smugglers who used
the poorly guarded Canadian border to circumvent government trade
restrictions. If Madison could conquer British North America, then his
country's power would increase immensely, as the United States would
become the sole source of North American commodities. With such a
trade monopoly, the United States could influence international affairs
to its own advantage. President Madison's interest in Canada, combined
with the desire for war by westerners and southerners, as well as internal
political problems that endangered Madison's hold on power, by late
1811 and early 1812 made an invasion of Canada an attractive alternative
to previous American policy, especially with Britain's military commitments in Europe making it unlikely that enough troops could be dispatched across the Atlantic to defend Canada adequately. In June 1812
the United States declared war.[39]

As had been the case in the American Revolution, this war would
engulf the Iroquois in a major conflict which, at its outbreak, would be
perceived by the majority of Iroquois only as another threat to their survival. The challenge for them was to anticipate and react to shifting geopolitical conditions, within the limitations and opportunities inherent to
their fluid and open political structures, with the objective of establishing
some sort of solid diplomatic and military stance to ensure their survival
as a people.

2

The Crisis of Alliance:
Spring and Summer 1812

The gloomy Day, foretold by our ancients, has at last arrived; – the Independence and Glory of the Five Nations has departed from us; – We find ourselves in the hands of two powerful Nations, who can crush us when they please. They are the same in every respect, although they are now preparing to contend.

An anonymous Seneca chief, June 1812[1]

Would the Iroquois go to war? If they did, whose part would they take? These were the primary questions on the minds of those British and American officials concerned about white–native relations in the months leading up to President Madison's declaration of war. The people of the Iroquois communities asked themselves those same questions, and a third: why should they participate in the strife among white peoples? As the clouds of war rolled across the horizon, peace chiefs tried to persuade their people to seek shelter from the coming storm in neutrality. However, the unfolding events, changing perceptions of their interests, powerful cultural pressures, divisions within their communities, and the broad personal freedoms enjoyed by individuals all combined to make it very difficult for the Iroquois to remain at peace once the Americans, the British, and the western tribes began to spill each others' blood. Most of the efforts made by the peace chiefs came to a failed end, and the War of 1812 saw the Iroquois perform their war dances within a few months – weeks in some cases – of the outbreak of hostilities on 18 June.

Earlier in the year the question of war or neutrality had been simplest for the Iroquois in New York. Confined to reservations within the boundaries of their ancestral territories, they no longer had an independent homeland to defend. The retention of their remaining land was tenuous enough in the face of aggressive settlement, unscrupulous speculators, and unsympathetic governments without inviting military reprisals. Moreover, peaceful relations with the United States were necessary to ensure that they continued to receive the annuities and gifts they needed to maintain their standard of living.[2] They could not contemplate allying with anyone but the United States, despite their own unhappy legacy of American–Iroquois relations and the ongoing animosity in the United States towards native peoples, as demonstrated so clearly at Tippecanoe in 1811. Fortunately, the Americans simplified the issue because they told the Iroquois that they did not want aboriginal allies. Just after the outbreak of war, the government's agent to the Six Nations, Erastus Granger, informed them that America's warriors were so numerous, 'like the sand on the shores of the great lakes,' that they soon would overwhelm the outnumbered redcoats across the border in Canada on their own. Not needing Iroquois help, Granger advised them to stay home, cultivate their fields, and take care of their property.[3]

Granger's advice was not motivated by kindness or generosity. Rather, he and his government assumed that the only options the Iroquois considered were neutrality or an alliance with the British. Therefore, at the same moment he asked them to remain quiet, he threatened the already insecure tribespeople: if they took up arms against the United States, then the Americans would take away their land, and the British, sure to lose Canada in the coming months, would have no alternative territory to give them as they had in 1784. Once that happened, the Six Nations could expect no mercy, but, 'deservedly,' would be 'cut off from the face of the earth.'[4] Perhaps some of the people who listened to Granger's speech remembered similar words he had spoken at the distribution of their annuities in 1808 when war seemed likely following the naval confrontation between HMS *Leopard* and the USS *Chesapeake* in 1807: 'If we go to war with Great Britain, and you join them, destruction will follow.'[5]

The antagonism behind Granger's threats underlined American suspicions that British Indian Department agents had deployed their diplomatic skills successfully to pull the Iroquois in New York into the British orbit. Fear tore through the border in 1812 as a result of this anxiety, and settlers on the American side of the Niagara frontier fled at the outbreak of hostilities because they expected the Six Nations in New York to join their old British allies and fall upon their isolated farms and villages. Along the St Lawrence River to the east, whites panicked whenever people at Akwesasne left their reservation in search of food. The state of New

York therefore supplied five hundred rations per day to that predominantly Mohawk community and gave cash bonuses to chiefs to keep their people at home.[6]

What the Americans did not comprehend was that British agents exercised little influence over Iroquois external affairs. The Iroquois made their own assessments of geopolitical realities and developed foreign policies to fulfil their objectives within the limits of what they thought was possible. The peace chiefs in New York knew that an alliance with the British would be suicidal because of the power the Americans wielded over the Six Nations in the state. Furthermore, historical experience told them that they had no strong reasons for supporting the British. As Anglo–American relations degenerated towards war after 1807, most of the peace chiefs embraced a two-point policy to protect their people and landholdings. They agreed not to take to the warpath for either side, and they decided to use their influence on behalf of the Americans to counter British attempts to win over other nations.[7] Externally, this strategy reflected their desire to maintain possession of their reservations without having to purchase American benevolence by fighting for the United States against the interests of other aboriginal peoples. Internally, it responded to the pacifist sentiments that had taken hold of those communities where the prophet Handsome Lake exercised his greatest influence, and, more broadly, to the sensitivities of the people who had been wounded grievously in the last Anglo–American war and who wished to avoid a repetition of the old miseries. Yet the chiefs knew they had to do something to prove their good intentions towards the United States. And they believed their security could be enhanced by keeping other aboriginal nations out of the impending conflict because the Americans had a history of using aboriginal resistance to push friendly as well as belligerent natives off land coveted by white settlers.

A good diplomatic target for the Iroquois in New York was the Six Nations community on the Grand River Tract in Upper Canada. Unanimity did not exist on the Grand: British, American, and neutralist parties vied for the support of the unaligned, and many people had decided to adopt a neutralist policy in the wake of the *Chesapeake* affair, although they continued to assure British officials of their ongoing goodwill towards King George III. The Iroquois from New York thought they might be able to swing the balance of opinion on the Grand solidly to neutrality, secure the safety of both themselves and their relatives in Canada, win American goodwill, and, in the process, strike a pose that clearly differentiated the Six Nations Iroquois from the predominantly

Algonkian western tribes, whose animosity towards the United States had already led to hostilities. (The Iroquois in New York were not the only ones who tried to sway the people of the Grand. In 1811 diplomats from the Mingo nation in Ohio had tried, but failed, to encourage the Six Nations to move west and join the western alliance under Tecumseh and Tenskwatawa.)[8]

British officials had told the Grand River people that the Americans planned to take their land away from them. However, most of the tract's inhabitants were not sure if this was true. Furthermore, they had good reasons to be suspicious of what the king's men said in light of the disasters of 1783 and 1794. Unless the Americans proved themselves to be a genuine menace, many people wanted to lie low and not align themselves to either power.[9] Experience and logic told them that the apparently irresistible expansion of the United States probably would continue, with the fall of Upper and Lower Canada occurring in due course, especially, as was common knowledge, because the great European war against Napoleon prevented Britain from sending significant numbers of reinforcements to Canada. If British North America fell, the Iroquois did not want to forfeit their homes by having fought on the losing side. Even within the British party there seem to have been some who found themselves torn between their attachments and a rational assessment of American might.

British supporters on the tract were vulnerable on other accounts as well. There was an old debate between Joseph Brant's followers and opponents which had divided the community since the 1780s over how closely they should ally themselves with the Crown, how much acculturation they should accept, whether or not land should be sold, how much leadership Brant should be allowed to exercise, and even if Brant could be trusted to represent the interests of the Iroquois rather than his own.[10] Although Brant placed greater importance on the historical alliance to the king than others did, sometimes his relations with Upper Canadian officials could be severely strained, which at least helped assuage fear that his pro-British leanings would prevent him from putting the interests of his people first. Perhaps the most dramatic example occurred in 1797 when Brant marched on the provincial capital of York (now Toronto) with three hundred armed warriors to intimidate a virtually defenceless government to make concessions over granting the Iroquois the freedom to sell land without government restrictions.[11]

After Brant died, in 1807, discord within the Grand River community seems to have deepened as his followers increasingly came under the influence of the Anglophile John Norton, who tried to create strong links between the community and the British army. Norton, who was probably born in Scotland about 1760, was the son of a Cherokee father and a Scottish mother. He had come to North America in the ranks of a British infantry regiment in the 1780s, left the army, and found employment with the Society for the Propagation of the Gospel as a schoolteacher at Tyendinaga. Finding teaching tedious and enjoying the aboriginal way of life, he resigned in 1791 to work in the fur trade in the Ohio country. He subsequently returned to Canada and became an interpreter for the Indian Department at Niagara in 1796, after being recommended for the post by Joseph Brant. Under the latter's sponsorship, Norton was adopted into the Mohawk nation, became Brant's 'nephew,' and rose to become a diplomatic and war chief around 1799 under the name of Teyoninhokarawen. During a visit to England between 1804 and 1806, Norton improved his standing in both white and aboriginal society when he secured the patronage of the Duke of Northumberland and other influential individuals in the evangelical Clapham Sect.[12]

British authorities realized that tensions along the Grand had to be calmed if they hoped to recruit significant numbers of warriors. Nevertheless, they failed to do so in the years leading up to the war. Aside from Six Nations reticence to participate in hostilities, there was a dangerous rift between the two Crown organizations connected to native affairs, the army and the Indian Department, which further weakened British influence on the tract. The army, in its somewhat naive tradition of dealing with war chiefs and its single-minded desire to defend Canada as effectively as possible, focused its attention on cultivating John Norton and the Anglophile elements on the tract. Army officers were loath to leave the Indian Department to its own devices in maintaining the Iroquois alliance, because they distrusted its agents, thinking them corrupt and self-serving – as did many residents of the Grand River, including John Norton. For Norton, allying with the army presented an opportunity to undercut his enemies and promote the positive British–Iroquois ties he desired but could not achieve through the department or through Upper Canada's civil authorities. For instance, he was well aware of the fact that the department had worked furiously and successfully in the years before Brant's death to thwart his efforts to assume the leadership of all the tribes in Upper Canada, including such non-Iroquoians as the Mississaugas. The department's motivation stemmed, in part, from fears that a powerful Brant could wreak havoc with the white population should he decide to turn on the government.[13] Such was official nervousness in the light of the events of 1797 that the lieutenant-governor appointed to the province shortly afterwards was instructed to impoverish the Six Nations, break their alliances with other tribes in British territory, and 'bring them to that temper and state of mind' to enable the government to control them effectively and to force them to sell part of their 1784 land grant on the government's terms.[14] In contrast, Norton thought that positive relations with the military could be used to advance Iroquois interests in the colony harmoniously. Furthermore, collaborating with the military gave Norton access to at least some of the Crown's power and prestige, since neither the provincial government nor the Indian Department wanted to patronize him. Beyond calculated reasons for aligning himself with the army, a careful reading of Norton's journal indicates that he enjoyed the company of military men and thought them more reliable and honest than other officials.[15]

The department's agents often were married to aboriginal women or were integrated into native society and, therefore, usually understood the Iroquois better than the army's officers did. They combined their more nuanced view of white–native relations with their interest in protecting their positions and emoluments and, in some cases, profiting dishonestly from their offices. Thus, they were well-positioned to undermine the army's efforts if they decided to do so, particularly in the early stages of the War of 1812, when the authority of the peace chiefs was stronger than it might be later. Indian agents seem to have interpreted Norton's close identification with the military as a liability for the maintenance of the Iroquois alliance, because they knew people would question his commitment to protecting Six Nations' interests if they thought his army connections were strong enough to confuse his loyalties. Moreover, they realized that patronizing war chiefs could be interpreted by natives as an affront to civil chiefs. The department preferred to cultivate good connections with a wider community, including the peace chiefs and other influential people whose support for the British was weak, as well as with those along the Grand River who opposed the Brant–Norton party.[16]

Personal differences between Norton and the Indian Department's senior local official, Deputy Superintendent-General William Claus, made a bad situation worse. Claus, one of the colony's most prominent men, with close connections to the civil authorities, was a cautious person whose distrust of the romantic and charming Norton extended back for over a decade and was tied to his earlier conflicts with Brant. He worried that Norton would make extravagant financial and territorial demands on the Crown through a strong and independent course of action (as he believed Brant had done) if army patronage elevated Norton's stature among the Six Nations too highly. In their struggles with provincial officials, Brant and Norton were tainted further in the government's mind, as they had both called for Claus to be replaced and they had both patronized independent land speculators and opposition politicians who posed a threat to the power of the local elite. Moreover, this elite sometimes had difficulty distinguishing dissent from disloyalty.[17] Claus also seems to have suspected Norton's loyalty because of an untrue story that in 1794, during the war in the Ohio country, he had warned the garrison of an American fort of an impending native attack.[18] For his part, Norton shared Brant's view that Claus was 'our implacable enemy' and he believed as well that Claus was an unimaginative and dishonest incompetent who wished to keep the tribes under Indian Department control to prevent the Six Nations from realizing their aspirations if these differed from the Crown's or even Claus's own interests.[19]

Because of the conflicting concerns of the army and the Indian Department, the British divided their supporters along the Grand and sent mixed messages to the rest of the community at the very time they needed to solidify what support they could muster. The Norton–Claus conflict further weakened British military goals because the distribution of government presents and rewards to the tribespeople in 1812 reflected the department's desire to thwart its opponents rather than to convince the Iroquois to take up arms. In addition to the Crown's clumsiness in dealing with the Six Nations, the people of the tract also continued to receive annuities from the Americans for lands they had sold in New York, which may have given the American and neutralist parties additional leverage against the British party. For people associated with the American and neutralist parties on the tract, the presence of two factions within the British party presented opportunities to align with or oppose one or both of these groups as it suited their particular agendas at any given time. This additional manoeuvring room added strength to the Iroquois side in bargaining with the British.[20]

The content of the messages from the Indian Department before Madison's declaration of war further weakened the Crown's prestige in aboriginal eyes. Before June 1812 the department encouraged the tribes to maintain peace with the United States as part of a larger effort to avoid an Anglo–American conflict, but the department also tried to ensure that enough pro-British sentiment persisted among the aboriginal peoples to secure their support should hostilities break out. The department's policy was odious because it reminded natives of the Crown's behaviour in 1794, when Britain all but abandoned them in their hour of need at Fallen Timbers. The military commander-in-chief and acting civil administrator of Upper Canada, Major-General Isaac Brock, thought the department's position was absurd because it contributed to Britain's declining influence over the tribes at the very moment the Americans were doing their best to overawe the native peoples. Unless a strong alliance could be maintained with them, Brock believed Upper Canada was doomed to fall into American hands.[21]

Brock experienced first-hand how weak British support was on the Grand, how complicated Six Nations politics were, and how the Indian Department had made a difficult situation worse when he attended a council on the tract in the spring of 1812. He met with a cold response when he suggested that the Iroquois form three companies of warriors and rotate one each month to the Niagara Peninsula to help guard the border. An Onondaga chief, Raweanarase, tried to make Brock squirm by saying the Iroquois would not act unless their land claims were settled to their satisfaction first.[22] The problem with Raweanarase's outwardly simple statement was that the community was badly divided on what satisfaction meant, which undercut Brock's ability to do anything that would win widespread Six Nations support.

Raweanarase and other Grand River residents who hoped to maintain traditional ways as much as possible did not want to sell land or have large numbers of whites live among them. One source of protection against alienating their property was the Royal Proclamation, which, while allowing the Crown to acquire land, offered a better chance to minimize and control sales than would be possible if, as other Iroquois argued, the Six Nations held the Grand River Tract under freehold tenure with autonomy to sell to whomever they wanted on whatever terms they could negotiate. The people who favoured the restrictions of the proclamation also believed that those who had already sold parts of the tract had not obtained a broad consensus to do so legitimately and sometimes had disposed of land for personal benefit rather than the community good. For example, in 1811 the prominent hereditary Mohawk chief Henry Tekarihogen had tried to engineer the sale of some property to his white son-in-law, Augustus Jones. Raweanarase had opposed the transaction, arguing that the land should remain in Six Nations hands.[23] Tekarihogen was dismissed, or dehorned, from his chieftainship in light of the scandal, with one Mohawk declaring that he had 'done very wrong.'[24] Complicating land sales even more was William Claus's own consistently reprehensible behaviour. In 1805, for instance, he kept a significant portion of the proceeds of a Grand River sale to a group of Mennonites as 'expenses,' contrary to orders. On another occasion, in 1811, he took it upon himself to cancel the obligation to pay the Grand River people twelve years' worth of interest on a defaulted land purchase so that he could facilitate selling the property to another buyer, a move he made against the legal opinion of the attorney-general of Upper Canada, who held that such an action could not be taken without the approval of the Iroquois themselves. [25] Frustrated, Tekarihogen complained that 'we have been most grievously deceived, and to our great surprise and grief we find ourselves by the contrivance of artful faithless and wicked men stript of our property – what little is yet left us we are denied the lawful right of controlling or disposing of without our master's leave.' [26] However eloquent this statement was, it came, of course, from the mouth of a man whose own land dealings were suspect.

For its part, the Indian Department endorsed the Royal Proclamation's restrictions on the sale of lands and held that most private buyers did not have adequate financial resources to pay the prices they offered. Thus the department thought that private sales would entangle the land in lengthy and expensive legal disputes, in contrast to the certainties that came with purchases by the Crown, although these took place at a lower rate. The department also realized that the government, as the intermediary between native vendors and white purchasers, could enhance its revenues and prevent potentially disloyal people from acquiring property close to the Six Nations. Furthermore, Indian Department agents, who played a central role in negotiations, could exercise some control over who purchased the land to oblige their friends. Meanwhile, across the border, the Americans insisted that the Iroquois within the United States had full rights to sell their property as they saw fit. While outwardly pleasing to someone like an exasperated Henry Tekarihogen, the ultimate impact of this policy was that the Six Nations in New York ended up selling far more land than they could afford to lose, and they did so under considerable pressure from white purchasers without adequate government protection. In Upper Canada, Brock had tried, but failed, to resolve at least some of the issues affecting Grand River land the previous winter, although he did arrange to speed up the delivery of some of the interest earned on money that the government managed for the Grand River people.[27]

John Norton, as a leader of those who wanted to sell land outside of the Royal Proclamation, was not tainted the way others were by conflicts between personal and community concerns. He and the supporters of

freehold tenure rejected the pre-revolutionary claims of British sovereignty over Iroquois territory in New York, argued that the Grand River
Tract had been given to them under the same conditions that had
applied before 1776, and asserted that they could do what they liked with
their property without government interference. As well, they generally
agreed with Brant's old policies of selling land to build up the community's financial resources while encouraging white settlement to provide
examples of modern agricultural practices for Iroquois farmers to emu-
late. In addition, they believed that they could make more money
through private sales than through disposing of parts of the tract within
the government's restrictions, because the Crown paid only a few pence
for each acre it then resold to whites for several shillings. [28]

The supporters of freehold tenure tended to be divided between the
strongest advocates of a pro-British stance, as exemplified by Norton, and
the promoters of a pro-American alliance, as represented by Tekarihogen. Both of these men drew their core support from within the Mohawk
community on the tract. Those who did not want to sell land, the majority
of the population, tended to dominate the non-Mohawk villages and to
endorse neutrality.

Raweanarase also asked Brock if the Iroquois, after the coming war,
would find themselves in the same desperate situation they had experienced at the end of the American Revolution. To emphasize Six Nations
discontent by using a pointed reference to the crisis of 1794, he
demanded to know if Britain would help the western tribes should the
Americans not invade Canada. Raweanarase's question implied that the
Iroquois planned to take up the king's cause if the British supported the
western tribes. [29] However, just after the war broke out and the British
allied themselves militarily to the western tribes, most Iroquois continued
to remain neutral or quietly supported the Americans. This suggests the
Grand River people sought opportunities in their meeting with Brock to
put the British at a diplomatic disadvantage that might be useful to force
more concessions from the government than they otherwise might have
been able to secure. That they could unite for this purpose while dis-
agreeing sharply among themselves as to what the concessions should be
is an indication of the genius of Iroquois diplomacy.

Brock's situation was difficult. The best he could do was repeat the
unsatisfying arguments of the Indian Department, which he opposed,
even though he knew it would not encourage the Grand River people to
take a belligerent attitude towards the Americans. He told them he did
not have the authority to assist the western tribes while Great Britain and

the United States remained at peace. However, should Canada be invaded, then he would be able to act with vigour. Given their fear of American power and anger over land issues, this reply simply was not acceptable to most people, and their hostility prevented the pro-British Mohawks from giving the strong speech in favour of the king's cause that they had planned to deliver at the close of the council.[30] Instead, what Brock heard was the fatalistic speech of one old man, Blind-Warrior, who said, 'Brothers, – when our ancestors first saw the English, they took each other by the hand, and became friends; – since that time, they have risked in every War, and many have fallen: – We are now much reduced in Number, but we are, notwithstanding, determined to conquer or fall in espousing the same cause for which our Ancestors have fought and bled.'[31] Blind-Warrior's pessimistic words did not even represent majority opinion which at best was reticent to align with the Crown and at worst supported an American alliance. But the speech at least was polite, which, from his knowledge of aboriginal diplomacy, must have reminded Isaac Brock that the door had not been closed on a potential change of heart depending on British behaviour, American aggression, and changing circumstances.

Brock was not surprised by the response. He readily acknowledged that Claus's frauds had alienated some of the Grand River leaders, although he also believed that a number of the Six Nations chiefs were less than honest themselves in guiding community affairs. Nevertheless, he felt that the behaviour of both the Indian Department and the provincial government had been such that the imperial authorities in London would have to intervene to protect Iroquois interests (and in the process helped affirm Norton's faith in General Brock and the army). On the larger military and diplomatic fronts, Brock had earlier told the governor-in-chief of British North America, Lieutenant-General Sir George Prevost, that the bitter memories of the 1790s were so strong that the aboriginal peoples would not support the Crown until the British proved their sincerity and strength in combat. Despite his lack of optimism at the beginning of the council, he must have been disappointed in failing to muster the support of the Grand's four hundred warriors, who would have been a welcomed addition to the sixteen hundred regulars he had under his command in Upper Canada as he tried to scrape together a respectable force to repel the imminent American invasion.[32]

In early June 1812, shortly after Brock's meeting but before the outbreak of war, a deputation of Iroquois from the American side of the border travelled to what was supposed to have been a secret council to solidify neutralist opinion along the Grand River.[33] As it was, the Iroquois in New York had been sending 'private messages' for several months in support of neutrality.[34] The delegates repeated the argument the Americans had used to persuade them to remain at peace: the British cause was hopeless given the gross imbalance of strength in favour of the United States, especially since the majority of settlers in Upper Canada were American immigrants who probably would welcome the forthcoming invasion. Furthermore, there was no reason to support the British given their abandonment of the aboriginal nations in 1783 and 1794.[35] Captain Strong, a Seneca chief from the Allegany Reservation, used this argument and warned the people of the Grand to be mindful of the king's 'smooth mouth,' which he would use to 'deceive' them to their peril. Captain Strong informed his audience that his people had 'determined to take no more notice of the King' and he invited the Grand River people to unite with their New York relatives because the Iroquois had no reason to align themselves with either white power.[36] Another Seneca chief, Little Billy, underlined Captain Strong's views when he said: 'We know that neither of these powers have any regard for us ... Why then should we endanger the comfort, even the existence of our families, to enjoy their smiles only for the Day in which they need us?' These words must have struck a chord with those stung by the Indian Department's machinations. To the probable agreement of many of those listening to him, Little Billy recommended that they 'sit still' at home, 'unhurt & unobserved by the enraged Combatants.'[37]

The Grand River people took the customary two days to formulate a reply to the delegation from New York. During this time there were numerous debates over what they should do and opportunities to mould opinion by spreading rumours of how quickly the Americans would overrun the British colony.[38] Some discussions were simple. In one, a British Indian Department official, who had found out about the council and attended the proceedings, dismissed American might with impatient disdain: 'The United States talks loud, brags, and has a great mouth.'[39] Others were more sensitive, such as the exchange between John Norton and two Seneca chiefs from the United States. The Senecas told Norton that they viewed him with 'apprehension and suspicion': they feared that, because of his ardent support for the British, he would persuade the Grand River people to take up arms, without considering the terrible consequences that might ensue from such an action. Drawing on the prophetic heritage of the Iroquois, one of them told Norton that the 'gloomy Day, foretold by our ancients,' in which the independence and glory of the Iroquois had disappeared, had arrived. The Six Nations now lived precariously between two powerful but identical nations who could crush them out of existence when they pleased.[40] The Senecas reinforced the comments made during the formal sessions, saying that their relationships with whites had been marked by heavy wartime casualties, no white compassion for Iroquois widows and orphans, the loss of native independence, and white neglect for aboriginal interests. They counselled that the best policy was a pacifism similar to what they had seen the Quakers practise during the American Revolution. In response, Norton told the Senecas that the Iroquois in New York had no choice but to be neutral because the Americans surrounded their reservations, making it impossible for them to join their natural allies, the British. However, for those in Canada fighting alongside George III was the honourable route because the king had been generous in giving them protection within his dominions after the revolution. Moreover, armed resistance to American expansion was the only viable course, since other responses simply did not work, as witnessed by the murders of natives who had attempted to follow non-violent models, as had occurred at Gnadenhutten in 1782, when revolutionaries brutally massacred ninety-six pacifist Delawares. In 1812 refugees from that horror lived west of the Grand at Moraviantown as an enduring indictment of American perfidy. Furthermore, the recent battle of Tippecanoe was ample proof of America's continuing hostility towards the aboriginal nations.[41]

When the council met to hear the answer from Grand River, the tract's neutralist party withdrew from the proceedings to signal a lack of consensus and to undermine the legitimacy of the militant policy of the Mohawk-dominated British party that was to prevail, at least officially and for the benefit of the Indian Department agents on the scene, although everyone must have realized what the absence of so many people meant. The speaker for the Grand River repeated Norton's arguments and dismissed the fear of American strength that dominated opinion by expressing a providential theology, that it was the Great Spirit who determined events, not the earthly might of temporal powers. He warned the people from New York that the American call for neutrality was probably a fraud, just as it had been in the revolution when the rebels persuaded the Oneidas to embrace a neutralist posture at first, but then made them take up arms against the other nations of the Iroquois Confederacy. Remembering that event, he encouraged the people of New York to restrain their young men from joining the Americans because the Grand River people would 'be ashamed of our Tribes' if any fought alongside 'the common enemy of our race.'[42] Another Grand River speaker expressed his resentment towards the visitors because they had not moved to Canada after the revolution but had instead fallen under American domination. He told them that they had 'broken with us, with Great Britain and with Indians,' that if they listened to the Americans, they would be 'destroyed and made slaves like the Negroes,' and that, ultimately, the United States would deceive them, stop paying their annuities, and take their land from them. That was not the fate he wanted for himself. He declared proudly: 'The President wants you to lie still and hold down your heads. But I am a Mohawk. I will paint my face and be a man and fight Yankees as long as I live.'[43]

The council ended in apparent disunity, as the visiting delegation failed to achieve its objective. After asserting that friendship between the Iroquois in New York and those in Upper Canada had ended – again presumably for the benefit of the Indian Department – the people from New York went home. However, they knew British support among the Grand River population was frail and they had quietly used their time in Canada to help the cause of the neutralist party on the tract.[44]

About three weeks after war broke out, another delegation from New York, composed of Onondagas and Senecas, crossed into Canada to try to persuade the Grand River people, or at least the British party, to accept neutrality. This group met the Grand River representatives at the border village of Queenston, on the Niagara River, because General Brock would not allow them to go to the Grand where they might gather intelligence and sow discord. Brock also seems to have tried to control the meeting by calling on John Norton to pick reliable people to accompany him in Queenston. In New York, Erastus Granger was not happy about this council either, although it was the American military commander on the Niagara frontier who had suggested the mission. Like their British counterparts, American Indian agents and army officers sometimes did not coordinate their efforts. Presumably Granger suspected that the Iroquois from New York either might be misled by Norton's party or were plotting some strike against American interests, even though they had just told him that they were peacefully disposed towards the United States.[45]

The delegation from New York took a more conciliatory and sensitive approach than they had at the previous council in order to convince the British party that Iroquois interests would be served best by neutrality. One speaker was Arosa (or Silver Heels), a Seneca, who tried to sway opinion by speaking of the miseries and destruction of war and of the tragedies of fighting old friends. He concluded with an almost pathetic plea that seems to have been designed to appeal to the understanding at Grand River of the differences between themselves and the Iroquois in New York: 'remember, we are in the power of the Americans, & perhaps when you shall have spread Destruction through their Ranks, they will change their Language, and insist upon us to join them: – they may compel our young Men to fight against their kindred, – and like devoted animals, – we shall be brought to destroy each other.'[46] (Perhaps the delegates from New York at that moment were thinking about a speech given a few days earlier by Granger; he had suggested that while the United States did not need Iroquois support, two hundred warriors could enrol in American service if they gave up their 'cowardly' way of war and conformed to American military standards.)[47] Arosa also conveyed the view of the matrons who favoured peace: 'Listen to the words of our Mothers, they are particularly addressed to the War Chiefs, they entreat them to be united with the Village chiefs and to have a tender regard for the lives and happiness of their women and children and not to allow their minds to be too much elated or misled by sentiments of vanity and pride.'[48] These words sought to bolster the standing of those who argued for peace by linking their views to the authority of the clan matrons and by denigrating the motivations of those who favoured war to mere 'vanity and pride.'

A Grand River delegate countered by speaking of the need for a pan-tribal defence against the Americans, noting that the western tribes had been forced to take up arms to protect their families and that it was impossible for the Iroquois 'to remain unconcerned spectators at the destruction of our Brethren.' However, he then contradicted himself by suggesting that his people would not venture outside Upper Canada. This inconsistency perhaps reflected some sort of consensus reached between some of the opposing interests on the Grand before Norton's delegation travelled to Queenston.[49] Another member of Norton's party was an Onondaga chief who noted that the separation of the Iroquois in New York and Canada meant that they now had separate destinies. Because the Grand River people had sought the king's protection when they were 'overhung by the power of the Americans,' they would have to share their fate with the king's forces, whether it be the 'Shout of Victory' or 'the Grave.' He finished by commending the decision of the people in New York to remain quiet, since they could have no interest in the American cause and regretted the coming separation between the two Iroquois groups.[50] With the rejection of the mission, Arosa concluded with a plea

for decency in battle: 'Let the Warrior's rage only be felt in combat, by his
armed opponents; – Let the unoffending cultivator of the Ground, and
his helpless family, never be alarmed by your onset, nor injured by your
depredation.'[51] His party then recrossed the Niagara River to the United
States.

Despite Isaac Brock's attempt to control contact between the Six
Nations in Upper Canada and the Iroquois of New York, as shown by his
actions at the Queenston council, unobserved individuals slipped quietly
back and forth across the border with little difficulty. There can be no
doubt that the tribespeople in New York knew how weak the British party
was on the Grand River Tract. By early July at the latest, the Americans
also knew about the plight of the British party, the existence of an American party, and the probability that the majority of people on the Grand
favoured neutrality, having been informed of these details by a Grand
River Delaware, Pitris. Another who probably spied for the United States
was Tekarihogen, who worked as an interpreter for the British Indian
Department, despite his leadership of the American party.[52]

Armed with this information, American officials were poised to strike a
fatal propaganda blow against the British party. They made their move at
about the same time the leaders of that party were away from the Grand
in Queenston. On 12 July an American army, commanded by Brigadier-
General William Hull, began the invasion of Canada when it crossed from
Detroit into British territory. A proclamation from Hull quickly reached
the Grand River, telling the Six Nations that their lands and rights would
be guaranteed if they stayed peacefully at home. Along with the proclamation came word that the tribes in the Detroit area had decided to
remain neutral rather than join the other nations of the western aboriginal alliance against the United States. These fragments of intelligence,
manipulated by the American and neutralist parties, destroyed much of
the pro-British sentiment on the Grand River. For those inclined to mistrust the British because of the events of 1783 and 1794, the one major
reason for war – the protection of their homes – probably did not exist,
contrary to what the king's representatives had claimed. For many people
on the Grand, the bitter memories of their own land controversies with
Indian Department officials presumably helped them accept Hull's words
despite the history of American–Iroquois relations since 1783. Addition-
ally, their immediate aboriginal neighbours to the west had concluded
that neutrality was in their best interests, notwithstanding the possibility
that military success might lead to the creation of a homeland for them
and independence from both white powers. These people presumably

assumed that a homeland was a mere dream, since Britain would lose the war. Their views likely resonated well among the people of the Grand.[53]

With an American army now on British soil, and little more than a small garrison in Amherstburg standing between William Hull and the Grand River, many Iroquois on the tract had to consider whether it even might be wise to make a radical change in policy and move from neutrality to active support for the American invasion to demonstrate their friendship for the conquerors who soon might control their destiny. Yet they realized they had to tread carefully so long as Upper Canada remained British and a British party enjoyed legitimacy on the tract. Most of the British party persisted in expressing amity for the king, but even they held back from answering Isaac Brock's call to join him at Fort George (at today's Niagara-on-the-Lake), claiming that they needed to attend to their crops. This lack of support may have been indicative of considerable pessimism among British supporters and a desire to save themselves from retribution if the war progressed in favour of the Americans. As it was, Hull's presence in Upper Canada escalated tensions among the different parties to the point where members of rival groups threatened their opponents with dire consequences depending upon which white power triumphed.[54]

A sign of the strength of the neutralist and American parties was a decision to send warriors to the mouth of the Grand River on Lake Erie, ostensibly to watch for an American water-borne attack that might threaten the tract and isolate the Amherstburg garrison. Tekarihogen recommended this course of action to his people, falsely claiming to speak for the British.[55] Although guarding the Grand might be viewed as a gesture of solidarity with the king's cause, it was a sham. Everyone knew the British Provincial Marine was in control of Lake Erie. As one frustrated Cayuga announced, 'I will go to the West, where I am assured I shall meet the Enemy, – but why should I go to the Mouth of the River, unless to catch Fish? The Enemy will not cross the Lake so wide, while the ships of the Great King hold the command.'[56] This young warrior missed the point of the exercise. The Iroquois had to appear to help defend Upper Canada to avoid a charge of treachery so long as British authority in the province remained intact. Isaac Brock, for example, told them early in August 1812 that he wished to know who were his friends and who were not. Beyond a simple attempt to recruit people, this statement sent a signal to the Iroquois to remind them that he was aware of their equivocation and intended to gather the information he needed to take action against his enemies.[57] But if William Hull enjoyed success, the warriors could either melt away before his troops got to the Grand or swing behind the American party and fall on the retreating British to put Hull in their debt. Converging at a relatively safe location may also have been a compromise between the opposing parties to temper the tensions within their community. Neutralists wanted everyone to stay out of the conflict, and this was a way of keeping the warriors away from potential hostilities. Members of the British party wanted to support the king's forces, but had to respond to pressure from others who wished them to express their alliance in such a way that would not imperil their lands should Hull defeat Brock. Adherents to the American party also had to recognize the strength of the other parties while they awaited the forthcoming confrontation between British and American forces.

An angry Isaac Brock of course knew about this shift in Grand River policy, and his own understanding of North American history told him that neutrality was impossible among aboriginal people. Therefore, he assumed that it would only be a matter of time before the Grand River Iroquois became combatants. Based on captured enemy correspondence, he also believed that the chiefs had held face-to-face meetings with William Hull. For his part, John Norton only admitted that the Americans had captured an intoxicated Oneida (who had gone to Detroit to discuss the outbreak of war with the tribes of that region) and had sent him back to the Grand with Hull's proclamation to the Iroquois. However, given the party spirit on the tract it does not seem likely that American or neutralist supporters would not have used their time in the west to establish contact with William Hull. In fact, communications from the Americans led the Six Nations of the Grand to call together a council at which they decided that the best way to protect their interests was by not fighting the Americans. Because Brock was convinced that American intrigue (along with additional pressure exercised by pro-American white Upper Canadians who lived near the Grand) lay at the root of Six Nations policy, and because he also knew that Tekarihogen had generated the idea of assembling at the mouth of the river, he told Sir George Prevost the Iroquois would show their true disposition if the Americans won a battle in the west by cutting the British line of retreat from Amherstburg. If that happened, he expected them to commit 'everything horrid' in an attempt to buy off the Americans.[58] In the provincial capital, the well-informed rector of York, the Reverend John Strachan, wrote that the Iroquois were 'preparing to join the enemy who had invaded us with a much stronger force than we could bring against them. Not that they preferred the enemy, but they considered our case desperate and they thought that by joining the Americans early they might preserve their lands.'[59]

Brock's frustration stemmed not only from the danger posed by the Iroquois themselves but also from the impact their behaviour had on others. The neighbouring Long Point militia, which Brock wanted to employ in his counter-attack against Hull, refused to assemble, in part because they feared the warriors might assault their families if they were left unprotected.[60] Sharing the anxiety of the ordinary citizens, the local magistrates and militia officers would not compel their men to obey the militia law. As Brock noted, the militia officers 'became more apprehensive of the internal than the external enemy, and would willingly have compromised with the [American] one, to secure themselves from the other.'[61] The demoralized militiamen, knowing that at least some of the western tribes would fight alongside the British, also had to consider a threat issued in a proclamation William Hull had directed at the Euroamerican population of Upper Canada: '*No white man found fighting on the side of an Indian will be taken prisoner.* Instant destruction will be his Lot.'[62] Brock's anger at the Six Nations led him to hope to punish them by expelling them to the west at the earliest opportunity 'out of the reach of doing any mischief.'[63] However, to prevent any further erosion of support, he was careful not to show his frustration when meeting people from the Grand River's British party.[64]

General Brock knew that he had to try to suppress anti-British sentiment quickly and strike successful blows against the Americans to counter the pervasive defeatism in Canada and to convince the natives that Britain was willing to prosecute a vigorous war against the United States. To fight anti-British feeling and win over the aboriginal population, Brock sent several people to the Grand to do what they could. One of them was the opposition politician Joseph Willcocks, who had befriended the anti-Claus people on the tract before the war. There was logic in Brock's decision to send Willcocks because of the politician's connections, but Brock inadvertently made a mistake. Several weeks later the courts charged Willcocks with sedition, claiming that he had intended to use his influence with the Six Nations to support the American conquest of the province. In fact, Willcocks fought alongside the Iroquois and British at the battle of Queenston Heights in October, but afterwards deserted to the Americans. Another person Brock sent was William Kerr, an Indian Department officer married to Joseph Brant's daughter Elizabeth. Kerr assessed the mood on the tract and concluded that the situation was dangerous. He learned that in addition to Pitris and Tekarihogen's efforts, people in the Tuscarora community also passed intelligence to the Americans through their relatives in New York whose reservation sat close to the Niagara River. Brock also asked the provincial legislature to suspend *habeas corpus* so that he could move quickly against subversives and slackers, including the pro-American white people near the Grand, but a nervous legislature refused to grant the request.[65] As well, he entered the propaganda war with a proclamation of his own, in which he tried to link the aboriginal and white population in a common cause, with equal rights to protect their lands and liberties from the invaders, especially since the natives faced 'a ferocious and mortal foe, using the same warfare' against them 'which the American commander affects to reprobate.'[66]

Militarily, Brock ordered the commandant at St Joseph's Island in Lake Huron to capture the American post of Fort Mackinac at the head of Lake Michigan to knock the Americans out of the upper lakes and thereby help secure the alliance of the northern nations. Brock himself organized an expedition from Fort George to reinforce Amherstburg and drive Hull from Canada. Accompanying this force of 50 British regulars and 250 Canadian militia was John Norton at the head of 60 warriors; he had rejected the consensus reached at the recent council and was willing to fight enthusiastically for the British despite land issues, being content to put them aside until the return of peace. However, as many as thirty in Norton's party changed their minds and went home before advancing very far. Some of them had been persuaded to desert by a pro-American Mohawk, perhaps Tekarihogen himself. This was a disappointment for Brock, who had hoped that the British party might muster 150 men for the expedition despite the tensions at Grand River. (About 100 had gone to Fort George to get weapons and other equipment early in July and had given assurances that the rest would appear when called.) Given the consensus among the Six Nations not to fight the Americans, and their feigned support of the British in guarding the mouth of the Grand River, Norton's expedition was a private act of war and a gesture of defiance against the broader community decision. Thus, the success in persuading half of Norton's men to desert may have stemmed from an appeal, whether honest or manipulative, to get them to follow the consensus reached along the Grand. Some others who remained with Norton seem to have gone along for no other purpose than to undermine his leadership and prevent the warriors from doing anything that might bring about American punishment.[67]

While Brock brooded over the Iroquois, Hull's invasion began to collapse. Logically, Hull's first objective should have been the capture of the fort in Amherstburg, to deprive the British of a base in the west and to demoralize the civilian and native populations in Canada further. However, he moved slowly once on British soil and engaged only in some minor skirmishing. Meanwhile, he worried that his army was not strong enough to accomplish its tasks, because only one of his regiments consisted of regulars, the others being mere militia from Ohio. His one naval vessel on Lake Erie fell into British hands and his overland supply line ran several hundred kilometres through territory over which Tecumseh's hostile forces ranged. To the north, British regulars, fur traders, and natives (including a few from Kahnawake) captured Mackinac without a fight on 17 July. Some Ottawas who were present at Mackinac demonstrated the fragility of native support for the British by sitting out the affair until they saw who won. When word of the American surrender reached Hull, he assumed that the natives of the Detroit area would abandon neutrality unless he quickly captured Amherstburg to nullify the impact of the Mackinac disaster. As it was, the news from the north helped the previously neutral Wyandots near Detroit to decide to ally themselves to the British. Hull asked for reinforcements so that he could adopt a more aggressive stance in his front, but ordered the garrison at Fort Dearborn (now Chicago) far in his rear to abandon that post in the face of a possible widespread native uprising. Next, Hull's plan to attack Amherstburg foundered when he learned that an American advance against Montreal, designed partly to support him by dividing British defensive resources, had been postponed, that Tecumseh's people had attacked a supply column on its way to Detroit and had dispersed a force sent to rescue it, and that Brock was on his way to Amherstburg with reinforcements. A nervous Hull evacuated most of his force to Detroit on 8 August and then decided to reopen his supply route to the south. He sent six hundred men towards Ohio to accomplish the task, but a British and native force ambushed it on 9 August. The Americans beat off the attack but failed to open communications and suffered heavy casualties. As they retired towards Detroit, the British Provincial Marine subjected them to a barrage along those portions of the road that ran past the shoreline. Demoralized, Hull withdrew his remaining troops from Canada on 11 August and locked up his army inside Detroit's defences to await Brock's attack.[68]

Isaac Brock arrived in Amherstburg on 13 August. From captured letters he knew that William Hull worried about the native threat, especially because the civilian population in Michigan was vulnerable to hit-and-run raids by small war parties. Brock also realized that the men in Hull's army were terrified of the natives and had little or no confidence in their commanding officer. On 15 August Brock demanded Hull's surrender, playing on American fears by holding up the spectre of a massacre: 'It is far from my intention to join in a war of extermination,' he informed Hull, 'but you must be aware, that the numerous body of Indians who have attached themselves to my troops will be beyond control the moment the contest commences.'[69] As Brock expected, Hull refused the summons, although the British commander undoubtedly hoped that he had at least intensified his opponent's fears. Brock then ordered his artillery to bombard Detroit. On the night of 15–16 August, he crossed the Detroit River in preparation for an assault on the American defences. His force, combining his Niagara region reinforcements with the Amherstburg garrison, numbered three hundred regulars and four hundred militia. The six hundred natives with him included Tecumseh's Shawnees, Miamis, Delawares, and Potawatomis from the south, the Detroit region Wyandots, and Norton's contingent of Iroquois, strengthened by some Ojibways and Ottawas who had joined Norton on his march to the west.[70]

While Brock supervised the landing that night, Hull began to behave strangely. Perhaps unnerved at the prospect of Brock's promised massacre, undoubtedly horrified by the sight of two of his officers being sliced apart by a British cannon ball, and probably debilitated by narcotics and alcohol, Hull, who probably had not recovered fully from a stroke he had suffered earlier, became disoriented, his speech became indistinct, he dribbled incessantly, and he ran and crouched in the corners of his fort whenever the British fired a cannon. In the morning Brock advanced on Detroit, but before his troops could get close enough to start shooting, Hull's nerves gave out. The Stars and Stripes over Detroit came down, to be replaced first with a white flag, then the Union Jack. Hull surrendered twenty-two hundred soldiers, twenty-five hundred stands of arms, thirty-nine cannon, large quantities of supplies, and the whole of the Michigan territory. The day before, on 15 August, four hundred Potawatomis destroyed the Fort Dearborn garrison as it abandoned its post in obedience to Hull's orders. Brock had achieved his objectives. He secured communications to the northwest by taking Mackinac, eliminated the American threat on his western flank for the time being, acquired large quantities of desperately needed supplies, took Michigan, won over the support of many of the tribes, and proved that Upper Canada could be defended – all with fewer than fifty British and native casualties.[71]

After Hull's surrender, John Norton asked Isaac Brock if he could stay in the west because he was so disheartened by the divisions on the Grand River. Brock, however, wanted him to return home, where he thought the Mohawk chief could do more good for the British cause by rallying support among the Six Nations. Expecting the next American thrust to occur on the Niagara Peninsula, Brock needed Iroquois help. He also wanted them to join his troops to assure the militia that they could leave their families without having to worry about what the Six Nations might do while they were away from home. As well, a decision by the Iroquois to join the British might inspire the neighbouring Mississaugas to deploy their 150 warriors, just as Iroquois circumspection a few weeks earlier had influenced that tribe to remain neutral. Although General Brock continued to harbour doubts about the Iroquois, he thought the magic of Mackinac, Dearborn, and Detroit, which had solidified aboriginal support in the north and the west, would work on them because they were clear proof of Britain's willingness to fight, and to fight decisively, instead of pulling back from the brink as had happened in 1794.[72] Despite his frustrations, Brock thought the Grand River people were uncomfortable with their pre-Detroit policy because it made them look cowardly in comparison with their white and native neighbours; he wrote that 'they appear ashamed of themselves, and promise to whipe away the disgrace into which they have fallen by their late conduct.'[73] News of the capture of Mackinac, already spread by William Kerr, had inspired sixty additional Grand River men to step away from the tract's consensus and march west to join Norton's expedition. Others proceeded to Fort George and scouted for the British, going so far as to cross onto Grand Island in the Niagara River in American territory. Within a few weeks, over three hundred of the Grand's four hundred warriors took to the field in support of the British, and, unlike Norton's war party at Detroit, they went with the sanction of the majority of the Grand River leaders.[74]

This was an astonishing change for the people of the Grand. It demonstrates the freedom individuals exercised as circumstances changed, and it reveals their uncertainty as to how they could protect their interests until some decisive moment had passed to enable them to assess conditions more clearly than had been possible before Brock's victories, when unsubstantiated rumours and partisan pleading dominated debate. In addition to bolstering the British party, Brock's successes discredited the pro-Americans and probably undermined the neutralists, because a refusal to support the king's cause might bring British retribution down upon the Iroquois, especially as other natives who had previously been reluctant to take up arms now were doing so. Less cynical people could celebrate the string of victories and hope to participate in a glorious cause that, if successful, would see native interests safeguarded in a successful war against the United States, the 'common enemy' of the aboriginal 'race,' to use the words of a Grand River speaker quoted earlier. Furthermore, the events in the west showed that the strength of the United States, which had been proclaimed so loudly to keep the Iroquois out of the war, was not nearly as formidable as had been feared, thus allowing previously cautious pro-British people to express their attachments with confidence.

The resolution of some of the Detroit-area tribes to join the British served as a model for Grand River behaviour in the same way their neutrality earlier had help sway the Iroquois. As it was, Norton returned home with parties of Delawares, Ojibways, and others who helped inspire the Grand River people to adopt an actively pro-British stance. [75] Brock's successes seemed to have held out the promise of establishing a native homeland in the Michigan territory. Although this promise would have been more beneficial to the western tribes than to the Iroquois, and while the Iroquois's perceptions of their role in the frontier war of the 1790s may not have been accurate, there was at least enough of a sense of pan-tribal solidarity that the Six Nations could rejoice in the possibility of stemming the western growth of the United States just when the anti-American passions that had been building up among them since the 1770s burst forth. Perhaps more important, Brock's successes seem to have focused the natives on the fundamental issues of the war for them as a people – American hostility towards natives and the likely consequences to aboriginal land tenure should the United States emerge triumphant. Providing needed reinforcements to the hard-pressed British in order to counter American aggression and protecting their own lands in the process were strong reasons for Iroquois leaders to muster support for a national war effort, within the limitations of their non-coercive structures and while remaining open to making further changes in policy if necessary should the course of the war change dramatically. Not only was there the memory of the sad outcome of the American Revolution and of the subsequent events leading up to Tippecanoe to remind the Iroquois how great a threat the United States posed, but other, more recent signs also suggested that there was a serious problem in flirting with either neutrality or an American alliance. For example, there were Hull's two proclamations to reconsider after the capture of Detroit. On the one hand, Hull had sent the Six Nations a warm message offering them friendship and guaranteeing them possession of their land, while on the other, he had communicated to white Upper Canadians that ' *No white man found fight-*

ing on the side of an Indian will be taken prisoner. Instant destruction will be his Lot.' How could these proclamations be reconciled, and what fate could aboriginal combatants expect if white allies of aboriginal forces were to be treated so cruelly? For many Iroquois looking back over the history of American–aboriginal relations, the first proclamation had to be considered a fraud, while Hull's words to the white population had to be assumed to reflect American opinion, an opinion marked by a savage hatred of native peoples.[76]

Given the magnitude of the turnaround within the context of difficult British–Iroquois relations, as exemplified by the decision by three hundred of the tract's four hundred warriors to take to the field when only thirty had gone to Detroit, the change in policy on the Grand also probably reflected the impact of internal and cultural forces on the Six Nations beyond larger issues of external relations. These ranged from the traditional and spiritual ways many people interpreted earthly events to the prospect of personal gain to be realized by participating in hostilities, to the deep-seated military legacies of the Six Nations, and to the ongoing vitality of the old-style struggles between peace and war chiefs.

Significantly, the nature of Brock's successes possessed the essential characteristic necessary to be interpreted as great victories from a native perspective: they were achieved at very little cost. Aboriginal people did not understand white concepts of victory, because Euroamericans were willing to suffer heavy casualties to achieve their objectives.[77] Whatever the reasons for war, aboriginal people often framed their motivation within a convention of avenging deaths suffered by their community through one of several methods: killing and scalping members of the enemy community, capturing people for adoption into the tribe, or capturing and torturing them. Avenging a death appeased a dead person's lust for revenge and enabled him or her to find a haven in the next world. In this world, the village 'condoled' the family of the deceased by offering a prisoner for adoption, a scalp for symbolic adoption, or a captive for torture. Traditionally, the best way for an Iroquois to avenge a death had been through the adoption of a prisoner to renew the population base and to strengthen the spiritual force of the tribe by transferring the power of a lost loved one to the adopted individual.[78] Adopting prisoners, as well as torture, had become less common among the Iroquois by the time of the American Revolution, and the growing strength of white society in the post-revolutionary era, both legally and demographically, made it difficult to avenge murders committed by Euroamericans outside the confines of war. Killing and scalping enemies during hostilities, however, remained a viable option.[79] Yet, if natives incurred heavy casualties during the avenging process, then many new families experienced the dreadful calamity of death and had to suffer through the horror of grief and bereavement until the new losses could be avenged. Moreover, while it is likely that the requirement to avenge deaths had been weakened by the changing world of the Great Lakes region in the late eighteenth and early nineteenth centuries, by the years of peace before 1812, and by the spread of Christianity, the important underlying principle of minimizing casualties unquestionably remained strong. With a small population and a powerful sense of the spiritual worth of each individual, the people of an aboriginal nation simply could not afford high casualties if they hoped to maintain their viability as a society. Therefore, if many lives were lost in action while avenging old deaths, even in a tactical or strategic victory or in one that fulfilled national objectives, native people interpreted the battle as essentially indistinguishable from defeat.[80] At the same time, the providential world-view of the Christian Iroquois residing in Canada probably led to an interpretation of Brock's stunning successes as an expression of divine will and a sign of the justice of the king's cause, while traditionalists may have interpreted these victories as evidence of the ability of British soldiers to harness sacred powers; in contrast, in earlier conflicts natives had witnessed spiritual failures that were evident by the comparatively high casualties among their white allies.[81]

Another aspect of Brock's victories of significance to the Iroquois was the enormous quantity of supplies and armaments captured at Detroit. War had taken on a material character among natives over the contact period as a way of enriching warriors through plundering enemies and by earning money and presents from allies. The Iroquois were no exception and regularly seized enemy property. On one typical occasion during the American Revolution, a combined Kahnawake and loyalist force captured a revolutionary village in New York. The commanders allowed the inhabitants to equip themselves with enough supplies to get to the next settlement, then let the warriors take whatever they wanted, 'a thing they allways look upon as their undoubted right,' according to an officer on the scene. Later in the expedition, the same witness noted that looting the enemy was so important that the natives, 'finding they were not likely to get any more plunder resolved to Quit us, which they Accordingly did.'[82] While this man's opinion may have been scornful because he did not understand Kahnawake thinking, and while there are accounts of aboriginal leaders trying to prevent the plundering of non-combatants, there was some truth to his comments.[83] In the 1790s the few Iroquois who participated in the frontier war with the Americans took prizes, sometimes as souvenir trophies. A visitor to Joseph Brant in 1792, for instance, saw a valuable rifle 'taken by an Indian boy from an American whom he shot dead in the action of the 4th of November last.' [84] During the same war, warriors captured black slaves while raiding American settlements in the Ohio Valley and took them to Canada to sell for profit. [85] The practice of looting continued throughout the War of 1812. The extent of native pillaging is characterized in an account by an American officer who saw a party of prisoners that was returned to the United States in 1813: 'they were stripped of all their clothes by the Indians, not a man had a hat or cap on his head, and very few had any shoes ... in fact they had nothing but some old duds the people of Canada had given them as a charity.'[86] A year later, an American officer seized by a group of warriors (possibly Norton's war party) recorded that the first thing they demanded after disarming him was his money, then they took his watch and all his clothes except his shirt and pantaloons. The amount of cash taken from him and two others captured at the same time was a princely one thousand dollars. [87]

The Iroquois also profited by demanding presents and payment from their allies, which acted as a further inducement to fight. Among the great quantities of goods given to natives by whites were weapons, hunting supplies, clothing, cloth, body paint, jewellery, cooking utensils, and food. [88] In addition to goods, natives wanted money. At the beginning of hostilities, John Norton told Isaac Brock that a 'regular stipend' to free warriors from the need to care for their families would be required to keep men in the field for any length of time. [89] This request illustrates the importance of the cash economy that had begun to influence Iroquois society significantly in the mid–eighteenth century. [90] Across the border, the outbreak of war saw the Americans lose access to the British blankets and other manufactured goods that they had traditionally given to natives. Thus, when they recruited native allies for combat roles, they tended to rely more on cash payments and military wages as supplements to gifts. Army pay was low in comparison with what civilians earned, although officers' salaries for chiefs could be attractive. Low military wages could inhibit aboriginal participation in a campaign unless whites provided additional incentives, because men could find more lucrative employment on farms and elsewhere in the frontier economy. Privates in the American army, for example, received eight dollars per month compared with the fifteen paid to farm labourers in western New York. [91] The Stockbridges, who lived with the Oneidas, were typical in trying to maximize the compensation they might receive. In the spring of 1814, when the United States tried to assemble as strong a force as possible to invade Canada at the time of an enlistment crisis, they wrote to the Americans asking 'what premiums we shall receive ... over & above the troops of the United States, which will be a great incouragement to our young men to turn out.'[92] If the amount of service performed for payment was small, warfare could be very profitable. For some, bluffing Euroamerican allies into giving away valuable goods and foodstuffs without receiving any help at all was at least some compensation for white exploitation of aboriginal peoples. This attitude likely motivated some of the Grand River warriors who went to Fort George for presents early in the summer of 1812 but then did not muster for the Detroit expedition. Warriors who had weapons, clothes, and supplies often left everything at home and joined their allies, claiming poverty so they could acquire as many presents as possible from those responsible for outfitting them.[93]

Beyond purely economic gain, native peoples saw gifts as rewards for past assistance, as manifestations of the giver's power, as expressions of affection towards friends in need, and as compensation for not being able to hunt, trade, or farm while on campaign. Some interpreted the receipt of presents in a very traditional way as establishing reciprocal cross-cultural bonds, as exemplified by the many council speeches in which native orators expressed friendship towards a white monarch or leader, and then asked for material assistance to relieve some distress. Stinginess, in comparison, could be interpreted as a sign of hostility. Whites often understood the distribution of presents as a straightforward prepayment for services. At times, Euroamericans used gift-giving to undermine neutralist initiatives within a community. They knew, for example, that women played a major role in decisions to go to war and offered them presents as a way of cementing support for military action.[94] In 1812 General Brock seems to have thought, in addition to presents, he might have to pay war chiefs army officers' salaries and give them 'bribes' to obtain their assistance, as had been common practice for at least two decades.[95] At another point he thought that 'much management and large bribes' would be necessary to keep the Six Nations allied.[96] His assumptions suggest either that some native leaders may have used their status for personal reasons by enlisting warriors without regard for wider tribal concerns or that they sought wealth to give to their followers, as Iroquois leaders had done in times past in order to secure their standing through establishing reciprocal obligations between themselves and their followers.[97]

Another cultural condition that sometimes led the Iroquois to jettison neutrality was the strain between the ambitions of hereditary peace chiefs on the one hand and, on the other, war chiefs who, with few exceptions, achieved their authority by winning community recognition of their prowess as wartime leaders. However, in the case of the Grand River in the late summer of 1812, the tribes' decision to fight after the fall of Detroit does not seem to have pitted peace chiefs against war leaders, although there may have been some incentive to adopt a belligerent stance because of pressure brought on by the war chiefs. John Norton's decision to lead a party on the Detroit expedition before that decision was made by the Grand River leadership may have fitted into the traditional pattern of conflict between different kinds of leaders. Because of the peace chiefs' hereditary hold on authority, a man who wanted to rise in esteem and influence had two main avenues open to him. One was to be elected or accepted as a pine tree chief because of his personal political talent as a kind of adviser to the hereditary leadership. Some pine tree chiefs, such as Red Jacket of the Senecas, outshone the hereditary peace chiefs and dominated tribal or village society. The other path to leadership was to become a war chief by demonstrating bravery and leadership in battle. If a community decided to go to war, the peace chiefs experienced a diminution of their stature because they had to defer authority to the war chiefs when on campaign. Some war chiefs, such as Joseph Brant, who exercised dynamic leadership and who won the confidence of both white authorities and traditional leaders in diplomacy as well as in war, maintained considerable control at the expense of other leaders after a return to peace. (In Brant's case, however, marriages to important women also were significant in solidifying his claims to leadership.) Even future peace chiefs could use their battlefield prowess to help attain office because there usually were several hereditary candidates for each position and the women who chose the chiefs based their decisions, in part, on the military exploits of the candidates.[98] Thus, as the military situation changed about the middle of August 1812, established and aspiring war chiefs had an excellent opportunity to pursue their ambitions and they found a ready source of support among men anxious to demonstrate their manhood and among women desirous of having deaths suffered by their families avenged.

There were certain traditional patterns of going to war at the national or tribal level that reached back through the contact period to prehistoric times and that the Iroquois likely followed in 1812.[99] The process probably started when a number of chiefs and other influential people decided the time had come to act, and then called everyone to a council and began to lobby important people to try to align potentially divergent views. On receiving the message, the women in the different villages along the Grand, if they favoured hostilities, prepared food and moccasins for the warriors while the men cleaned and repaired their weapons and equipment. Thus, a pro-war impetus could be created even before deliberations began and might be solidified further by its advocates, who could use their family, clan, or other affiliations to increase support for their position. At the council, either the momentum could be maintained by the opening statements of a speaker who would propose a belligerent course, or debate might start with a discussion on the motives for and against war.[100] Presumably, the content of the opening statements reflected an assessment of what was possible given the feelings of those present. Through dialogue dominated by the most influential people, the council attempted to achieve a consensus. One way of obtaining agreement was to have the most respected chiefs speak last so that they could fuse the diverse views expressed and the multiplicity of personal and larger reasons for wanting to go to war into some conclusion that would enjoy widespread acceptance.

Iroquois communities, despite the integrative characteristics of their social structure, respect for individuals, and the search for consensus, could become badly divided over an issue. Some early-nineteenth-century Iroquois people also tried to exclude their opponents by holding secret or semi-secret councils within a community; afterwards they would claim more authority for the decisions that had been taken than the conditions under which the councils had been held would suggest was appropriate. Another technique to exclude opponents from a council was to declare that they had no authority to participate in the first place. A third way of undermining rival opinion was to expand the definition of who could participate in order to incorporate a large body of supporters and to isolate adversaries in numerically small groups. For example, before the War of 1812, Joseph Brant found himself under pressure from his opponents on the Grand and from the Indian Department, and so he temporarily reconstituted a unified trans-border Six Nations Confederacy council at Buffalo Creek in New York, which, however, ended up siding with his enemies. That council soon ceased functioning when the Grand River people rekindled their own confederacy council fire at the Grand's Onondaga village.[101]

Women, particularly older ones who headed the lineages and clans where a community's attempt to reach consensus regularly began, played an important role in deliberations as influential lobbyists for whichever side they supported. If women favoured war, they might use their eloquence to convince men to raise the tomahawk in retaliation for deaths suffered by their families in the past, aside from any geopolitical reasons that might motivate them. In fact, because of their responsibility for avenging deaths within their families, women could demand that warriors launch private hostilities exclusive of the initiatives of male leaders. Women without formal power could weep and display enormous emotional upset to convince men to agree to avenge a death. If this did not work, they might offer material rewards to warriors or shame them into acting by accusing them of cowardice in front of their friends and families.[102] Beyond these methods of making their views known, women also seem to have had, at least in certain circumstances, the right to make policy decisions if a consensus could not be reached through normal processes. In 1809 one man from the Grand, Old Patterson, explained how this worked, saying that when an issue came forward the chiefs first attempted to resolve it, but would refer the issue to the warriors if they could not arrive at a consensual agreement. If the warriors also failed to resolve the issue, then, 'the women take it up.'[103]

In the discussions over joining the British, it seems likely that the neutralist and American parties in Canada found themselves in an untenable situation, at least for the moment. Tekarihogen, for one, slipped across the border to join the Americans at about this time. However, he later had a change of heart, returned to Canada, regained his chieftainship, participated on the British side in the battle of Beaver Dams in 1813, and helped suppress the American party on the Grand River Tract. After the war, his continuing unhappiness induced him to move to Ohio in 1820, but he again came back to the Grand in 1823 and remained there the rest of his life where he was active in the life of the Church of England. To some degree, Tekarihogen's behaviour is representative of the strains that permeated the tract. He had fought as an ally of the loyalist cause during the American Revolution, presumably because he felt that a Crown victory would benefit the Iroquois more than if the rebels won. Yet in 1812 he found hope for the future as a leader of the militant American party during the uncertainties that pervaded Upper Canada before the fall of Detroit, in an atmosphere poisoned by his dehorning and by his disputes with both the Indian Department and his enemies within the Six Nations community. Such a posture made sense, as the expected American conquest of Canada would pave the way for his return to power, ruin his enemies, and allow him to protect his people once they fell under American jurisdiction. Then, in the wake of Detroit, Tekarihogen left Canada, perhaps to save himself, as political assassinations were one method the Iroquois occasionally employed to rid themselves of perceived troublemakers; he knew Joseph Brant had had an attempt on his life during an earlier political crisis on the Grand. Afterwards, perhaps disillusioned by his American experiences, Tekarihogen returned to the Grand River, where he re-embraced his older pro-British attitude. [104]

Finally, when it was clear that the council had decided in favour of war, messengers carried wampum, tomahawks, and war clubs to communicate the decision to neighbouring villages and allies, and sometimes to the enemy. With receipt of the notice, war chiefs went through their communities, sounded the war cry, and showed some wampum to those they hoped to recruit. Anyone could join a war party but nobody was forced to do so, although community pressure to fight might be intense. War parties typically formed among men from the same clan but warriors could enlist under any chief they liked. Chiefs might attract as few as three men or dozens of warriors, depending upon their stature and the potential number of recruits. [105]

Usually, chiefs had little trouble attracting warriors because of the social influences which drove men between the ages of about twenty-one and fifty to fight when the opportunity arose. [106] The pressure to prove oneself in combat was so great that even in times of general peace small groups of individuals often formed war parties, without the sanction of their community councils, to fight another, often distant, aboriginal nation with whom the tribe was not officially at peace and with whom an old feud remained unsettled. The commandant at Fort Niagara just prior to the outbreak of the American Revolution, towards the end of a ten-year period of relative peace, recorded one candid Seneca remark that exemplifies the connection between manhood and combat experience: 'The old ones ... when in their cups & off their guard can not help saying that this long peace will be the ruin of their nation, that their warriors are loosing [sic] their manhood & that their youth must become women, having no opportunities of exercising themselves in war.' [107] The expectation that boys and youths would be warriors when they grew up was so powerful in Iroquois society that it is difficult to imagine how neutralist opinion could have prevented significant numbers of men from going off to fight when their communities decided to support the British war effort. [108]

The Iroquois recognized the warrior's worth in the reverence they paid to the legends and legacies of the community's military history and by creating a distinctive battle dress that affiliated the wearer with previous glories. Traditional religious practices affirmed the legitimacy of war (for instance, food brought on the warpath was treated as a divine gift), as did the prayers and sacraments of the Iroquois Anglicans and Roman Catholics in Canada. The rich symbolism of going to war further attested to the community's expectation that able-bodied men would fight when called to do so by the matrons and war chiefs. When the anonymous individual quoted earlier made the outwardly simple assertion, 'I am a Mohawk ... I will paint my face and be a man and fight Yankees as long as I live,' he was in fact expressing a rich and complex consciousness of his role within society. In contrast, an individual who chose to reject the will of his clan or village to fight an enemy would be exposed as a failure in one of Iroquois society's fundamental tests of manhood, and his failure would be made all the more painful because it would occur under the accusing eyes of the women, many of whom accompanied the warriors on campaign (but not normally into battle) and thereby continued to make their views felt. With all these pressures, many men found it difficult to avoid joining a war party, although once in the field, individuals could leave their chiefs and drift home if they wished. [109]

The people of the Grand River were not the only Iroquois to go to war in 1812. The Seven Nations communities abandoned neutrality before the end of the first season's hostilities, probably for the same reasons that had influenced the Grand River people. Kahnawake, Kanesatake, and Akwesasne together had eight hundred warriors, representing a significant augmentation to the Crown's forces in the Canadas. [110] However, when approached by British officials before the outbreak, the Seven Nations echoed the attitudes of the Grand River people, saying that they were willing to defend their lands if threatened but that they preferred 'to hunt beaver rather than go to war,' as they had during the American Revolution. [111] Their statement was not quite accurate, given that their people had fought on both sides during that conflict. Complicating any decision for them were the facts that they, like the Grand River people, received American annuities and came under intense pressure to support the American cause from outsiders as well as from prominent people within their communities, such as Thomas and Eleazer Williams in Kahnawake, and Colonel Louis and Captain Francis in Akwesasne. (The latter two were considered so friendly to American interests that the United States, uncertain about Seneca views in western New York, employed them to try to convince the Senecas to side with the Americans.) [112]

The people of Akwesasne had to be particularly careful. Their community straddled the international border, and British and American parties competed for the affections of the residents. At the same time, neutralists hoped to keep everyone quiet and to avoid the intense internal strains that might explode should one or both of the other parties succeed in recruiting warriors. Any hostile action they might take could lead to an attempt by whites to confiscate their land because of the community's strategic location astride the St Lawrence River – Upper Canada's lifeline with the rest of the British Empire. They also had to be cautious because both the British and the Americans gave them presents and they did not want to endanger either source. Governor-in-Chief Sir George Prevost recognized the precariousness of the situation should Akwesasne support the British and thereby invite an American occupation that could cut his links to the west. Therefore, he tolerated the neutralist party and agreed to continue issuing presents to keep the people favourably disposed towards the British.[113]

The residents of Akwesasne, nevertheless, found themselves drawn into the war as local British and American officials ignored both orders from their superiors and Iroquois expressions of neutrality. On 1 October a contingent of New York militia tried to occupy Akwesasne but without success. Subsequently, a small Canadian militia force moved into the community. The Americans returned later in October, routed the Canadians, and took a large quantity of British presents intended for the Iroquois. Then they threatened to burn down the village if anyone sided with the British. Next they built a blockhouse to exercise control over Akwesasne. Eighty outraged warriors promptly joined British forces operating on the north bank of the St Lawrence River. Sadly, these people found themselves ostracized by their opponents when they returned home. Despite the rejection, they remained unrepentant and continued to serve alongside the king's forces throughout much of the war.[114]

In November 1812, 250 Canadian militia and thirty natives marched on Akwesasne and forced the American garrison to surrender. Some American party members of the community warned the New Yorkers of the attack, but it is not known if they fought beside the Americans. In the aftermath at least one prominent pro-American resident felt he had to flee to save himself from the British party. At the same time, both white powers exacerbated Iroquois divisions by recruiting Akwesasne warriors. Isaac LeClaire of the British Indian Department sought recruits, although unauthorized to do so, and threatened to torch the village if men did not come forward. The Americans used the same tactic and managed to enrol twenty men after plying them with alcohol and presents, but when the warriors sobered up, only three actually went off to war. These and a handful of others fought alongside the Americans throughout the war, being engaged on both the Niagara and St Lawrence fronts. Other Akwesasne people worked for the American army, making snowshoes, spying, or otherwise providing useful services. Among the pro-British people of Akwesasne, two groups of leaders arose in 1812. A more traditional group followed the neutralism endorsed by the governor-in-chief. The other followed the militant Isaac LeClaire. Both parties vied for control, using wartime divisions to seize their opponents' property while attempting to solidify their influence over the people of the badly divided community.[115]

Many of the Iroquois in New York also decided to go to war in 1812 but most did so in support of the United States (although some Senecas had gone west to join Tecumseh in 1811). Aligning themselves with the American cause seems curious because of the history of poor American–Iroquois relations and because the United States enjoyed no successes in the opening weeks of the war comparable to General Brock's. To some, therefore, allying themselves with the Americans would have been analogous to rejecting the revelations of the Great Spirit. However, there were reasons and pressures that influenced the Iroquois in the United States to fight, including the deep warrior tradition in which many men wanted to partake, especially in communities where the pacifism of Handsome Lake had not gained widespread support. Even before the outbreak, chiefs recognized that they could not restrain all the warriors who wanted to take up arms. Afterwards, they believed they had to let men join the Americans because the obligation to demonstrate prowess in battle was so strong that they feared significant numbers of them otherwise might attach themselves to tribes hostile to the United States and thereby endanger the property of Iroquois in New York. Senior American officials recognized this possibility; they ordered New York's agent to the Onondagas to organize them for combat if he could not keep them 'quiet' and told the commanding officer on the Canadian front to recruit other Iroquois men rather than let them join the British since they thought that it would be impossible to stop them from taking up arms.[116]

Some tribes in New York had political or historical reasons for allying themselves to the American cause. Oneidas and Tuscaroras had fought with the rebels in the American Revolution and probably had memories of unavenged deaths and insults brought on by loyalists to spur them into action, or, at least, saw the British in Canada as a natural target for avenging deaths, however caused, because of their status as old enemies. The Senecas felt they had to protect their own land after some Mohawks from Grand River occupied Seneca-owned Grand Island in the Niagara River. Judging from comments by the Seneca leader Red Jacket in August 1812, the decision to fight did not stem from a desire to ally with the Americans, at least at that point, but rather to defend Iroquois interests. Neither the United States nor the state of New York recognized Seneca ownership of the island.[117] Therefore, protecting their property was a key factor in taking to the warpath. As Red Jacket told the Americans: 'Our property is taken possession of by the British and their Indian friends. It is necessary for us now to ... drive the enemy from it. If we sit still ... the British (according to the customs of you white people) will hold it by conquest, and should you conquer the Canadas you will claim it upon the same principle, as conquered from the British.'[118] The Seneca war chief Little Billy echoed his sentiments, saying, 'we ... shall now prepare to defend ourselves against the common enemy. It is true we have friends on the other side, but we are exposed to the blow as well as you are, and must prepare to meet it. We know of no other way to preserve peace but to rise from our seats and defend our own firesides, our wives and our children.'[119]

Seneca intentions at the tribal level were purely defensive at that point. Nevertheless, the chiefs recognized that some of their warriors might want to seek glory across the border but they wished to minimize the potential hazards of operations in Canada by restricting the number of men who might go. Little Billy continued: 'We hope you will not ask us to cross over. Those that do go over must go at their own risk. If our men go they must go voluntarily. We wish to act only on the defensive.'[120] Other people communicated a similar reticence while trying to preserve Iroquois–American relations and limiting the extent of their commitments to combat. At a council held at Onondaga, one Iroquois speaker told the Americans: 'Having been told repeatedly by your agents to remain neutral, we were very much surprised and disappointed ... at being invited to take up the tomahawk. We are not unfriendly to the United States, but are few in number and can do but little, but are willing to do what we can, and if you want us, say so, and we will go with your people to battle.'[121]

Part of the change in the actions of the New York Iroquois arose out of a shift in American policy. While the Americans had been happy enough to obtain aboriginal neutrality at the outbreak of hostilities, some officials decided to recruit natives once the optimistic predictions of an easy conquest of Canada began to sour and the realization came to them that their opinions of British influence over the Six Nations were exaggerated. On the Iroquois side, some leaders presumably agreed to move away from neutrality towards belligerency as a way of distancing themselves from their pro-British relatives in Canada in order to avoid American retribution, although recruiting efforts met with less success at Allegany and Tonawanda, where Handsome Lake had convinced many of his followers that the loss of Seneca lands had stemmed largely from participation in white wars. (Handsome Lake's hostility to warfare had been so strong that he even tried to change the old, spiritually charged rituals of going to war, such as certain dances, away from their original functions and convert them into ceremonies for peacetime medicine societies.) In contrast, the majority of warriors from Buffalo Creek, where his support was weak, went to war.[122]

Thus, within a short time after the outbreak of hostilities, the Grand River people, the Seven Nations of Canada, and the Iroquois in New York raised the tomahawk, despite the efforts of the peace chiefs to keep them neutral and a widespread belief that whites either could not be trusted or would ignore Iroquois interests after their services were no longer needed. For the Senecas in New York and the residents of Akwesasne there was an immediate need to protect their lands to motivate them. For other Seven Nations people and the Grand River Iroquois there was the potent image of British and western tribal victories to entice them to take to the warpath as well as a recognition of the hazards that a victorious United States might pose for them. For Iroquois everywhere, there was the need to show support for the white power that exercised power over them. To these reasons must be added the strong military incentives and culture of early-nineteenth-century Iroquois society as fundamental reasons why warriors joined the dances of their war chiefs, despite the greater collective benefits that many thought could be achieved by sitting out the Anglo–American confrontation.[123]

The decision to go to war was not easy, as illustrated by the contortions that took place on the Grand River over a ten or twelve week period. As events unfolded, the British, American, and neutralist parties on the Grand each had a cadre of ardent supporters, but the majority of people based their primary loyalties on their village, clan, or some other foundation. Therefore, while most people entered the war supporting neutrality, their sentiments were not fixed. As a result, the influence of the hardliners in the opposing parties on the majority ebbed and flowed with considerable speed as circumstances changed and as public debate evolved. As might be expected, the Iroquois continued to respond with the freedom and fluidity they had demonstrated in the opening weeks of hostilities as new opportunities or disasters arose, as the horrors of war began to make people reconsider the virtues of neutrality, and as the Iroquois faced the imperatives of making the right decisions in a most uncertain world to ensure their survival as a distinct people.

3

'We Wish Not to Be Sold': The Iroquois Way of War

I explained to them the manner the British and Americans fought. Instead of steal-ing upon each other, and taking every advantage to kill the enemy *and* save their own people, *as we do, (which, with us is considered good policy in a war chief), they marched out, in open daylight, and* fight, *regardless of the number of warriors they may lose! After the battle is over, they retire to feast, and drink wine, as if nothing had happened.*

Black Hawk, a Sauk veteran of the War of 1812[1]

Just as the Iroquois decided to go to war in ways that reflected their dis-tinct values and concerns, the modes of warfare they practised likewise differed from those of the opposing white powers. Two dominant factors determined how aboriginal peoples fought in the early nineteenth cen-tury. The primary one was cultural: they were anxious to balance larger objectives with their desire to minimize casualties and provide opportuni-ties for individual warriors to display initiative and heroism. The second was the widespread use of Euroamerican technology, which had contrib-uted to fundamental changes in native warfare since the early seven-teenth century. What had developed by 1812 among the Iroquois and other natives of the Great Lakes region was a form of warfare that was very different from both white combat of the same period and from aboriginal tactics at the time of contact two centuries earlier.

In order to appreciate the distinctive qualities of native warfare it is necessary first to understand Euroamerican military technology and how it was used on the battlefields of the Napoleonic era. The land war around the Great Lakes was primarily an infantryman's struggle. Gener-ally, only small numbers of artillery supported the infantry, and cavalry fulfilled only minor roles. The Iroquois did not use artillery and rarely fought on horseback, although some owned horses and rode them to get to battle.[2]

The principal firearm in the British and American armies was the muzzle-loaded, smooth-bore, single-shot, flintlock musket. Using paper cartridges containing a lead ball and gunpowder, a trained soldier could load and fire his musket two or three times per minute. In action, a musket could be accurate at forty or fifty metres and effective at 150. Further than that, it rapidly declined as a deadly weapon and became almost useless against an enemy standing two hundred metres away. Accuracy and firepower diminished as a battle wore on because loading became sloppy in the stress of combat, gunpowder residue clogged the firing mechanism, and the sharp-edged flint (used to generate sparks to ignite the powder by hitting a piece of steel when the trigger was pulled) wore out. The most effective way to overcome the musket's limitations was to stand troops shoulder-to-shoulder in tightly packed lines and to pump massed volleys into their opponents at close range. Ideally, these volleys would shatter the enemy line and shake its resolution so that the winning side could use its secondary weapon, the bayonet, to chase its adversaries from the field. In colonial environments (and in the rough or enclosed terrain of much of Europe), armies adjusted to local circumstances by thinning these tight lines somewhat, although the fundamental principles of massed volley fire and unified action remained intact.[3]

As effective as these dense formations of disciplined soldiers were – and it was these troops who won or lost the big battles – they could not respond to all of the situations in which infantry needed to be engaged. Therefore, both the American and the British armies trained a portion of their soldiers as light infantry. These troops increased a commander's flexibility, because they possessed skills needed to address conditions that called for skirmishing, ambushing, and guarding the line's front, flanks, and rear. Normally, light troops fought in extended order – a type of very thin line – to allow their small numbers to cover a larger frontage than the formations they protected. Their fundamental weakness was an inability to produce the same volume of destructive firepower that line troops could deliver. In battle, light infantry tried to preserve the main body from harassment by covering the latter's manoeuvres so that it could approach the enemy in as fresh a state as possible in order to inflict its deadly volleys effectively. Light infantry also might try to harass enemy line troops and thereby blunt their fighting edge before the rest of their own force came into action. In retreat, light infantry could fight a delaying action to hold off pursuing troops long enough to allow the main body to escape to fight again another day. In an advance, light infantry (and cavalry if available) could move ahead of the line infantry to prevent the enemy from recovering from a bayonet charge, to round up prisoners, and to capture bridges and other features for securing the army's advance.[4]

Although most light troops in the War of 1812 carried muskets, some used rifles, particularly a few Canadian militia companies, American regular rifle regiments, and some American militia and volunteers. British regular army riflemen did not serve on the Canadian front during the war. Rifles differed from muskets primarily in that their barrel interiors were not smooth but spiral-grooved. This gave them greater range and accuracy when combined with a more tightly fitted and carefully loaded bullet than muskets used. Military rifles were accurate at twice the range of muskets and were dangerous at 275 metres. However, rifles took a minute to load and fouled from gunpowder residue so quickly that only a few shots could be fired before they became unserviceable until cleaned. The musket, with its superior rate of fire and the capacity to fire dozens of rounds between cleanings, was a more useful weapon until later in the nineteenth century when technological advances overcame the rifle's limitations. Further, battlefield tensions and the rifle's more complicated and physically demanding loading procedure usually decreased the rifleman's steadiness and aim, thus eliminating most of the rifle's accuracy. Except for the British Baker Rifle, rifles did not carry bayonets, mak-   ing riflemen vulnerable when attacked by musketmen equipped with bayonets. According to veterans of the Niagara campaigns and early- nineteenth-century experts, the rifle's main value was limited to sniping from inaccessible locations or for use in ambush.[5]

Weapons technology not only dictated tactics but influenced the design of soldiers' uniforms. Today, with the massive firepower, range, and accuracy of modern weapons, troops need camouflage uniforms to hide from their enemy. In 1812, with the poor firepower, restricted range, and limited accuracy of the weapons, dress concerns were different. Uniforms on both the British and American sides tended to be highly distinctive and flamboyant to make the wearer appear impressive, physically large, and aggressively masculine within the cultural framework of the period. With troops moving in tightly packed lines close to their enemy, attempts to camouflage soldiers generally would have been pointless anyway. These dashing uniforms helped boost the morale of the wearer, intimidated the enemy, and reduced the chances of shooting at people on the same side on the smoke-shrouded battlefields of the period. Distinctive uniforms were also part of a larger process to socialize recruits into their corps. If successful, the integration of the individual's self-perceptions with those of his regiment's and its heritage would help make the soldier capable of standing his ground during the carnage of battle so that he would be able to achieve the regiment's objectives and maintain its honour. Some light infantry uniforms, such as the dark green clothing of some British corps, were designed to make the wearer inconspicuous because of the different nature of their combat, but they still retained the impressive tailoring and tall cap of conventional design to exploit the psychological value of early-nineteenth-century military fashion. [6]

It was impossible for the Iroquois to fight in rigid linear formations because of their small numbers and the priorities of their culture. They could not afford the casualties that line troops often experienced, and individual warriors would not subject themselves to either the danger or the disciplined command structure necessary for successful linear operations. Instead, the Iroquois fought as a kind of light infantry force and regularly went into action alongside white light infantry. As light troops, the Iroquois often surpassed Euroamerican regulars and almost always were superior to militiamen. What seems to have given the Iroquois their advantage was better training.

The Iroquois prepared people for war from childhood, and warlike skills were useful in hunting and other non-combative pursuits. In contrast, whites rarely experienced much military instruction before enlistment, and the soldierly arts were mainly useless outside of the army. The long training period and greater application of warlike abilities to the needs of native society tended to contribute to increased prowess and a higher sense of the value of that prowess among warriors than it did among the rank and file of white armies. From an early age Iroquois boys learned such hunting skills as stalking, mastering the ambush, survival techniques, proficiency with knife and hatchet, and good marksmanship. These skills not only enabled Iroquois men to feed their families but also equipped them to fight their enemies. Children and youths honed their skills and developed warlike attitudes through their games and by sharing in the warrior culture in such activities as accompanying war parties for part of the way from their homes. Adult males kept fit and trained for combat through hunting and such leisure activities as tomahawk-throwing and lacrosse. The keen sense of independence and competence in a hostile environment and the excellent physical development and stamina resulting from the native way of life were superb preparation for the warpath. [7]

Marksmanship was one area in which the Iroquois seemed to have been superior to whites. As early as the 1660s Europeans commented on how well the Iroquois handled their firearms.[8] Natives even modified European technology in order to improve their marksmanship by carving out part of the comb on their gunstocks (where a person's cheek bone rests when aiming) so that they could sight their weapons better by being able to line up their eyes along the barrels more easily.[9] The Iroquois scoffed that whites did not know how to shoot, accusing them of holding 'their guns half man high,' meaning that whites did not aim as carefully as they did.[10] In contrast, one contemporary Euroamerican observer wrote that natives 'are taught the use of the rifle when very young; at the age of ten they are of considerable use in the hunting parties & can Shoot with great accuracy.'[11] A post-war writer thought that it was the 'unerring fire of their rifles' that made natives a serious threat in the field.[12] Moreover, the Iroquois often selected officers as targets because they believed the lower ranks could be thrown into confusion without their leaders.[13] The accuracy of the Iroquois in using firearms came with experience from years of hunting and contrasted starkly with the experience of British and American troops. Few British soldiers and not many more American regulars had used firearms extensively before joining the army. Once enlisted, a typical British infantryman might receive only sixty blank and thirty ball cartridges each year for practice, although light troops usually had more. The majority of American infantry had even less musketry training.[14] Many American and Canadian militiamen and volunteers from frontier environments had experience with firearms, but only a small proportion of them had had as much practice as natives. In addition to being good marksmen, the Iroquois showed considerable skill with their edged weapons, especially the tomahawk. One soldier at the siege of Fort Erie in 1814 saw warriors throw tomahawks as far as twenty metres at American troops 'with unerring aim and great force' and bury 'the head of the hatchet up to the eye in the body of their opponents,' something that could not have been done without considerable practice and physical strength.[15]

To be effective, training for battle had to move beyond preparing individuals for combat to include tactical training for the cooperative manoeuvring of organized war parties and for the control of these parties by their leaders. Although there are few records of formal military instruction taking place among the Iroquois, their performance in combat indicates that it must have occurred. Furthermore, deer hunting regularly was a large-scale collaborative enterprise that took place through

rough terrain and that required skills similar to those for combat. [16] At the
time of European contact in the seventeenth century, the Iroquois used a
double-line tactic that required both leadership and training. In battle,
one line, armed with bows, discharged volleys of stone-tipped arrows at
the enemy. If shock was needed, the second line, protected by wood or
hide armour, charged and used clubs to knock down their adversaries.
The archers, not wearing armour and thus being more mobile, then
assisted the other line by rushing into the fray to use their clubs to kill, or
preferably capture, anyone who tried to run away.

The introduction of firearms, metal arrow- and spear-points, and European edged-weapons forced the Iroquois to change their tactics because
the new weapons inflicted more grievous damage with less human energy
than native weaponry did. They abandoned armour and developed different modes of fighting to use the new technology effectively by empha-
sizing mobility and ambush, although they retained the basic concept of
deployment in line. [17] In the 1750s one person described aboriginal warfare in a way that assumes the existence of tactical training and effective
command. He wrote that they moved in a loose, spread-out line similar to
that employed by light infantry, with each person observing the movement of the warrior on his right. This allowed a force to move along a
frontage of up to fifteen hundred metres with at least enough cohesion
that it could redeploy effectively once the enemy was sighted. They also
formed circles, semicircles, and squares as required. These skills in moving and controlling large bodies of warriors through wooded terrain
survived to the War of 1812. At Chippawa in 1814, for instance, three
hundred Iroquois and other tribesmen from New York, with two hundred
white volunteers, advanced across a one-thousand-metre front through
thick forest against a force of Canadian militia and natives allied to the
British. [18] Some leaders controlled the line from its extremities; others,
playing a more direct leadership role, moved twenty metres in front of
their war parties, while scouts marched ahead of them. Bird and animal
calls enabled different components of the force to communicate with
each other. According to the commander of the white forces present,
these signals conveyed 'notice through the whole line with incredible
rapidity' that danger was near; the warriors instantly dropped to the
ground and remained quiet until their leaders assessed the situation and
gave orders to take advantage of the circumstances at hand. [19]

Another important aspect of military training was the development of
martial attitudes to sustain someone in the terror and confusion of battle.
In Euroamerican armies a soldier acquired these sensibilities by his

socialization with his regiment through friendships with other soldiers, by wearing a distinct uniform, and by sharing in the traditions, martial music, barrack-room lore, training, and discipline of army life. Likewise, the Iroquois warrior experienced a socialization for war as part of his military development. As noted before, warfare gave an Iroquois male an acceptable opportunity to prove his manhood and win esteem for himself and within his community. The example of advancement based on wartime leadership and the traditions associated with martial exploits, along with the recognition men received for skills that could be applied to combat, were part of the process of preparing individuals for battle. Religion and wartime ceremonies were also rich in morale-boosting qualities to equip people emotionally to be effective warriors. Individuals presumably internalized this process through their desire to conform to the community's ethical and moral standards, which acknowledged the value of the warrior spirit and which assumed that men would fulfil their combatant duties when required to do so.[20]

The Iroquois used a variety of weapons: muskets, rifles, pistols, bows and arrows, tomahawks, clubs, knives, swords, spears, and bayonets. The most common were firearms, tomahawks, and knives.[21] The British gave their aboriginal allies four different types of firearms: common guns or muskets, chief's guns, pistols, and rifles. Common muskets were lighter than military muskets, fired a slightly smaller ball, and had a somewhat shorter barrel. Although the quality of the firearms the British gave their native allies was not much different from their own, the smaller calibre and shorter barrel of native arms meant that they were not as powerful as the army's muskets, and their lighter construction meant that they were not as robust as military arms. The differences between army and aboriginal firearms likely reflected some combination of aboriginal preferences for certain styles of firearms and the desire of the British to avoid providing military-grade weapons to people who might turn against them. For a native, lighter, smaller-calibre weapons were easier to carry in rough terrain, were better suited to hunting conditions, and used smaller quantities of hard-to-get gunpowder. Chiefs' guns were weapons of better quality than common muskets and resembled sporting guns, but they usually had the same barrel length and fired the same calibre ball as common guns. The wrist on the stock of these muskets was decorated with an inlaid silver medallion showing the likeness of a native. Pistols issued by the British were similar to those used by their light dragoons. The rifles presented by the British normally had longer barrels than muskets and had seven-grooved barrels. These rifles were more accurate and fired greater distances than the army's Baker Rifle, but had less stopping power because they fired smaller bullets. Aboriginal rifles could not carry bayonets. [22]

Although firearms normally were loaded with only one bullet or ball, the Americans sometimes fired a ball plus one, two, or three tiny buckshot pellets. Buckshot rarely caused serious injury because it was so small, but it could inflict an annoying wound. The British gave buckshot to their Iroquois allies. Although natives probably used most of it for hunting small game, the Americans suffered some buckshot casualties during the war, possibly from Iroquois weapons. [23]

Complete records of the weapons issued to the Iroquois do not exist. Nevertheless, there are some statistics that give an impression of the relative importance of each kind of firearm. One source of aboriginal arms was the Board of Ordnance which sent 26,800 firearms to Canada for Britain's native allies between 1813 and 1816. Of these, roughly 47 per cent were common guns, 38 per cent were chiefs' guns, 10 per cent were pistols, and 6 per cent were rifles. [24] It seems that the proportion of rifles represented by the Ordnance supply was lower than normal since contemporary eyewitnesses often spoke of the Iroquois who were allied to the British as carrying rifles. [25] Another list, from 1814, gives a sense of the proportion of edged weapons to firearms issued by the British. It ordered from England five thousand chiefs' guns, five thousand common guns, one thousand pistols, two thousand swords, two thousand pipe tomahawks, and one thousand spears or Indian lances. [26] As well as receiving firearms as presents, the Iroquois obtained weapons by other means, such as through trade or as battlefield trophies. Therefore, it would not have been unusual to see either British or American military firearms and non-standard weapons in the hands of warriors. Bayonets were likely acquired only on the battlefield along with soldiers' muskets. Since native and military muskets had different barrel diameters, bayonets would not have fitted snugly enough on aboriginal muskets for them to be used. [27]

The Iroquois allied to the Americans used the same range of weapons from similar sources as those in Canada, with the principal difference being that a much larger number of warriors, perhaps the majority, carried rifles rather than muskets. This is not surprising as the Americans tended to issue rifles in greater quantity than the British to troops who performed light infantry roles. Brigadier-General Peter B. Porter, who incorporated a large body of Iroquois in his brigade in the 1813 and 1814 campaigns, even believed muskets were unsuitable for native warfare. Like the rifles issued by the British to their allies, they were hunting-style rifles rather than military-grade Harper's Ferry rifles. However, they were both sub-standard in their manufacture and inferior to the weapons the Iroquois acquired privately. Muskets issued by the Americans also were inferior but were made to look like British weapons in an attempt to appeal to native preferences for the better quality British arms, although it seems unlikely that anyone fell for this trick. These poor quality muskets may have been degraded further, because the Americans seem to have issued coarse cannon-grade gunpowder to their musket-equipped aboriginal allies instead of more suitable medium-grade powder. However, they did provide appropriate fine-grade powder for Iroquois rifles. The Americans also issued carbines (short, light muskets) to their native allies. Carbines normally were cavalry weapons, which raises the question of why they gave them to people who fought on foot. Possibly they were meant to be used in conjunction with the spears some tribesmen carried, in the same way that some American troops experimented with reviving the use of pikes as their primary arm and used sawed-off muskets as a secondary weapon, but perhaps carbines were preferred by warriors simply because they weighed less than a standard musket.[28]

Although firearms were the primary shooting weapons, some Iroquois used bows and arrows in combat. Bows still had a use in hunting and in socializing children for war in this period; some warriors preferred to carry these traditional weapons, and bows sometimes were used when men ran out of ammunition for their firearms.[29]

At close quarters, the Iroquois used different kinds of tomahawks, clubs, spears, swords, and knives. Except for clubs and some spears, these weapons came from white sources. British inventories of material sent to Upper Canada for the natives included pocket knives, clasp knives, butchers' knives, spears or 'Indian lances,' chief's swords, hangers (short, usually slightly curved swords), half axes (a kind of tomahawk), and pipe tomahawks (a tomahawk with a pipe bowl). Tomahawks, made of either brass or iron with steel blades, were normally used as striking weapons, although they could be thrown. An older French-style tomahawk also continued in use; it looked like the head of a spontoon, a type of pole arm that resembled a small firefighter's axe with a hook and an axe head as well as a thrusting spear point. The British Indian Department supplied spears and some warriors made their own, either by attaching blades to the end of poles or by carving a point on the end of a shaft and hardening it in a fire.[30] Although spears could be thrown, warriors used them chiefly as thrusting weapons. It seems likely that spears would have been desirable weapons in hand-to-hand combat because most natives did not

have bayonets and otherwise may have been at a disadvantage against soldiers equipped with bayonets. It is impossible to know how widespread
the use of spears was, but one account from the American Revolution
claimed, probably with some exaggeration, that all Iroquois carried them,
while a document from 1813 seems to support widespread use.[31] Traditional wooden clubs were still in use during the War of 1812. The most
common was the ball-headed club, so-called because the striking end was
a solid ball of wood. Some ball-headed clubs had a metal spike at their
striking end for additional effectiveness. Another traditional club was the
gunstock club, which resembled an inverted gunstock and which typically
had a metal striking point on its underside. A variation of this club used a
short, sharpened deer horn as a striking point and was noted for its ability to inflict deep wounds. Clubs often bore carved representations of the
owner's exploits, likenesses of his guardian spirits or of spirits identified
with war or the underworld, or his clan affiliation, and they were painted
and decorated with feathers.[32]

Iroquois dress in combat had many of the same functions as the battle
dress for whites. It provided suitable clothing in relation to the available
technology and consequent tactics, looked forcefully manly, identified
the warrior with his military heritage, boosted his morale, and intimidated the enemy. A major divergence was that the Iroquois wore far fewer
clothes in combat. Since the introduction of new technologies that had
rendered aboriginal armour obsolete in the seventeenth century, men
normally stripped for battle. As a result, they suffered fewer encum-
brances than did their white adversaries whose equipment might weigh at
least twice as much. In close combat, the Iroquois also may have gained
an advantage by smearing bear's grease on their bodies, partly as protection against the weather and insects, but mainly to make themselves slip-
pery and hard to grab. In combat, a warrior usually wore only a breech
cloth, leggings, and moccasins or white soldiers' boots.[33] To these he
added his accoutrements, consisting of a long plaited vegetable fibre belt
that could be used to tie up prisoners, a powder horn if he used a rifle, as
well as a pouch for ammunition, spare flints, and other necessities.
Images of guardian spirits (such as thunderbirds, underwater panthers,
and horned serpents) typically decorated these pouches.[34] When on campaign but not in combat, warriors wore more clothes, representing a
cross between traditional native dress and the clothes white militiamen
wore. One Onondaga who served with the Americans in the war, for
example, sought payment for having provided his own clothing and
accoutrements because he had not received government-issued supplies.

His claim included such mixed white and native items as a hat, a coat, leggings, shirts, stockings, a canteen, a knapsack, and moccasins. [35]

Just as white troops sported costume features that were without practical value but that served to heighten self-esteem and group identity, Iroquois warriors used body paint, feathers, and other ornamentation for the same purposes as well as to associate themselves with sources of spiritual power. They regarded feathers, for example, as signs of war powers received from the thunderbirds. [36] One person who saw some Tuscaroras from New York in 1795 noted that the warriors decorated themselves with 'feathers of all possible species of birds' and supplemented the feathers with horsehair. [37] Warriors also painted their bodies, red being the favourite base colour, over which they usually added coloured streaks, with black being the most common. This was an appropriate combination because of the association of red with life and of black with danger and death. [38] Although these two colours predominated, some people chose others. A British army surgeon who saw warriors on the Niagara Peninsula painted for war recorded that a favourite pattern 'was to blacken their faces, from a line drawn from ear to ear across the upper lip; above this dark base they drew a streak of red an inch broad; which they surmounted alternatively with lines of yellow white and red.' He also saw Iroquois children painting their faces with red and yellow ochre, perhaps as part of their socialization for their adulthood as warriors. [39] The description of the Tuscaroras in 1795 gives another impression of how natives might paint themselves for combat: 'In general they prefer the harshest colours, paint one leg white, and the other black or green, the body brown or yellow, and face full of red or black spots, and their eyes different colours.' [40] Some Iroquois wore tattoos, with representations of guardian spirits or geometric patterns being common. Tattooing usually occurred at puberty after a boy experienced a successful vision quest as part of his adult formation. [41]

Another important decorative feature used to boost morale and identify the warrior with Iroquois military tradition was the scalp lock. An Iroquois scalp lock was not the famous 'Mohawk' haircut of popular imagination that looks like a brush running along the centre of the scalp from the front to the back of the head. (Other natives wore those.) Rather, it was a ring of long, easily grabbed hair, located at the centre of the back of the scalp on the warrior's otherwise shaved head, decorated with domestic and imported feathers, horsehair, silver, and other ornamentation. Worn, theoretically, to taunt an enemy into trying to take it, the scalp lock probably served more to heighten the warrior's self-esteem and to link him emotionally to Iroquois military tradition. Even children wore them as part of their military development. [42] The Iroquois seem to have believed that spiritual power was concentrated in the scalp lock. This assumption had serious implications, because a warrior had to keep his own scalp out of fear that he might be denied peace in the next world if he suffered a violent death and lost his scalp. But, if he could scalp an enemy, his people would acquire that person's spiritual power while devastating his opponent's hopes for a happy afterlife. [43] Another distinction among the Iroquois to mark warriors was the practice of cutting and stretching the outer rims of their ears after their first experience in combat as a mark of their veteran status. [44]

A popular ornament was a circular gorget, worn on the chest. Originally made of white shell or wampum, most gorgets were silver or gilt by 1812. Gorgets often were made to represent an image of the sun, an appropriate wartime symbol because of the sun's association with war. Shell, and its analogue, silver, were considered to be spiritually charged gifts of underworld spirits. Many warriors wore European-style gorgets (in white society they served as token pieces of armour to link officers to the knightly ideals of mediaeval times). These crescent-moon devices likely appealed to the warriors' sense of their own importance because of their association with military leadership. [45]

When on the warpath, native peoples took steps to prevent their being surprised and to create situations in which they could overwhelm their enemy. As much as possible, they engaged in reconnaissance to assess enemy strength before committing themselves to a particular action. From their hunting experience, warriors were adept at analysing the number of people in a group and the length of time since they had passed by a spot by examining the condition of the ground over which they had trod, unless the numbers were very small, leaving little trace of their passing, or rain had obliterated the evidence. [46]

The classic Iroquois tactic, as was the case with neighbouring tribes, was ambush. Immediately before going into action, the senior war chief usually made a short speech advising his followers to be brave but not rash. Traditionally, they preferred to surround their enemy in darkness in order to launch a surprise assault at dawn. The purposes of this form of attack were to confuse and to overextend their opponents. By accomplishing these goals, they could cripple the enemy's ability to respond effectively and thereby increase the chances of victory with few casualties. An example of this tactic in operation on a large scale was the assault on the American army beside the Wabash River on 4 November 1791. The natives attacked at dawn, threw the Americans into a confused and vulnerable defensive posture, then proceeded to decimate the white force, inflicting over nine hundred casualties on the fourteen hundred soldiers present while losing only sixty killed and wounded themselves. In another ambush tactic that was used against an enemy on the move, natives concealed themselves in a semicircle across their opponent's path, where they would wait until the enemy fell into a trap from which escape might be very difficult. They used these same principles when attacking an enemy in situations where ambush was impossible. As the warriors got near their target, they usually moved forward rapidly and silently with the objective of unnerving their opponents by the suddenness of their appearance. To make it difficult for the enemy to outflank them, they often divided into several files spread over as wide a frontage as was practical.[47] Sometimes they did not use surprise to frighten their enemy but exploited their terrifying reputation to scare their opponents by singing war songs as they advanced. These songs, one witness noted, 'most commonly signify what they have before done against the people whom they are going to attack, or what they intend to do or what number of scalps they will bring away.'[48]

Once engaged, according to the Mohawk chief, John Norton, they kept up the pressure on their enemy by advancing in relays, the first line moving forward with loaded firearms, to be replaced by the second when the first had discharged its weapons.[49] Individuals also liked to move to a new position immediately after each shot, using the thick smoke from the firearm's discharge as cover. Ideally, this caused the enemy to shoot at a vacant spot rather than at an occupied one and to overestimate the number of Iroquois engaged against them.[50] William Dunlop, a British army surgeon who witnessed native warfare in 1814, corroborated these descriptions. He saw warriors minimize casualties by changing their positions, while upsetting the enemy and boosting their own morale by declaring each casualty they inflicted: 'It seemed to me to be a point with them at every discharge of their rifle to shift their position, and whenever they knocked a fellow over, their yelling was horrible.' If the enemy broke, the warriors gave chase. Dunlop continued: 'When the enemy retired the Indians who had shown so much wariness in the fight ... suddenly seemed to lose all their caution, and bounded forward with a horrible yell, threw themselves on the retreating enemy with their tomahawks, and were soon out of our sight; but as we advanced, we saw they left their trace behind them in sundry cleft skulls.'[51] Dunlop expressed surprise at the natives for abandoning their concern to take cover when pursuing the Americans. However, the warriors probably realized that soldiers fleeing in terror posed little threat. Furthermore, this show of bravado provided an excellent but relatively safe opportunity for men to impress their friends, inflict more casualties, take more prisoners or scalps, and capture more booty than would be possible with a timid pursuit of a beaten foe.

If a war party failed to achieve its objectives and had to retreat, it tried to minimize losses and attempted to prevent a rout through a careful fighting withdrawal using natural obstacles as defensive positions to slow the adversaries, and through an assessment of the enemy's strength along the retreat so that an ambush might be laid to destroy the attackers if they did not send enough men in pursuit. Sometimes war parties feigned a retreat in order to pull their opponents into a vulnerable position. The warriors also did their best to remove their dead and wounded from the field so they would not fall into enemy hands, although no plans were made before battle to deal with casualties and therefore this was done on an ad hoc basis.[52]

These modes of warfare suited Iroquois society, in which military virtues included individual heroics and initiative. Furthermore, it was only through employing these methods that the desire of the Iroquois to suffer few casualties was possible. If pressed hard, they normally retreated. Such tactics were appropriate for a society with a small population in which adult males were only part-time warriors but full-time providers. However, these tactics also limited Iroquois capabilities and made them vulnerable to Euroamerican adversaries in certain circumstances. In battle, a warrior acted more independently than a white soldier because of his personal aspirations for glory, measured by the exercise of individual judgment and daring. Chiefs, therefore, usually exercised less authority over their followers once in action than white officers did over their subordinates, although the men, because of their training, tended to know what was expected of them to accomplish their goals and, because of their society's integrative practices, usually were able to act cooperatively with their friends and relatives in combat without close supervision. Once an individual warrior met his immediate needs for displaying bravery or acquiring scalps and plunder, however, he was free to go home even though broader strategic objectives might not have been achieved. Men could also leave their chiefs if they became dissatisfied, if they received an omen warning them of disaster, or if they felt that the action in which they had participated was all the Great Spirit had intended for them on a particular campaign.[53]

Good professional soldiers, in contrast, were subject to a much stricter control that idealized the subjugation of individual concerns to those of the regiment. The priority was the unit's acquisition of honour through achieving its objectives as dictated by its commanders. Properly disciplined soldiers would suffer comparatively heavy casualties to achieve their regiment's goals and were capable of changing their focus in unison as the conditions of a battle changed, especially within the format of Napoleonic tactics where they typically operated under their commanding officer's close management. Attaining the level of discipline required by regular armies, along with the corresponding willingness to suffer heavy losses, was possible in societies with a large pool of labour from which soldiers could be drawn and separated almost entirely from the broader requirements of civilian society. The United States, for example, responded to the destruction of its army in 1791 by raising another in 1792 to continue the war. Losses among the Iroquois similar to those suffered by the Americans on the Wabash would have shattered their social viability. White societies therefore could defeat native ones simply through attrition. More economically, white armies could defeat aboriginal adversaries if they could upset the natives' equilibrium by inflicting or threatening to inflict heavy casualties.

Competent British and American officers understood native combat and took appropriate action to counter aboriginal threats. In the mid–eighteenth century, for instance, Colonel Henry Bouquet of the British army identified three principles of native warfare: fight scattered, surround, and give ground when hard-pressed. Therefore, he recommended that a prudent commander deploy scouts and light infantry to watch for signs of ambush and arrange his command so that it could deploy itself quickly in a square in order to defeat native attempts to surround and hit weak points. If attacked, a commander had to maintain his force's equilibrium because the key to success was a disciplined counter-attack using coordinated firepower and bayonet charges that were pressed with vigour to force the natives to retreat. An example of this approach occurred in 1794 when the American army sent to replace the one lost in 1791 met the natives at Fallen Timbers. At first, the advanced guard stumbled into the native ambush and recoiled in confusion. However, instead of falling into a defensive position where they would be vulnerable to destruction, as had occurred in 1791, the Americans re-formed and advanced steadily and aggressively under fire while maintaining their discipline to drive the natives from the field. If white troops forced natives into a situation from which retreat was impossible, such as a trap in which the warriors' families were endangered, defeat could be complete.[54]

Another serious weakness in Iroquois warfare was a high desertion rate. In two typical engagements, at least one-half of the warriors at the first part of the battle of Queenston Heights and two-thirds of those at the battle of Fort George deserted their fellow warriors just before going into action. Such potentially disastrous haemorrhaging of combat strength probably stemmed from the lack of a disciplinary structure to keep people in the field, the relatively independent manner in which the Iroquois fought which made it easy for people to slip away under fire, and the great fear of an unhappy afterlife traditionalists faced should they lose their scalps. But it is also possible that there was another problem: Iroquois society, with its emphasis on personal stoicism and bravery, may have failed to address the instinctive fear that a person feels when preparing to engage in mortal combat.[55] At the beginning of the battle of Fort George, one Iroquois tried to rally the warriors with the simplistic declaration, 'The Warrior knows no anxiety for his safety.'[56] This was rhetoric, not the truth, and it was dangerous rhetoric because it conflicted with the immediate experience of the people who heard it. Fear, and its attendant symptoms, such as uncontrollable trembling or bowel movements, are due to rapid involuntary muscular action designed to warm up the body for the anticipated fight. Most combatants experience such symptoms, yet warriors seem to have grown up hearing only about the fearlessness of their ancestors and the courageous exploits of the war chiefs without reference to the reality of fear in anything but contemptuous terms. Therefore, when they had to confront their own terror, some presumably believed they were cowards, not the 'men' of their culture's tradition, and they responded by fleeing if they could not bring their fear under control. In contrast, white soldiers usually came under the close supervision of their officers and had fewer opportunities to shirk their duty. As well, soldiers who were well-informed about the naturalness of fear, or who could admit it and discuss their anxieties with their friends, could recognize its symptoms, place them in context, and, usually, carry on.[57]

John Norton wrote about the consequences of personal failure on the battlefield in an account of the murder of some wounded American prisoners by western tribesmen in 1813 during the siege of Fort Meigs. A 'worthless' Ojibway and 'a number of wretches like himself' killed the prisoners, along with the British sentry guarding them, because they did not have the 'courage to kill their Enemies while in arms' but wanted to win the prestige associated with combat by acquiring scalps to show off as

The Mohawk Village, by Elizabeth Simcoe (watercolour, 1793). Iroquois communities in the 1812 era usually consisted of log and frame buildings, as seen in this painting of a village on the Grand River. The structure with the flag is Joseph Brant's house. The steeple of the still-extant Anglican church built in 1787 is on the right. (Archives of Ontario, F47-11-0-109)

GEORGE WASHINGTON
PRESIDENT.
1792.

The U.S. government presented this silver medal to the Seneca leader Red Jacket in 1792. Although it was offered in friendship, its design suggests subjugation: George Washington's pose seems to declare his dominance over the supplicating native, whose forest world falls victim to the advancing plough. (Courtesy of the Buffalo and Erie County Historical Society, 70-445r)

The Seneca Chief Corn Planter, or Ki-on-twog-ky, by F. Bartoli (oil, 1796). In this portrait, Cornplanter, an important but reluctant U.S. ally in the war, is shown wearing typical Iroquois clothing of the period (with the exception of the tomahawk, which is fictitious). His cut and stretched ears indicate that he is a veteran warrior. (© Collection of The New-York Historical Society, 6338)

Tonaventa Peter de Bufalo, by the Baroness Hyde de Neuville (watercolour, 1807).
This image shows Peter of Buffalo in conservative Seneca dress of the early 1800s,
including a European shirt and coat. Note the leggings, spontoon-type tomahawk
(exaggerated by the artist), string of wampum (left hand), and scalp lock. (© Collection of The New-York Historical Society, 37255)

Fair Indian of the Buffalo Tribe, by the Baroness Hyde de Neuville (watercolour, 1808). The Seneca in this image is dressed in a more European style than Peter of Buffalo, reflecting the differing levels of comfort among Iroquois people with respect to adopting Euroamerican ways. Long hair was common: men tended to wear scalp locks only when going to war or to council meetings. (© Collection of The New-York Historical Society, 37254)

Costume of Domiciliated Indians, by George Heriot, engraved by Joseph Stadler (1807). Depicting a temporary hunting and fishing camp, this print shows a mix of native and white technologies (cradleboard and musket); Euroamerican goods used in aboriginal products (native-style skirts made with cloth); and objects manufactured by Euroamericans for aboriginal consumers (pipe tomahawk/trade silver). (National Archives of Canada, C-012781)

Thayendanegea (Joseph Brant), by William Berczy (oil, c. 1807). While the men in *Domiciliated Indians* carry muskets, Joseph Brant is depicted here with a rifle. War parties used both kinds of firearms, giving them the combined advantages of the volume of fire that fast-loading muskets could deliver and the accuracy of the slower-loading rifles. Note the clothing, the powder horn, and the hunting bag. (National Gallery of Canada, 5777)

John Norton, Teyoninhokarawen, the Mohawk Chief, by Mary Ann Knight (watercolour on ivory miniature, 1805). John Norton proved to be one of the best friends the British had on the divided Grand River during the war. He is depicted here wearing characteristic Iroquois clothing of the period: a turban decorated with an imported ostrich feather, silver earrings, a coat encrusted with trade silver, and a blanket. (National Archives of Canada, C-128832)

Bust of a Mohawk Indian, by Sempronius Stretton (coloured wash and ink drawing, 1804). The colours of this Grand River Mohawk's face paint, from the centre of his cheek outwards, are red, black, yellow, and red. His cut and stretched ear is painted red, and his silver ornamentation includes a nose bob, earrings, a sun gorget, a chief's medal, and a crucifix. (National Archives of Canada, C-14827)

Deputation of Indians from the Mississippi Tribes, by Rudolph Von Steiger (water-colour and gouache, 1814). Warriors from Algonkian tribes often fought along-side the Iroquois. The black warrior pictured here is symbolic of the 'multicultural' nature of native society in the early nineteenth century. Painted in Quebec, this image also reflects the fact that women often accompanied men on long journeys, even into war zones. (National Archives of Canada, C-134461)

Detail from a photograph of a British Board of Ordnance 'common gun' (1811–16) produced especially for aboriginal allies. Both the Americans and the British supplied flintlock muskets, rifles, and other firearms to native forces. (Collection of the Toronto Historical Board, 1960.137.2A)

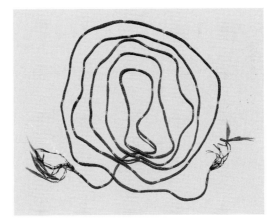

A pre-1822 Mohawk matunip line, used for tying up prisoners. It is six metres long, made of braided vegetable fibre, dyed black, and decorated with tin cones, red-dyed moosehair, and red, black, and white porcupine quills. (Royal Ontario Museum, 918.35.1)

A wooden ball-headed club, c. 1775–1815, with an iron spike added to make it more lethal. Sixty-three centimetres long, it is stained red and decorated with personalized motifs that are typical of the period and that may have been related to a vision quest. (Royal Ontario Museum, 970.15)

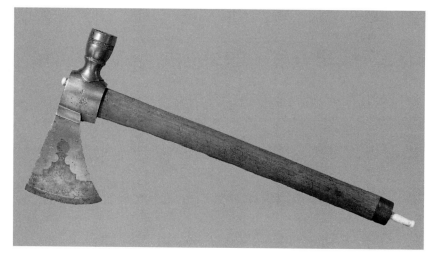

A tomahawk of the 1775–1815 period, with a functioning pipe bowl (representing peace) and a deadly blade (symbolic of war). Most tomahawks were about fifty centimetres long, although this one is only thirty-seven. Most were made of iron with steel edges, but some, like this one, were brass with a steel edge. Engraving and inlays of brass or silver were common on both blades and hafts. (Royal Ontario Museum, 924.46.4)

The design of this wooden Iroquois gunstock club (date undetermined) with a metal striking point is typical of the 1812 period. When new, it was probably decorated with paint. (Royal Ontario Museum, 27050)

This scalp (pre-1815) is stretched onto a wood frame and painted red on the hairless side. Originally it would have had somewhat more skin. (Collection of the Toronto Historical Board, 1974.60.70)

Detail from *The Death of General Wolfe*, by Benjamin West (oil, 1770). Though romanticized and dating from an earlier period, this painting is interesting in that it shows 'combat dress' typical of the 1812 era. Note how little clothing was worn (although moccasins would have been normal) and observe the scalp lock, enhanced with red-dyed feathers and other ornamentation. (National Gallery of Canada, 8007)

United States Infantry, by Charles Hamilton Smith (watercolour, 1816). Although soldiers dressed differently from warriors, white society, like aboriginal, used distinct and flamboyant dress to express its culture's concepts of aggressive but sanctioned masculinity, and to reinforce men's connections to their nation's military heritage. (By permission of the Houghton Library, Harvard University)

View of the Falls of Niagara, by George Heriot, engraved by F.C. Lewis, 1807. The Niagara River region was the site of the greatest Iroquois involvement in the War of 1812. This print shows the river from the Canadian side, not far from the bloodiest of the Six Nations' actions, Chippawa. (National Archives of Canada, C-12797)

Queenston, 1814, after a c. 1805 watercolour by Edward Walsh. Queenston Heights was the most important battle of 1812 for the Six Nations. After the Americans established themselves at the top of the hill (cleared of trees by 1812) facing the village, the Iroquois, unseen, ascended the heights in the dense forest just to the right of this image. They attacked the American rear, then kept the invaders pinned down until British reinforcements assembled on the high ground to the right of the upper background for a final devastating charge. (Metropolitan Toronto Reference Library, T 32723)

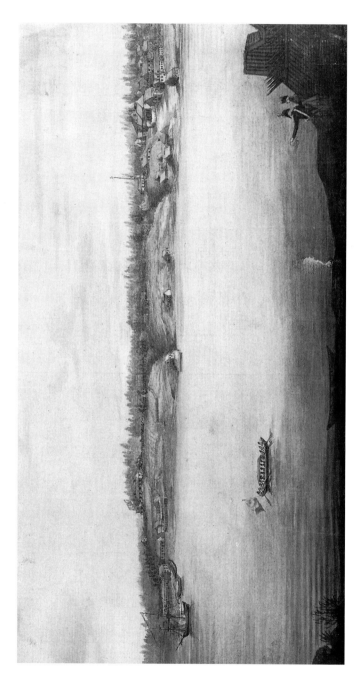

Detail from *A View of Fort George*, by Edward Walsh (watercolour, 1804). This painting shows a corner of Fort Niagara on the American bank of the Niagara River. On the Canadian side is Fort George at the top of the hill on the left, with the British naval station in front, by the waterfront. In the right background is the Town of Niagara. (Courtesy of The William L. Clements Library, University of Michigan, 198C)

Seneca School House, by Dennis Cusick (watercolour, 1821). A Tuscarora artist created this image of the school on the Buffalo Creek Reservation after the war, when acculturation pressures had increased dramatically. Adults led children to the school, practising traditional hunting skills on the way. Inside, a white schoolmaster taught writing and other subjects, while his wife instructed the students in such craft skills as carding, spinning, and knitting. (Courtesy of a private collection, New York City)

Three Grand River Iroquois veterans of the War of 1812, photographed in 1886. From the left: Jacob Warner (aged ninety-two), John Tutlee (ninety-one), and John Smoke Johnson (ninety-three). (Courtesy of the Woodland Cultural Centre)

proof of their bravery. Norton affirmed that such behaviour was unusual among native peoples, despite American propaganda to the contrary. There also are records of warriors warning prisoners to take precautions against the possibility of robbery or violence by other natives. [58] Another account describing the consequences of fear dates from the American Revolution and involved the famous Seneca Red Jacket. During one battle, he became frightened and ran away. To avoid accusations of cowardice, he secretly killed a nearby cow with his tomahawk, then showed the bloody weapon to others as proof of his bravery. However, someone with a loose tongue saw what he had done and the incident was to haunt him for years afterwards. [59]

Torture, massacre, and scalping have been associated with native warfare, and North American history provides ample proof that such practices were common on both sides of the aboriginal–white divide, but they were neither customary among all peoples nor in place at all times. Some of the western tribes, for example, had bowed to British pressure and stopped torturing prisoners in the early stages of the American Revolution. However, the custom revived after some revolutionaries brutally murdered ninety-six aboriginal pacifists at Gnadenhutten in 1782. Although the Iroquois still tortured captives during the American Revolution, the practice was dying out and does not seem to have survived the conflict. However, some Iroquois continued to murder prisoners and many scalped enemy dead to the end of the War of 1812, although customs varied tremendously. For example, many Grand River warriors at the battle of Queenston Heights in 1812 scalped the American dead, but some, like John Smoke Johnson, an Anglican Mohawk, did not because he thought the custom was brutal and useless. [60]

Scalping was not considered to be a form of torture because scalps were removed from people thought to be dead. Nevertheless, there are accounts of wounded individuals being scalped and surviving the ordeal. This was possible because scalping removed only the skin, tissue, and hair from the top of the head, leaving the skull intact. [61] The Canadian novelist John Richardson saw a scalping at the battle of Moraviantown in 1813 and described what happened. A warrior pursued an American until he got within fifteen paces of his enemy. He then 'threw his tomahawk ... with such force and precision ... that it opened the skull' and knocked the soldier 'motionless on the ground.' The warrior laid down his rifle, drew his knife, removed the tomahawk from the dead man, and 'proceeded to make a circular incision throughout the scalp.' He next put the knife between his teeth and placed his knees on the victim's back, fastened his hands in the dead man's hair, and tore the scalp off 'without much apparent difficulty.' Richardson remarked in astonishment or admiration: 'All this was the work of a minute.'[62] One man who served on the Canadian front during the war added that the Iroquois did not consider scalps (about the size of the palm of someone's hand) to be genuine unless the skin had the hair on it where it divided at the crown of the head. [63]

Once acquired, scalps usually became prized trophies, treasured by warriors for years and displayed in their homes. As gifts to the family of a dead person, the scalp – painted red and mounted on a little half-moon wooden frame – became a constant reminder of the departed, a source of spiritual power, and an acceptable proof that the dead person's life had been avenged. Sometimes scalps served other purposes. After the victory over the Americans on the Wabash, the tribes sent the scalp of a famous soldier to Joseph Brant to chide the Grand River people for not participating in the battle.[64] As well, scalps sometimes could be sold to white allies for profit. However, in 1813, when the Iroquois in New York joined the American army on the Niagara Peninsula, some officers attempted to discourage them from scalping British troops – although scalping natives was permitted – by paying bounties for prisoners but not for scalps. The British likewise tried to stop scalping and murder by offering higher payments for unharmed prisoners than for wounded men and by refusing to pay for dead soldiers and scalps.[65] Scalping served another purpose in aboriginal warfare – that of making the Iroquois appear as ferocious and terrible enemies. In addition, mutilation of enemy corpses was a technique used occasionally to make natives appear fearsome. If the enemy's morale could be subverted by exaggerated fears of aboriginal prowess, warriors then could go into battle with a significant psychological advantage to help overcome the problem of generally being outnumbered. [66]

Whites also practised scalping during the War of 1812. One American officer, George McFeely, described what he saw at Fort Niagara while entertaining a recently paroled prisoner (a Kentuckian captured in early 1813): 'He had two Indian scalps that he had taken at Frenchtown [now Monroe, Michigan], and had concealed them in the waist band of his pantaloons while a prisoner. While in the fort with us he ripped open his waist band, took out the scalps, fleshed them with his knife, salted them, and set them in hoops in true Indian style. He said he had twenty-eight scalps at home, and these two would make thirty he had taken off with his own hands in his time, and that he would raise fifty scalps before he would die.'[67] In November 1812, when the Americans planned to cross the Niagara River into Canada, the American commander offered a forty dollar reward (equal to five month' pay for a private soldier) for the weapons and scalps of British native allies.[68] Whites also scalped other whites. In 1814 some Kentuckians on the north shore of Lake Erie 'killed and mutilated' Sergeant Collins of the 41st Foot and Private Barto of the Canadian militia 'in the most horrible manner,' according to a contemporary report. Barto 'was actually butchered' with no evidence of having been shot beforehand, and both men were 'scalped and cut shockingly.'[69]

Sometimes aboriginal people expressed confusion over the contradictions between what whites required their native allies to do and how the whites themselves behaved. When reprimanded by the British in 1813 for mutilating an American corpse, a group of western tribesmen complained that the Americans had disinterred native dead and chopped up the bodies: 'If the Big Knives when they kill people of our color leave them without hacking them to pieces,' said one chief, 'we will follow their example.'[70]

Despite discomfort by many white officers over native warfare, few commanders willing to employ aboriginal warriors tried to contort Iroquois tactical doctrine to follow white practices.[71] On the one hand, these efforts would have been counter-productive because the Iroquois were impressive combatants in their own right (despite such weaknesses as their high desertion rates) and could be used with considerable effect against whites and other natives. On the other, the Iroquois, with a few exceptions, simply were unwilling to surrender their own styles of making war to what they considered to be inferior white techniques. As the Seneca war chief Little Billy told the Americans in September 1812, 'we must act under our own chiefs; according to our own customs,' and 'be at liberty to take our own course in fighting.' Independence in command and tactical practice was important, especially after Brock's capture of Detroit. Little Billy continued: 'You know what took place at Detroit; an army was sold. We wish not to be sold.'[72]

4

The Niagara Campaign:
Autumn 1812

I invoke thee, that thou wouldst be favourable to my enterprise, and have compassion upon me and my tribe. I likewise supplicate all the good and evil spirits, those who inhabit the air, who perambulate, and who penetrate the earth, to preserve me and those of my party, and to grant, that after a prosperous journey we may return to our own country.

An Iroquois war chief's invocation, n.d.[1]

A lull in the fighting occurred after the Detroit campaign because the British governor-in-chief, Sir George Prevost, negotiated a ceasefire with the American commander on the Canadian border, Major-General Henry Dearborn. Prevost hoped that negotiations could bring the war to a quick close because Britain, just before learning about the American declaration of war, had made diplomatic concessions to address American maritime grievances. President James Madison, however, disavowed the truce and hostilities resumed in early September. Later in the month, the Grand River people performed their war dances and travelled to the Niagara Peninsula. In mid-October, the Americans launched an assault across the Niagara River. The Six Nations played a critical and outstanding role in the subsequent battle of Queenston Heights, and in the process exposed some of the serious inadequacies that plagued the American army during the war. Despite the effectiveness of the Grand River Iroquois, their conduct in the battle also displayed some of the weaknesses inherent in their modes of combat. The Seven Nations also saw action before the new year. The Iroquois in New York, however, played only a minor role during the war's first fighting season.

Major-General Isaac Brock heard about the truce on his way back to Niagara from Detroit. He worried that the news might arouse native suspicions about British intentions and consequently make his aboriginal allies less willing to fight should hostilities recommence. As it was, many of them went home when they learned of the armistice, although they did not give the British commander any indication that they were unhappy about the situation.[2] Yet General Brock feared they would 'study in what manner they can most effectively deceive us' if they thought the British were to arrange a peace with the United States without representing aboriginal interests or were to display an inability 'to prosecute the War with spirit' should hostilities resume. These concerns, combined with the strength of the native position in the west following the Detroit campaign, led him to think the tribes should be included in any negotiations that might take place.[3] Such a policy would avoid rekindling the sense of betrayal the native peoples had felt in the treaties of 1783 and 1794. However, Madison's rejection of the truce meant that Brock did not have to worry about these issues for long.

John Norton met Isaac Brock on 6 September 1812 at Fort George just after news of the resumption of hostilities reached Niagara. After his briefing, Norton sent word to the Grand for the rest of the chiefs and warriors to assemble at the fort with all possible speed because Brock thought an American attack was imminent.[4] Shortly after, the rituals of going to war enlivened the Grand River communities as Iroquois men demonstrated their decision to take up the tomahawk and join the British. Typically, a ceremony began when warriors formed around a war chief dressed and painted for combat. The chief struck his hatchet in a war pole and each man gave the chief he wanted to follow a piece of wood, painted red and marked with an emblematic figure as a symbol of his commitment to the coming campaign. As part of the process of purifying themselves for combat and to guide them to victory, they raised spiritually charged songs and ate sacrificial dogs or pigs, the broth and meat symbolizing the blood and flesh of the enemies they would consume in battle. The songs depicted their enemies as enraged and dehumanized, celebrated the bravery and exploits of the warriors and their ancestors, and included invocations asking for supernatural protection so the warriors could enjoy a successful campaign and a happy return to their families.[5]

A war dance followed in which the chief and his followers demonstrated their decision to go on campaign. The dance was a physically exhausting and emotionally powerful exercise that helped bolster solidarity among men who would soon fight alongside one another in combat. Somebody who once saw John Norton perform it wrote that his 'whole appearance was instantly changed.' As some warriors sang and played their drums and turtle rattles, Norton joined others in a frightening pantomime of combat in which his normally mild and humane demeanour changed to take on 'a most savage & terrific look.'[6] Considering that he was half Scottish and was one of the leading Anglicans on the Grand, Norton's enthusiasm is an arresting manifestation of the strength Iroquois tradition exercised even among those who were most Christianized and acculturated to Euroamerican ways. Throughout the ceremony, the men consumed huge quantities of tobacco, food, and alcohol; and, when it was over, most fell asleep, exhausted and drunk.[7]

When everyone recovered, the men assembled at the homes of their chiefs dressed in their finest attire. Each leader delivered a short speech, repeating words Iroquois males had heard since their boyhood about the honour, pride, and independence that marked the warrior spirit, on the necessity of following their chiefs' instructions, and on the need to be of good cheer, as well as issuing strictures against molesting captured females, making offensive jokes, or indulging in other evil practices that might diminish the war party's spiritual powers. Then the chief moved to the front of his party and ceremoniously led the way, singing a song of death, while the others followed in silence. Outside the village, the women awaited them with the supplies and provisions needed for the expedition. Once fully equipped, the war party continued, someone fired a shot, and the chief continued his song until they lost sight of their homes. Thus, the Grand River warriors, many accompanied by their families, began the journey to the mouth of the Niagara River, arriving at British headquarters a day or so later.[8]

About five or six hundred warriors joined the British on the Niagara Peninsula that September, comprising Grand River Iroquois, their Mississauga neighbours, and the Delawares and Ojibways who had joined Norton on his way back to the Grand from Detroit.[9] Although their numbers represented a significant addition to British strength, Isaac Brock remained unimpressed with the military capabilities of the Iroquois and other aboriginal people of Upper Canada, sniffing that 'They may serve to intimidate otherwise expect no service from this degenerate race.'[10] Brock's attitude was curious. On one hand, he neither trusted them nor thought they were effective combatants. On the other, he felt the shame of the 1783 and 1794 treaties and wanted to guarantee that a peace settlement would address aboriginal concerns equitably. His views were shaped in part by his experience of the Detroit campaign, where the western tribes in territory claimed by the United States had proved to be so formidable in combat in striking contrast to the limited support he had received from the natives within British territory and the considerable anxiety they had caused him. Even after the majority of Grand River people had allied themselves with the British, Brock still thought they might commit 'evil.' Therefore, he felt it would be necessary to remove them from the Grand to a less strategic and vulnerable part of Upper Canada at some appropriate point in the future.[11]

Despite his mistrust, Brock used the warriors as a fast-moving reserve that he could deploy quickly to bolster any threatened spot along the border that he otherwise guarded from fixed positions garrisoned by his regulars and militia. Occasionally, scouting parties crossed to Grand Island and onto the American mainland to observe enemy movements and skirmish with American pickets. For the most part, though, the Niagara Peninsula generally was quiet. Discouraged by supply shortages and a lack of action, the aboriginal force diminished as the weeks passed. Only three hundred warriors remained by 9 October as many of them took up the chase with the approach of the autumn hunting season.[12] Meanwhile, the Americans assembled sixty-three hundred regulars, volunteers, militia, and Iroquois allies along the Niagara River in preparation to invade Canada. Brock's force of regulars, militia, and natives opposing them numbered fifteen hundred supplemented by six hundred militia and warriors in reserve. Brock was not concerned about the combat capabilities of the warriors in the American camp, numbering between two and three hundred men, because his Grand River allies had told him that they would not act 'with any spirit.' However, he did fear that the Six Nations in the United States might cross the Niagara River to assault and plunder the civilian population if he suffered defeat and had to retreat.[13]

Major-General Stephen Van Rensselaer of the New York militia led part of the American army from his headquarters at Lewiston, half way between Niagara Falls and the mouth of the river to the north. He had 900 regulars and 2,650 volunteers and militia under his command, but they were badly equipped and poorly trained.[14] Thinking he had little time to act before what effectiveness his army possessed disappeared because of bad weather, spreading sickness, and desertions, he decided to capture the village and heights of Queenston ten kilometres to the south of Fort George. His objectives were to wipe away Hull's disgrace, break Canadian morale, cut British communications between Lakes Ontario and Erie, drive Brock from the border region, and take superior British barracks for winter quarters. To ensure success, Van Rensselaer wanted the senior American regular army officer on the peninsula, Brigadier-General Alexander Smyth, to attack Fort George simultaneously with the Queenston assault. Smyth, unwilling to serve under a militia officer, refused to cooperate. Instead, he wanted to cross the border at Buffalo where Lake Erie empties into the Niagara River. Once on Canadian soil, he planned to march down the Canadian side of the river and push the British out of the peninsula. Van Rensselaer objected to Smyth's plan because the British had defensive works all along the border and could slow an army by pulling up bridges while native forces crippled the Americans from the forests which ran parallel to the river fifteen hundred metres or less from the shoreline. Because of the disagreements between the two officers, most of Smyth's troops were to sit out the battle of Queenston Heights.[15]

The heights at Queenston are part of a massive natural ridge that forms the Niagara Escarpment. They run at a right angle from the river one hundred metres above the water level. The village of Queenston lies at the bottom of the north side of the heights twenty metres above the Niagara River. At the village, the river separating British from American territory is four hundred metres wide. Around three in the morning on 13 October, Van Rensselaer began to send his troops across the river towards Queenston in the thirteen or fourteen boats he had at his disposal. The British opened fire with artillery and musketry as soon as they spotted the attack. At that point, American batteries at Lewiston and at Fort Gray to the south of Lewiston began to bombard the British positions. The American barrage, however, could not stop Queenston's defenders from inflicting heavy casualties on the Americans as they crossed the river. Despite this solid defence, the Americans persisted, and landed five hundred men on the sheltered beach below the village.[16]

General Brock, at Fort George, heard the firing, and hurried to the battlefield. There, he rode up to a gun located in a redan part way up the heights to determine if the attack on Queenston was a feint, with Fort George being the real target. As it was, British and American batteries had begun pounding each other along the fifty-kilometre length of the Niagara River. Concluding that the Queenston attack was the main thrust, Brock sent word to his second-in-command, Major-General Roger Sheaffe, to hurry from Fort George with all the regulars, militia, and warriors he could spare from the fort.[17]

As daylight approached, one of Brock's officers, assuming that the Americans could not scale the cliff, called the soldiers on the heights down to the village to support the hard-pressed troops in Queenston. However, three companies of American regulars found a path from the landing to the heights. They climbed to the top, formed a line, and charged down the north side of the hill. The surprised British spiked the redan gun and retreated hastily to the village. Brock, deciding the redan had to be recaptured, led 190 men in a charge up the hill. Before reaching the battery, he fell, mortally wounded. His aide-de-camp, John Macdonell, took command and continued the charge, but the attack faltered after he too was shot and the Americans received reinforcements from the landing which enabled them to outflank the British. Brock's force of regulars and militia withdrew to another artillery position, fifteen hundred metres north of the landing site at Vrooman's Point. More American reinforcements rowed across the river and two artillery pieces arrived at Lewiston from Buffalo to support the crossing. By mid-morning the Americans had thirteen hundred men and a six-pounder gun on Canadian soil on top of the heights under the command of Lieutenant-Colonel Winfield Scott. An engineer began to lay out field fortifications and the Americans unspiked the redan gun and turned it towards Queenston.[18]

The relief force Sheaffe had ordered south to Queenston included 160 Grand River men. The rest of the natives remained behind to defend Fort George in case of an attack from Fort Niagara, located across the river from the British post. Led by John Norton, William Kerr, and Joseph Brant's son John, the Iroquois rushed towards the heights in advance of the British regulars and Canadian militia trudging along the river road to Queenston. When the warriors got within four kilometres of the battlefield, Norton heard that the Americans had gained the heights and were marching on Fort George through the forest several hundred metres back of the river on Norton's right. He thought this was impossible because the woods were too thick and snarled with fallen trees to allow troops to move through them with any speed. Nevertheless, he decided to enter the forest to investigate and perhaps prevent an ambush. [19]

As the Iroquois disappeared into the woods, the Americans stood on top of the heights, in line, facing north towards the village of Queenston with an advance party located at the redan battery. The Niagara River rolled past them far below the heights on their right, the forest loomed on their left. Expecting the British to make another frontal assault up the heights as Brock had done, Colonel Scott did not post any light troops in the forest to cover his left flank. He stationed skirmishers only in his front and rear, the latter detachment having been ordered to watch for British reinforcements who might come from Chippawa and other posts to the south.[20]

Before the Iroquois got close to Queenston, a two-gun detachment under Captain William Holcroft of the Royal Artillery, supported by some men of the 41st Foot, re-entered the village. They pushed the American light troops back up the heights and, with the support of the gun at Vrooman's Point, recommenced a destructive barrage against the boats ferrying between the American and Canadian shores. In the forest the Iroquois divided into five or six files so they could search out the enemy and avoid being surprised. If all went well, this manoeuvre would achieve the classic native tactic of surrounding and surprising the enemy, as well as creating a diversion to give the British enough time to concentrate more troops for a counter-attack. On their way, the warriors found no Americans, only some panic-stricken Canadian militiamen who told them there were six thousand Americans on the heights. Some warriors reacted to this startling report with a boastful 'The more game the better hunting.' Half of the native force, however, became alarmed, and anxious for their families at Niagara, they quietly slipped away. To boost morale, one chief, probably Norton, tried to rally the warriors with a speech. 'Be men,' he told them, 'remember the fame of ancient Warriors, whose Breasts were never daunted by odds of number; – you have run from your Encampments to this place to meet the Enemy, – We have found what we came for.' He tried to assuage their concern about their families by telling them that the women and children could run to safety easily enough, and concluded with a heroic, 'Haste, – Let us ascend by yon Path, by which, unperceived, we may gain their rear; your Bullets shall soon spread Havock and dismay among those Ranks that form so proudly ... Let not their numbers appall you: – look up, it is He above that shall decide our fate.'[21]

The warriors climbed the heights through the forest, hidden from view. Once on top they took a position behind Scott's line to gain the advantage by upsetting the Americans' equilibrium. The Iroquois concealed their movements so well that, when they attacked, the Americans assumed that they had come from Chippawa, south of Queenston, rather than from Fort George to the north. The American rearguard, composed of militia riflemen, stood between the Iroquois and Scott's line. The warriors advanced; the riflemen fired, withdrew, halted, and fired again. The natives then pursued them at a rush and pushed the militiamen back to the main line. When the senior American officers heard the shooting in their rear, they re-formed their line behind a fence with its back to both the village and the river to withstand the oncoming natives. Some soldiers on the right of the re-formed American line moved forward, perhaps in the hope of turning the native left flank.[22]

At this point, Van Rensselaer's invasion began to falter. The majority of soldiers in Lewiston lost their nerve and simply refused to cross into Canada. They were frightened by the sight of casualties being carried back from the earlier fighting, the continuing British artillery fire, rumours of the Iroquois presence, and glimpses of Sheaffe's reinforcements marching south along the banks of the river towards Queenston.[23] Back on the heights, the chiefs manoeuvred their followers in the direction of the American right to get beside or behind it and to thwart Scott's flanking movement. With the small number of warriors present, there was little else they could do but hit one of the flanks. This operation also opened up the possibility of surrounding at least part of the American force if the battle progressed in favour of the Iroquois. The Americans fired heavy volleys at the Six Nations men moving in the scrub in advance of their line, but the shots passed over them as the warriors used the rough terrain for cover. The tribesmen, as John Norton recalled, 'returned the Fire of the Enemy with coolness & Spirit, – and altho' their fire certainly made the greatest noise, from the Number of Musquets, yet I believe ours did the most Execution.' Under pressure, the American right flank retired to join the main body behind the fence.[24]

By this time General Sheaffe's column began to reach the battlefield. Instead of making an assault up the steep hillside from the village as Brock had done, Sheaffe veered inland so he could march to the top of Queenston Heights out of range of the Americans and attack across flat ground. In the village below, Captain Holcroft increased his firing, lobbing shrapnel shells up the heights at the invaders. The Iroquois misinterpreted the artillery fire, thinking Sheaffe had decided to move up the heights against Scott. Therefore, they pushed forward with greater boldness than was prudent to distract the Americans. Some warriors fell as a consequence, while others retreated and took cover in a ravine in the rear. Those who moved forward hid in the bush 'within a Javelin's throw' of the Americans and opened a deadly fire into the crowded ranks. The American line 'raged like a Hive of Bees disturbed,' wrote Norton, and began to pump volleys into the brush. Acknowledging that it was 'rather too hot,' Norton and his followers retired to the protective cover of the ravine where they found some of their party hiding. They tried to hearten them with a gentle chiding: 'Where are now those fierce Spirits that at the Village Feast, were wont to boast their prowess? Why now so calm? Come forward whoever holds a manly heart.'[25]

Harassed by the Iroquois from the top of the heights and from the artillery below, and dispirited by the heavy casualties inflicted by the warriors in the bush, the Americans decided to attack the Iroquois and chase them out of their secure position. The charge forced the warriors back and provided some relief to the Americans.[26] According to one rifleman, the natives 'were compelled to fly for safety,' but the advance did not boost American morale. He continued: 'By this time, I thought hell had broken loose and let her dogs of war upon us. In short, I expected every moment to be made a "cold Yanky" as the soldier says.'[27] Following both good light infantry and native tactical doctrine, the Iroquois had retreated from their untenable position. But once the Americans got into the woods, the Iroquois began to regroup and snipe at the troops while managing to hide from American fire. Scott's force did not have the necessary light infantry force to advance ahead of the line and drive off the warriors. Rather than continue the charge, Colonel Scott decided to improve his security by increasing the distance between the edge of the woods and the American line by withdrawing to a new position one hundred metres closer to the Niagara River than the one he had occupied at the beginning of the Iroquois assault. This gave the Americans some respite because the natives could not approach within range nearly as well without exposing themselves dangerously. One officer remarked, 'After this movement was accomplished, the fire of the Indians was of course less general and fatal, but it was never intermitted during the rest of the day.' Continued Iroquois harassment led the Americans to launch a second, half-hearted, and ultimately aborted charge against the Six Nations men.[28]

A pause in the battle followed as John Norton and the other chiefs concentrated their followers in a ravine to rest and wait for General Sheaffe to finish his ascent up the heights unhindered by American opposition.[29] That Sheaffe could perform this manoeuvre was due, as he noted, to 'the judicious position taken by Norton on the woody brow of the high ground.'[30] The Iroquois thus far had fulfilled the fundamental objectives of effective light troops in battle. They had knocked out Scott's light infantry, thereby eliminating the American line's protective screen and allowing Sheaffe to gain the heights unmolested to enter the battle on the most favourable terms possible. They had prevented the Americans from moving inland, which allowed British reinforcements from Chippawa to the south to unite with Sheaffe's troops from the north for a concentrated counter-attack. They had pushed Scott into what would become a perilous topographical position once Sheaffe advanced into action. And finally, the Grand River men had upset the American line's equilibrium and weakened the invaders' capacity to take on the unharassed British line.

Once Sheaffe arrived on top of the heights, Norton dispatched a messenger to outline events as they had occurred up to that point and to let Sheaffe know where the Iroquois had posted themselves. The British commander in turn sent an officer to Norton for more information. After he reported back, Sheaffe dispatched one hundred light infantry from the 41st Foot and a company of black Canadian militiamen to support Norton. At the same time, eighty Cayugas from Fort George also reinforced the Iroquois on the heights.[31] Sheaffe's intelligence gathering extended beyond his contact with Norton. According to the Americans watching his movements, the British manoeuvred 'with great caution ... to reconnoitre our whole front and left in part, always skirting the woods and presenting themselves in line on our right flank.'[32]

The Americans, exhausted and running out of ammunition, were in a virtual state of collapse by the time the British regulars and Canadian militia paraded in front of them. To make matters worse, Van Rensselaer continued to be unable to persuade reinforcements to cross the river and had to content himself with sending some ammunition to the troops stranded in Canada. At about three in the afternoon Colonel Scott responded to Sheaffe's menacing movements by withdrawing closer to the cliff edge. While his men moved, and thus were vulnerable, Sheaffe attacked.[33] One Upper Canadian militiaman recorded: 'we rushed through the woods ... The Indians were first in advance. As soon as they perceived the enemy they uttered their terrific warwhoop, and rushing rapidly upon them commenced a most destructive fire. Our troops instantly sprung forward from all quarters, joining in the shout. The Americans gave a volley, then tumultuously fled by hundreds down the mountain' towards the river bank.[34]

At this point, the warriors moved forward on the British left flank and worked their way behind the Americans on the cliff to prevent their enemies from reaching the river and making their escape. As Winfield Scott's command collapsed under the weight of Sheaffe's attack, the Iroquois ferreted out Americans trying to hide along the bank, scalped dead men, and completely stripped some of the casualties. Some of the American wounded seem to have been killed by tomahawk blows during this time and some Iroquois may have used excessive violence in securing the surrendering Americans.[35] One British officer reported that the British had 'much trouble in restraining the Indians.'[36] However, John Norton claimed that the invaders 'had no reason to complain of cruelty this day.'[37]

The British victory was decisive. The Americans suffered as many as five hundred killed and wounded, and surrendered 960 men as prisoners-of-war. Another eight hundred to one thousand disheartened soldiers in New York deserted over the course of the next week. The Americans also lost their six-pounder, its ammunition wagon, the colours of the Thirteenth Infantry, and a huge quantity of weapons. One witness thought the British captured twelve hundred firearms and the Iroquois another four hundred.[38] Sheaffe's force of 800 white and black troops and 240 natives (including those who deserted before coming into action) lost nineteen killed, including five Iroquois, and eighty-five wounded, of whom between seven and nine were Six Nations warriors. Twenty-one were missing, of whom eight or ten, including an Iroquois chief, were taken prisoner. Sheaffe subsequently arranged the exchange of at least the chief for some American prisoners. The five Iroquois killed were two Cayugas, one Onondaga, and two Oneidas. John Norton was slightly wounded.[39]

General Sheaffe thought the magnitude of the British success ensued from Norton's decision to position the Grand River men on top of the heights early in the battle because it allowed British forces from Fort George and Chippawa to unite for a crushing final assault. Following the battle, Sheaffe made special mention of the Six Nations in his dispatches, proclaiming that they deserved 'the highest praise for their good order and spirit,' and he particularly singled out John Norton for recognition. [40] It would be incorrect, however, to oversimplify by claiming that the participation of the Iroquois in the battle was the single most important factor in the British victory. The artillery played a critical role in making the Niagara River too dangerous to cross for a large portion of the American army either to reinforce their comrades stranded in Canada or to evacuate them. It was the regulars and militia who kept the Americans out of the village of Queenston, which cut off the invaders' northern escape route to the landing should things go badly for them on top of the heights; and Holcroft's shrapnel fired from the village helped demoralize the Americans on the heights at the same time as Norton's men kept the American army pinned down. In the final charge, three-quarters of the troops in Sheaffe's force were militia or regulars. Yet the victory would not have been as easy or as decisive without the Iroquois, and the battle serves as an example of how well natives and non-natives could function together in action. The Grand River people proved to be excellent fighters by helping to prevent the Americans from consolidating their position and by contributing to the destruction of the invaders' military cohesion. The achievements of the Iroquois were all the more remarkable because they had only eighty men engaged against a far larger number until the last stages of the battle.

One factor that helped make the Six Nations so effective was topography. Norton wrote that the 'Ground on which we had fought was well adapted to favour a small number against a stronger force' because it gave the Iroquois room to manoeuvre and because the extensive amount of cleared land where both Iroquois flanks were stationed enabled them to watch Scott's movements and thereby protect themselves from a surprise counter-attack.[41] Another consideration affecting the Iroquois success was the incompetence of the American force. In the early stages of the battle, when the invaders formed on the heights facing the village below, Winfield Scott posted no light troops on his left in advance of his line to guard against a flanking manoeuvre. Given that the Americans knew the British force included natives and that the warriors likely would come from Fort George, this was a serious blunder that enabled the Iroquois to climb the heights and move behind the Americans undetected. Once the Iroquois attacked, the militia skirmishers in the rear did not provide effective cover for the main body. This was probably due mainly to the skirmishers' lack of skill and discipline in comparison with that of the Iroquois force. As well, these militiamen were all armed with rifles, which meant that they could not respond to the Iroquois, equipped with both rifles and muskets, with an adequate volume of fire. Good light troops, particularly if they outnumbered the warriors, should have been able to keep the tribesmen and the main body of Americans apart. Had they done so, the American skirmishes would have preserved the line in a reasonably fresh state to meet Sheaffe's regulars and militia, or at least they would have given the line a chance to escape back across the river. Another example of the inadequacy of Scott's force was the poor quality of its musketry. Although the Iroquois evaded most enemy bullets by keeping close to the ground in the bush, the Americans also fired too high. Properly trained troops would have been drilled sufficiently to present their muskets low enough to fire directly into the brush sheltering the Iroquois. Firing high – a common problem among troops with poor musketry training – would continue to be a problem for the American army in the war.[42]

The Americans did not learn the right lessons from their defeat at

Queenston Heights. When, a few weeks later, they planned another invasion an officer wrote a letter in which he boasted that no 'savages' (American-allied Iroquois) would cross with them 'to tarnish our ungathered laurels by ruthless deeds,' that the officers were to dress like the men 'so that they could not be distinguished from them at 150 paces,' and that the soldiers were to be 'drilled in squatting or lying down and loading their pieces.' He also wrote that the army expected to be reinforced by fifteen hundred to two thousand militiamen from Pennsylvania. [43]

Several points in his statement are remarkable. One is the anti-native rage of the letter. Presumably, Iroquois actions at Queenston galled American sensibilities, perhaps because they were so harrowing and possibly because American biases were inflamed as a result of the American defeat at the hands of 'savages.' This was an interesting issue. On the one hand, early nineteenth-century American propaganda constantly vilified the aboriginal peoples by describing native barbarities in lurid detail; on the other, this propaganda frightened rather than bolstered American troops. At Queenston Heights 'the name of Indian,' as one combatant noted, was an important element in stopping reinforcements from crossing into Canada. [44] As well, many people may have been able to accept the defeat of their troops only by believing it was the result of British perfidy in using natives rather than from any incompetence of their own. This sort of attitude, of course, was not conducive to making the reforms necessary to ensure future success. The order for officers to dress like the lower ranks – which is not the same as wearing camouflaged uniforms – implies that the Iroquois chose their targets carefully and were accurate marksmen. The directive to teach the soldiers to load lying down or squatting, which good light infantry could do, likely reflected the problem the Americans experienced when the warriors, under cover, inflicted heavy casualties among the troops standing in line. Yet fighting lying down would have been redundant if Scott had had effective light infantry to keep the Iroquois from getting to his line troops. Furthermore, loading lying down took more time than loading from a standing position and the line's primary strengths – its ability in performing quick uniform action and providing a high rate of heavy volley fire – would have been compromised significantly by adopting such a measure. Also, effective well-directed volleys aimed low would have forced natives or light troops to withdraw because of their complete inability to respond with a similar volume of fire. Last, the author of the letter looked forward to the arrival of the militiamen. The number expected was impressive, but because they were militia they would have been at a serious disadvantage to well-trained British and Iroquois light forces. The lessons the Americans learned at Queenston Heights were poor ones indeed, and would come back to haunt them in 1813.

On the Iroquois side the battle not only illustrated their effectiveness, but also their weaknesses. Two flaws stand out. One was the desertion rate. Half of the initial contingent left before firing a shot, and Norton's account makes it clear that many of those who remained hid during the action and had to be cajoled by their chiefs to fight. The second, though unclear, implication of weakness is a hint that Iroquois scouting skills could not provide the information a white commander required. When Sheaffe ascended the heights he did his own reconnaissance of the enemy line before attacking, choosing not to accept Norton's assessment without verification, as was characteristic of his cautious character. Sheaffe had spent a large part of his career in the Great Lakes region, knew native people well, and seemed to like them, and so his decision to perform his own reconnaissance presumably was based on experience rather than prejudice. Yet even with these negative assessments, and allowing a large portion of the warriors' success to have been a result of American failings, it is clear that the performance of the Grand River men was outstanding. It is difficult to imagine a like number of white troops performing as brilliantly against such odds as the Iroquois warriors did on 13 October 1812.

Roger Sheaffe succeeded Isaac Brock as the civil and military leader of Upper Canada. From this dual position, Sheaffe rewarded Norton for his service by granting him the title 'Captain of the Confederate Indians' of the Grand River, the same rank the legendary Joseph Brant had held during the American Revolution. This appointment meant that Sheaffe had designated Norton as the British army's choice as leader of the Iroquois. The army could back up its decision by channelling a large proportion of government presents and rewards through Norton to the Grand River people, but it could not force the Six Nations to accept Norton's leadership. For that reason alone, it was a bold move. Moreover, it was a striking attempt to undermine the Indian Department on the Grand by connecting the tract's military resources directly to Sheaffe through Norton even though such a move might cause additional problems because the department had a significant body of friends within the Six Nations. However, the logic to Sheaffe was obvious because the department had not been aggressive enough in mustering Iroquois support and had devoted much of its energy to subverting John Norton, the army's best friend on the tract. Administratively, the reorganization would have been difficult without a wartime emergency because the Indian Department had been transferred from the authority of the commander-in-chief to the civil lieutenant-governor in 1796. However, in 1811, when the governor sailed for England on leave, the British government, seeing the war coming, had amalgamated military and civil leadership in Upper Canada in the most senior army officer in the province to ensure that a military mind dominated executive leadership in the colony.[45]

Despite Sheaffe's recognition, Norton continued to have to struggle against the Indian Department for dominance over the pro-British groups on the Grand because the political situation was too fluid and the influence of the department was too pervasive for an administrative decision alone to deal a mortal blow to the department. At the same time, the new order was frustrating for Indian Department officials, who had exercised so much power in white–native relations for decades. The disappointment must have been great when its officers saw people like Norton, a former common soldier of obscure origins, being courted by the army while their own people, such as Lieutenant-Colonel William Claus, a prominent figure in colonial society and the senior Indian Department officer on the Niagara Peninsula, were shunted aside. The point that Norton was a brave and skilled chief seems to have left Indian Department officials unimpressed. All they saw was the loss of their dominance to a man whose stature had been raised by army officers from Europe who would leave the colony once the fighting ceased.[46] (Later Mohawk memories of Norton remembered him as a 'good natured man' with a 'very good character' who 'was a great warrior & very brave.')[47]

Roger Sheaffe and Stephen Van Rensselaer arranged a local truce following the battle. Sheaffe thought he had little choice because he had so many prisoners on his hands while Van Rensselaer believed he could not offer effective resistance should the British invade New York. Like Brock at Detroit, Sheaffe received a baronetcy for his victory at Queenston but, unlike his predecessor, he lived to hear the news. A large number of the native warriors – who felt 'grief' and 'gloom' at Brock's death – attended the funeral and lined the route of the procession, 'resting on their arms reversed' as part of the guard of honour.[48] Along with this Euroamerican show of respect, they offered their traditional condolence ceremony to the British to help 'wipe away the tears' occasioned by the loss of the famous general.[49] As an outward show of respect for their fallen adversary, the Americans fired a salute from their cannon at Fort Niagara in response to the British artillery salute. Inwardly, the senior American commander on the Canadian front, Major-General Henry Dearborn, thought, or at least hoped, that Brock's death would undermine the morale of the Canadian militia and Britain's aboriginal allies.[50]

Major-General Van Rensselaer resigned shortly after his defeat and Brigadier-General Smyth negotiated an extension of the truce. With the renewal of the ceasefire, Sheaffe let the militia and natives return home, and by early November only Norton and a handful of followers remained at Fort George with the regulars. Alexander Smyth cancelled the armistice on 20 November. Eight days later an advance party of Americans rowed across the Niagara River to secure a landing site a few kilometres south of Fort Erie for another invasion of Canada. Other troops attempted a landing downriver to destroy a bridge and slow the arrival of British reinforcements from posts to the north. However, the invasion quickly fell apart: the soldiers assigned to wreck the bridge failed to achieve their objective, and British troops from Fort Erie drove the other party away. Norton's men at Fort George rushed to the scene but arrived too late to participate, although other natives, probably Mississaugas, joined some British light troops in a reconnaissance of the landing site. A few hours later, the Americans called off the attack. After giving his troops a two-day rest, Smyth tried to invade Upper Canada again, but cancelled this attack in its early stages. He then went on leave and never returned to duty.[51]

Iroquois from the New York reservations achieved the only success the Americans enjoyed on the Niagara Peninsula after the battle of Queenston Heights. At the end of October or early November one hundred warriors crossed the border for the first time in the war and stole a vessel from a dock near Fort George. Some Cattaraugus warriors also undertook patrols to guard the Lake Erie shoreline near Buffalo from British raids.[52]

John Norton's party continued to serve along the Niagara Peninsula until Christmas, by which time Sheaffe thought the Americans would not attack again until the spring because ice on the river made a crossing too dangerous to attempt. After receiving Sheaffe's congratulations and thanks, the warriors went home, loaded with presents from the Indian Department stores and knowing that Sheaffe had ordered the department to send more supplies to meet their requirements. The Six Nations needed these gifts, as they had failed to harvest most of their crops because the warriors and some of their families had spent the autumn at the front rather than at home attending to their farms. [53]

Beyond the capture of Fort Mackinac, Detroit, and other smaller victories gained as part of the Detroit campaign, the triumph at Queenston Heights, and the repulse of the November attacks on Fort Erie, the British and their native allies achieved a number of other successes in 1812. The western tribes, in addition to destroying the garrison of Fort Dearborn, waged an incessant and largely successful campaign against American settlers on the western frontier. In the east, supplies kept moving up the St Lawrence River to support British and aboriginal forces despite American efforts to cut the province's link to the rest of the British Empire. More important for Canadian defence, Major-General Henry Dearborn's long-awaited invasion of Lower Canada from Plattsburgh collapsed after the Canadian Voltigeurs and 230 Kahnawake warriors repulsed the American vanguard at Lacolle in late November. Among other endeavours on the eastern front, warriors from the Seven Nations supported French-Canadian militiamen in a skirmish at L'Acadie in December. [54]

The outcome of the 1812 campaigns was not the one most people had expected when the United States declared war in June. The Americans lost every significant engagement and suffered losses in territory, manpower, supplies, and prestige of huge proportions in comparison to the resources the British had applied to achieving their victories. What successes the Americans did enjoy, such as their autumn raid on Akwesasne, were nullified by subsequent British actions. [55] The Americans achieved only one triumph of consequence during the first campaigns of the war. Towards the end of the shipping season, the newly created United States squadron on Lake Ontario chased two British vessels into Kingston harbour. It was a small affair and casualties were minimal. However, it signalled something important: the Americans seemed ready to seize control of the lake, an event that could cut Upper Canada off from its source of reinforcements and supply in the spring of 1813. [56]

5

The Twisted Road to Beaver Dams:
January–June 1813

*But we did not hold this position long, – in two days we moved on to Burlington.
The Lower part of the Grand River becoming more exposed to the Enemy by this ret-
rograde movement, – the Warriors all left me to place their families in a place of
Security; – there only remained with me my young Cherokee Cousin, a few Delawares, some Chippawas, one Mohawk, and a Cayuga.*

John Norton on the British evacuation of the Niagara Peninsula in May 1813[1]

The first half of 1813 was an extremely anxious period for the Grand
River Iroquois. Ongoing difficulties between the Indian Department and
the British army continued to exacerbate animosities through the winter
of 1812–13. In the spring the Americans won a series of battles that
forced the British to abandon the Niagara Peninsula towards the end of
May. At that point the Grand River Tract sat dangerously exposed to
direct American assault. Once again, many of the people along the
Grand, in desperation, seem to have been prepared to abandon their
British alliance in favour of an American one in the hope of buying peace
with the invaders. In June, however, the British counter-attacked, reoccupied most of the peninsula, and reversed the strategic situation. Therefore, the Six Nations continued to fight alongside King George III's
troops as the immediate threat to their community evaporated. Then, on
24 June, Grand River, Akwesasne, Kahnawake, Kanesatake, and other warriors united to go into battle in what became the most famous Iroquois
action of the war, Beaver Dams.

Both Great Britain and the United States took measures to strengthen
their forces in the Great Lakes theatre over the winter of 1812–13. Despite

its commitments in Europe, the British government managed to spare five additional infantry battalions, part of a cavalry regiment, and other reinforcements for the war in North America. Within the Canadas, the government began to form incorporated militia units for full-time service as well as special corps, such as the Provincial Dragoons. The Royal Navy took over the Great Lakes squadrons from the less competent Provincial Marine, and 450 officers and ratings arrived on the inland waters to bolster British naval strength. On the Atlantic front, naval officers received orders to attempt a diversion in favour of the Canadas by blockading and raiding the American coast. In the United States, the Madison administration raised its first war loan, authorized the creation of twenty new infantry regiments, and approved an expansion of the navy. Madison appointed a more energetic secretary of war and initiated reforms to improve American prospects in the upcoming campaigns. With most of the United States Navy blockaded in Atlantic ports, the government sent hundreds of seamen to the Great Lakes to form the companies needed to sail its newly built warships which the American government assumed would help bring victory in the upcoming campaign.[2]

The first actions of 1813 favoured the British cause. On 22 January a force of regulars, militia, and western tribesmen, including some Mingo Iroquois, crushed the advance guard of a strong American army sent to retake Detroit at Frenchtown on the Raisin River in Michigan. The Americans lost nine hundred killed, wounded, or taken prisoner to 185 British, Canadian, and native casualties. However, British losses probably were higher than necessary because the commanding officer, Brigadier-General Henry Procter, passed up an opportunity to launch a surprise attack, choosing instead to open fire with his artillery first which gave the Americans time to form for battle. Despite his casualties, Procter's victory reduced the threat to the vulnerable British right flank for the next several months until the Americans could recover from their defeat and dispatch a fresh force to contest the region. To consolidate his gains, Procter organized the western tribesmen and some Grand River Iroquois attending a council near Amherstburg, including John Norton, to harass the American army as it retired. However, the expedition had to be cancelled when warm weather thawed the rivers and lakes over which the warriors had expected to travel. To the east, the British captured Ogdensburg on the St Lawrence River in February to stop the Americans from threatening the Canadian side of the river. Thirty Akwesasne warriors fought alongside the British at this battle. The victors torched schooners and gunboats stuck in the ice and took supplies and armaments.[3]

In early March the British asked the Grand River people to return to the Niagara Peninsula in anticipation of the upcoming spring campaign. However, only a small number responded. The Six Nations complained that an invasion was not possible so early in the year because ice floes on the Niagara River made an American crossing unlikely. The Iroquois were busy producing maple sugar, and some of them thought that if the warriors were mustered so often as to affect their ability to take care of their families they might not turn out when needed to oppose a real threat. Others stayed home to protest the Indian Department's failure to deliver the quantity of presents they expected to receive for their services in 1812. If John Norton's account is to be believed, the department wanted to undermine the authority of the army after Major-General Sir Roger Sheaffe moved to negate the department's influence when he appointed Norton to the command of the Grand River people after the Battle of Queenston Heights. He claimed that the department's agents even attacked the army's credibility by condemning Procter's performance on the Detroit frontier. Presumably, these agents worked with their supporters within the Six Nations and took advantage of Norton's absence in the west to sabotage confidence in both him and the army. While their objective was to force Sheaffe to let them resume their former position of power, they probably contributed to the decision of many Grand River people to stay away from the front lines. When Norton returned to the Grand for a few days in March he found he could recruit only a handful of men to go with him to Fort Erie where the British expected an assault (but which the Americans cancelled in its early stages). [4]

After the Fort Erie incident John Norton walked to the provincial capital at York to meet General Sheaffe and to convince him to send more provisions to the Grand River. Apparently Sir Roger was surprised that supplies ordered previously had not been dispatched and immediately sent a letter to Lieutenant-Colonel William Claus, ordering him to rectify the problem. Perhaps Norton's information was the first news Sheaffe had received about the insubordination of the Indian Department. However, the main purpose behind Norton's visit was not to address the problem of presents but to obtain Sheaffe's permission to take a war party to Amherstburg to join the western tribes operating against the enemy. Norton considered the plan necessary to consolidate British success in the west before the Americans could muster enough strength to threaten the Niagara Peninsula and compel the outnumbered British to fight on two fronts at once. Sheaffe agreed, but only reluctantly, because he thought Norton was the linchpin in maintaining a strong Iroquois presence in the Niagara region. Sir Roger had little faith in either the Indian Department or the majority of the Grand River chiefs and considered Norton to be the only leader from the tract in whom he could have any real confidence. He therefore urged Norton to return to Niagara as soon as possible. John Norton left York about 13 April and headed for the Grand to assemble warriors for his western expedition.[5]

The new American secretary of war, John Armstrong, developed a Canadian strategy that called for the capture of Kingston and its naval squadron as the first step in the upcoming campaign. This would cut Upper Canada's links with the rest of the Empire and force the British to move troops and supplies along the miserably slow land routes, thus destroying their ability to strengthen threatened points quickly. In such a predicament, the province likely would fall because there would be no way for the British to rebuild their lost squadron and regain control of Lake Ontario. However, the American commanders on the northern front, Major-General Henry Dearborn of the army and Commodore Isaac Chauncey of the navy, were afraid to assault strongly held Kingston. Instead, they proposed an alternative plan for the conquest of Upper Canada. They wanted to attack York first, then invade the Niagara Peninsula, and finally take Kingston as the last effort in the 1813 campaign. They believed that the capture of York would be much easier than assaulting Kingston and that seizing two warships thought to be in York would swing the balance of power on Lake Ontario to the United States. The acquisition of the ships would facilitate the second and third phases of their plan because the British squadron would be too weak to challenge the Americans on the lake. The scheme was a poor one in comparison to Armstrong's. As long as Kingston remained in British hands, with its squadron supplied from Lower Canada, any American successes further west might be of only temporary importance because Kingston's dockyard gave the British the capacity to build more warships and support a counter-attacking army. Even if the first two phases of the plan were successful, the Americans would still have to take either Kingston or Montreal late in the season with an army depleted from several months of campaigning. Despite these strategic problems, political imperatives led Armstrong to accept the plan. The pro-war Republican governor of New York sought re-election in April 1813 but was in trouble because many voters were angry at the lack of success in 'Mr Madison's War.' In Washington, the government believed a military victory on the Canadian front could swing the electorate away from the anti-war Federalists. Politically, York was a good target. Victory could almost be guaranteed because of the weakness of its defences, and the seizure of the provincial capital would have excellent propaganda value.[6]

The Americans attacked York on 27 April. After a hard-fought and costly battle, they captured the town and a large quantity of naval supplies destined for the British squadron on Lake Erie. However, they did not get their ships: one had left before the battle, and Sheaffe burned the other before retreating to Kingston. Ice on Lake Ontario had prevented the action from occurring before the election as planned, but the pro-war Republican governor nevertheless won by a small margin, partly because his supporters circulated victory proclamations in advance of the attack to an unsuspecting electorate and partly because Dearborn did not take most of his New York troops to York with him, preferring instead to leave them behind to vote for the Republicans.[7]

At the time of the raid, the commanding officer at Fort George heard the cannonade from the battle and sent word to the Grand River warriors to march to York with all dispatch – a distance of one hundred kilometres. By about 3 May over three hundred men had advanced as far as the Head of the Lake (today's Burlington, Ont.). There, they cancelled the expedition when they learned that the Americans had re-embarked on their vessels. The Iroquois then were asked to reinforce Fort George since it might be attacked next. In fact, Dearborn had planned to assault it immediately after York, but diarrhoea and dysentery among his men forced him to return to his base at Sackett's Harbor to allow the troops to recover. The warriors, though they had been willing to counter-attack if the Americans still occupied the provincial capital, would not go into garrison duty with less certain prospects of a fight and leave their families 'to starve,' because, as Norton wrote, 'the present Season was that of preparing their fields for planting the Maize.' Furthermore, the Iroquois were put off by the local militiamen who showed little zeal in obeying orders to muster. Therefore, only a quarter of the Grand River force went to Fort George.[8]

These warriors did not have to wait long for a battle. On 25 May, in carrying out the second phase of the Dearborn–Chauncey plan, the guns of Fort Niagara and the United States Lake Ontario squadron began to bombard Fort George. The barrage destroyed the fort. Two days later, four to five thousand American soldiers assaulted the combined British, militia, and Iroquois force of one thousand, defeated them, and sent them in retreat towards Beaver Dams (today's Thorold). Norton's party halted five kilometres north of Beaver Dams along Twelve Mile Creek where two hundred recently arrived reinforcements from the Grand

River had assembled after receiving word of the earlier American bombardment. Norton's men were weary and hungry after heavy fighting but, along with the fresh warriors and the light company of the 8th Foot, laid an ambush for the night in case the Americans attempted to pursue the British. The next day the British fell back to the mouth of Forty Mile Creek and Norton's people followed, arriving the following day. There, Norton found all of the British troops from the Niagara River, who had assembled after destroying and abandoning their posts along the border. However, Norton was pleased with what he saw because he thought the local topography was well-suited to defeat the Americans when they continued their invasion attempt and moved inland. On the British right flank was the impassable high ridge of the Niagara Escarpment, on the left, Lake Ontario, and to the front, open ground that was commanded by the Royal Artillery. However, the British decided against making a stand there. Instead, the troops continued their retreat back to Burlington Heights (where Dundurn Castle now stands in Hamilton) to regroup in a safe location. The Iroquois covered the withdrawal, but the Americans did not harass them, contenting themselves at that point with occupying the recently abandoned British forts.[9]

With the fall of Fort George and the British retreat to Burlington, the Americans had gained a significant lodgement in Upper Canada. Once inside their adversaries' former headquarters, the Americans stood poised to cut Upper Canada in half. Should they succeed, not only would the Niagara Peninsula fall, but communications links to the west might be severed and the war in that theatre might be brought to a close. As it was, the evacuation of Fort Erie allowed the Americans to sail naval vessels from Buffalo, where they had been trapped by Fort Erie's guns, to Presqu'Isle, where the Americans were building a squadron to challenge British dominance on Lake Erie. The Americans also demonstrated their growing strength in the southwest in early May, when Henry Procter found himself forced to lift a siege he had undertaken at Fort Meigs (in today's Perrysburg, Ohio). The situation looked bleak on Lake Ontario as well. Not only had the British burned an important frigate at York, but an attack they launched on Sackett's Harbor at the end of May failed. (A number of Iroquois in New York fought on the American side while Seven Nations and Mississauga warriors served with the British at that engagement.) The assault on Sackett's Harbor nevertheless caused Commodore Chauncey to sail his squadron away from Niagara to protect his base from another strike. Chauncey's move gave the Royal Navy an opportunity to cruise west from Kingston to support John Vincent, the

British commander at Burlington, during the difficult days following the loss of Fort George.[10]

For the Iroquois, especially those with traditional religious views, the successive British defeats at York, Fort Meigs, Fort George, and Sackett's Harbor seemed to indicate that the king's men were losing their spiritual powers. The only mitigating factor was the success of the Fort Meigs expedition, despite its overall failure, in inflicting massive casualties on the Americans – over one thousand compared to just sixty British losses – which the Grand River people could interpret with considerable approval as balancing the debt with their old enemies. Yet they had to look with apprehension on what was happening on the lakes. Although there had been no victories in the naval war, the Americans seemed ready to seize control of the vulnerable waterways. As prodigious consumers of British food, munitions, and other supplies, the Six Nations could clearly see what would happen if the lakes fell.[11]

The retreat to Burlington Heights was particularly worrisome for the people of the Grand. Their villages and fields now sat exposed to attack from either Fort George or Buffalo since there was nothing to stop the Americans from marching against the tract. Vincent's motive in halting at Burlington and not farther east at York or Kingston stemmed partly from his desire to show some support for the Six Nations, but the Iroquois were not impressed. Most of them probably shared the common Upper Canadian view that the British would soon abandon everything west of Kingston.[12] As the Iroquois began to assess the consequences of such a move, they left Vincent, and did so at the same time the few Canadian militiamen remaining with the army deserted, 'considering our situation as desperate & all as lost' according to one British officer.[13] Once home, the warriors drove away their livestock and hid their families in the forest in fear that Major-General Henry Dearborn would dispatch a punitive expedition against them just as Major-General John Sullivan had done during the American Revolution. Lieutenant-Colonel William Claus followed the warriors to the Grand to try to convince them to return to Burlington, but they would not listen to the king's officials during those dismal days.[14]

Although the record is unclear, it seems that the Grand River people had become profoundly demoralized. And, as they had done in 1812, they thought about abandoning the British to join their old enemies in hopes of avoiding American vengeance. General Dearborn, ensconced in his new headquarters at Fort George, took comfort in the absence of any native harassment, and wrote that the Six Nations were 'quiet for fear of losing their valuable land on Grand River.'[15] He could write fairly accurately about Iroquois affairs because some people from the tract had opened communications with the Americans.[16] Given the importance of omens for many Iroquois, the shock of 350 British casualties at Fort George, the strategic situation on the peninsula, and the history of American success in the revolution and in the frontier war of the 1790s, it is no wonder the Six Nations saw their future threatened and contemplated extreme measures to preserve their vulnerable society. With the British party on the Grand in disarray because of the recent disasters, it was the perfect time for the American party to reassert itself to protect Six Nations interests.

At this critical point General Dearborn decided to attack the sixteen hundred British soldiers on Burlington Heights. He sent thirty-seven hundred infantry, cavalry, and artillery from Fort George to Stoney Creek on 5 June, where they camped within striking distance of British headquarters. At the same time, the Grand River warriors moved towards Burlington Heights with undetermined intentions. Should the British be defeated, the Iroquois were going to be in an excellent position to strike at their old allies and attempt to purchase American forgiveness by falling upon the retreating redcoats, just as they would have been in the summer of 1812 when they had assembled at the mouth of the Grand at the time of Isaac Brock's move against Detroit.[17]

During this very tense period, Lieutenant-Colonel John Harvey reconnoitred the American camp and concluded that it was so poorly laid out that it sat perilously open to a surprise attack. He consequently obtained Vincent's permission to assault it. As British officers organized their troops, they seem to have realized that there was a serious problem with their Iroquois allies. Therefore, they asked for thirty or forty warriors to assist in the Stoney Creek attack, probably to test the mood of the Six Nations as well as to acquire hostages to prevent a native strike against them. The Six Nations people refused to send anyone. For his part, John Norton did not try to muster support beyond the handful of warriors who continued to follow his leadership. His militant British party had lost almost all of its influence, and he and his followers chose instead to distance themselves from the problems at Burlington by tormenting the advancing Americans rather than by participating in difficult negotiations. William Claus made another attempt to enlist Iroquois support, but failed. The Iroquois told the British that they had to protect their families instead of attacking Stoney Creek. While that statement might seem plausible given that a road, Dundas Street, which connected Burlington to the

Grand, could be used by the Americans to attack the Six Nations if the British retreated, it lacked logic because a combined British–Iroquois strike would have had a better chance of success than an assault by the heavily outnumbered redcoats alone. Did the Iroquois plan to make up their minds only after the outcome of the battle became known, as the Ottawas had done at Mackinac in 1812? Were they going to fall on the British if Vincent suffered defeat and leave the United States Army in control of central Upper Canada? Perhaps the future of the province as a British colony never hung more precariously in the balance than it did when British troops left Burlington Heights to march on Stoney Creek on the night of 5–6 June. It was a desperate move: seven hundred soldiers (accompanied by Norton's little war party) were going to attack thirty-seven hundred Americans.[18]

The British learned the American password and used it to get close enough to the unsuspecting sentries to bayonet them. Shortly after two in the morning the redcoats stormed the camp. Confusion reigned in the ensuing fight: friend shot at friend and the two American brigadiers-general who commanded the expedition were captured when they walked into the hands of the British. In the end the British had to withdraw from the field, but their underlying objective for the attack had succeeded because the invaders abandoned their assault on Burlington Heights and retreated to a camp on the Lake Ontario shore at Forty Mile Creek between Stoney Creek and Fort George.[19]

The outcome of the battle sent a message to the wavering Iroquois that the king's men were still a potent military power. Yet the still formidable American force camped at the Forty had the potential to rally, and casualties had been heavy on the British side, which made it difficult for the Six Nations to interpret Stoney Creek as an unqualified triumph. One limited British success was not enough for them to forsake their anxiety about their future on the war-torn Niagara Peninsula.

At this point John Norton met the chiefs and warriors to suggest a plan that would take the Iroquois away from potentially dangerous contact with both Vincent's troops and white civilians, but that would demonstrate continued Six Nations support for the king's cause and thus undo some of the damage they may have done to their British alliance. He urged them to advance towards the American camp through the thick woods on the top of the Niagara Escarpment which ran parallel to the lakeshore lowlands where the British and American forces operated. From the heights they could watch American movements on the plain below and strike whenever an opportunity arose. Some warriors liked the idea and prepared to go with 'alacrity,' as John Norton wrote. However, others objected, notably, and surprisingly, some hitherto pro-British Mohawks who, Norton wrote cryptically in his unedited journal, 'had received a suggestion from a certain Quarter' and who delayed the departure by proposing to hold a council meeting first. [20] (A few months later a group of Grand River chiefs sent a petition to Colonel Claus asking him to exclude 105 people – mostly Mohawks – from the Crown's gift-giving, claiming they had influenced people to abandon the British cause.) [21]

At the council, speakers, whom Norton described as forming a 'Cabal' (which, for him, was an uncharacteristically severe term), enumerated 'several difficulties' and obviously tried either to prevent the expedition from moving forward or at least to organize it in such a way as to offer the Americans some reason to think the Grand River Iroquois had changed sides. For example, they did not want the war party to proceed without some British regulars accompanying them. Presumably, this was an attempt to acquire hostages either to protect themselves from British retribution or to turn over to the Americans depending on circumstances. It also may have been an angry gesture in response to the British request for a war party which they could have used as hostages during the attack on Stoney Creek. Norton expressed his disapproval of the idea of bringing whites along. He skirted the issue of hostages by saying the British did not have any surplus men to deploy with the Iroquois and he claimed that the escarpment route was too rugged for them to use in any case. He also appealed to the warriors' sense of honour by reminding them that 'we should attempt something alone, as in the last two Battles we had aided our father's Troops with a very few Warriors indeed.' [22]

Norton's arguments seem to have been strained given that the British normally deployed light infantry alongside their native allies. Did he think the Iroquois still might forsake the British despite the victory at Stoney Creek and fall upon the soldiers? One historian has suggested that, at the very least, the Iroquois did not want to rejoin the British until it became clear that the Americans really were on the run and no longer posed a threat to their homes. [23] Unfortunately, the Iroquois archival record is too thin to be conclusive, as might be expected from a society that produced few written documents and in which the contemplation of desperate measures called for circumspection. There is, however, a fragment in Six Nations oral tradition that seems to address the tensions of this period because it reads like the redemption part of a 'fall and redemption' story in its description of a skirmish with the Americans immediately after this council. [24] About all that exists in Norton's memoir other than his curious arguments is a mysterious comment written about the events immediately before the battle of Stoney Creek: 'I expected with great anxiety the return of our people from the Grand River, & happened to be absent when the first report reached Head Quarters of the Enemy's having advanced to Stoney Creek.'[25] Why was Norton so apprehensive? Logically, it was because he suspected the tribesmen's motives. One even might wonder if Norton detached himself from the rest of the Iroquois before Stoney Creek in order to save his own skin from the American party that was apparently in the ascendant.[26]

If a crisis had been brewing, the American withdrawal from Stoney Creek stopped problems from reaching the boiling point for the moment, and then, combined with subsequent events, they led to a reconfirmation of Grand River support for the British. While the Americans licked their wounds at the Forty, a dozen of Norton's Onondaga and Seneca followers ambushed some dragoons, killed one and wounded another. The warriors pursued the rest of the cavalrymen into the main American camp, causing panic despite their small numbers. At about the same time, the Royal Navy's Lake Ontario squadron sailed past the camp and unleashed a bombardment on the hapless Americans.[27] Though the barrage proved to be ineffective and a detachment from the Thirteenth Infantry drove off the Iroquois, these events helped to persuade the Americans to fall back to Fort George. They left in such haste that they abandoned substantial quantities of supplies and equipment. They withdrew out of fear that the British squadron carried reinforcements who might land in their rear and cut them off, a contingency made all the more terrifying because of a rumour that large numbers of tribesmen had marched from the west to join the British on the Niagara Peninsula.[28]

Meanwhile, at Fort George, General Dearborn expected a major counter-offensive and gave orders to evacuate Fort Erie, Chippawa, and Queenston so that he could concentrate his resources at the mouth of the Niagara River. The British army pursued the Americans and reestablished itself in Fort Erie, Forty Mile Creek, and near Beaver Dams. Major-General John Vincent hoped that this move also would serve as an encouragement to Upper Canadians who, he wrote, were 'everywhere rising upon the fugitive Americans,' taking prisoners, and withholding supplies.[29] During the British advance, three hundred Six Nations and other natives, confident that the Americans now were on the run, raced ahead to capture enemy stragglers and a good part of the abandoned equipment. Colonel Harvey thought most of the American baggage fell to the natives, although a considerable proportion found its way into the hands of local white settlers. Colonel Claus thought Iroquois enthusiasm for the pursuit stemmed purely from a desire for plunder. According to one American officer, the natives also killed or made prisoners of the wounded and sick who fell behind during the retreat. The warriors and some Provincial Dragoons took prisoners right up to the skirts of Fort George, further demoralizing the Americans and giving the British an advanced position from which they could watch Dearborn. [30]

Following the American retreat, the Iroquois deployed sixty men at Beaver Dams and another 240 at Forty Mile Creek to participate in the developing blockade of Fort George. This was a temporary move because two-thirds of them had returned to the Grand River by 20 June. However, other native reinforcements began to arrive to take their place. Sir John Johnson, the superintendent-general of the Indian Department, organized a Seven Nations expedition from his headquarters in Montreal and sent them west to join the British in Upper Canada. The force comprised 160 men from Kahnawake, 120 from Kanesatake, and 60 from Akwesasne, accompanied by Captain Dominique Ducharme and lieutenants Jean-Baptiste de Lorimier, Gidéon Gaucher, Louis Langlade, Évangeliste Saint-Germain, and Isaac LeClaire. In addition to these men, 380 Mississaugas, Ojibways, and western warriors had joined the British on the Niagara front by the end of June. Between these reinforcements and the Grand River people who remained with William Kerr, John Brant, and John Norton (who had regained some of his standing following Stoney Creek), total native strength exceeded eight hundred, a significant augmentation to Vincent's little army. [31]

Vincent concentrated most of the Grand River and Seven Nations people near Beaver Dams for picket duty along with the light companies of the 8th and 104th regiments and the Provincial Dragoons. From Beaver Dams they patrolled the Niagara River and harassed the Americans whenever possible. One typical incident occurred on 23 June when twenty-five Seven Nations warriors assaulted some American troops at a tavern near Fort George, killed four and took seven prisoner. They lost one killed as they escaped while being pursued by American dragoons. The same day, another patrol scouting the banks of the Niagara River opened fire on a barge full of Americans, killing two and taking six captive. [32]

The Americans responded to this harassment by organizing a secret expedition to destroy the forward British position at a defensible farmhouse, known as DeCou's, that was near Beaver Dams, an area of ponds and marsh beside a branch of Twelve Mile Creek, where the British had deposited a considerable quantity of stores. Lieutenant-Colonel Charles G. Boerstler led six hundred Americans from the Fourteenth Infantry, detachments of the Sixth and Twenty-Third, a company of light artillery armed with a six- and a twelve-pounder, twenty officers and men of the Second Dragoons, and forty mounted volunteer riflemen who had recently scouted the area. A detachment of riflemen scheduled to accompany the expedition did not do so, which weakened Boerstler's light infantry and scouting capabilities. He chose a circuitous thirty-kilometre route from Fort George via Queenston in the hope of reaching the farm undetected. As part of his plan, he left Fort George at night and sent his cavalry ahead to Queenston to prevent the civilian population there from warning the British. However, a woman, Laura Secord, overheard some American officers discussing the raid. She escaped through the bush to alert the British, giving them time to deploy the Grand River, Seven Nations, and other natives across one of the possible routes the Americans might take, and to send word to the Grand River for reinforcements. [33]

As the American column swung away from the Niagara River towards its destination, scouts spotted two Seven Nations warriors between Queenston and St Davids just after daybreak on 24 June. They killed one but the second escaped. The survivor ran into the native camp and gave the death cry to alert everyone to the impending threat. Waiting for the Americans was a force of 465 men, composed of 180 Seven Nations and 203 Grand River people, along with twelve men from the Thames River, seventy Ojibways and Mississaugas from the Rice Lake region, and a few militiamen. They formed an ambush in the forest beside the road the Americans were marching along. The tribesmen hid on just one side of the road because the other, consisting of low-lying cleared fields, did not offer much cover. Captain Dominique Ducharme, the senior white officer on the scene, sent word to the closest British positions to marshal the scattered companies of light troops and pickets to come to his aid. [34]

Closer to Beaver Dams, the Americans saw some redcoated officers in the distance observing their movements and heard British bugles and muskets sounding the alarm. Although he had lost the opportunity for surprise, Colonel Boerstler decided to proceed anyway. The mounted riflemen led the line of march, followed by the Fourteenth Infantry, artillery, wagons, the Sixth, and the Twenty-Third, with the dragoons at the rear. Skirmishers moved ahead on either side of the column to prevent surprise. Somehow, the scouts failed to discover the natives. The American force marched to a point along the road beside the waiting warriors, and, amazingly, halted to interrogate some captured Canadian militia-men brought in by the skirmishers. It was about 8:30 or 9:00 a.m. [35]

Suddenly, the Grand River Mohawks on the native left flank ran out of the forest and formed a loose line on the road down which Boerstler's force had just marched. If successful, an attack on the American rear would demoralize the column by threatening to cut off its retreat. One officer near the back of the column was Major Isaac Roach of the Twenty-Third Infantry. He wrote that, as they stood on the road, a soldier cried out 'the Indians!' Roach turned around and saw 'a large and close body of Indians moving rapidly across the road.' He wheeled his company into line and marched against the warriors while the dragoons charged ahead of him with sabres drawn. But as soon as the cavalry came close, the Mohawks 'fired a smart volley.' The cavalry wheeled around and plunged back through Roach's line, 'knocking down and breaking about one-third of each platoon.' Having stopped the American cavalry charge with good form, the warriors rushed forward to strip and scalp the dead. [36]

With this encounter, the main body of natives in the bush beside the road opened fire. Colonel Boerstler faced the Fourteenth Infantry to the right towards the forest, while his wagons moved to the safety of the fields on the left side of the road and the artillery unlimbered their guns to sup-port Roach at the rear. The artillerymen opened fire with canister shot at the Grand River men but fired high, so that the balls passed harmlessly over the warriors' heads. At this point, one or both of the companies of the Sixth and Twenty-Third at the rear let loose a volley as the Mohawks were redeploying to get off the road. The volley hit hard; the Mohawk force collapsed and the majority of survivors retreated out of danger. Wil-liam Kerr and John Brant followed to try to persuade the warriors to return to the fight. [37]

Other tribesmen moved into the deserted Mohawk position at the American rear to keep up the harassment at the back of the column. Colonel Boerstler ordered the two companies at the rear to file into the open field, but this brought them under close aboriginal fire. At the same time, the remaining natives on the right side of the road assisted their comrades at the American rear by increasing their fire to keep the Four-teenth Infantry pinned down so that it could not march to the aid of the other units. Boerstler's mounted volunteers at the head of the column panicked and rode out of harm's way into the field by the wagons after a brief encounter with the warriors. [38]

Colonel Boerstler responded to the native harassment of the Four-teenth with the classic regular army response to native forces – a disciplined bayonet charge. The regiment attacked the warriors in the woods at the quickstep and drove them back. After enjoying initial success, however, the Fourteenth experienced a sudden and furious attack on its left flank where the tribesmen had regrouped. The Americans changed their focus obliquely to the new native position and chased the warriors for a considerable distance. The Seven Nations continued to demonstrate their discipline by withdrawing, regrouping, and counter-attacking in spite of the charge. What the Americans had failed to do was press the charge with sufficient vigour to prevent the natives from regrouping or to force them to retreat by threatening to inflict heavy casualties. [39]

Yet, up to this point the fight had been fairly even with neither side conceding a tactical advantage to the other. Many of the Grand River Mohawks had retreated, but the Americans had suffered heavier casualties and had not extricated themselves from the ambush because the rest of the aboriginal force had stayed in the field. Major Roach recorded the progress of the action as it then developed at the column's rear. The natives 'behaved with uncommon bravery, several times dashing out of the woods to within 30 or 40 yards, as tho' confident of their numbers,' while the two companies of infantry and the artillery under his command fought as best they could. His troops performed well but came close to running out of ammunition. Someone brought up more cartridges from the wagons. While the rank and file exchanged shots with the natives, the officers replenished the men's cartridge boxes, and the drummers carried the wounded back to the wagons 'to prevent their falling into the hands of the Indians when we should move' and, as Major Roach continued, because, 'It is also an advantage to remove from the line the wounded, to prevent making an impression on the others.' [40]

Gradually, the battle began to shift in favour of the aboriginal force. Boerstler could not dislodge the tribesmen from their secure positions in the woods despite the Fourteenth's two bayonet charges because he lacked adequate light infantry resources to move ahead and consolidate his success. Finding 'that musketeers unaccustomed to fighting in any other than a regular order, could not maintain so unequal a combat without great loss,' he deployed as many skirmishers as he could to cover the bulk of the regiment as it withdrew to the open field beside the road where the soldiers formed a new line behind a fence. Captain Ducharme recorded the aboriginal perspective of this phase of the action: 'the Indians, enraged at the loss of their brethren, fought savagely, and finally their horrible yells terrified the enemy so much that they retired precipitately, infantry and cavalry, into a hollow.' [41]

A lull in the fighting occurred, giving the Americans time to load the wounded onto the wagons and to form into a column of platoons in preparation for a fighting retreat along a side road in order to regain the main road back to Fort George. However, images of defeat loomed large within the American ranks at that point. Boerstler had suffered two wounds and many soldiers joined the mounted volunteers in shirking their duty. Those who continued to fight were ready to collapse after two hours of combat without water or refreshment on a very hot summer's day following the long march from Queenston.[42]

The officers decided to give everyone a whisky ration to help steady morale. However, before it could be distributed, the chiefs and warriors renewed the attack.[43] Captain Ducharme had ordered the war parties to surround the hollow. Once in place, they opened fire and the Americans withdrew deeper into the field. 'But,' as Ducharme wrote, 'hemmed in on one side by a swamp and on the other by our Indians,' Boerstler 'found himself unable either to continue the action or his retreat.'[44] As the Americans watched the natives manoeuvring around them, they began to doubt whether a fighting withdrawal was at all possible. The officers thought that no more than a quarter of the force would be able to escape because they would have to 'retreat in regular order along the road while the immense number of Indians would constantly hang on our flanks and rear and shoot us down at pleasure without our being enabled to injure them more especially when our few remaining cartridges should be expended.'[45] Colonel Boerstler believed the situation was desperate. He attempted to surrender by sending forward a flag of truce, but the warriors continued shooting despite requests from Ducharme to stop.[46]

Shortly afterwards, the first detachment of British regulars arrived on the scene, led by a company of the 49th Foot under Lieutenant James Fitzgibbon. To impress Boerstler with the hopelessness of the American position, Fitzgibbon manoeuvred his men in plain view across the American line of retreat. The Americans lobbed a few ineffective artillery shots at the redcoats but realized their chances were getting worse with the arrival of fresh British troops. However, Fitzgibbon's appearance coincided with the withdrawal of many of the Seven Nations men from the battle. Why they left is not known. Some probably were afraid, while others had achieved their personal goal of killing and scalping an American. Many undoubtedly were exhausted. Others may have run out of ammunition, and those equipped with rifles instead of muskets likely had fired all the shots they could before their weapons became inoperable from gunpowder debris clogging the barrels.[47]

Captain Ducharme had a brief discussion with Lieutenant Fitzgibbon. They agreed that Fitzgibbon should negotiate the capitulation since Ducharme, a francophone, did not speak English very well.[48] Fitzgibbon assumed that the Americans still might be willing to fight or attempt a breakout despite the earlier gestures to surrender because they seemed to have rallied somewhat at that point, perhaps in response to the slackening fire from the warriors. With only forty-seven soldiers at his disposal, Fitzgibbon decided to meet the Americans and exaggerate British strength. By parleying he also might be able to retard the start of an American withdrawal until more reinforcements arrived. Carrying a flag of truce, he advanced towards the enemy while his bugles sounded the ceasefire. After a short discussion, Fitzgibbon coaxed Colonel Boerstler into capitulating to prevent the annihilation of his command, as he had convinced the American colonel that native reinforcements from the northwest were arriving who would massacre the Americans because they, unlike the Iroquois, could not be controlled.[49]

The three-hour battle was over. The terms of surrender stated that private property would be respected and that American officers could retain their side arms. This was not what Ducharme had wanted, as he had hoped his warriors would be able to take the officers' possessions.[50] But before the British could secure the Americans, the tribesmen descended on the defeated soldiers to rob them. Apparently the Grand River Mohawks returned at that point and did much of the looting. Major Roach found himself surrounded by warriors and slipped his sword under his coat in hopes of saving it, 'but one Indian demanded it while another very significantly made a flourish of his gun over my head and took my sword.'[51] The American soldiers, according to one of the volunteer riflemen, 'were stripped of every article of clothing to which the savages took a fancy.'[52] Not all the loot went to the Iroquois: a young lieutenant, John Le Couteur, whose light company of the 104th Foot was part of the second wave of arriving British reinforcements, got himself 'a capital black horse for a charger on this occasion, saddle & Bridle & Pistols and all.'[53] (The Americans also enjoyed looting when they had the chance. Immediately after the battle of Fort George, their camp followers stripped every article of clothing and equipment from the dead lying on the ground while American soldiers plundered the town of Niagara.)[54]

Major Roach claimed that the tribesmen killed the American wounded later in the night. He seems to have exaggerated the gruesomeness of the situation, while British accounts praised the natives for their restraint. However, the warriors killed at least one person during the negotiations between the end of the shooting and the formal American surrender, according to Le Couteur, who saw someone tomahawk an American during that period. Roach's comments may have been motivated by his outrage at the scalping of the American dead after the action. Le Couteur recorded Colonel Boerstler's disconsolate reaction in seeing his scalped men: 'as he passed the Indians and saw numbers of his poor men Scalped, He first asked: "Oh! What are those? What is that?" I made no answer but turned away my head for I felt for Him. He was badly wounded and seemed horror struck, the tears rolling down his handsome countenance.'[55]

Total casualties among the aboriginal force are not known for certain. One record lists seven killed, but it is possible that as many as twenty lost their lives. There were twenty severely wounded out of thirty or more wounded, including five chiefs. The Americans lost their artillery, the colours of the Fourteenth Infantry, their equipment, and supplies, and they suffered thirty killed, seventy wounded, and five hundred more taken prisoner.[56] At least one prisoner found himself adopted by an old Mohawk chief who had lost a son earlier in the war. It is not certain what the chief planned to do with him. Some British officers thought, perhaps mistakenly, that the chief planned to burn the captive, so they gave the Mohawk money and presents to spare the soldier's life. The chief took the money and said he would adopt the man if he behaved well. A few days later, Le Couteur saw the prisoner, 'stripped of his Uniform and toggery of all sorts and clothed in an Indian dress. His hair was shaven, a tuft left on it which was ornamented with Feathers and Horse hair.' The British advised the man not to try to escape for a year or two or he would probably be killed, but thought they could do nothing more for him. As Le Couteur noted: 'Rescue Him we dared not, it would have lost us an alliance of seven hundred Indians, most invaluable allies as they were – no surprises with Nitchie on the lookout.' ('Nitchie' was slang for natives, and came from the Ojibway greeting, 'Shaygo Niigii,' meaning 'Hello Friend.')[57]

The battle of Beaver Dams was a major aboriginal victory and was the largest engagement of the war in which the Iroquois (and the other natives with them) inflicted defeat on an enemy without the significant participation of white troops. Part of the reason for their success was the decision to launch an ambush from cover. This made the best use of their skills while hindering the Americans. The decision to make a two-pronged attack – at the rear and at the right of the column – was also important because it limited the distance the Americans on the right could charge into the forest: it would have been folly to divide the force and leave those fighting at the rear on their own. The American counterattacks were solid responses, since the firepower, discipline, and bayonet charge of the line were perfect foils to light infantry harassment. However, the warriors were skilled enough to conduct a sharp fighting withdrawal and they did not have to face either a continuation of the line's advance or a significant body of American light infantry who otherwise could have followed up the charge to prevent the warriors from reforming. Thus the natives were able to rally, counter-attack, and push the Americans into a perilous situation.[58]

After the battle, the Seven Nations people on the Niagara Peninsula made it clear that they did not think the British had given them an appropriate quantity of praise and presents for so important a victory. While the British might condemn the warriors for seizing plunder, the Iroquois from Lower Canada said they needed to take prizes because they did not receive pay to cover the losses they incurred by fighting instead of remaining in their villages to look after their families. According to John Norton, most of the warriors, thinking 'their service had been prized too lightly,' went home, stating that 'their families would suffer in their absence for the want of their support.'[59] Thus the British found themselves deprived of a particularly effective fighting force.

If the Iroquois told their white allies the truth and did not merely claim poverty in order to magnify the quantity of gifts they could receive, then the extent of aboriginal distress may have been quite serious. At a council held after the battle, the Iroquois said they were so destitute that they did not even have shoes to wear while scouting. (The regulars were suffering likewise in war-torn Upper Canada; one report noted that the men of the 41st Foot were dressed 'in rags and without shoes.')[60] The warriors also complained that the absence of cash payments drove them to rob local farms to sustain themselves – an act they believed justified because destitute whites stole from native people. They also complained that they had not received money for turning in captured soldiers or supplies as they had been told they would by General Brock in 1812, and they demanded to know how their families would be cared for if they died in the war.[61] Furthermore, the Seven Nations said there was no reason to remain on the Niagara Peninsula because there seemed to be no immediate opportunity for another battle, but a chance for action might emerge in Lower Canada should the Americans attack closer to their homes. The small number of Seven Nations warriors who had not already returned home told the British on 5 July that they would leave within ten days unless another chance for combat emerged.[62]

The British tried to appease the Seven Nations by issuing shoes and promising prize money equal to the value of captured enemy property. Warriors received the same bounty as private soldiers and chiefs the same as subalterns. (Privates received one 'share' of prize money and subalterns eight. At Detroit, for example, each share was valued at three pounds and at Mackinac a share was worth ten pounds.) The army also instituted a payment schedule for prisoners: five dollars for each healthy captive brought in, half that amount for wounded soldiers, but nothing for dead men or scalps. In addition, the British established compensation rates to help the families of those killed or wounded. A chief who lost an eye, limb, or suffered a wound of equal seriousness would receive an annual pension of $100 in cash or presents. The pension for warriors was $70. One-time payments to widows of those killed in action were $200 for chiefs and $140 for warriors. These amounts, limited as they were, compared favourably to the relief given to whites. The Loyal and Patriotic Society of Upper Canada usually gave militiamen's widows no more than a one-time payment of one hundred dollars. To counter the desire of the Seven Nations warriors to go home to attend to their crops, the Indian Department promised to provide help at harvest time. The army issued a general order expressing its admiration of the native performance at Beaver Dams in an attempt to assuage aboriginal unhappiness over not receiving enough praise for their victory. In the end, however, the British could not supply the gifts and money the natives wanted because of delays brought on by the precarious state of communications and the wartime shortages. Even had the army given enough presents, it seems unlikely the British could have retained the bulk of the Seven Nations on the Niagara Peninsula, as it was normal for Iroquois war parties to go home after a major action. The majority of Seven Nations people left before the end of July, probably annoyed at British stinginess, but undoubtedly satisfied at their own achievements.[63]

6

Iroquois versus Iroquois: July–December 1813

We, the Chiefs and Counsellors of the Six Nations of Indians, residing in the State of New York, do hereby proclaim to all the War Chiefs and Warriors of the Six Nations that war is declared on our part upon the provinces of Upper and Lower Canada. Therefore, we do hereby command and advise all the War Chiefs to call forth immediately their warriors under them and put them in motion to protect their rights and liberties which our brethren the Americans are now defending.

Iroquois declaration of war, July 1813[1]

In the second half of 1813 wartime shortages continued to make life hard for the Iroquois, and prejudice and ignorance on the part of their white allies was a source of despair. In addition, as some had warned when trying to keep their people neutral in 1812, Six Nations warriors found themselves in the position of being asked to kill each other by their American and British allies. Towards the end of the year American victories on Lake Erie and at Moraviantown threw the Grand River Tract onto the front lines again and forced the Six Nations people to flee from their homes as refugees. Across the border, the last outburst of fighting in December 1813 led to the burning of the Tuscarora Reservation near Fort Niagara by Grand River warriors and the looting of the Tonawanda Reservation in western New York by its residents' own American allies.

Following the battle of Beaver Dams, the new commanding officer in Upper Canada, Major-General Baron Francis de Rottenburg, advanced closer to American-held Fort George to constrict the American foothold on British territory. De Rottenburg did not have enough men to be able to lay siege to the post with any hope of retaking it, but he thought he could blockade the Americans inside its defences. If he could stop them from occupying more than an insignificant piece of Upper Canada, while preventing their army from doing damage elsewhere until cold weather brought an end to the campaigning season, then the 1813 Niagara campaign would be a British success. His task was made easier by orders sent to the American army from Washington after the Stoney Creek and Beaver Dams debacles. Secretary of War John Armstrong ordered his officers to avoid engaging the British unless absolutely necessary. Instead, the army was to spend its time on much-needed training. [2]

At first, most of the Grand River Iroquois decided not to participate in de Rottenburg's advance. 'According to the ordinary custom,' wrote John Norton, 'whenever the seat of action is not very far distant they returned home to revisit their families before they would prepare for another enterprize.'[3] As the warriors and other people who had gone on campaign approached their homes, they presumably followed tradition and let those who had remained behind know about their imminent arrival by sending someone ahead to alert the population with shouts of victory. The people in the villages then assembled to greet them and to honour their bravery and heroism. Each war party made a record of its exploits on a piece of bark by painting a picture of a longhouse (symbolizing the Six Nations) along with pictures of headless bodies equal to the number of the enemy they had killed and of bodies with heads to represent the prisoners they had taken. Before they could go to war again, there were condolence ceremonies to solemnize, victory feasts to celebrate, and war dances to savour.[4]

Back in the British lines, 150 Ottawas and Ojibways from Lake Huron, led by the Ottawa chief Black Bird and Lieutenant-Colonel Matthew Elliott of the Indian Department, joined de Rottenburg on 5 July. Major-General Henry Procter had sent them to de Rottenburg, telling his colleague there were some 'very fine fellows' among them. De Rottenburg – one of the British army's foremost light infantry experts – was suitably impressed, describing them as 'a most ferocious and savage set.'[5] With this reinforcement, de Rottenburg moved closer to the American lines 'on account of the Indian warriors' who, he wrote, 'must be actively employed, and are now daily engaged with the enemy's outposts harassing and teasing them the whole day long.'[6] At the same time, the Royal Navy blockaded the mouth of the Niagara River for part of July and occasionally cruised the American shore of Lake Ontario to intercept supplies, while British forces made forays across the Niagara River to destroy American depots.[7]

On 8 July a British and native force, including Grand River men who had returned to the lines, moved close to the American defences to retrieve medical supplies that had been buried during the retreat from Fort George in May. John Norton and Black Bird led the native contingent of fifty Delawares, thirty Onondagas and Cayugas, a few Mohawks, thirty Ottawas, and thirty or forty Mississaugas and Ojibways. As the British and natives reached their objective, Norton's followers moved ahead towards the American pickets to cover the regulars who had been assigned to secure the supplies and take them back to camp. Norton learned that the Americans had sent two hundred infantry and cavalry forward of their pickets to search for the British. He therefore 'dressed an Ambuscade with the design of allowing them to pass before we should assail them' along the edge of a road near Ball's Farm, about two kilometres from Fort George. Some men spoiled the plan when they opened fire on their own initiative and thereby warned the Americans. The Americans then advanced cautiously in battle order. Norton withdrew in the hope of encouraging the enemy to amalgamate their columns and march far enough from Fort George to make escape difficult. He sent a request to the British for reinforcements in case his adversaries fell for the ploy.[8]

The Americans followed the natives but soon recognized Norton's plan for what it was. They stopped short of the new ambush, laid at the edge of a forest, and formed a line along a fence in a neighbouring field facing Norton's people. The cavalry charged the aboriginal position, but the natives stood firm. Just before coming close enough to use their sabres, the dragoons wheeled about and rode away under fire. The American infantry next commenced firing at the ludicrous range of 275 metres, which did nothing more than let the warriors know that their enemy's fire discipline was weak. Consequently, as one Canadian officer on the scene noted, the Iroquois attacked, 'shouting in the most hideous manner.'[9] Although the Americans subjected the tribesmen to heavy volley fire, they shot too high, as they had done at Queenston Heights, and wounded only two people. The Americans fell back to a wood on their own side of this no man's land. The warriors followed but thought the Americans probably had laid a trap for them. They were right. The native force therefore split in two. One part manoeuvred to draw the fire and attention of the ambush; the other moved around the American position, attacked it in the rear, and captured or killed a large portion of the patrol.[10]

After this success, the tribesmen withdrew to a safer position to await the counter-attack the Americans seemed to have contemplated by sending out a large force towards their outlying pickets. British cavalry and infantry reinforcements arrived to support the natives at this point. However, since most of the chiefs and warriors had left, they retired without seeking a further encounter when they saw the Americans pulling back as well. Casualties were one interpreter and two warriors wounded on the native side compared to sixty or seventy Americans killed, wounded, or taken prisoner. To help the natives celebrate their victory, General de Rottenburg provided funds for a 'war feast' for everyone engaged in the skirmish.[11]

This 'Affair of the 8th' differs from many War of 1812 battles in that records survive to document the viciousness of the fighting and the use of terror to instil fear into an enemy. During the action, an officer in the Thirteenth Infantry and two of his men fell into the hands of a young Ottawa. The warrior first aimed his musket at the officer, who made a sign of submission by dropping his pistol arm. But when the warrior turned his attention to the others, the officer raised his pistol and shot his captor. More warriors arrived on the scene just in time to see what had happened and instantly tomahawked the Americans in retaliation.[12] When the angry natives, particularly Black Bird's followers, captured more Americans, they threatened their prisoners with 'instant death, accompanied by gestures not of the most pleasing or agreeable description,' according to a Canadian officer, William Hamilton Merritt. These acts completely broke the prisoners' morale. 'The poor devils,' Merritt continued, 'were crying and imploring me to save their lives as I was the only white man they saw.' The Ottawas, however, told him that they would spare the prisoners 'and would only frighten them a good deal to prevent their coming again.'[13] The horror felt by the Americans must have been extreme as the tribesmen scalped and mutilated the soldiers' dead friends in front of them and taunted the survivors all night before turning them over to the British.[14]

In defence of this practice, Black Bird pointed to the history of the Americans in committing atrocities against natives and he described how they had insulted his people by mutilating aboriginal dead in the field and by digging up graves and scattering native remains over the ground. What he did not say was that terror was a necessary part of aboriginal warfare to enable their small populations to magnify their military reputation in the eyes of their white opponents.[15] One can imagine the effectiveness of this form of terror by considering the thoughts that likely passed through the minds of the Americans sent to retrieve the casualties from the 8 July action. One officer wrote that nothing could have prepared his men for what he described as a 'scene of wanton and revolting barbarity.' The warriors, he recorded, 'had left on the ground nearly half of the detachment, most of them dead, but some of them still breathing, though scarcely sensible. Every body was utterly stripped, and scalped, and mangled and maimed in a way that looked as if there had been a sort of sportive butchery among the dying and the dead.' One man had 'more than a dozen of these gashes and lacerations.' His head was 'denuded from the eye-brows to the back of the neck' but he 'was still breathing and sensible when our party reached him.' Brought back to camp, his 'exquisite agonies were terminated a few hours after.'[16]

De Rottenburg tightened his blockade of Fort George following the 8 July success. He positioned his headquarters and right flank at St Davids, a short distance inland from Queenston on Four Mile Creek, and located his left near the mouth of the same creek on Lake Ontario. To prevent the Americans from attempting a surprise attack by crossing the Niagara River upriver of St Davids, he dispatched a strong body of Ojibways towards Fort Erie to watch for any American activity that might pose a problem from that direction. The British commander had good reason to worry, the Americans having moved part of their Fort George garrison to Buffalo in mid-July and deployed their native allies in and around the town. If used with some boldness, these people might compel de Rottenburg to loosen his blockade or even fall back to Burlington.[17]

The British and their aboriginal allies continued to harass American patrols at Fort George and it was a rare day when the warriors did not bring prisoners or scalps back to the British lines.[18] So effective was this harassment that one frustrated American officer recorded in disgust that 'we have had an army at Fort George for two months past, which at any moment of this period might by a vigorous and well-directed exertion of three or four days have prostrated the whole of the enemy's force ... and yet this army lies panic-struck, shut up and whipped in by a few hundred miserable savages, leaving the whole of this frontier except a mile in extent which they occupy, exposed to the inroads and depredations of the enemy.'[19]

Henry Dearborn, in one of his last acts before the American government recalled him from the Canadian theatre in mid-July, asked Erastus Granger, the Six Nations agent in Buffalo, to muster 150 Iroquois for service at Fort George to help relieve the demoralizing harassment of his pickets. Up to that point the American-resident Iroquois generally had been disinclined to cross the border although they had been willing to serve within the United States. The reluctance to fight in Upper Canada seems partly to have originated in a treaty arranged between some of them and the aboriginal people in Canada early in July. At a council held in Queenston between the two groups, the Tuscaroras asked the natives allied to the British what their intentions were towards the tribes in New York.[20] An Onondaga from Grand River, Katvirota, gave the reply: 'This will depend on yourselves. If you take no part with the Americans we shall meet you with the same friendship we ever did, and we look for the day when you will see our faces on your side of the water. We have no contention with you; it is the King and the Americans, and we have taken part with the King.'[21] The council concluded with the Tuscaroras telling the Upper Canadian natives that they wanted to 'sit quiet and take no part' in the war. However, they warned that another council, scheduled to take place in Buffalo a few days later, might lead to other Iroquois people deciding to invade British territory. The Tuscarora chiefs seem to have agreed to participate in local defence but not to invade Upper Canada. This made strategic sense because their reservation was located only a few kilometres from the hardest fighting and therefore was vulnerable to attack, particularly if a British sortie into New York were to be inspired by Tuscarora operations in Canada. The Senecas, however, already had a reason to go to war because of the questions the Grand River invasion of Grand Island had raised about their ownership of the island in 1812, and therefore they may not have shared these attitudes.[22]

Shortly after the Tuscarora council some Senecas saw combat when Erastus Granger used an anticipated British raid onto American soil to help promote what presumably was a growing belligerency among some tribal leaders. General de Rottenburg had decided to destroy the American supply depot at Black Rock near Buffalo. He assigned 220 regulars and militia to the task under the command of Lieutenant-Colonel Cecil Bisshopp. Granger learned about the raid from deserters before it took place and saw it as an opportunity to fulfil Dearborn's directive to recruit warriors for Fort George. The evening before the attack, Granger invited some Senecas to his house three kilometres from Black Rock. Forty men with Young King, Farmer's Brother, and Red Jacket at their head came before midnight and Granger got them armed and ready.[23]

At about two in the morning on 11 July, Bisshopp crossed the river and quickly dispersed the Black Rock garrison. His men loaded large quantities of arms, munitions, and supplies into their boats, destroyed guns and other equipment, and took or destroyed seven bateaux and a scow. They burned the naval yard, a large schooner, the barracks, and a blockhouse. Bisshopp, impressed by the quantity of desperately needed supplies to be taken, spent too much time loading the boats when he should have obeyed orders to row back across the river as soon as possible. At about sunrise, word of the British landing reached Granger. Farmer's Brother gave a speech, telling the warriors they had to fight because they had common interests with the people of the United States and that the time had come to show their friendship for the Americans, not just in words but in deeds as well. The Senecas then marched on Black Rock. On the way, they joined 250 regulars and militia commanded by a prominent congressman, Brigadier-General Peter B. Porter, who were also advancing to repel the British. Porter was surprised to see the warriors. It seems that Granger had not shared his knowledge of the attack with the army. If he had, there would have been no reason for the Americans to have suffered the losses they had already sustained at Black Rock.[24]

Near the landing site, Porter formed the regulars and militia in line to attack while the Iroquois moved ahead as light infantry. The warriors stole into the woods undetected and opened fire. The British shot back but could not dislodge the Senecas without a bayonet charge, which they did not want because they did not know how many opposed them and they feared significant losses if trapped. Therefore, they withdrew to the landing site and re-formed. However, the native force continued the attack and Porter's men soon came into action. Realizing the hopelessness of the situation, the British got into their boats to recross the river under intense Iroquois fire. Some warriors, according to Porter, saw one boat that looked vulnerable and 'actually plunged into the water, seized upon the gunnels ... and would have brought it to shore, but from the fire from the rear, which obliged them to desist.'[25] During this period, one British officer surrendered but was tomahawked and robbed nonetheless; he later recovered from his wounds. Whether or not the Senecas took scalps is uncertain. In one document Porter said they did not, while in another Granger wrote that they did but that they did not mutilate the dead or hurt the wounded. In the initial raid, the Americans suffered fourteen killed, wounded, or taken prisoner. The Senecas lost two men wounded in the action, including Young King. British casualties were comparatively heavy. Most, if not all, occurred while fighting the Senecas. Total losses were forty-six killed, wounded, or taken prisoner, including Colonel Bisshopp who died of wounds in Canada a few days later.[26]

On 25 July representatives of the majority of Iroquois in New York met in council and declared war on the Canadas. This followed the decision by 143 chiefs and warriors of the different tribes immediately after the Black Rock affair to form a sort of volunteer company in the American army. Four Senecas received commissions: Farmer's Brother became a captain at forty dollars per month, Little Billy and Captain Pollard received lieutenants' appointments at thirty dollars, and Black Snake became an ensign at twenty dollars. Four other chiefs were designated as sergeants at eleven dollars per month, and 135 warriors became privates at eight dollars. Later, when enough Iroquois enrolled to form a small battalion of about 400 men, Farmer's Brother became its colonel and some other men received commissions. Their enlistment into the American forces at that time was more an administrative act to create a mechanism for providing rations and pay and to place them under a general military command structure at the brigade level than a move to replace Iroquois leaders or modes of combat.[27] It also seems to have been an attempt to eliminate at least some of the need for dependence upon what one American official called 'premiums, presents and plunder.'[28]

To a certain extent, the recruitment of the Six Nations was remarkable given the frustrations of the warriors who did not feel obliged to follow the agreement reached by the Tuscaroras at Queenston and who instead wanted to join the American forces in the weeks previous to the Black Rock raid. They had been pressured to abstain from taking up arms by fellow Iroquois opposed to participation in the war. Moreover, those who were influenced by signs and omens had to contend with the resilience of the outnumbered British in defending their side of the Niagara River. Perhaps most significantly, the warriors who wanted to fight alongside the Americans found their white allies to be arrogant and inconsiderate towards them. Undoubtedly, many remembered the haughtiness of Granger's words in 1812 when he told them that they could fight with the whites only if they gave up their 'cowardly' style of warfare. Compounding this and other insults were the words of Secretary of War John Armstrong in April 1813. He wrote to the chiefs telling them not to worry about the impact of the war on their families because the United States would move the Iroquois away from the border and look after them if the British invaded New York, and in fact he recommended that they move to their lands in the southern part of the state. This message belittled the concerns of the Iroquois with maintaining their homes rather than becoming refugees, and it conveyed an attitude that did not acknowledge the warriors' obligations to protect their families.[29] It is also possible that Armstrong was more interested in getting the Iroquois away from the front lines to prevent them from joining the British than from any real concern for their safety, because he wrote the letter in the wake of the Frenchtown disaster, when British troops, Canadian militia, and American-resident natives threatened United States sovereignty in north-west Ohio within striking distance of the Niagara Peninsula.

The Americans insulted the Iroquois further when between three and four hundred men assembled ready for battle at Fort Niagara, as requested by the Americans, at the same time that de Rottenburg received his own aboriginal reinforcements from the west. As soon as they arrived they were told that the army planned to use them as mere bargaining chips to persuade the British to stop employing natives, otherwise the Americans would unleash the tribesmen of New York in Canada.[30] Disgusted, the warriors refused to cooperate and went home. The Americans soon called them out again, but then decided against employing them and sent them away without even compensating them for their travel costs. Exasperated, the Iroquois told their allies that they felt 'injured' and would stay home until they got a satisfactory explanation for such callousness.[31] It is no wonder that when Dearborn made his request for native help, it took the warriors from one reservation, Allegany, two weeks to assemble. Yet they did gather, most likely because of a combination of their sense of honour, their desire to make a stand which clearly differentiated them from the British-allied peoples, internal cultural imperatives to engage in combat, and a desire to benefit from American presents and rations, especially as they probably thought they could control the extent of their participation in order to minimize their losses once in the field.[32]

Those Iroquois warriors who were willing to invade Canada wanted their white allies to know that their support was conditional on receiving proper rewards and treatment. In a speech at the Buffalo council where they declared war, Red Jacket told the Americans that the support of the Six Nations was not unqualified: 'The part we take in this war is not voluntary on our part; you have persuaded us into it ... Your voice was for us to sit still when the war began, but you have beat us – you have got us into the war.'[33] Perhaps this was not completely true – being the opinion of the peace chiefs rather than that of the war leaders – but such assertions reflected the diversity of opinion within the communities, gave them diplomatic manoeuvring room, and improved the chances of getting generous quantities of presents. At the same council, Cornplanter, a Seneca, told the Americans: 'You must pay well. You must open your purse. You must pay some now; and do not let your taverns supply our warriors with spiritous liquors. We feel some anxiety that there is no provision made for the families of our men who fell in this war,' a reference presumably to Black Rock. The condemnation of alcohol may have been made in anticipation of soon going into battle.[34] Cornplanter's son, Henry O'Bail, told the Americans: 'We can not stand [it] in battle. You can drink and fight. Our forefathers fought without liquor.'[35] Beyond these demands, the Iroquois wanted shoes, shirts, and instruction as to what they could take as lawful plunder. They also asked the Americans to treat any captured Iroquois humanely and to turn them over to the tribes in New York, except for Mohawk prisoners of war. In exchange, they promised to give up white prisoners to American authorities. The exclusion of the Mohawks is curious, since people from all of the Iroquois communities in Canada fought as British allies. However, the Iroquois of western New York may have felt little affinity for the Mohawks, given that few of them had connections to that nation. They also may have had a plan to protect their non-Mohawk relatives in Canada from reprisals through creating the image that only the Mohawks were responsible for the belligerency at Grand River, just as they had blamed that tribe alone for the Grand River people's decision to fight the Americans in 1812. The tribes at the Buffalo council pledged assistance from the Buffalo Creek, Cattaraugus, Caneadea, Squakie Hill, Tonawanda, and Allegany reservations. Some communities, however, such as Allegany, where the anti-war sentiments of the prophet Handsome Lake were strongest, only committed a small number of men. Allegany, for example, sent only seven warriors whereas Buffalo Creek had 162 under arms at the time of the council.[36] The absence of a pledge from Tuscarora reflected the decisions made at their council with the Upper Canadian Iroquois.

One of the Americans who was most enthusiastic about employing natives was Peter B. Porter of the New York Militia. However, he thought the natives would need better opportunities to fulfil their combat goals than would be possible if they were confined to defensive picket duty at Fort George. Therefore, he suggested that they should be encouraged to take offensive action and be allowed to keep a large share of any property they might capture. If these conditions could be met, Porter believed nine-tenths of the warriors would cross the border. Despite Porter's enthusiasm for the Iroquois, many other officers did not want to use aboriginal combatants in Canada. Some regarded them as too terrible a force to unleash.[37] One person who opposed recruiting natives was Brigadier-General Alexander Smyth. He expressed his opinions in an address to wavering white troops to encourage them for an invasion of

Upper Canada in the autumn of 1812: 'Must I turn from you and ask the men of the Six Nations to support the Government of the United States? Shall I imitate the officers of the British King and suffer our ungathered laurels to be tarnished with ruthless deeds? Shame, where is thy blush? No! where I command, the vanquished and peaceful man, the child, the maid, and the matron shall be secure from wrong. If we conquer, we will "conquer but to save."' [38] Although Smyth had left Niagara in 1812, many American officers shared his views. Others believed aboriginal allies were of limited value. One expressed his thoughts following a tour of the battlefield after the capture of Fort George: 'their Indians are not of much use to them. They run as soon as the battle grows hot. I saw but one of the Indians and one negro ... dead on the field, a proof that neither their *black* nor *red* allies are very potent or brave.' [39]

As Porter attempted to determine how the American-allied Iroquois could be deployed effectively, other officers worked to prevent the warriors from crossing the border by resurrecting the idea of using them as bargaining chips. Erastus Granger revived the notion of negotiating a withdrawal of Britain's native allies in return for a commitment to refrain from deploying American-allied aboriginal forces against 'the defenceless inhabitants' of Upper Canada. [40] However, British commanders could not countenance such a proposition: the dismissal of the tribes would hurt the king's cause far more than a reciprocal gesture would damage American interests because a much larger proportion of the British force was native and because aboriginal warriors were employed so much more effectively by the British than by the Americans. Lieutenant-Colonel Winfield Scott tried to get around the British–American impasse when he asked the Six Nations in New York to speak directly to the British-allied tribes to get them 'to return to their native wilds – leaving the white belligerents, alone, to kill each other in the settlement of their own peculiar quarrel.' [41] Some negotiations did take place between the tribes to discuss the American proposal, but nothing came of them at that point. One of the men the Americans sent was Joseph Willcocks, the Canadian opposition politician who had been a friend of the Six Nations before the war in their struggles with the provincial government but who had deserted to the Americans. Willcocks commanded a force of Canadian traitors, many of whom had been neighbours of the Grand River Iroquois, and therefore sending him represented a solid choice for establishing contact between the United States and the Six Nations. [42]

The British blockade of Fort George began to falter at the end of July but the Americans did not take advantage of the situation to try to break British resolve even though they continued to outnumber them four thousand to two thousand men. De Rottenburg's main problem was a lack of supplies and money, which led to some loss of discipline among his troops and contributed to the general unsteadiness of his native allies. The American squadron, bolstered with a new warship, reappeared at the western end of Lake Ontario and threatened de Rottenburg's supply line. The Americans planned to cripple him by attacking his main depot at Burlington Heights. However, the British marched enough men to the American landing site to chase them away and preserve their precious stores. Disappointed, the Americans sailed to undefended York and burned barracks that had been left standing at the time of the attack in April. Although the American efforts were of minimal consequence, the sight of the United States Navy hovering off the mouth of the Niagara River demoralized the natives and many of them left the British lines. Others became discouraged because de Rottenburg could not supply enough food and supplies to meet their requirements, and some went home simply because they had become disenchanted with the campaign. To keep as many of them with him as possible, de Rottenburg scraped together what resources he could and hosted a feast for the warriors and their families. However, the supply problem continued to worsen, and by 13 August he had even run out of money. [43]

Many soldiers and warriors fell sick in the hot, humid Niagara summer and a large number of unhappy men deserted. The 104th Foot, recruited in New Brunswick, alone lost forty soldiers this way during the blockade. [44] To stop the drain and prevent the Americans from gathering helpful information from deserters, de Rottenburg deployed his native allies to capture anyone who tried to run away. The tribesmen were so effective that the Americans thereafter lamented that the warriors were kept 'so constantly scouring the woods of our vicinity that we gain no deserters nor intelligence.' [45]

A large number of natives met their needs during the blockade by stealing from the civilian population. According to Lieutenant-Colonel William Claus, the Six Nations spent most of their time roving the countryside where they plundered the settlers, destroyed livestock, and took spoils back to the Grand. General de Rottenburg believed that it was the western tribesmen rather than the Iroquois who did the most harm, while one military surgeon thought both groups were to blame. [46] The amount of property lost was substantial. In one collection of war losses, 321 people in the Niagara and Home districts, where the Iroquois were most active, submitted claims totalling a substantial £29,000 for theft and damages by natives allied to the British during the war. The information recorded in these claims shows that they stole small amounts of household property and committed isolated acts of vandalism, but most of the depredations were connected to basic subsistence: they took foodstuffs and livestock to eat, trampled fields and meadows when they made camp, and burned firewood, fences, and trees for fuel.[47] White soldiers aggravated the problem by purchasing stolen goods from natives to meet their own desperate needs.[48] The warriors and their families were not the only ones to steal from their allies. The Grand River people also sustained property losses during the war at the hands of looters from the white community. While the extent of their losses is uncertain, the provincial government awarded compensation of £2,786 to 268 Grand River people after the war.[49]

Faced with robberies by natives, some settlers defended their properties by firing warning shots at aboriginal people. Occasionally they resorted to murder. In one incident in 1814, a gang of ten men near Stoney Creek killed three Delawares who had camped for the night and who may have robbed the home of a man by the name of Green. The natives came from the Grand River, although originally they may have been residents of the Cattaraugus Reservation in New York. (A fourth Delaware, although wounded, escaped.) The murderers then hacked away at the dead with bayonets and axes. At least two parties of natives investigated the incident, apprehended some men, and sent them to the provincial capital for trial. However, the court released the prisoners for lack of evidence and the government offered a reward of one hundred pounds for information that would lead to the apprehension of the criminals. Nobody was arrested, perhaps because the perpetrators had fled to the United States.[50]

It is telling that these murders were premeditated crimes shared by a number of whites who felt justified killing people for thievery, and that the natives chose not to react violently within the tradition of the blood feud but instead investigated the crimes and turned their suspects over to white authorities. The aboriginal reaction may have reflected a degree of acculturation among the particular natives on the scene but it is nevertheless curious because the Upper Canadian legal system had generally failed to provide justice in cases where whites committed crimes against natives.[51] These murders also help confirm the existence of a general mistrust of the aboriginal peoples that was felt by significant numbers of Canadians despite the contributions of the natives to the colony's defence. That such hostility existed is no surprise. The majority of the population consisted of first or second generation non-loyalist immigrants from the United States whose upbringing had been steeped in the anti-native attitudes of their old country. (For example, the largest single group of men in the Upper Canadian militia whose origins and birth dates are known were born in the United States after 1790.) [52] Some of these immigrants openly espoused a pro-American view, and on at least one occasion a senior British officer in the secret service utilized natives to suppress sedition, an act that undoubtedly increased hostility towards aboriginal peoples. The officer later recorded: 'I actually knew one parish to walk in procession with a drum and American flag, in a critical moment of war; and I only prevented a repetition of this treason, by threatening to send my Indians to teach them better manners.' [53] Furthermore, stories of violence committed by aboriginal peoples against whites circulated freely, and often Upper Canadians could not tell American- and British-allied warriors apart. On one occasion, some warriors, who almost certainly came from the Grand River, shot an Upper Canadian during a robbery in Niagara at the time of the battle of Fort George. The people who witnessed the crime did not know which side of the border the murderers had come from. [54] Many soldiers also held prejudiced views. Sergeant James Commins of the 8th Foot was typical of the lower ranks when he dismissed native allies as people who did not stand their ground in combat but who fled, only to return after the fighting to plunder the dead and wounded. [55] A Canadian militiaman echoed these views, writing, 'I hate these savage barbarians. You cannot place confidence in them without a sufficient force to keep them in check, they are more plague than profit.' [56] Lieutenant John Le Couteur of the 104th Foot thought some natives, such as the Ottawas and Kahnawakes, were 'Brave, generous and honorable,' but dismissed the Grand River people as 'mostly cowards, thieves and dirty.' Sharing Sergeant Commins' prejudices, Le Couteur did not understand aboriginal warfare and complained that warriors would never stand their ground in combat if faced with serious opposition. [57]

Morale began to improve in the British camp before the middle of August when the Royal Navy returned to the western end of Lake Ontario to challenge the American squadron. In the ensuing manoeuvring, the Americans lost four schooners: the British captured two, the others capsized and sank during a storm. Yet the American squadron was still more powerful and the British commodore, Sir James Lucas Yeo, would not risk his ships and schooners in an uneven battle unless the weather and other variables gave him a significant advantage. If he did engage the Americans and lost, Upper Canada probably would fall because its marine links to the outside world would be cut. With the continuing American menace on the lake, only limited quantities of supplies moved west to General de Rottenburg's needy forces on the Niagara Peninsula.[58]

While de Rottenburg's army suffered from supply shortages, American commanders continued to work at convincing their Iroquois allies who were mustered near Buffalo to cross the border. In early August Erastus Granger, frustrated at their lack of enthusiasm for participating in the defence of Fort George, angrily told them that their only reason for joining the Americans was to eat government rations. Therefore, the sooner they returned home, the better it would be for the American cause. Granger adopted this stance because he knew the Iroquois on the reservations were starving and he believed those on the Niagara frontier would fight so that their families could join them to receive army food. He miscalculated and hurt their pride. The next day many of them packed up and prepared to go home. Brigadier-General Porter, however, succeeded in placating them with a proposal more in keeping with their objectives. He told them he wanted to perform a reconnaissance in strength on the British side of the Niagara River from Chippawa to St Davids. If the Iroquois participated, they could keep any publicly owned livestock they might capture. Porter actually had a more ambitious scheme in mind. He wanted to cross the river with a combined militia, regular, and native force of twelve hundred, knock the British out of Chippawa, then march on de Rottenburg's right flank at St Davids at the same time the Fort George garrison sortied to support Porter and break the blockade. In the end, however, Porter only got permission to lead a minor demonstration at the head of two hundred Onondagas, Senecas, Delawares, and Oneidas and an equal number of militia and regulars. On 7 August he landed six kilometres north of Fort Erie, and then marched north to take civilian prisoners, plunder homes, and seize cattle and horses. Most of the livestock was private property rather than public, but Porter believed he had to allow the warriors to keep the animals. Porter was overruled and the tribesmen had to give them up. This decision, combined with American tardiness in paying wages, later caused resentment among the warriors that festered for many months.[59]

However, this taste of war seems to have engendered enthusiasm for more combat. A few days later Porter led 140 Iroquois and 220 volunteers to reinforce Fort Niagara because of nervousness generated by the presence of the Royal Navy off the mouth of the Niagara River. The next day more warriors and volunteers arrived to double the size of his command. A day or so later, with Farmer's Brother leading the Six Nations, the Iroquois crossed into Upper Canada and joined the American garrison at Fort George, where they formed a battalion of a small brigade that was otherwise composed of volunteers under Porter's leadership. [60] Immediately afterwards, the Iroquois took up picket duty in advance of the fort and forced the British to loosen their stranglehold a little. Brigadier-General John Boyd, who had replaced Dearborn in command at Fort George, wrote to the secretary of war on 13 August that 'Yesterday I had the honor to address you a letter detailing the conduct of the Indians in a late skirmish. Their bravery and humanity were equally conspicuous. Already the quietness in which our pickets are suffered to remain envinces the benefit arising from their assistance.' [61] Not only does this statement indicate the effectiveness of the Iroquois, but it underscores how badly off the Americans were for good light infantry protection because they could not relieve the pressure on them before the arrival of their aboriginal allies.

The Iroquois allied to the British held a council on 12 August to discuss the change in the behaviour of their relatives in New York. The Grand River people, choosing for some now unknown reason not to differentiate the Tuscaroras from the others in New York, decided that the tribes in the United States had violated the 5 July agreement and therefore should be regarded as enemies. [62] Five days later Iroquois warriors from the Grand River and New York fought each other for the first time in the war.

On the rainy morning of 17 August, three hundred volunteers and Iroquois under Peter B. Porter attempted to chase British pickets from their advanced position at Ball's Farm. Some cavalry of the Second Dragoons and two hundred soldiers of the Sixteenth Infantry supported Porter's mixed white-native force, and they were joined later by men of the First Rifle Regiment. Immediately, the British rallied for a fight. To prevent the Americans from turning his flanks, the picket commander divided the natives who were with him into two detachments, sending the Iroquois to watch his right and the western tribesmen to his left. He took this action despite protests from William Claus that separating the warriors might undermine their morale. [63]

John Norton led one of the war parties that arrived after those on picket duty had taken up their positions. When he and his followers approached the scene, Norton decided to move ahead of the British line and to get behind the American dragoons. As he advanced, he came across some Ojibways lying in ambush who already had sent a party of warriors forward to encircle the cavalry. Norton's men therefore hid with this rearguard to prevent the Americans from spotting them before they could spring the trap. While they waited, an American scout stumbled into the group. They chased and shot him. Not far behind the scout were the Iroquois from New York, mainly Senecas, who attacked the natives allied to the British.[64] Norton at first thought they were the Ojibways who had gone on ahead and that they were retiring in the face of the American advance. 'But,' he wrote, 'their appearance soon undeceived me, – I suspected them to be the Indians of the opposite side of the Water, who had now undertook to support the Enemy; – I was about to challenge them, when I saw them level to fire, – there were no more than six or seven men near me, – We returned their fire, & retreated on a more advantageous position about one hundred paces in our rear.' Next he tried to assemble the British-allied tribesmen who had scattered through the woods and fields, but failed and had to continue his retreat to take up a new post farther in the rear; 'from thence,' he noted, 'we gave them another fire, after having taken Several Shot from them.' However, Norton did not hold this spot long but continued his retreat because American forces were reported to be passing in strength on his left, threatening to cut him off just when another rumour spread that the British picket had fled.[65]

According to William Claus, the party of American volunteers passing on the left coordinated their efforts with their native allies and nearly ambushed Claus, Norton's party, and the Ojibways. Other natives with the British forces, including some from Kahnawake, fell into a trap set by this same group when they ran to the scene of the shooting unaware of the presence of American-allied warriors.[66] According to one American account, the Iroquois from New York 'set up a most dreadful whooping and yelling, calling on the Indians of the enemy to assist them. The stratagem answered the intent, as they advanced and when within about five or six rods our Indians commenced firing on them and immediately rushed on with their tomahawks.' The tribesmen on the British side 'endeavored to retreat, when our men on the flanks formed in their rear and commenced a most dreadful fire on them.'[67]

This episode cost the British-allied natives five killed, three wounded, and ten taken prisoner. The Indian Department lost Jean-Baptiste de Lorimier and John Livingston, both of whom were wounded and captured. Livingston received a bullet in the thigh, lost the sight in one eye from a tomahawk blow, and suffered spear wounds to his head and shoulder. Captured, he obtained no medical attention until his wounds swarmed with maggots. At another part of the skirmish, a British officer commanding thirty men lost his nerve when he was assaulted by ten New York Iroquois. Instead of ordering his men to fire, he ran off. After the battle, he was arrested and imprisoned for his misconduct. [68]

During the fighting, the Sixteenth Infantry held back at a critical point and thereby crippled the attack. The British forces, including natives, returned to their former position and the Americans withdrew back within their lines after setting fire to a farmhouse, barn, and outbuildings. When the Americans reached the town of Niagara, they were reinforced by fresh troops and marched back towards the scene of the action. However, they met stiff resistance from British reinforcements outside the town and retired to Fort George. Apparently, the Americans suffered their heaviest loss during this part of the engagement. It is impossible to determine total casualties, although British losses likely were higher than those suffered by the Americans. The Americans withdrew in a spirit of triumph, thinking they had seriously damaged the British picket, and they even thought they had killed 'the famous Chief Norton,' who in fact had escaped unharmed. [69] The sight of the prisoners and scalps boosted American morale. Colonel Winfield Scott wrote that when the Iroquois brought in their captives, 'each closely pinioned and led by a string, the novel spectacle produced such roars of delight as to be heard from camp to camp.' [70]

Within the British lines, the western tribes, having suffered four killed, declared angrily that the Iroquois were responsible for their losses. No longer trusting the British-allied Six Nations, they moved fifteen kilometres away from the front lines. [71] John Norton observed that the Iroquois from New York 'spread no small Dismay among the Warriors attached to the British Army' and that the Ojibways, respecting the Iroquois 'for their ancient celebrity in arms,' had not fought 'with the firmness that might have been expected from the Gallantry and lively Courage they had formerly evinced in repeated combats with the Americans.' Instead, the American-allied Iroquois had thrown them into a 'distracted state,' making Norton 'despair of being able to bring the Warriors to act collectively and consistently against the Enemy.' [72]

For their part, the Iroquois from New York were not pleased with the lack of close support they got from the American regulars in action. They said the troops lacked courage and wished to sacrifice the warriors in battle. Disgusted, they returned to the American side of the Niagara River. However, Porter persuaded most of them to return to Fort George. On

18 August, the day following the battle, Porter launched another attack on the British picket at Ball's Farm. The skirmish was almost a repeat of the previous day's work. The natives and volunteers in the American force did all the fighting while the regulars held back, and the Six Nations again censured the Americans. British casualties were seven killed (including four natives), one wounded, and fifteen taken prisoner. The Americans lost four Iroquois killed and one captured, as well as several warriors and a few volunteers wounded. After this engagement, many in Porter's force, both natives and whites, went home. [73]

Soon afterwards, Governor-in-Chief Sir George Prevost arrived in Niagara from Quebec to determine if the British could change their objective from blockading Fort George to recapturing it and expelling the Americans from Canada. On 24 August Grand River and other warriors participated in a probe of American defences organized by Sir George. Because of the earlier difficulty in identifying British-allied natives from those serving with the Americans, Colonel Claus gave the tribesmen some 'distinguishing mark' to avoid the same sort of confusion that had caused problems at Ball's Farm. The chiefs and warriors formed part of the skirmishing force along with the light infantry and the 19th Light Dragoons. As the British and natives advanced, the American pickets collapsed. The demonstration was a success in terms of driving in the American pickets, of taking significant numbers of prisoners at very little loss to the British, and in providing a good opportunity to do a careful survey of the American defences. However, the British concluded they could not take Fort George with the resources that were available to them and decided to continue the blockade. [74]

Before leaving Niagara, Prevost attended a small dinner party hosted by General de Rottenburg at which John Norton was a guest. Presumably the three men discussed Norton's ongoing frustration with Colonel Claus and the Indian Department over who should control British–Grand River relations, as Norton was 'highly gratified with the candor that shone throughout' the conversation. Perhaps Norton expressed his opinion that Indian Department intrigue was partially responsible for the fact that warriors were leaving the lines and going home. Norton had continued his efforts to gain ascendancy over Claus throughout 1813 but had not been particularly successful. The department's influence along the Grand remained strong because its agents exploited their connections to the community with skill in subverting Norton and his army patrons. Norton therefore recommended an administrative change whereby Claus would cease to exercise a leadership role. He suggested that Claus should instead become a kind of general administrator of the department in Upper Canada, 'in no manner peculiarly attached to the Five Nations or any other tribe,' and that Claus should be prevented from having 'any right to interfere with the people that I am to lead.'[75]

General de Rottenburg supported Norton's ambitions, believing that his service was 'the most efficient of any in that Department.'[76] Despite this endorsement, de Rottenburg could also look critically at Norton and recognize that the Indian Department had its value. When his efforts to bring some measure of harmony between Norton and Claus failed, de Rottenburg noted with frustration that all his work to reconcile the two men had been in vain. He saw Norton as 'a great intriguer,' but also as a 'fighting man' who could 'do a great deal of mischief if not supported.'[77] The last comment perhaps indicated an ongoing nervousness over the health of the British–Iroquois alliance and may have represented de Rottenburg's acceptance of at least some of the suspicions surrounding Norton's actions in 1794.[78] For his part, Prevost thought the Indian Department was run by a self-serving clique. Thus, in May 1813 Prevost had written an encouraging letter to Norton, praising his actions and letting him know that he planned to bring his achievements to the attention of no less a personage than the Prince Regent. A few months later the future King George IV sent the Mohawk chief a sword and a pair of pistols as a token of appreciation. During this time, when he enjoyed the army's support, Norton advocated policies to benefit native combatants. It was his idea, for example, to give extra rewards to the wounded and to the families of the killed after the Battle of Beaver Dams.[79]

Whatever Prevost, de Rottenburg, and Norton discussed over dinner, the governor and his senior general in Upper Canada agreed to change the way gifts were distributed to native allies. This represented a move beyond Roger Sheaffe's decision in 1812 to link the military resources of the Grand to the army through Norton. Henceforth, officials who did not participate with the tribesmen in action lost all right to distribute presents unless they had certificates or other signs from 'the Officer or Chiefs of Renown' who had led the men personally. Instead, war chiefs would be given presents to distribute according to 'their respective merit.'[80] William Claus believed John Norton had designed the new policy specifically to undercut his authority by excluding him from being able to give presents, his responsibilities as a militia officer rarely allowing him to lead warriors in battle. Possibly de Rottenburg arranged Claus's duties specifically to keep him away from the Grand River people. Claus was right, in so far as the policy followed Norton's recommendations.

Norton's objectives, however, were broader and arose mainly from his wish to support the British cause by giving power over the distribution of material rewards to the army's best friends in the native communities. To achieve his end, he thought getting Claus out of the way was essential. [81]

Although the army championed Norton, he lost most of his influence over the Grand River people during the remainder of 1813. How this came about is not known, but the loss presumably stemmed from some combination of Indian Department activity, the ebb and flow of alliances among the different parties on the tract, suspicions among the Six Nations that Norton's relations with the British were too intimate for him to protect Iroquois interests effectively, and the irritation native people sometimes felt towards individuals who claimed too much authority for themselves. During the autumn Norton withdrew from public life, citing illness as the reason, although it seems that his health may have been merely an excuse to preserve some of his reputation during a period when Colonel Claus regained the upper hand despite the army's efforts.[82] Even Norton's marriage in July 1813 provided an opportunity for Claus to attack his rival. Robert Addison, the rector of Niagara and missionary to the Six Nations, married Norton to a Delaware or Onondaga woman, Karighwaycagh or Catherine. Claus sniffed that she was 'the daughter of a deserter from the Queen's Rangers, and a common woman,' and that Norton, instead of contributing to the war effort, 'did nothing but ride about the country with madam and a posse of his connections.'[83] The Iroquois society in which the very pretty Karighwaycagh grew up accepted considerable freedom in a young woman's premarital relations with men. This provided some whites with an opportunity to attack her morals and indirectly to degrade Norton's status. One group of Canadian militia officers closely connected to Claus, who had been taken prisoner by the Americans, amused themselves one dull afternoon by taking advantage of common gossip to create a list of everyone they thought had slept with her.[84]

The next recorded skirmish involving the Iroquois occurred on 6 September when some warriors in American service attacked a party of British soldiers sent to harvest oats at Ball's Farm. In this small action, some Glengarry Light Infantry and Grand River men ran to the aid of the foraging party while American riflemen supported their native allies by covering their retreat at the end of the three-hour skirmish. Losses amounted to five on the British side: two Mohawks and a Delaware wounded, a Tuscarora killed, and a Cayuga captured. The American side suffered two Oneidas killed, two wounded, and a white man wounded by a Delaware while the former was scalping one of the Grand River casualties.[85]

By this time many of the natives attached to the British had returned home, as the prospects of battle diminished and a new hunting season was beginning. Towards the end of September the British decided to lift the blockade because they assumed that the Americans would likely not be able to renew their offensive in the Niagara campaign with the approach of cold weather. After making their decision, however, the British heard that the Americans intended launching a strong attack on their lines. Therefore, they packed up their equipment in case they were forced to retreat and got their troops ready to respond to the threat. Somehow, nobody told the Grand River people about the situation. When the warriors witnessed the white troops' actions, some thought the British were about to fall back and, according to William Claus, became 'uneasy' and went home. Others objected to the lack of respect shown to them by not keeping them informed, protesting that their 'eyes were always kept shut, which was not the case in former days.'[86] In fact, the Americans did not attack, and although Claus did what he could to keep the Iroquois happy, fewer than sixty warriors decided to stay with the troops. On 6 October the British withdrew to more comfortable quarters on Burlington Heights.[87]

Shortly before the British retired, the Americans showed some increased vigour when Major-General James Wilkinson assumed command at Fort George in September. One of his first acts was to call a council of the Iroquois in New York. About four hundred chiefs and warriors assembled at Fort George in October. The Americans contemplated pursuing the British to Burlington Heights and wanted one thousand Iroquois and militia volunteers to participate in the advance. In the end, the Americans marched only as far as Twelve Mile Creek and accomplished little more than the burning of some barracks because the British were too well entrenched at Burlington to be dislodged.[88] Afterwards, Wilkinson and most of his troops withdrew east to participate in a two-pronged attack on Montreal that was designed to cut Upper Canada off from the rest of British North America. However, British, Canadian, and Iroquois forces defeated the much larger American contingents at Châteauguay and Crysler's Farm in October and November. At Châteauguay, Kahnawake warriors participated in both the preliminary skirmishing and in the pursuit of the defeated Americans as part of a larger light infantry force. The American army included a small number of Akwesasne warriors. At Crysler's Farm, thirty Tyendinaga Mohawks fought with distinction alongside the British light infantry. Elsewhere on the St Lawrence front, pro-British Akwesasne warriors served on picket duty, conveyed flags of truce between the opposing sides, and spied; at the same time, pro-American men from the same community assisted the United States through accomplishing the same services as well as through piloting boats on the St Lawrence and helping to procure food for American troops.[89]

Despite their failures on the Niagara Peninsula and along the St Lawrence in 1813, the Americans enjoyed military success in southwestern Upper Canada. On 9 September 1813 the American and British squadrons on Lake Erie met in battle. The United States Navy triumphed and cut the already inadequate supply line to the western frontier. With the loss of the lake, Major-General Henry Procter destroyed the military works at Detroit and Amherstburg and retreated east towards Burlington. Major-General William Henry Harrison pursued Procter with 3,500 men, including 250 warriors, among whom were some Sandusky Senecas. Harrison caught up with Procter near Moraviantown on the Thames River on 5 October, where he defeated the nineteen hundred men in the British and native force. One of those who fell in the action was the great Shawnee leader, Tecumseh. The Moraviantown disaster and the consequent expulsion of the British from southwestern Upper Canada tore the heart out of both the western tribal confederacy and the dream of an independent aboriginal homeland south of the Great Lakes.[90]

Harrison's victory also meant that the path lay open for a move against the Grand River. The Six Nations, hearing stories of American atrocities committed against native peoples and believing Harrison would strike almost immediately, abandoned their homes and fled to Burlington Bay behind the British post on Burlington Heights. There, fourteen hundred Grand River men, women, and children camped near the home of Joseph Brant's widow, Catharine, along with the aboriginal refugees from Moraviantown.[91] Willcocks's traitors, known as the Canadian Volunteers, took advantage of the crisis to raid the Grand River in late 1813. However, their commanding officer on this occasion, Benajah Mallory, spared Iroquois property, perhaps out of respect for his pre-war friendship with the Six Nations or some consideration that leniency might help Grand River–American relations later.[92]

The flight to Burlington as the weather degenerated towards winter must have been immensely dispiriting for a people who remembered the miserable days of the American Revolution when a rebel army had forced them to abandon their ancestral homes to live in the squalor of refugee camps outside Fort Niagara. To many people that autumn, the slow struggle to re-establish themselves on the Grand since the 1780s must have seemed like a cruel joke, especially because they thought the British planned to retreat eastward if the invaders threatened Burlington. To others, the decision to reject earlier American-initiated peace offers must have seemed like a great blunder. John Norton captured some of their gloom at the prospect of a retreat farther east, writing that the Iroquois told their redcoated allies that 'if we yet continue to fly from the apprehension of an enemy, our Women & our Children, – should they travel in their present distressed Situation, will perish from fatigue & the inclemency of the season. What then will it avail us to live, – would it not be better for us to fall gloriously in combating for Victory, – which may preserve their Lives?' Thus, they told Major-General John Vincent, who commanded British forces on the Niagara Peninsula in General de Rottenburg's absence, to 'have confidence' and make a stand, because, they warned, they could not follow if he marched east.[93]

After the battle of Moraviantown the British did consider retreating to York or Kingston, and John Norton's comments probably were in reaction to British suggestions that the natives participate in the withdrawal. Vincent wanted to keep them with him lest they abandon the British and join the Americans. Yet, in light of Harrison's victory, it did not seem possible to be able to retain Burlington because the Americans could bypass the Niagara Peninsula and get behind the defences at Burlington from the Grand River. Furthermore, through administrative confusion, presents for the natives had been directed away from Burlington, and so Vincent had little to give the natives either to meet their needs or to demonstrate British power.[94] In the end, it may have been only the threat of the loss of the native allies and the fear that the natives, as one prominent Upper Canadian noted, 'would purchase peace with the enemy by the massacre of the population' that made Vincent remain at Burlington instead of retreating.[95] Assuming that General Vincent stayed put because of this danger – whether real or implied – then this is an interesting example of Iroquois ability to use the threat of violence against their own allies to achieve strategic objectives. For his part, John Vincent found it necessary to try to keep his aboriginal allies – now almost completely dependent on meagre British supplies – in line with a warning that 'it is my decided determination to be governed in my future conduct and liberality towards the six Nations and their families, by the support that is afforded to me by the Chiefs and Warriors in carrying out the King's Service.'[96]

Fortunately for the British, they did not need to abandon the Niagara frontier that autumn. Satisfied with his victory over Procter, Harrison failed to consolidate its potential with an attack on Burlington Heights. Instead, he retired to Amherstburg, dismissed most of his volunteers, and sent the bulk of his regulars to Buffalo where they strengthened the forces on the Niagara frontier for a short while before moving east to take part in the ill-fated Montreal campaign. The British continued operations out of Burlington and retained control of most of the territory east of the Niagara Peninsula despite worsening supply problems exacerbated by the large numbers of white, black, and native refugees in their lines. [97]

In an attempt to rebuild aboriginal confidence in the British, Vincent decided to demonstrate some offensive spirit by dispatching a mixed native and white force to establish a forward base at Stoney Creek. From there, strong patrols penetrated deeper into the Niagara Peninsula to assert British vigour and acquire supplies while preventing the Americans from enjoying the region's 1813 harvest. With the Grand River people stranded behind British defences at Burlington, Vincent's initiative seems to have been critical in thwarting American efforts to open communications with the demoralized Six Nations in the hope of negotiating their withdrawal from the war. On one occasion in November, Vincent's troops intercepted a captured Kahnawake messenger sent by the Americans to Burlington. Later in the month, the senior American commander on the peninsula, Brigadier-General George McClure, again tried to entice the British-allied tribes to a council. He led fifteen hundred men, including one hundred Iroquois, on a demonstration from Fort George to Twenty Mile Creek, and then sent two hundred dragoons onwards to create confusion so that the Iroquois from New York could slip through the lines and speak to the British-allied natives. However, this effort also met with no success. [98]

Afterwards, the Iroquois from New York returned home for the winter. Many were exasperated because they had not received the wages they had been promised. Some even charged that the local American commanders had not been authorized to pay for their services in the first place. In addition to these complaints, they were unhappy because of the war's impact on their families. Their annuities had been delayed, the closure of the Bank of the United States reduced the income they derived from their investments, and severe wartime inflation undermined the purchasing power of what little money they did get. In contrast, they probably knew that the British continued to pay the Grand River people annuities from the sale of some of their land in the 1790s despite the war's disruptions. When the American government finally did pay what they owed the Six Nations, it was at a discount because of the increased cost of presents – costs that had been inflated because of the successful British naval blockade of the Atlantic coast. During this period of economic hardship, some Senecas, led by Cornplanter, Red Jacket, and Blue Sky, demanded reimbursement before continuing on service. Others, such as Little Billy, Farmer's Brother, and Young King, were more understanding of the difficulties of the Americans. [99]

There was one more outbreak of fighting along the Niagara Peninsula before the year closed, an outburst that brought the war directly to two Iroquois reservations in New York. With the movement of American troops eastward for the Montreal campaign and the expiration of the terms of service of many militiamen, the garrison in Fort George had dropped to under six hundred men by 9 December. At that point, the British decided to recapture the post. At the same time, a wild rumour, that the British had captured an American patrol and, gruesomely, had turned the soldiers over to their native allies for torture, shot through the American camp. (In fact, a patrol had been ambushed by some warriors who killed and scalped two men.) Consequently, Brigadier-General McClure decided to abandon the fort and consolidate his forces within the United States. To strengthen his defences, he asked Peter B. Porter to organize as many Iroquois as possible to guard Buffalo. Erastus Granger met with Farmer's Brother and other chiefs who thought they might be able to rally two hundred men, since there were many Iroquois dependents in the frontier town at that time. Within a day, one hundred warriors assembled at Buffalo and the neighbouring village of Black Rock. [100]

McClure made a disastrous blunder before evacuating Canadian soil. He turned the residents of Niagara out of their homes on a cold winter's night and burned their houses, ostensibly to prevent the British from housing their troops over the winter and to improve Fort Niagara's defensibility. The next day, American artillery at Lewiston destroyed part of the village of Queenston with hot shot. A new British commander in Upper Canada, Lieutenant-General Gordon Drummond, arrived on the Niagara Peninsula on 16 December. Three days later he began the process of avenging the burning of the Canadian towns when he ordered Lieutenant-Colonel John Murray to cross the river and take Fort Niagara. Murray launched a surprise night assault on its sleeping garrison. The fort and its vast quantities of weapons and stores fell with only eleven British losses compared to over four hundred Americans killed, wounded, or captured. The British found some prisoners inside the fort, including a few Kahnawake and Grand River people who had been captured during the summer. Immediately after this victory, Drummond sent reinforcements across the river, including warriors from the western tribes, to clear the Americans out of the region completely. At the same time, large numbers of frightened American militia deserted, while civilians pack up their possessions and fled the border region.[101]

After Murray's attack on Fort Niagara two men from a party of thirty warriors from the nearby Tuscarora Reservation went to investigate what had happened. At about sunrise on 20 December the warriors who had remained at the reservation heard shooting at Lewiston, a short distance to the west, and they rushed to the scene where they found British and American forces in action. After some sharp fighting, the Americans evacuated Lewiston and deployed the Tuscaroras to cover their retreat eastward through the reservation before turning south towards Buffalo. British forces soon afterwards looted and burned Lewiston's abandoned homes and shops, and many of the warriors and soldiers got drunk on the liquor they found. Once the village fell, a small party of western tribesmen led the British vanguard in pursuit of the Americans. Three kilometres from Lewiston, they came into contact with the retreating Tuscaroras, who stood their ground long enough to allow the rest of the American force to escape. While the main body of Tuscaroras held their position, three warriors moved past the western tribesmen's left flank, blew a horn, and fooled their enemies into thinking they were being surrounded. The British-allied warriors fell back, and the Tuscaroras resumed their withdrawal, halting seven kilometres closer to Buffalo, where they again slowed a party of warriors long enough to save a supply of gunpowder. This time they tried to dupe their opponents into thinking the Tuscarora force was much larger than it really was by moving constantly between a storehouse and a nearby thicket in view of their opponents.[102]

With Lewiston secured, some Grand River men crossed the Niagara River and moved inland to assault the Tuscarora Reservation, which had been abandoned following the capture of Fort Niagara. They stole livestock, looted the village, and burned the council house, church, and homes, presumably out of some sense that the Tuscaroras had betrayed them by promising peace just before other Iroquois in New York crossed the border and inflicted casualties among the Grand River people during the blockade of Fort George. Left destitute in the depths of winter, the Tuscaroras lived out the rest of the war in other Iroquois communities in New York, with the majority going to the Oneida Reservation near Rome.[103]

As panic spread through the Niagara frontier, George McClure in Buffalo tried to rally his native allies for a counter-attack through a speech in which he told them, falsely, that 'Your Red Brothers and the British' had massacred women and children in cold blood. He asked them to 'Avenge yourselves on the authors of such barbarities' and attempted to provide further incentives by inviting them to take whatever private property they could in the process.[104] McClure's exhortation did not work. On 29 December the British marched on Black Rock and Buffalo. With a combined force of fifteen hundred soldiers and western tribesmen, Drummond easily defeated the Americans and sent them retreating in disorder. The American-allied Iroquois, assigned to hold an important defensive position, offered little resistance and melted away before the British could engage them in close combat.[105]

The fall of Buffalo was a welcome event for the nearly destitute western tribesmen who pillaged the town, as John Norton wrote, 'to alleviate the distress and poverty into which the War had thrown them.'[106] However, there were no widespread incidents of assaults or murders of civilians, despite American charges to the contrary, although a handful of civilians died tragically during the various actions associated with Drummond's invasion. Four men, for example, were killed at Lewiston by some western warriors who got drunk with some regulars and then engaged in a fit of brawling and looting that also left two of the tribesmen dead and two soldiers in the British force wounded. Much of the looting at Buffalo was the work of American militiamen, and some retreating American troops stopped long enough to take advantage of the confusion to rob the Senecas at Tonawanda before continuing their withdrawal from the border region. Fortunately, much of the Tonawanda people's food supply had been hidden in traditional buried bark barrels below the floors of their homes and was saved.[107]

Following his success, Drummond decided to continue his winter campaign along the south shore of Lake Erie to destroy the American Lake Erie squadron and recapture Detroit. If he were successful, he might nullify the American victories of Lake Erie and Moraviantown, restore British supremacy in the western theatre, and resurrect hopes of creating a native homeland in the Old Northwest. However, he had to abandon his plan when a January thaw melted the ice on the rivers that he had intended to use for quick movement and surprise.[108]

Thus, with the burning of Buffalo, the 1813 Niagara campaign came to a violent end. The American offensive, which had started so promisingly with the capture of York and Fort George, had been brought to a halt at Stoney Creek and Beaver Dams. The first of these engagements was crucial in helping preserve Grand River support for the British; the other, mainly an Iroquois victory, was decisive in destroying the invaders' willingness to venture far from Fort George. The subsequent blockade of Fort George kept the American army immobile through the critical summer campaigning season. Even the American victories on Lake Erie and at Moraviantown were of limited value because William Henry Harrison did not seize the opportunities they provided to threaten the British rear, relieve Fort George, knock the Iroquois and western tribes out of the war, and expel the British from the Niagara Peninsula. The autumn withdrawal of American troops for the attacks on Montreal weakened Fort George to the point where McClure could only abandon it in panic. These actions sowed the seeds for the British counter-attack which took Fort Niagara, destroyed the American presence along the peninsula, and brought retribution to the American and Tuscarora populations of the region. Although the British did not have enough troops to hold all of the American side of the Niagara River, they maintained a garrison in Fort Niagara for the rest of the war, which gave them complete control of the strategic mouth of the river and, in the process, rendered the Tuscarora Reservation virtually uninhabitable.

For the Iroquois, 1813 was a tragic year. Those who lived in the United States experienced economic hardships and even starvation, whether or not they supported the American war effort. The Tuscaroras lost their village during a direct attack, while the Tonawanda Senecas endured the indignity of having their homes looted by their white allies. The rewards the Six Nations in New York and Pennsylvania received for fighting did not equal their losses, although mercifully their battle casualties were not heavy. They fought with distinction, even if against their relatives in Canada, but the impact was slight because of weak American combat support. They also experienced a large degree of frustration at the hands of their unsympathetic allies. The Grand River people, for their part, fought hard throughout the campaign and contributed substantially to the defence of Canada, but endured deep internal divisions in the wake of the debate over changing sides after the battle of Fort George. After Moraviantown they faced the horror of abandoning their homes to retreat to Burlington, where they suffered the food shortages and other privations of living as refugees close to the front lines. Of all the Iroquois, the Grand River people suffered the heaviest battle casualties. Tyendinaga and Seven

Nations warriors fought well, although they did not experience the same traumas as their Grand River and American-resident relatives did, with the exception of the Akwesasne people where the sad divisions that had torn the community apart in 1812 continued to make life burdensome throughout 1813.

7

The Last War Dance:
1814

The Loss of our friends gave us all a gloomy appearance.

John Norton on the Battle of Chippawa[1]

The year 1814 was the last time the Iroquois fought independently under their own leaders in a major war. It was the bloodiest campaign for them, and the carnage the Iroquois from New York inflicted on their Canadian relatives at the battle of Chippawa demoralized Six Nations people on both sides of the border. Magnifying the tragedy of Chippawa was the ignorance of the white allies (and their posterity), who wrote off Iroquois sacrifices, both at that action and in the conflict as a whole, despite the contributions they had made during the three years of the conflict. Neutralist sentiment regained the ascendancy after Chippawa and the majority of warriors on both sides of the border withdrew from hostilities except to defend their homes and families when threatened directly. At the same time, the ongoing feud between the British army and the Indian Department proved to be too complex and ruthless for John Norton, who suffered complete defeat in his quest for control of relations between Grand River and the Crown.

In 1812, with the British preoccupied by the European war, the Americans thought they would overrun the outnumbered defenders of the Canadas quickly and annex the provinces to the United States. However, they underestimated the capabilities of the British and at the same time placed too much confidence on their larger but poorly trained and inadequately led army. After two years of hard fighting, the Americans lost the opportunity to expand north even though the odds ran heavily in their favour. Moreover, events in Europe helped tip the balance against the United States. Following Napoleon's expulsion from Russia in 1812, the French emperor suffered a serious defeat at Leipzig in 1813 and retreated west into France. To the south, British, Portuguese, and Spanish armies pushed up towards French territory. In March 1814 allied armies marched into Paris, and in April Napoleon abdicated. After France and Britain resumed political and commercial relations in May, the British could turn their attention to the American war. The Royal Navy, with dozens of ships freed from European service, expanded its blockade of the Atlantic seaboard and increased raiding with the objectives of taking pressure off Canada and making Mr Madison's unpopular war even less bearable for the American people. Other reinforcements set sail to British North America to shield the colonies from conquest and carry the war into the United States.[2]

The Americans, to gain as good a bargaining position as possible in peace negotiations, had to take advantage of the time available before the arrival of British reinforcements towards the end of the summer. Logically, they should have concentrated efforts on an early capture of Kingston. However, such factors as confused orders from Washington once again led the Americans to focus their offensive operations on the Niagara Peninsula. In early 1814, as a result of the battles of Lake Erie and Moraviantown, the centre of American strength on the border was Lake Erie. The Madison administration therefore decided to use Detroit and Buffalo as bases for a renewed invasion of Canada. The government ordered its forces at Detroit to sail north and recapture Fort Mackinac to regain control of the north and far west. From Buffalo, the army was to cross Lake Erie and establish a foothold at either Long Point or the mouth of the Grand River. Using the Grand to move supplies and troops inland, the army was then to march along Dundas Street to seize Burlington Heights. If successful, this move would isolate British forces on the Niagara River and allow American troops, supported by the Lake Ontario squadron, to take York and Kingston. If all went well, they would knock the British out of Upper Canada before reinforcements arrived from Europe. Madison could then try to persuade the British that a difficult reconquest of the province would not be worth the effort. The net effect would be the acquisition of Upper Canada and the elimination of a rival power that could help the aboriginal nations resist further westward expansion. However, more strategic confusion and delays led the Americans to subvert their chances of success on the Niagara front by ignoring the opportunities offered through exploiting the Grand River–

Burlington axis. Instead, the final plan for 1814 called for the army to cross the border from Buffalo, take Fort Erie, then march down the Niagara River and take as much British territory as it could.[3]

Before the Americans could put this plan into operation, there were a number of actions in the east, as the opposing sides attempted to achieve strategic advantages in preparation for the upcoming Niagara campaign. An American army crossed the border south of Montreal in March but withdrew when it could not dislodge a small force at the Lacolle River. Among the British losses in the action were two warriors from a Seven Nations contingent. In February the British raided American communities along the St Lawrence River to seize supplies, and in May they captured Oswego at the southeastern corner of Lake Ontario and took a large quantity of stores. An expedition against Sackett's Harbor to destroy or capture the American squadron, however, had to be cancelled for lack of men to carry out the plan. Towards the end of May, at Sandy Creek near Sackett's Harbor, 120 Oneidas helped defeat a British attempt to capture an important bateaux convoy on its way to Sackett's. The supplies reached their destination and helped the navy arm the USS *Superior,* a sixty-two-gun warship, which would give the United States dominance on Lake Ontario towards the end of July.[4]

In the months leading up to the American invasion of the Niagara Peninsula, the British worried about supply shortages that might cripple their defensive efforts. Faced with a serious want of flour as early as March, the hard-pressed commissariat contemplated reducing rations to aboriginal allies in the Burlington refugee camps, especially with local farmers not being able to supply adequate foodstuffs in the war-ravaged peninsula to take the place of imported supplies. At the same time, sickness at Burlington carried off two or three native people every day. To the west, American foraging parties from Amherstburg exacerbated the situation by removing provisions from the north shore of Lake Erie. At one point the American government even thought of organizing its native allies to ravage and depopulate the civilian settlements along the Lake Erie shore in order to deprive the British of needed foodstuffs permanently, but then it decided against the plan. Much of the food that did get to Burlington came from farmers in New England who were attracted by the better prices paid by the British for their produce and livestock. A major conduit for smuggling American food into Canada ran through Akwesasne. Conditions were so grim at Burlington that the army encouraged many natives to go home and cultivate their fields, even though this lessened the number of warriors available for military service. As it was, some of the refugees from the west had planted crops near Burlington and two-thirds of the Grand River people returned to their farms despite American control of southwestern Upper Canada. However, no immediate relief from the food shortage could be expected from these efforts. In April flour supplies ran out completely and the natives had to go without bread for several days. So desperate were these people for food, shoes, and other necessities that British officials worried that they might resort to violence or defect to the Americans to relieve their woeful condition.[5]

During this period of distress, the old conflict between the Indian Department and the army further aggravated the problem of retaining native support. Although John Norton possessed the army's confidence, he still could not generate significant support among the Grand River people. During the winter he went to Quebec to confer with Governor-in-Chief Sir George Prevost on how best to maintain aboriginal forces in the field. Sir George made one last attempt to end the Norton–Claus feud by forbidding the department's agents from communicating with the people of the Grand River Tract altogether unless they did so through Norton. He also reaffirmed Norton's status in the army's eyes as 'Leader of the Five Nations Grand River Indians or Confederates,' and showed his satisfaction with the Mohawk chief by adding the Thames River warriors to his command. To prop up Norton's crumbling position, Prevost gave him complete control over the distribution of presents to the Grand River people, allotting three-eighths of Upper Canada's entire supply of aboriginal gifts for 1814 to him to dispense as he thought best.[6]

John Norton left Quebec for Upper Canada. By the time he got to Kingston, however, the spring thaw turned the frozen winter roads into impassable muddy quagmires, which prevented him from returning to the Niagara Peninsula until early in May after the supply problem had contributed to the growing discord. On his arrival, Norton may have worsened both the supply-induced tensions and his own precarious position by advocating that presents be withheld until the warriors went on active service in order to maximize the impact gift-giving might have in encouraging their participation in the war. Such a policy must have seemed mean to native people, who believed that friends should share what they had with those in want and who interpreted stinginess as an act of hostility or as a breach of the reciprocal obligations that existed between allies.[7] Meanwhile, the Indian Department simply refused to accept Sir George's new attack on its authority and carried on its own efforts to retain power. The department seems to have used Norton's absence and the food crisis to try to convince the Grand River people that its agents had to replace him in the intermediary role with white authorities. In April three tribes expressed dissatisfaction at Norton's appointment, accusing him of being nothing but a 'disturber of the peace and harmony.'[8] It seems that the Mohawks, Oneidas, and Tuscaroras sided with the department, while the Onondagas, Cayugas, and Senecas generally supported Norton. The historical record does not reveal how the Delawares and other residents of the Grand felt, although the aboriginal people of the Thames River rallied behind Norton.[9]

Clearly, these divisions could have serious consequences for the upcoming campaign. The Indian Department saw the situation as desperate. Lieutenant-Colonel William Claus thought the army's interference had created a crisis in which the British could lose Grand River support entirely. Was his view purely self-serving, or did he detect divisions that threatened the Iroquois alliance because of the army's support for a particular party on the river? Unfortunately, evidence is lacking to draw a conclusion. The details of the power struggle that followed Norton's return to the Grand do not survive either, but in June representatives from the community misled the British, saying they had resolved the crisis. All Six Nations outwardly recognized Norton as their principal representative with white authorities and sent Prevost a string of wampum from each tribe to affirm its decision. Yet eighty Mohawks persisted in allying themselves with the department against Norton. Defections continued, and in July only half of the Grand River fighting force assembled at Niagara Falls where Norton had established his camp. The rest absented themselves from the front entirely. Of the two hundred Grand River warriors and one hundred western tribesmen in Norton's camp, one hundred refused to accept his leadership. The people from the west with Norton were motivated to follow him, or at least stay close to him, partly because of the large quantity of presents he had under his control.[10] As one of their chiefs remarked pungently: 'He speaks loud, and has Strong Milk, and Big Breasts, which yield plentifully.'[11] Among the men who joined Norton was Tecumseh's prophet brother, Tenskwatawa, who himself had lost much of his credibility after the battle of Moraviantown.[12]

As well as these three hundred men, another six hundred western tribesmen gathered at Fort George, and two thousand soldiers under Major-General Phineas Riall garrisoned Fort Niagara in New York as well as the posts on the Canadian side of the Niagara River between Niagara and Fort Erie. Riall's orders were to defend the peninsula as best he could, but if the Americans compelled him to withdraw, he was to deploy the militia and natives to cover his retreat and slow the enemy. Ideally, Riall could hold out until September when reinforcements would arrive from Europe.[13]

Major-General Jacob Brown commanded the American army gathered at Buffalo in the spring of 1814. By the beginning of July he had five thousand soldiers and six hundred warriors organized into three brigades. Senecas formed the majority of Brown's aboriginal force, but he also had Onondagas, Oneidas, Tuscaroras, and some Algonkians in his camp. Brown's army was different from those the Americans had deployed earlier in the war. His white troops were more thoroughly trained than before and his Iroquois allies were better disposed towards fighting than they had been in 1813 because they wanted to avenge their battle losses and the destruction of the Tuscarora village.[14] According to Peter B. Porter, the Iroquois were 'impatient to take up the hatchet' in their exasperation at 'the late barbarities of the enemy.'[15] Even men who normally advocated neutrality joined the campaign.[16]

American officers worried about how to make their native allies obey white commanders in battle or stay in the field when American desires might conflict with aboriginal ways of war or strategic objectives. This attitude, expressive of a desire to exercise more control over their aboriginal allies than previously, represented a significant shift in American thinking from 1813. Although the warriors were reluctant to accept white leadership in combat, Brigadier-General Porter thought they would not be 'efficient' without white direction. Therefore, he recommended that American commanders, disguised as staff officers, be assigned to them because the natives 'would be jealous of a direct command,' while quartermasters and the like might not pose a threat since the Americans thought they could be passed off as mere administrative and logistical support for their native allies.[17] The way General Brown organized the tribesmen into an 'Indian Volunteer Corps' was indicative of this concern. Company officers were native, but field and other officers, except for Red Jacket, were white. The battalion colonel was Indian agent Erastus Granger, in contrast to 1813 when Farmer's Brother commanded the regiment. Granger was supported by two other Indian agents holding the rank of captain and three other whites in staff positions.[18] The British, in contrast, tended to accept the fact that warriors would only fight under their own leaders, following their own customs. As one prominent Upper Canadian noted, natives were 'the best light troops in the world,' and it would have been foolish to have attempted to change their modes of fighting or to have tried to assert authority over them.[19] Even the Indian Department agents who fought alongside natives functioned more as socially integrated war chiefs or as allied advisers and liaison officers than as white overseers. Many of these men, unlike the vast majority of their American counterparts, had aboriginal blood in their veins. Some, such as Lieutenant John Brant, were entirely native.[20] The restraints that did exist tended to be based on rewards and appeals to the natives' sense of right rather than attempts to impose close white management at the lower operational level.

Despite the organizational plan, Porter faced a difficult task in reconciling white control with native aspirations for independence. On one occasion, he attempted to achieve his objectives by offering rewards before stating the government's restrictions, which he then enunciated with great care. He told the warriors that President Madison offered them the same wages, supplies, and rations as white volunteers which, he said, was merely just. (Native allies, however, often expected more.) Furthermore, Porter assured them, curiously, that their participation would strengthen their 'title' to lands in Upper Canada (presumably a reference to the Grand River and Tyendinaga tracts). Then he acknowledged that they might be 'apprehensive' about the army's 'rigid systems of discipline and our modes of conducting war.' Yet he conceded only a little, while making it seem like a lot. What Porter offered was freedom from army discipline but not autonomy to fight according to native custom if it conflicted with American desires because he wanted the chiefs to serve under white officers rather than exercise independent command. Lest they refuse to fight under these restrictions, he tentatively offered an insult, saying that if his conditions should cause them to decide to go home, then 'Let us hear no more of you as warriors, and we will not only take care of ourselves but we will defend you and your women and children from the enemy.' The carrot that followed this stick was: 'But if you love your country and wish to defend your families and property with your own arms; if you wish to brighten the chain of friendship between yourselves and your white brethren by partaking with them in common dangers and successes; if you are ambitious to support the military fame of your ancestors of the Six Nations, go back, arm, and prepare all your young warriors ... and we will sweep the enemy from the country.'[21] In the end, five hundred men decided to cross the border as part of Porter's brigade. There also were at least twenty Oneida women on the army's pay list, presumably to fulfil the cooking, washing, nursing, and the other duties women performed in armies of the period, although it is possible they assumed combat roles, as had a handful of Iroquois women during the American Revolution and the Seven Years' War. [22]

The 1814 American invasion of Upper Canada began on the morning of 3 July when Jacob Brown crossed the Niagara River and attacked Fort Erie. The 170-man garrison put up only a token resistance before surrendering in the face of the overwhelming force brought against it. Phineas Riall was at Fort George when news of the American invasion – but not of the fall of the fort – reached him a few hours after Brown's crossing. He rushed south to Chippawa, part way between Fort Erie and Niagara Falls, with five companies of the 1st Foot to bolster the five hundred men of the garrison stationed there. John Norton's Iroquois and western tribesmen marched from Niagara Falls to Chippawa where they joined one of the flank companies of the 100th Foot before continuing south to watch American movements. Finding the Americans on Canadian soil in strength, the 100th retired to Chippawa while Norton's people withdrew farther north to guard the British rear in case the Americans crossed the Niagara River from Grand Island. Riall initially hoped to counter-attack that night but postponed his plan when reinforcements from the 8th Foot did not arrive in time. [23]

On 4 July one of Brown's brigades, commanded by Brigadier-General Winfield Scott, marched north to seize the bridge across the Chippawa River while British light troops harassed the Americans and destroyed bridges in advance of Scott's movements. By late afternoon the British retired to the security of the north bank of the Chippawa River to await reinforcements after destroying the bridge, along with buildings on the south side of the river, that might provide cover for Scott's men. Norton's people joined the British at Chippawa about the time the redcoats crossed to the north side of the river. As the river was seventy-five metres wide and protected by a battery mounted behind a fieldwork and as it was late in the day, Scott decided not to press the British. Instead, he withdrew three kilometres south and camped on the south bank of Street's Creek for the night. There, the Americans' right flank rested on the Niagara River, while on their left, twelve hundred metres across a flat plain, was forest. Street's Creek covered their front. General Brown arrived with a second brigade at eleven at night. Porter's mixed volunteer and aboriginal brigade arrived the next day. Only 350 of the 500 warriors who had crossed the Niagara River remained with the American army, the rest having gone home after the fall of Fort Erie. [24]

John Norton's warriors spent the night of 4–5 July on the British right flank near the forest. In the morning Norton led a small party through the woods to scout the American lines. Before he could complete the reconnaissance, other parties of militia, Iroquois, and western tribesmen initiated a general skirmish when they went on ahead and opened fire on the American pickets from the forest. Norton thought the American left flank was vulnerable because it had pulled back to avoid the sniper fire, which left their camp exposed to attack from troops operating from the cover of the bush.[25]

While Norton, Riall, and others scouted the American lines, the 8th Foot marched into the British camp. This brought General Riall's strength up to fifteen hundred regulars from the 1st, 8th, and 100th Foot, the Royal Artillery, and the 19th Light Dragoons, as well as three hundred natives and two hundred militia. Norton and Riall consulted with each other after performing their scouts. They both underestimated American strength, partly because of faulty evaluations, partly because they assumed that Fort Erie had not fallen and that therefore a significant number of Americans were investing the place, and partly because Porter's brigade arrived after Norton had returned to the British lines. As well, they assumed that Brown's combat capabilities were weak, based on previous experience against the American army. This led Riall to decide to attack. Once he defeated Brown, he planned to march to the relief of Fort Erie. Therefore, with two thousand men Phineas Riall prepared to attack thirty-five hundred Americans, not the two thousand he believed were in place.[26]

Riall sent his natives, militia, and light infantry through the woods to join the snipers already in place and to commence a very heavy flanking fire on the American left. With the Americans' attention thus engaged, Riall would march the rest of his army across the plain between the camps and attack the American front. The natives, militia, and light infantry moved through the woods in three parties: one group of natives and militia moved ahead close to the forest edge, the rest of the whites marched behind them, and Norton's men travelled deeper in the bush on the right of the white and aboriginal force. At four in the afternoon Riall crossed the Chippawa River and sent most of his regulars up the river road.[27]

General Brown, still unaware of the threat because forest covered Riall's river crossing, earlier had decided to eliminate the ongoing harassment on his left flank. Because few of his regulars could perform as light infantry, he sent Porter's brigade to dislodge the snipers. At three in the afternoon Porter took sixty regulars, two hundred volunteers, and three hundred warriors into the forest eight hundred metres south of the American camp out of sight of the snipers. To distinguish friend from foe, the volunteers left their hats behind and the warriors wore white cloths on their heads. Once in the woods, the warriors and volunteers cautiously led the way, moving in a single, extended line of one thousand metres. The regulars followed in reserve. Red Jacket commanded from the left of the line, Porter from the right, while the lesser chiefs advanced fifteen or twenty metres ahead of their individual war parties and scouts moved on beyond the chiefs. Captain Pollard was considered the first in command of the native force, but his location during the advance is not known.[28]

Once they spotted their aboriginal enemies – consisting mainly of the snipers already in place – Porter and Red Jacket redeployed their men in order to take the best advantage of the situation for the attack, and then they continued their march until they received a volley of musketry. Next, according to Porter, the Iroquois-American force 'rushed forward with savage yells' and pursued their retreating foe 'for more than a mile through scenes of indescribable horror, few only of the fugitives surrendering themselves as prisoners, while others believing that no quarter was to be given, suffered themselves to be overtaken and cut down with the tomahawk, or turned upon their pursuers and fought to the last.' Those who were captured were quickly secured with a matunip line (or prisoner tie) and rushed to the rear. The sight of the warriors bringing their prisoners back at a trot at the skirts of the woods caused many of the American troops to think that a much larger number of Iroquois deserted under fire than was the case.[29]

No sooner had the Americans and Iroquois driven off the British-allied snipers than they were brought to a halt by a 'tremendous discharge of musketry' from the militia and warriors underway to participate in the British flanking movement. At first the Iroquois-American force thought the volley came from the people they were pursuing and who had re-formed for a counter-attack. Realizing the mistake and thinking he was outnumbered, Porter ordered everyone to retreat, but a short while later his force rallied and returned to engage their opponents in a hot exchange of bullets. Porter then saw fresh British light troops advancing rapidly to join the action. The latter soon opened fire with a tightly disciplined volley before continuing their spirited advance against the Americans. Porter's men then fled. On the British far right flank, Norton's men had ventured too far into the woods to participate in the action up to this point because they had intended to execute a circular motion to get behind the American lines undetected. Nevertheless, Norton and his followers shifted direction towards the fighting and engaged Porter's left flank to rescue 'many that were just overtaken by the exulting Enemy' and to participate in the British advance through the forest, which turned Porter's retreat into a rout.[30]

Although the British light troops and warriors had stopped Porter and Red Jacket, Riall lost the opportunity to surprise Brown with his main force. Brown, assuming he was about to be attacked because of the size of the engagement in the woods and the sound of the British light troops' disciplined volleys, ordered Scott to march the Ninth, Eleventh, Twenty-Second, and Twenty-Fifth regiments of his brigade with artillery support across the field against the British who were advancing against the Americans. Before the two sides could clash on the open fields, Porter's brigade ran out of the forest, pursued by the natives, militia, and light infantry. The British–aboriginal force took up positions on the skirts of the woods and opened fire on Scott's advancing force. Norton recorded that 'We now saw the Columns of the Enemy advancing through the field with colours flying, – we fired among their condensed Ranks, – and they returned it with Grape & Musketry.'[31] The Americans deployed the Twenty-Fifth Infantry to protect their left, but the regiment found the British and native fire too devastating for them to be able to stand and return volleys from their exposed position in the field. The Twenty-Fifth therefore charged the skirmishers at bayonet point. The British and natives, outnumbered and not deployed to take a tight linear charge, retreated. Once they drove away the British light forces, the Twenty-Fifth sent skirmishers after them to prevent a rally while the rest of the regiment returned to the plain. The few American-allied Iroquois who remained in the field at this point joined the Twenty-Fifth in the charge and fell upon the rear and right flank of Riall's forces. Meanwhile, on the open ground the British and American infantry and artillery clashed in a classic linear battle. The combined fire of the American artillery and infantry halted the British advance. A stationary, close-range firefight ensued. About twenty minutes later, General Riall realized he had been defeated and ordered a retreat.[32]

Casualties at the battle of Chippawa were heavy: the British regulars and Canadian militia lost five hundred killed, wounded, or missing; the American army suffered 325 casualties. In addition, the warriors from New York lost between nine and twelve killed, four wounded, and ten missing. Native casualties on the British side are not known, but there is no doubt that they were heavy enough to be catastrophic from an aboriginal perspective. If American statistics are correct, the Grand River people and western tribesmen suffered as many as eighty-seven killed, five taken prisoner, and an unknown number wounded.[33]

The Americans were jubilant at their victory – a triumph that they have since heralded as a turning point in the professionalization of their army because their regulars displayed the skill of well-trained troops for the first time in the war. For their part, the British seemed surprised at the new level of competence in the American army. Yet General Brown did not make the most of the battle's potential because he failed to deploy one of his brigades early enough in support of Scott to ensure complete success by cutting off the British retreat. Furthermore, the Americans might have been soundly trounced had Porter's men not blundered into the British light force because it was that incident which warned Brown about the seriousness of Riall's attack. [34]

Both the Americans and the British gave their native allies a poorer rating for their participation in the battle than seems appropriate. Perhaps the American general, who could not see the Iroquois action because of the forest, wanted his regulars to absorb as much of the credit for his singular victory as possible, while the British commanders may have hoped to deflect some of the blame for the defeat away from themselves. Rather than praising the American-allied Iroquois discovery of the British flanking movement, Brown's report to Washington emphasized how their retreat left his flank exposed and how he had to send his dragoons to stop 'the fugitives' from running from the battlefield altogether. On the British side, Riall's superior, Lieutenant-General Gordon Drummond, did not take into account the unanticipated presence of Porter's brigade in assessing the failure of the flanking movement, and declared that the natives 'proved of little service' because they penetrated 'too far into the woods to offer the assistance required of them.' [35]

Both armies returned to their former positions after the battle: the British to the north bank of the Chippawa River, the Americans to the south side of Street's Creek. The next day, 6 July, the American-allied warriors presented Peter B. Porter with the scalps they had taken, believing he would reward them for these trophies, perhaps remembering Brigadier-General Alexander Smyth's 1812 offer of forty dollars for each British-allied native scalp turned in. Porter had different sensibilities than Smyth and he 'refused to examine or count these unseemly trophies.' Instead, he ordered them 'to be buried or thrown into the river,' which he claimed 'was immediately done.' [36] Given the importance of scalps as prizes and sources of spiritual power, however, it seems unlikely that the warriors threw them away. Porter gave the natives a small ransom for the prisoners they had taken. The warriors in Porter's brigade then returned to the battlefield to search for their dead. In the process, they found three mortally wounded British-allied tribesmen, slit the throats of two of them, but gave the third a canteen full of water while he waited to die because he was a former resident of one of the New York reservations. When upbraided for the murders, the warriors told Porter that 'it did seem hard to take the lives of these men, but that we ought to remember that these were very hard times.'[37]

Phineas Riall realized that he would have to fall back to Fort George, and consequently he had the wounded and baggage transported north to the mouth of the Niagara River. According to John Norton, most of the natives were wholly demoralized by their casualties and the sight of the British preparing to retreat. In the rueful aftermath of the battle, many tribesmen sought solace in looted drink to the point of becoming 'entirely devoid of reflection.' Within two days of the defeat, all the natives left Riall except for fifteen or twenty men, including a few from the Grand River. Concerned to preserve a strong light infantry capability, General Riall asked Norton to persuade as many warriors as possible to return. Norton, with John Brant's assistance, did his best but only managed to bring total native strength in the front lines up to fifty.[38]

On 7 July General Brown followed up his victory by bridging the Chippawa River under cover of his artillery, volunteers, and remaining warriors. The flank companies of the 1st Foot tried to stop the Americans. The odds, however, were too great, and towards evening General Riall retreated to forts George and Mississauga (the latter being a new work on the Canadian side of the mouth of the Niagara River). The Americans crossed the Chippawa River that night and marched to Queenston on 8 July, where they camped to await the arrival of their Lake Ontario squadron for a final push to drive the British out of the peninsula. Some of the warriors who stayed with the American army for this portion of the campaign joined their white allies in looting and burning Canadian farms and villages, torching thirty or forty homes in St Davids alone, perhaps in retaliation for the destruction of the Tuscarora Reservation in December. They also seized fifty or more barrels of wine, brandy, and other stores that the British had hidden, but the American quartermaster took these supplies away from them against their will.[39]

On 8 July Riall asked John Norton to go to Burlington and bring back warriors who had withdrawn from the peninsula. There, Norton met Colonel Hercules Scott of the 103rd Foot, who had mustered the five hundred men of his regiment and one thousand militia to march to Riall's aid. This force moved closer to the front lines, joining five or six hundred natives from both the western tribes and the Grand River at Forty Mile Creek in preparation of swinging behind the Americans and attacking their rear if Brown advanced on Fort George. However, the Grand River people who had not already gone home were dismayed by their losses at Chippawa and refused to leave the relative safety of their camp at Forty Mile Creek. [40]

Likewise, the experiences of most of the American-allied Iroquois in the battle undermined their willingness to continue with General Brown. They had fulfilled their obligation to avenge the destruction of the Tusca-rora village. More important, they were horrified that they had butchered so many of their Canadian relatives and friends on behalf of the United States. In melancholy reflection of the aboriginal blood spilled, the Iro-quois, led by Red Jacket, Cornplanter, and Blue Sky, began to reconsider both the neutrality they had failed to maintain in 1812 and their later decision to fight only in defence of their homes within American terri-tory. Their thoughts led them to arrange a council with the Grand River people near Burlington in mid-July. [41]

Two Senecas, one of whom had moved from the Grand River to New York in 1810, spoke for the American-allied Iroquois. They claimed that they had tried to stay neutral at the outbreak of war and that the Ameri-cans had let them adopt that stance because they thought they did not need aboriginal help. But as the war progressed, they found themselves compelled to take up arms because the Americans wanted to use them either to counter the impact of British-allied natives or to force these peo-ple out of the war. Therefore, the tribes in New York were told either to join the Americans or to be considered enemies of the United States. Since they could not move away, they felt coerced to fight. As one of them said: 'We are in their power, we cannot withdraw our families from among them, but we are certainly much averse to help them in War, for in so doing, we are brought to fight against Relatives and friends.' [42] This state-ment may have exaggerated the pressure the United States put on them while minimizing their own desires to go to war; if not, it is difficult to account for the intensity of their participation at Chippawa.

John Norton countered by reiterating his old position that the Ameri-cans were the enemies of all aboriginal peoples and that therefore no native could have a valid reason to fight on their side. He insisted that the Americans used warriors 'as a Hunter used a Dog, pushing them always forward in the greatest Danger, – without allowing them any Share of glory.' He concluded by telling the people from New York that they should leave their villages and retire to the woods to hunt if they could not evade the compulsion to fight, stating that 'any expedient is better than to allow those who have got the most of your lands, now to have your Lives at their disposal; – If by this means they can effect your utter Destruction, they will be highly gratified, – there will then be only Women & Children remaining to claim the little Land which yet remains your property.'[43] Given the number of people involved and the horticultural foundation of Iroquois society, Norton's suggestion to disappear into the forest simply was not realistic, but it made sense to him because of his intense fear that American successes in war or diplomacy could only contribute to the destruction of native societies.

Norton's speech was probably unnecessary if he intended to encourage neutrality among the Iroquois in New York, and it was pointless if he hoped to keep the Grand River people in the field. The majority on both sides of the border – presumably influenced by reascendant neutralist parties – already had decided to go home. As the tribesmen departed, the British watched helplessly as their worsening supply situation prevented them from giving presents in sufficient quantities to encourage the warriors to stay in the field. After the council, Norton could persuade only sixteen Iroquois to remain with him and these people seemed unwilling to engage in hostilities. Even Norton's supporters among the western tribes seemed to have melted away, apparently suspecting the Six Nations of treacherous behaviour in light of their losses at Chippawa. Thus, most Iroquois were to miss the brutal fighting and high casualty rates that lay ahead for the British and American armies at the battle of Lundy's Lane and the siege of Fort Erie.[44]

General Riall was furious with John Norton and began to doubt his loyalty, believing that the Mohawk chief should have seized the American-allied emissaries and prevented the council from happening in the first place. For his part, Norton thought that he had no authority to stop the meeting and that it would have been dishonourable to apprehend men admitted within the British lines to parlay. Norton also argued that he had taken the precaution of controlling Seneca movements in order to prevent them from assessing the defences at Burlington.[45] Norton's handling of the Burlington council sealed his fate in the eyes of Drummond and Riall, coming so soon after the disaster at Chippawa, which they seem to have blamed partly on him in their criticism that the natives moved 'too far into the woods to offer the assistance required of them.'[46] The army had already become unhappy with the Mohawk chief because he had overstepped his authority by pulling warriors from the region west of the Detroit River into his command in addition to his authorized leader-

ship of the Grand River and Thames River people. With Norton's loss of
favour, the army lost its administrative war with the Indian Department,
and the department – with army assistance – began to undermine
Norton's remaining influence. Despite these blows, Norton continued to
fight with enthusiasm at the head of his own little war party until the end
of hostilities (and then he volunteered to sail for Europe to join the Duke
of Wellington on the road to Waterloo, although circumstances prevented him from taking on Napoleon's army). [47]

   The Americans did not want their native allies to leave at such a critical
point in the war either. On 25 July Brigadier-General Porter did his best
to persuade the warriors not to listen to the chiefs who wanted to withdraw but to remain in the field for the glory they were sure to win in the
coming battles. More ominously, he reminded them that the president,
who had the power to 'reward and punish,' would hear about their decision. [48] Nevertheless, the majority of warriors in American service upheld
their side of the agreement with their Canadian relatives and crossed
back into the United States. They seem to have tried to mask their intentions from the Americans, some saying they had to go home to do their
haying and to protect their families, others claiming that they would
return as soon as they received their pay. [49] As Porter noted, they left 'for
reasons which were plausible if not satisfactory.' [50] Attempts to encourage
them to return in strength failed and no more than fifty warriors, mainly
Algonkian Stockbridges, served with the army in Canada for the rest of
the war, although others remained in Buffalo where they burdened the
Americans with demands for food and supplies. [51] Apparently angry at
having killed fellow tribesmen, the warriors defiantly told American officials that, rather than return to Canada, it was 'their pleasure to ... eat
beef and get Drunk.' [52]

There seemed to be little that could be done to stop the Americans from
achieving their objectives once Jacob Brown's army camped at Queenston Heights (with pickets sent forward to within two kilometres of Fort
George where they had to endure rocket and artillery fire from the fort)
in preparation for a final push against forts George, Mississauga, and Niagara if carried out in cooperation with the United States Lake Ontario
squadron. However, Commodore Isaac Chauncey's ships and schooners
neither delivered the supplies and heavy guns Brown needed to attack
nor blockaded the mouth of the Niagara River to sever British communications. Chauncey claimed he could not leave Sackett's Harbor because
he was ill and would not entrust the squadron to anyone else. Further-

more, he declared the navy had a higher calling than that of merely supporting the army! Without naval support and faced with a deterioration of his army's strength because of sickness at the same time that the British began to receive reinforcements from Europe, Brown retired south to Chippawa on 24 July. The British advanced against the Americans and the two armies met at Lundy's Lane near Niagara Falls, where they fought each other to a bloody standstill on 25 July. The next day, the Americans retreated to Fort Erie. The British had checked the 1814 American campaign to conquer Upper Canada.[53]

On 26 July General Drummond ordered the 19th Light Dragoons, the Glengarry Light Infantry, the western tribes, and the small remaining Grand River contingent to move forward and watch the Americans. The rest of Drummond's army was too exhausted after the battle at Lundy's Lane to make a quick and decisive advance on Fort Erie and also it had to be held back to protect its rear because the American squadron had belatedly appeared off the mouth of the Niagara River. Drummond's delay gave the Americans time to strengthen Fort Erie. While British forces on the Canadian side of the river rested, Drummond ordered six hundred men from Fort Niagara to march south and destroy the American supply depots at Black Rock and Buffalo which overlooked the approaches to Fort Erie. However, they failed to achieve their objectives. Militia and the handful of American-allied Iroquois still in the lines spotted the movement and warned the Buffalo garrison in time to ward off the attack. Drummond therefore had to engage in a frustrating and costly siege of Fort Erie from early August until late September. Most of the natives present were British-allied western tribesmen, although a handful of Iroquois continued to serve on both sides. Despite his efforts, Drummond could not dislodge the Americans and he began to lift the siege towards the end of September and, in the process, dismissed the remaining tribesmen from service so that they could take up their annual autumn hunt.[54]

Shortly afterwards, one hundred Grand River warriors, perhaps surprisingly, given their despondency in July, assembled once again for combat in early October when the British learned that the Americans planned another attempt to seize control of the Niagara Peninsula.[55] The first wave of a large American force crossed the Niagara River near Fort Erie to advance against the British near Chippawa on 10 October. However, after British light troops bloodied their advanced detachments and before the rest of the American army could be deployed effectively, word reached General Brown that control of Lake Ontario had fallen decisively to the British with the launching of the 112-gun warship, HMS *St Lawrence* in Kingston. Believing that any victories they might attain would be of little value with the United States Navy now blockaded in Sackett's, the Americans retired to Fort Erie.[56]

The Iroquois returned to the Grand River when a false report reached the Niagara region announcing that the American Lake Erie squadron had landed troops at the mouth of the Grand. General Drummond dispatched reinforcements from the Lincoln Militia, the 19th Light Dragoons, and the 103rd Foot to help the Six Nations defend their homes. A real threat to the tract appeared shortly afterwards in the form of an overland attack. Brigadier-General Duncan McArthur led fifteen hundred mounted volunteers and seventy native allies from Ohio and Michigan along the north shore of Lake Erie to take and destroy property and foodstuffs. Included in his plan was an assault on the Grand River Tract and, if practical, either an attack on Burlington or a rendezvous with the American garrison in Fort Erie. McArthur succeeded in destroying property and looting foodstuffs in the white settlements that General Drummond had hoped to use to supply his forces over the winter. By 6 November McArthur reached Brant's Ford. (Meanwhile, on 5 November the Americans evacuated Fort Erie, blew it up, and returned to Buffalo; the British reoccupied the ruins a few days later.) With the Iroquois villages threatened, 225 British regulars, 150 militia, and 400 Grand River and other warriors took up a defensive position on the east bank of the Grand. The warriors' right to defend their homes clearly took precedence over the summer treaty. After an exchange of shots, McArthur decided not to cross the river under fire, claiming feebly that it was an unexpected rise in the water level on the river, not the men arrayed against him, that made him retire to Amherstburg.[57]

By the time McArthur's raid on the Grand River had been checked and the Americans had evacuated their last soldiers from Fort Erie, the November winds began to blow colder and everyone assumed that the 1814 campaign had come to an end. John Norton summarized his expectations for the next few months: 'We had reason to expect that we might pass the Winter in tranquillity, – unless a favourable opportunity should instigate to us to make Reprisal.'[58] Thus, the Six Nations returned to their villages, probably with a sense of considerable satisfaction in having saved their community from American depredation, but deeply sorrowful about the costs they had incurred in fighting alongside the British over the summer. Some of them, however, likely expected to take to the warpath in the spring, following their customary modes of fighting, to achieve their own traditional ends. What they did not know was that they had returned from the last major action they would fight as an independent force after two centuries of colonial warfare.

Despite the improved tactical performance of the American army, the 1814 Niagara campaign was another British strategic victory. The Americans failed to extend their Upper Canadian holdings beyond what they had occupied on the north shore of Lake Erie since late 1813. In the northwest, the Americans suffered defeat when they attempted to recapture Mackinac in 1814. The British followed up this victory with a number of successes in both the northwest and the far west, due in part to their ability to supply their western native allies from Mackinac by using fur-trade routes to bypass Lake Erie. In Lower Canada, Sir George Prevost, with reinforcements from Europe and Seven Nations warriors, crossed the border into the United States near Lake Champlain in September 1814 as part of the larger effort to bring the war to a close. He bungled the invasion and, after some inconclusive skirmishing at Plattsburgh, withdrew into Lower Canada when the Americans defeated the British flotilla on Lake Champlain. On the Atlantic seaboard, however, increased efforts by a strengthened Royal Navy were so effective that American international trade dropped by 90 per cent by 1814 from its pre-war levels. British troops also launched raids along the Atlantic coast to help force an end to the war by putting pressure directly on American territory. Although these attacks were of limited tactical value – the British captured Washington and occupied much of Maine, but lost battles outside Baltimore and New Orleans (the latter, a great disaster, occurring after the war had ended) – they helped to increase opposition to Mr Madison's War and speed peace negotiations underway in Belgium. [59]

As in previous wars the Iroquois between 1812 and 1814 had proved to be major players in the struggles for control over the Great Lakes region. Many of the British successes, particularly before sizeable numbers of reinforcements arrived in 1814, were due in large part to the efforts of Iroquois and other aboriginal allies. In the west, the diverse people in Tecumseh's alliance were so important during the crucial first year of hostilities that it is impossible to imagine the British enjoying the dominance they did in that theatre without native support until the autumn of 1813 (and in the far west until the end of the war). On the Niagara Peninsula, Iroquois and other warriors performed important roles in the defence of the region. Again, it is hard to envisage the British doing as well in that theatre without native help, when Iroquois actions are taken into account at such pivotal engagements as Queenston Heights, Beaver Dams, and the blockade of Fort George. To the east, where Sir George Prevost had concentrated British strength to guard Lower Canada, Seven Nations assistance was less decisive but nevertheless important to the preservation of British territory. In hindsight, the most important outcome of the War of 1812 was the successful defence of British territory, which meant that the Canadian experiment in building a North American society was not brought to a premature and violent end through American conquest. That outcome could not have been achieved without aboriginal support for the king's cause. [60]

On the American side, Iroquois allies provided the United States with a competent light infantry force in an army that fought without an adequate supply of such troops. Unfortunately for the Americans, they did not utilize their aboriginal allies effectively and, except for Sandy Creek and Chippawa, reaped few strategic benefits from having native combatants in their ranks. Long-standing Six Nations unhappiness with the United States and their reluctance to support the Americans limited the potential of the Iroquois to begin with, but within these restraints there were fundamental flaws in the way the Americans employed native allies which wasted the potential that did exist. Ambivalence towards aboriginal forces sapped Iroquois energy and either inhibited commanders from understanding the value of native assistance or stopped them from maximizing that potential when they agreed to deploy them in the invasion of Canada. In combat, the Americans generally did not provide enough close support for the Iroquois. This failure likely stemmed from a combination of their qualms about fighting alongside aboriginal forces, the general limitations in their military competence, especially before 1814, and the specific weakness in their light infantry arm throughout the war. Conversely, the poor performance of American light troops allowed the British-allied warriors to optimize their destructive capabilities against their enemies, as demonstrated in particular at Queenston Heights and during the blockade of Fort George. As well, the British practice of providing their own light forces to support native allies significantly improved the chances of achieving objectives and helped compensate for some of the weaknesses of aboriginal combat, such as a high desertion rate under fire. [61]

The value of the Iroquois in combat was all the more remarkable when two important points are factored into an understanding of their place in the conflict. The first was the capacity of the Iroquois to make major contributions despite the serious and ongoing divisions within their communities and the problems they faced with their white allies. Perhaps the best example of this capacity occurred on the Grand River where different parties competed for support and where the army and the Indian Department devoted considerable effort to subverting each other rather than rallying the Six Nations to fight the Americans. The second point is that it is not fair, in assessing aboriginal contributions, to compare warriors to regular troops instead of to militia and volunteers, because warriors, like militiamen and volunteers, were only part-time fighters with larger roles to play in their society. Yet they outperformed their white peers consistently throughout the war. By keeping this comparison in mind, and by remembering the Iroquois-centred motivations that lay behind their participation in the war, it is much easier to understand their apparent shortcomings and appreciate their combat successes. The weakness of Grand River support for the British in July 1812 and June 1813, for example, paralleled the coolness of their Upper Canadian neighbours for the king's cause at these same moments. This is an important consideration because historians generally have made the mistake of equating aboriginal forces to regulars and then found them wanting. [62]

There is a third point to consider as well. While it is true that the white population in Upper Canada did not consider a mass shift in its allegiance such as the Grand River people did at critical points in the war (although pro-American sentiment ran high among in the population), white Upper Canadians, unlike the Six Nations, did not have to face the prospects of having their land confiscated and their very viability as a society destroyed if the Americans won, and therefore they had no need to consider the same kinds of desperate measures that the Iroquois were forced to contemplate.

8

'Give Us Hopes of Finding Some Relief':
1815 and Beyond

We have now heard the pleasing sound of Peace; but the distress of our Families for want of provisions renders it insensible to all kinds of News unless it should be such as would give us hopes of finding some relief for them.

Grand River Speech, March 1815[1]

The Iroquois learned about the end of hostilities early in 1815. Like most people on the war-torn northern front, they were glad peace had returned and were anxious for a return to normalcy in their lives. The transition was not easy, not only because of the human and material losses but also because freak weather systems retarded the re-establishment of agriculture to pre-war levels and government officials were slow in fulfilling their obligations to the Iroquois. After 1815, on both sides of the border, massive white immigration overwhelmed the aboriginal population so that the Iroquois quickly ceased to be a potent military or diplomatic force. This change made it easy for the dominant societies to shunt their old allies aside. In Canada, most whites began to see native peoples as a dying race and as Crown wards who ought to be integrated into the broader society. The situation was worse in the United States, where the Six Nations had to fight a long and difficult rearguard action to keep at least some of their lands out of the hands of predatory speculators and hostile governments wanting to expel them to the west far beyond their traditional homelands. Within their own communities, the war exacerbated old internal divisions on the one hand, while, on the other, it reinforced pride in the warrior legacy, a pride that remained alive beyond the demise of the conflict's last veterans towards the end of the nineteenth century.

Serious diplomatic efforts to end hostilities between Great Britain and the United States got underway in the Belgian city of Ghent in 1814. During the opening stages of the peace talks, the Americans hoped to achieve their goals in going to war. However, the events of 1814 made their position untenable. The United States teetered on the brink of bankruptcy, the armed forces had failed to achieve their objectives, recruiting fell below the rate at which men were being lost, and a secessionist movement seemed to be forming in New England. The American delegation at the peace conference dropped its initial claims for the resolution of maritime controversies between the two countries, for restitution for the destruction of property during British wartime blockades and raids, for compensation for, or the return of slaves who had fled to British ships on the Atlantic seaboard, and, most important of all, for the cession of the Canadas to the United States. Instead, they merely sought to achieve a peace treaty that would not see the United States lose anything it had held before the war began.[2]

In addition to achieving their primary objective of retaining Canada, the British thought it might be possible to redraw the border to make their North American colonies more defensible in the event of future hostilities, primarily by creating a native buffer state in the Old Northwest. Such an agreement would right many of the wrongs of 1783 and 1794, especially if, as the British hoped, neither white power should later acquire sovereignty over the new polity which they assumed would ally itself to Britain. The king's diplomats suggested that the state's northern border be the existing British–American boundary, and its southern one be the line established in the 1795 Treaty of Greeneville. This 650,000-square-kilometre territory represented one-seventh of the United States land mass and was home to 100,000 whites and perhaps as many as 43,000 aboriginal people.[3] The Madison administration simply would not give up so much territory. In a letter to British negotiator Henry Goulburn, John Quincy Adams expressed the prevailing American view that it was inconceivable to leave such a vast region 'to perpetual barrenness and solitude' so that 'a few hundred savages might find wild beasts to hunt upon it.'[4] In this and other exchanges, the British diplomat recoiled at the severity of the American rebuttal of the proposal. He wrote that before coming to Ghent he 'had no idea of the fixed determination which there is in the heart of every American to extirpate the Indians & appropriate Their territory.'[5]

The British failures at Baltimore and Plattsburgh, along with American dominance in the Detroit theatre in 1814, weakened the case for a buffer

state and made it difficult to argue for a redrawn border without a corresponding willingness to continue the war longer than either the British
government or the king's subjects wished. As the negotiators quarrelled
over a treaty, a developing European crisis led the British to make a generous peace, mainly at the expense of the western tribes. Negotiations to
end the great European conflicts following Napoleon's abdication were
in trouble and the government installed in Paris by the allies stood ready
to collapse the moment Napoleon returned from exile.[6] Hence, it was
important to end the North American war and to get the troops back to
Europe, even if it meant giving up on demands for a better border and
an aboriginal homeland, so long as the British retained Canada. On
24 December 1814 the peace commissioners signed a draft treaty, with
both sides agreeing to return captured territory on the principle of re-
establishing the status quo that existed between the two powers and their
aboriginal allies before the war. News of the draft settlement reached
Upper Canada in February 1815, followed a few weeks later by word that
the British and American governments had ratified the Treaty of Ghent.

For most of the white population of the Canadas, this was good news.
The war was over and the defence of British North America had been
successful. These facts, combined with the superior performance of
the king's forces and his native allies, told Canadians that Great Britain
had won the War of 1812. For the United Kingdom, retention of the
North American colonies proved to be of enormous importance for the
empire's commercial and maritime greatness in subsequent decades.
Across the border, Americans too were relieved that peace had returned.
They forgot their reasons for going to war, the poor performance of their
armies, and focused instead on their successes at Baltimore, Plattsburgh,
and New Orleans to claim that they had won a second war of independence against British efforts to reverse the outcome of the American Revolution! To bolster their arguments, they pointed to the resolution of the
maritime disputes as proof of their success, but to do so they had to over-
look the fact that diplomacy had settled impressment even before hostilities had commenced and that the blockade of Europe ended simply
because Britain had defeated Napoleon. Furthermore, Britain did not
renounce its right to impose similar conditions in the future, and would
offend the United States a century later with a European blockade during
the early years of the First World War before America joined the Allied
cause against Germany.

Even though the British did not demand territorial adjustments and
the creation of a native buffer state, they had a section placed in the

treaty, Article IX, to prevent the Americans from punishing the tribes for their alliance with King George III. Instead, the natives were to have their territorial and other rights of the pre-war period returned to them. The British agreed to do the same with respect to the natives with whom they were at war, such as the Iroquois in New York and Pennsylvania as well as the Sandusky Senecas of Ohio, but the implications for them were insignificant because there were no hostile aboriginal nations living within British territory and no war-related land ownership conflicts with the native population. This article had to be forced upon the reluctant American diplomats, and their acceptance of it seems to have been one of the turning points in the negotiations to end the war because it led the British government to decide to continue with the peace talks rather than prosecute the war further.[7]

Ultimately, however, Article IX became a dead letter in the United States: the British were not willing to use armed might to enforce American compliance in the post-war years because it simply was not in the interests of Great Britain or her Canadian colonies to wage an enormous, perhaps doubtful, and certainly unpopular war to force the Americans to respect that article. (One historian has suggested that the Americans did not act in good faith in the first place in agreeing to it.)[8] Furthermore, the treaty merely stated that the tribes were to be returned to their pre-war status, but said nothing about enjoying that status forever. As early as 1816 the United States began to exclude the British from the Old Northwest in order to cut the ties between the tribes and the Crown that had proved to be so troublesome between 1775 and 1815. In 1816 Congress prohibited British subjects from trading with aboriginal peoples in American territory and the army established forts on the white–native frontier to block the trade routes from Canada. By 1817 the Americans negotiated treaties with the last of the western tribes who had fought against the United States. These treaties established peace and restored aboriginal rights, but placed them under American 'protection.' In subsequent years the United States displaced the natives of the Old Northwest despite the Treaty of Ghent, continued aboriginal visits to Canada in order to maintain their alliance with the British, and a few military acts of aboriginal resistance, such as Black Hawk's War in 1832.[9]

Article IX was not as important for the Iroquois as it was for the western tribes because most of them, with the exception of the Mingos, had fought alongside the white power in which their land was located. (In the end, the Sandusky Senecas who allied with the Americans were treated as badly by the United States as were the Mingos who had joined the British.) However, the treaty offered safety to individuals who had crossed the border to fight for the 'other side,' and it gave the Iroquois the same immunity from persecution that British subjects and American citizens enjoyed if they chose to enter the territory of their former enemies. As well, it restored the cross-border trading rights aboriginal people had enjoyed under the terms of Jay's Treaty of 1794. For the most part, the Treaty of Ghent confirmed the status quo of the Iroquois in their relationships with the white powers on their respective sides of the border. Those in New York, Pennsylvania, and Ohio continued to live within the jurisdiction of the United States; the Grand River, Tyendinaga, Kahnawake, and Kanesatake people continued to hold their lands within British North America; and the Akwesasne community remained divided by the international border. However, there were problems. One was a decision by the state of New York to ignore the treaty and to stop paying annuities for pre-war land sales to the Canadian-resident Cayugas because the tribe had sided with the British. Ultimately, the Cayugas had to wait until the 1920s for an international court to pass judgment in their favour, which was followed by financial compensation in the 1930s. [10] Yet this was a minor irritant compared to what probably would have happened if the Americans had won the war, since it is unlikely that the Iroquois in Canada would have been left alone on their valuable lands in the face of a victorious, resentful, and expanding America, as had been demonstrated by American behaviour on the frontier in the 1780s and 1790s and as would be manifested again in the post-1815 period.

The war largely confirmed the divided relationships between the Six Nations living across the white border from each other. It was almost unthinkable that the separate league council fires which had burned at Buffalo Creek and on the Grand River could now be united, chiefly because so much bitterness had developed between the Canadian- and American-resident Iroquois, but also because they lived under the suzerainty of two different white powers. While exchanges between the two branches continued after the war and representatives from both sides met to discuss common problems, as they had during the conflict, it would take many years for the war's legacy to ease the distrust between these separated people. [11]

The Canadas needed a much smaller garrison with the return of peace. Therefore, in addition to sending most of the regulars to Europe in the wake of Napoleon's return to France, the Crown disbanded the embodied militia, the locally raised professional regiments, and it encouraged native forces to return to peaceful pursuits. However, the experience of the war led to the transfer of the Indian Department in Upper Canada from the authority of the lieutenant-governor to that of the commander-in-chief in 1816 in order to avoid the problems that had troubled the generals during the conflict.[12] To ease the transition to peacetime conditions, Sir George Prevost kept supplies of government goods flowing to the tribes 'with a liberal hand' until traders could re-establish themselves, at which point the government planned to reduce gift-giving to peacetime levels.[13] In March 1815, just after learning of the return of peace, the Grand River's leaders made it clear that their destitute people needed a considerable amount of help. In March and April officials delivered tonnes of pork and flour along with cloth, tools, ammunition, utensils, and other supplies as part of their response to the request. [14]

To thank the natives as they returned to pursue their peacetime lives, the army and the Indian Department called the tribes together in council at various points along the border. The meeting for the Grand River people and those of the western nations then living in the Niagara region occurred in April 1815 at Burlington Heights. Lieutenant-Colonel William Claus, on behalf of the Crown, started with the traditional condolence ceremony required at the beginning of negotiations. With the end of the condolence, in which he symbolically dispelled the cloud that hung over the natives because of the loss of so many of their people, the council formally heard the news of the peace and the government's hopes for the tribes. Claus told them that hostilities were to cease 'for the sake of your Women and Children,' and that 'It is therefore my duty to inform all the Nations here assembled that the Hatchet which you so readily took up to assist your Great Father should now be laid down and buried, that it may not be seen – This is the earnest wish of your Father the King and I am confident you will comply with Cheerfulness.' Claus went on to say how sensitive the king was to the sacrifices of the tribes and how he would continue to maintain his friendship and provide gifts. More important he informed them that in making peace 'your interests were not neglected, nor would peace have been made' with the United States 'had they not consented to include you in the treaty which they at first refused to listen to.' Next, he read Article IX to them, which he said secured 'to you the peaceable possession of all the Country which you possessed before the late War, and the road is now open and free for you to pass and repass without interruption.' Claus concluded with his hope that the peace chiefs would resume their leadership roles, and he asked the warriors and war chiefs to take up non-violent pursuits. He also notified the natives that pensions would be paid to the widows and families of those who fell in the war and he requested the village chiefs to do their part in looking after these people. Finally, he advised them that they soon would receive more clothing and provisions. [15]

The tribes heard the words of the British and made their replies after condoling with the king for the loss of so many of his children in the conflict. One speaker was an Onondaga war chief, Sir Johns. His reply contained some exaggeration: 'At the commencement of the troubles We who live at the Grand River tho' a small people our Doors were open to your news, and putting confidence in the Great Spirit we did not hesitate to take up the Tomahawk – You are perfectly well acquainted with our conduct during the War – We consider ourselves of one Heart with the King and we joined him willingly.' [16] Although happy with the end of hostilities, Sir Johns and other speakers expressed disappointment that an independent homeland had not been created for the western tribes. His reaction was only natural given that the aboriginal people had seen the creation of a native state as a fundamental objective for fighting and because the British had assured their allies throughout the war that its creation would be a priority in negotiating peace with the Americans. [17] Yet, if the documentary record is reasonably accurate, there seems to have been less disappointment among the Iroquois in Canada over this issue than might have been expected, perhaps because a homeland in the Northwest was of symbolic rather than material importance to them so long as they could retain their existing territories and trading relationships. As well, fatigue, particularly after the Chippawa disaster of 1814, may simply have shifted opinion at the Grand River to a desire for the war to end, without significant concern over how it ended so long as the fundamental interests of the Iroquois in their lands were settled satisfactorily.

On a more modest level, the Grand River people complained that they still had not received bounties for their participation at Detroit and Beaver Dams or for the prisoners they had turned over to the British. In the end, they had to wait until 1817 to receive payment for the Beaver Dams prisoners, and as late as 1819 some still had not received their prize money for Detroit. (This sort of delay was typical for all combatants, white or native.) Reflecting the differences between native and white concepts of family, they requested that widows' pensions be extended to other relatives of the victims. They also wanted the government to give them food and farm implements to help them through to harvest time. As well, they asked the Crown to construct a grist mill, to supply cattle, and to re-establish a government blacksmith on their tract. They told the British that they considered the Grand River lands they had sold to white settlers who had subsequently fled to the United States during the war to have been forfeited back to the tribes. Finally, they asked the British to help arrange an exchange of prisoners taken at Chippawa between them and the Iroquois from the American side of the border.[18]

The end of hostilities between the two white powers did not lead automatically to peace between the divisions of the old Six Nations Confederacy. Therefore, the Iroquois of Grand River and of New York held a council at Fort George on 31 August and 1 September 1815 to negotiate peace between the two groups and between the king and the Iroquois in New York. At the council, they exchanged white wampum belts to formalize the end of hostilities and to symbolize that ill will had been removed from their hearts, thereby cancelling the need to avenge the deaths suffered at each others' hands. They condoled with each other for their wartime losses and metaphorically buried 'the Tomahawk to the depth of a pine Tree under ground.' Both Iroquois groups then went home loaded with British presents as gestures of the king's good will.[19]

Yet tensions continued between the Iroquois who were divided by the international border. The Grand River branch believed that they had formed a united league among themselves in the ancient way under the old laws when they moved to Canada in the 1780s. They claimed to be the true confederacy and to have shown the right spirit in fighting alongside the British, an attitude they could adopt comfortably given the outcome of the war. They considered the Iroquois in New York to be mere broken bands without any coherence as a confederacy, scattered as they were across New York State on their isolated reservations. The people from New York countered that the Canadian-resident Six Nations had left the confederacy and cut themselves off from the league by abandoning their ancestral homes. However, in the aftermath of the war many Iroquois in New York swore allegiance to the United States, perhaps subverting the strength of their argument, as people shifted their loyalties to the increasingly dominant white society whose settlers were filling up their old homelands with unprecedented speed.[20]

In early 1815 a delegation of Iroquois in New York travelled to Washington with Indian agent Jasper Parrish to see James Monroe, the acting secretary of war. They wanted the government to relieve their financial plight, made worse by the war, especially for the burned-out Tuscaroras, and to gather rewards for the sacrifices they had made serving the interests of the United States.[21] Monroe replied with soothing words, speaking of the 'great affection' the president held for those who had been 'faith-

ful to the United States in the hour of danger' and of how he mourned
the loss of those who had fallen in battle. He announced that a pension
of two hundred dollars would be granted to the families of the killed as
well as other recompense for the wounded, promised presents and payments to the tribes, announced a resolution of the financial problems of
the Senecas that stemmed from the suspension of the Bank of the United
States, and arranged special compensation for the Tuscaroras.[22] Sadly,
the American government did not act in good time, despite continued
protests by the Iroquois, and morale among the tribes in New York plum-
meted. They had fought for the United States, they had suffered losses,
but they found their needs ignored by those who had demanded their
help. As of 1816 some Iroquois still had not received their military
wages.[23] To make matters worse, freak frosts and snowfalls destroyed
crops in the summer of 1816 because volcanic ash from a massive erup-
tion in the southern hemisphere blocked much of the sun's light that
year. Indian agent Erastus Granger lamented: 'The situation of the Indians is truly deplorable. They have exerted themselves for the year past in
trying to raise crops, but have failed in their expectations. Their prospects have failed. Their hunting ground is gone. They have availed themselves of the money arising from their public funds, but they fall short.
They are in fact in a state of starvation.' Granger pleaded for increased
support and noted how the Iroquois received short shrift even in comparison to the way the government treated the tribes that had been at war
with the United States.[24] Money began to get through by 1817 with the
resumption of federal annuities (suspended since 1813) and the payment
of $3,000 in pensions and awards to various individuals. Meanwhile, Eras-
tus Granger found himself criticized for looking after his own interests
at Iroquois expense. The Tuscaroras protested when he kept $350 of
an $8,000 federal payment to them as compensation for the loss of their
village. Granger countered that he needed the money to cover his expenses. (New York State also gave the Tuscaroras $5,000 as compensation
for the burning of their community.)[25]

   Despite their alliance to the United States, the Iroquois in New York
continued to endure the loss of their land and other forms of exploitation. The war had slowed the migration of settlers, but the return of
peace in 1815 and the completion of the Erie Canal in 1825 saw a huge
increase in the flow of people into the region with its attendant threats to
aboriginal holdings. As early as 1817 the Iroquois watched helplessly as
white authorities did nothing to stop settlers from cutting valuable timber
on their property. Soon after that, they reeled under the coercive moves

of the Ogden Land Company to force them to sell their homes and move away from New York. (Their old brigade commander in the war, Peter B. Porter, was one of the company's prominent shareholders.) The actions of the Ogden Land Company heralded the beginning of a thirty-year crisis during which the Iroquois resident in New York were defrauded of much of their territory by grasping speculators supported by compliant officials. At the same time, the government pressured the Iroquois to abandon their ancestral land and move away to the west. Among one large group that went to Kansas in 1846, half of the people died within a year and the rest returned to New York, although other groups did stay in the west where many of their descendants live today in Iroquois communities in Wisconsin and Oklahoma. It was not until the 1840s and 1850s that the process of shoving the Six Nations off their homelands slowed, and reversed somewhat, with the return of parts of some of the lost reservations.[26]

Some Oneidas, whose families had fought alongside the Americans in both the revolution and the War of 1812, sold their territory to purchase a 2,200-hectare tract in Upper Canada near London in the 1830s. In the 1840s more Oneidas joined them in the face of pressure from whites to leave New York. Those who moved to Canada were influenced in part by a sense that the Grand River settlement had become the most important community of the old League of the Six Nations. They joined the Six Nations Confederacy centred on the Grand, which helped to ameliorate some of the disunion that had developed between them and the Iroquois in British territory over the alliance of the Oneidas with the United States. In Ohio, the Sandusky Senecas, Mingos, and some Grand River Mohawks who had emigrated there after the war ceded most of their land to the United States in return for three small reservations in 1819. In 1831 those who remained moved west of the Mississippi as part of the expulsion of aboriginal people from the eastern United States following the passing of the Indian Removal Act in 1830.[27]

With these encroachments on Iroquois villages, farms, and other reservation lands, along with the loss of traditional hunting grounds, there was an acceleration in adopting white ways of living in the years after 1815 on both sides of the border.[28] For some, this change did not occur without causing immense grief. One of those afflicted by the transformations was Cornplanter. In 1820, as he surveyed the stresses facing his people, he became morose and withdrawn. The Great Spirit told him in visions that his people should have nothing more to do with whites. Whites were crazy and it was wrong for the natives to follow their customs. Cornplanter burned his war trophies as symbols of the evils of the Euroamerican wars that had proved to be so calamitous for the Iroquois. He changed his name to Nonuk, meaning 'Cold' or 'Dead,' and lived in miserable poverty until his death in 1835.[29] Presumably other Iroquois looked back on their post-war experiences, and ruefully remembered the arguments of the neutralist parties at the outbreak of hostilities, words such as: 'Why ... should we endanger the comfort, even the existence of our families, to enjoy their smiles only for the day in which they need us?'[30] Some Senecas lost all confidence in their traditional leaders, whom they held responsible for the alienation of their land and the destruction of their culture. In 1848 the people of the Allegany and Cattaraugus reservations deposed their chiefs and created a Seneca republic with a written constitution and an elected government which continues to this day.[31]

The years after the war also proved to be wearisome for the Grand River people as they attempted to return to their agricultural endeavours after three years of wartime upset and the disastrously cold weather of 1816 which destroyed most of the harvest. Destitute, they sought assistance to survive. In 1816 and 1817 the government provided flour and corn from its own meagre stores, plus cash, seeds, twine to make fishing nets, and other supplies.[32] However, the government was slow to act and, in the process, probably contributed to the deaths of some people from starvation while alienating others who chose to settle in Ohio, to the consternation of some colonial officials who worried, with some exaggeration, that 'the American Government, after having for years unsuccessfully endeavoured to draw the Six Nations to the American side, have obtained their object, owing to the ignorance of a British Commissary.'[33]

John Norton, having lost his favoured position with the military command, became vulnerable to his enemies in the Indian Department and civil government. In December 1815 the lieutenant-governor of Upper Canada, Francis Gore, who had returned to the province after the war, was upset that the army had elevated Norton during the war, claiming that he had acquired 'a species of influence incompatible with that subordination of the Tribes to the views of His Majesty's Government, which it is so important to preserve.'[34] Lieutenant-General Sir Gordon Drummond, who had become fed up with the man himself, retired Norton with an annual pension of two hundred pounds plus rations, during pleasure (with provision to give his wife, Karighwaycagh, one hundred pounds should she outlive him). Part of the motivation for such a generous pension stemmed from a frank recognition of his outstanding efforts in the war; part, however, sprung from darker concerns. Drummond thought 'the character of this man is so strongly marked by great Ability, design, and Intrigue, that if tempted to change sides he might prove a most dangerous Enemy.'[35] This was an important consideration for someone like Drummond because most British and American leaders in 1815 suspected that the Treaty of Ghent was more of a truce than a permanent peace. He also wanted to end the divisions created by the Norton–Claus conflict and thought removing Norton from a position of power was the best way to do so. The army, knowing that control of the Indian Department would be transferred to the commander-in-chief from the civil authorities – to the civil government's great chagrin – no longer needed parallel leaders within the aboriginal community to counteract the department's influence.[36] Some of Norton's enemies even worked to prevent him from getting his pension, labelling him as an 'imposter' and claiming that his 'insolence and insubordination' had wrought havoc to the management of British–Iroquois relations.[37] Despite their hostility, they failed to deprive Norton of his money. For his part, Norton seems to have been content to escape departmental intrigues even though he knew it was he, not Claus, who had been sacrificed in the post-war restructuring of the government's administration of Grand River affairs. (At least the army tried to mitigate the blow by using the return of peace as an excuse to retire Norton gracefully rather than to dismiss him.) [38]

Colonel Claus's own position was enhanced by his appointment to the provincial Executive Council as well as by his decision to live on the Grand and by his appointment by the government to be the trustee of the Grand River community's investments. As he had done before the war, Claus continued to abuse his office for personal profit. In organizing the transfer of Iroquois land to a white speculator, for example, Claus offered to arrange the forgiveness of five years' worth of unpaid interest in return for a bribe. Oddly, his shameful peculation contrasted with an obvious individual dedication to service – even under fire – and with his family's personal losses in the king's services: one son, an officer in the 49th foot, was killed during the war, an adopted boy fell in the battle of Fort George, and a third died while serving as a lieutenant in the 54th Foot in the Cape of Good Hope.[39]

In 1815 John Norton and Karighwaycagh and one of their sons travelled to Britain, where John completed his important journal on aboriginal life, Six Nations history, and Iroquois participation in the course of the war. His wartime services led to the British government's decision to respond favourably to a request that he be honoured with a non-serving major's commission in the army.[40] (An American publication reacted to this news by writing: 'Norton, the Indian chief, celebrated for his murders on our frontier during the late war, has the ... commission of major from the British government.')[41] John and Karighwaycagh returned to Canada in 1816, John carrying letters of recommendation from the British government with him. Their son remained behind with John's Scottish relatives to attend school until 1820. Once home, John spent much of his time on the Grand working his farm, advocating social reforms to improve the lot of the Six Nations, and serving the church, including translating the Gospel of Saint Matthew into Mohawk. (He had already translated the Gospel of Saint John between 1804 and 1806 for the British and Foreign Bible Society; however, most Mohawk Anglicans preferred to have the Scriptures in English.) Drawing on his own standing within the Six Nations community as well as support from the British government and from such influential people as the Duke of Northumberland and William Wilberforce, Norton found time to reassert his leadership to a degree and to renew his fight with William Claus, especially in arranging pensions for Grand River veterans who had followed him during the war. Norton used his stature, both as a chief and, in consequence of his majority, as a retired army officer, to convince the governor-in-chief, Sir John Sherbrooke, to order the Indian Department to stop William Claus from showing favouritism to his supporters in the distribution of government largesse at the expense of Norton's people. As late as 1819 Colonel Claus received orders to get along with his nemesis.[42]

In 1823 a court found Norton guilty of manslaughter and fined him twenty-five pounds after he mortally wounded a man by the name of Joe Crawford (or Big Arrow) in a duel. Stories of what happened conflict, some suggesting Karighwaycagh may have had an affair with Crawford (a married man who lived with the Nortons and who had been one of Norton's warriors during the war).[43] For his part, John Norton claimed that Karighwaycagh had complained that Crawford had 'offered her the grossest insult a woman can receive'; however, he added mysteriously that he had disapproved of her behaviour as well as Crawford's and had told both of them to leave his house, but that they had refused to do so.[44] At first, Karighwaycagh maintained her innocence (other people were not convinced and she seems to have admitted her guilt later), condemned Crawford for his insults, and upbraided John for not protecting her honour. At that point, Norton said he had been challenged by Crawford to a duel, during which they both were shot at three paces. In the aftermath, Norton decided he had to get away for his own emotional well-being as well as from fear that Crawford's relatives would seek to avenge the death by killing him, even though the Nortons were prepared to follow Mohawk tradition by giving presents to the deceased's family in atonement.[45] He gave his wife a portion of his pension (which she collected until her death in 1827) and left the Grand. Norton, then in his sixties, journeyed far to the south with a Cherokee cousin who had lived with him since 1809. He apparently reached Mexican territory by 1826 and was on his way to the Pacific Ocean. At that point he disappears from the historical record, although a nephew believed he lived until 1831. William Claus only enjoyed Norton's absence for a short time. He died in 1826 after a five-year battle with cancer.[46]

John Norton's story is representative of that of most of the Grand River people immediately following the war in that they returned to their peacetime pursuits but continued to live with the legacy of the conflict in the forefront of their minds. That legacy could not be forgotten because of the reminders of the war years around them, from the deteriorated condition of their farms to the daily pains of those who had been wounded or who suffered ongoing health problems from the deprivations of living at the centre of the conflict and to the sad absence of familiar faces.

To the east, the Mohawks of Tyendinaga also resumed their peacetime lives after three years of wartime disruptions, although the transition was easier for them because their participation in the war had been limited and the community sat outside the main areas of conflict. The Tyendinaga people seem to have been forgotten by British authorities throughout much of the war. In both 1813 and 1814 they wrote to Sir George Prevost volunteering their services, but he seems to have failed to have taken them up on their offer. Aside from whatever service individuals contributed in small war parties, the only action they saw as a group was at Crysler's Farm in November 1813.[47]

The Seven Nations of Canada, like everyone in the Great Lakes region, were hit hard by the frigid summer of 1816 and needed government support. In January 1817 the government, with its own storehouses empty, turned down a Kanesatake request for emergency supplies. However, the community likely received relief at the same time Crown officials delivered foodstuffs to Kahnawake and Akwesasne in March. Shortages were so bad that the food – including biscuit, salt meat, and dried peas – probably came from Britain.[48]

In 1821 the Seven Nations experienced another serious setback in the preservation of their way of life. The North West Company of Montreal amalgamated with the Hudson's Bay Company of London and many

Seven Nations men consequently lost their jobs as traders, trappers, and employees in the fur trade in the Northwest. Several hundred people therefore moved west to settle in what today is Alberta (although similar numbers of Seven Nations Iroquois had already moved west in 1798). Others found alternate employment in the emerging Ottawa Valley timber trade.[49]

Of all the Seven Nations, the people of Akwesasne were most adversely affected by the war. The conflict ripped their community apart. Then, with the return of peace, they had to live with uncertainty while a British–American commission reviewed the location of the international boundary at Akwesasne as part of a process to mark the border with greater precision than had been done with inadequate information in earlier years. In 1817 officials told pro-British people at Akwesasne not to improve their holdings until the border could be defined accurately. At the same time, further anxieties about their future arose because some American-resident Iroquois sold a portion of their land to the state of New York.[50] The most enthusiastic supporters of the British during the war communicated their frustration in a letter to Crown officials in 1815: 'Immediately after the declaration of war, we and our children opened our doors and parted from our families to join the King's army and assist in opposing the enemy, since which time our wives, as you are aware, have been exposed to the inclemencies of the weather on islands and strange places, while we and our warriors were engaged in the constant service of our Great Father.' When peace returned, the warriors expected 'to return to the quiet of our homes and property,' but instead 'found to our great mortification that those who had joined the enemy and those who had remained neutral were in possession of the village.'[51]

As the years passed the divisions at Akwesasne hardened. The British refused to allow supporters of the American party to live on the Canadian side of the border, and both British and American officials paid annuities and gave presents only to their own supporters; prior to the war both governments had ignored the border in their dealings with the community. The British party got some relief when the Crown added new land to the Canadian portion of the community. However, the grant did not occur until after tensions had nearly degenerated into armed conflict between the American and British parties in 1818. For generations afterwards, these divisions poisoned relations among the Akwesasne people.[52]

In 1830 the British Indian Department ceased to be a military agency and became a civilian one, financed by the British government, controlled by the governor, but watched closely by colonial politicians. This change followed a shift in policy in the post-war years that attempted to reduce government costs for supporting native peoples by integrating them into the broader white agricultural society.[53] In 1816, for example, the lieutenant-governor of Upper Canada noted that the state did not interfere with the internal workings of the Grand River people but chose to respect their 'National Independence.' Yet by 1823 his successor argued that the time had come to assimilate the Six Nations into the body politic of the province because they now lived at the very centre of the organized and settled parts of the colony.[54] Both the public and the government – particularly in Britain – began to see aboriginal peoples not so much as valuable military or diplomatic allies, but rather as unsophisticated wards who should be encouraged to adopt completely the ways of Euroamerican society on foundations consisting of a mix of Christianity, economic liberalism, and individualism. In the 1820s and 1830s a combination of greed for 'undeveloped' aboriginal lands, a sense that natives had to be protected from moral and financial ruin at the hands of unprincipled Upper Canadians, and a growing view that the state had the right to exercise civil jurisdiction over native communities persuaded many people that the Iroquois in the province should be removed to a kind of government-controlled sanctuary on Manitoulin Island in Lake Huron. (Some native people also had advocated moving away from white influences to preserve their society from unwanted intrusions while others called for changes in aboriginal social structures to replicate white systems.) Although the Six Nations never moved to Manitoulin, the Iroquois of Akwesasne, Grand River, and Tyendinaga lost land during this period. Encroachments at Tyendinaga in 1820 and 1835, for example, saw that community shrink to 7,100 hectares from the 38,000 it had been at its largest. In the 1840s the Indian Department reorganized the Grand River lands, which had been infiltrated by large numbers of white squatters and other people, into a single 22,000–hectare block, plus some additional land scattered elsewhere on their old tract, representing less than one-tenth of the original grant in the 1780s. The consolidation took place over the protests of the Grand River people, who now were left with a limited land base of ten hectares per person. The Six Nations people who lived elsewhere on the lost land had to abandon their homes, move to the reduced reserve, and start their lives anew.[55]

To make matters worse, most of the proceeds from selling Six Nations land was lost to them when, against their will, they were were forced by the government to invest in the Grand River Navigation Company, which limped along on the brink of insolvency from its founding in 1832 to its bankruptcy in 1861. The company hoped to turn the Grand into a navigable river, and in the process flooded and expropriated some of the best agricultural areas and destroyed the fishery, again against the will of the Six Nations. Scandalously, their funds were invested by provincial government officials who were closely connected to the company's management and who seem to have abused their positions as trustees to protect their business friends and associates from financial ruin. Ultimately, the Iroquois held over 80 per cent of the company's stock, although they went unrepresented on its board of directors and never received any dividends. So consuming was the company of their funds that over the hard winter and global economic dislocations of 1836–7 some people perished from a want of food because no money could be freed to relieve their distress, while the government's inability to pay annuities on Iroquois investments over a seven-year period beginning at that time impoverished a great many others.[56]

Except for some minor activity in the Upper and Lower Canadian rebellions of 1837, when most of the Iroquois in British North America actively supported the government, the War of 1812 was the last time they fought in a major conflict as a distinct group. (Some Kahnawake people sided with the rebels in Lower Canada, while some Iroquois in New York joined rebels from the upper province in their camps along the Canadian–American border.)[57] When the Tyendinaga Mohawks rallied to protect the Crown during the rebellion crisis, they came 'not ... with tomahawk in hand, half-naked bedaubed bodies, and painted faces' according to one ethnocentric white observer, 'but armed with rifles, comfortably clad, and as orderly in their demeanour and appearance as any of their white comrades.'[58] Early photographs from the 1840s show the Iroquois with European hair cuts and clothing, documenting the transition away from the warrior dress of previous centuries.[59]

Yet a sense of their distinctive military tradition remained strong among the Iroquois. During the 1840s Upper Canadians raised money to construct a monument at Queenston Heights to commemorate the famous 1812 battle and to re-inter the remains of Sir Isaac Brock and his aide-de-camp, John Macdonell. This was the second monument on the heights, the original from 1824 having been blown up by a Canadian dissident living in the United States during the tensions that followed the rebellion. The aboriginal communities in the province participated in the subscription; most gave ten pounds, including the recently arrived Thames River Oneidas who had fought on the American side during the

war. The Grand River people made the largest native donation, seventy-
five pounds.[60] Along with these contributions, the different groups gave
speeches that revealed their understanding of the War of 1812, the
United States, and their own self-images at that time. The Tyendinaga
Mohawks made these observations about the Upper Canadian rebels
and their American friends in light of the destruction of the first monument: 'Our country has been insulted, and we are very angry at it. We
heard of the shameful conduct of our American neighbours, when some
bad people [the 1837 rebels] raised a disturbance here, and were forced
to run away they received these bad men as their friends, and gave them
every assistance to Stab and destroy our Mother [Queen Victoria]. But
defeat and shame followed their repeated attempts. We know the Americans of old – our father told us how they used *them*, and we see every
year how they are abusing and murdering our red brethren in the west.'
On the subject of their own military prowess, they said: 'although our
tomahawks are buried and we wish to sit-down, yet our warriors have not
forgotten the *war whoop*, and whenever it is raised at the call of our
Queen we will get up like *one man* to punish our enemy. Brother
Remember this: *we are always ready*.'[61] (One old chief from Tyendinaga
expressed a more sarcastic opinion when called out during the rebellion: 'White man fall out – then send for poor Indian whom he call dog,
to help him!')[62]

The Grand River address displayed similar views to those of the Tyendinaga people, although the language used in their presentation had lost
much of the 'Iroquois voice' of earlier documents. Part of it read: 'We
and our Fathers endured the fatigues and privations of war fighting by
the side of the illustrious dead and wish to contribute ... to forward the
speedy completion of the work to commemorate our veneration for the
name of the illustrious and valiant Brother deceased, and to record our
horror at the perpetration of so base a deed as the destruction of the
Tomb where his hallowed remains had been interred.'[63] There was, of
course, some irony in the Grand River readiness to donate money to
Brock's monument given the ambivalence towards the British alliance
many of them had felt during much of his time as commander-in-chief in
Upper Canada and his own negative opinions about them in contrast to
the respect he had felt for the western tribes. It seems that a good portion
of the military myths and loyalties of the broader society in Canada,
formed partly by a shared trial by fire, had been adopted by many Iroquois as their own by this time. Despite the difficulties of the Canadian-
resident Iroquois with white society, the even grimmer situation of the

Iroquois south of the border seems to have affirmed the validity of their decision to fight against the United States in the war. If the Americans could be so callous to their old allies, what protection could British-allied or even neutral Iroquois have expected if the United States had conquered Canada?

In New York, the aging warriors and their families could take satisfaction in their own exploits in the war, but seem to have been excluded from the larger American patriotism regarding the conflict. On one occasion, at a meeting of the New-York Historical Society in 1847, a white speaker gave an address in which he claimed that 'the Iroquois had left no monuments.' This offended a Cayuga in the audience, Waowowanoonk (or Dr Peter Wilson), who stood up and said: 'In your last war with England, your red brother – your elder brother – still came up to help you as of old on the Canada frontier! Have we, the first holders of this prosperous region, no longer a share in your history?'[64]

Towards the middle of the nineteenth century, Iroquois men who wished to pursue the way of the warrior had little choice but to abandon their distinct traditions and join white military establishments. A year before the Iroquois in Canada helped put down the rebellions, dressed and accoutred much like their white militia neighbours, Jacob Jameson, a Seneca from New York, died in the Mediterranean while serving as a surgeon's mate in the United States Navy. During the American Civil War, Iroquois men were integrated fully into the Union army as much as any other recruits. One Seneca, Ely Parker, became a brigadier-general. On the Canadian side of the border, in the 1880s fifty people from Kahnawake left their homes to serve as boatmen on the Nile River as part of the Canadian contingent that participated in the British army's relief of Khartoum. A photographer recorded a striking instance of this integration at that time. He took a picture of the Six Nations men of Grand River in their Victorian era fighting garb, consisting of the blue trousers, red coats, and white helmets of the Canadian militia. They stood in line, two ranks deep, at attention, while their officers, with swords drawn, stood in front. They did not even sport a culturally distinct version of a British uniform such as native regiments in India and elsewhere wore. Aside from their facial features, there is nothing in the photograph to tell the viewer that these men were not white.[65]

It is difficult to imagine anything other than a substantial amount of acculturation happening in the mid- and late-nineteenth century. Farming and logging finally replaced hunting, trade, diplomacy, and warfare as primary activities among Iroquois men, and the special customs, dress, and traditions of the Iroquois warrior faded from personal experience with the long years of peace after 1815. At the same time, white powers paid less respect to the Iroquois as a culturally distinct military force, Iroquois populations became insignificant militarily in comparison to the rapidly rising white population, and the removal of other native people south of the Great Lakes to the west eliminated most of the need by white powers for Iroquois diplomatic support. [66]

Despite the integration of the Iroquois into white military establishments, their distinctive heritage lived on in the old people who inspired their juniors with their stories of ancient glories. [67] At about the same time the Grand River militiamen posed for their photograph in their red coats, someone took another picture of three Iroquois veterans of the War of 1812, Jacob Warner, John Tutlee, and John Smoke Johnson. These men, all in their nineties, hold 1812–period weapons in their hands. They wear mainly white clothing, but their faces are unmistakeably native, and proud. [68]

Appendix

Iroquois Population and Combat Strength in 1812

Statistics for the Iroquois resident in Canada are limited for the 1812 period, but there are two documents that allow for a reasonable estimate of the number of Iroquois living in British North America on the eve of the war. The first is a two-year census of the Grand River that gives populations of 1,856 in 1810 and 1,928 in 1811. An examination of the document suggests that the 1811 version was compiled with more care than the other, which probably accounts for some of the change from 1810, although natural increase and immigration to the Grand from elsewhere likely were factors as well. The second document is a list of warriors in the different aboriginal communities in the Great Lakes region in 1812. It estimated, at a rounded figure, 400 warriors for the Grand.[1] Combined with the 1811 census, we have a ratio at Grand River of warriors to total population of 1:4.82, which fits within the 1:4 to 1:5 ratio historians commonly accept for the Great Lakes region in the seventeenth and eighteenth centuries. Based on this ratio, rough estimates can be made of the populations of the Iroquois communities covered by the warrior list in 1812 (see Table A.1).

It should be noted that at Kanesatake there also were 100 Algonkin warriors (or some 482 people in all) living separately from the Iroquois for a combined warrior population of approximately 250 and an aboriginal population of about 1,205. (In 1869 the Algonkins moved to Maniwaki, 300 kilometres to the northwest.) As well, some Iroquois in Canada lived outside of these communities, such as a few members of the Brant family who had a home at Burlington, but their numbers seem to have been small. Other people, because of intermarriage or other reasons, lived in non-Iroquois communities, both native and white, but there is no way of estimating how many of these people counted themselves as Iroquois. Still others, largely from Kahnawake, Akwesasne, and Kanesatake,

TABLE A.1   Estimated Population of Iroquois Communities, c. 1812

Community	Number of warriors	Population estimate
Grand River	400	1,928
Tyendinaga	50	241
Akwesasne	250	1,205
Kanesatake	150	723
Kahnawake	300	1,446
Total	**1,150**	**5,543**

TABLE A.2   Tribal and Village Affiliations, 1811 Grand River Census

Nation	Number of people	Estimated number of warriors
Aughquagas (Oneidas; possibly Tuscaroras and others)	158	33
Cayugas	412	85
Mohawks	436	90
Oneidas	47	10
Onondagas	225	47
Senecas	39	8
Tuscaroras	143	30
Akwesasne people	19	4
Total Iroquois	**1,479**	**307**
Plus		
Delawares	303	63
Tutelos	105	22
others (possibly including some Iroquois)	41	9
Total	**1,928**	**401**

found employment in the fur trade in the far west in what today is Alberta, British Columbia, and the neighbouring parts of the United States; they may not have been counted in these statistics, which might suggest a higher population for the Seven Nations Iroquois than stated above. (For example, 250 people from Kahnawake, Kanesatake, and Akwesasne went west in 1798.) [2]

The 1811 Grand River census divided the population of the tract by tribal and village affiliations, as shown in Table A.2.

TABLE A.3 Breakdown of Nations among New York and Pennsylvania Iroquois, 1816 Census

Nation	Number of people	Estimated number of warriors
Cayugas	125	26
Oneidas	1,031	214
Onondagas	450	93
Senecas	1,879	390
Tuscaroras	255	53
Total	**3,740**	**776**

TABLE A.4 New York and Pennsylvania Iroquois by Location, 1816 Census

Reservation	Nation	Number of people	Estimated number of Warriors
Cattaraugus	Seneca	328	68
Buffalo Creek	Seneca	474	98
" "	Onondaga	210	44
" "	Cayuga	125	26
Tuscarora	Tuscarora	255	53
Tonawanda	Seneca	282	59
Allegany	Seneca	445	92
Genesee River sites	Seneca	305	63
Cornplanter (Penn.)	Seneca	45	9
Onondaga	Onondaga	240	50
Oneida	Oneida	1,031	214
Total		**3,740**	**776**

In the United States an 1816 census enumeration of the New York and Pennsylvania Iroquois gave a population of 3,740 (which, given the above ratio, represented about 776 warriors). These figures seem to be somewhat lower than those for 1812, a result of wartime losses to disease, starvation, and casualties. The breakdown for this population (with an estimate of the number of warriors based on a 1:4.82 ratio) is given in Table A.3.

The 1816 census also listed 250 Brothertown people, 437 Stockbridges, and 65 Delawares (representing about 156 warriors). Because there were no Mohawks on the list, Akwesasne does not seem to have been included, although its people likely were covered in the 1812 British report on war-

TABLE A.5   Iroquois in Ohio, 1819

Community	Number of people	Estimated number of warriors
Sandusky Senecas close to the shores of Lake Erie	348	72
Mohawks and possibly other Six Nations from Canada at Honey Creek	57	12
Mingos at Lewiston	203	42
Total	**608**	**126**

riors. The population (and the estimated number of warriors) is given by location in Table A.4.

The total New York aboriginal population (exclusive of Akwesasne) was 4,492 (3,740 Iroquois; 752 others). That figure is in line with a rough figure of 5,000 in 1824 for the New York aboriginal population, which may have included the American-resident Akwesasne people. With one exception, the above figures conform to other reliable data. The exception is related to the Tuscaroras, who may have been under-represented: a source from 1796 enumerated 400 Tuscaroras in New York, and a record dated 1818 placed the number at 314.[3]

A list of the Iroquois in Ohio dating from 1819 enumerated 608 people living in three communities, to which Table A.5 adds the estimate of the number of warriors. The Honey Creek Mohawks moved to Ohio between 1815 and 1817 and therefore were resident at the Grand River in 1812.[4] The figure of 608 people compares reasonably well with an 1824 figure which listed the Ohio Iroquois population as 688; divided by tribal affiliation rather than place of residence they numbered 380 Cayugas, 100 Senecas, 64 Mohawks, 64 Oneidas, and 80 Onondagas.[5]

While the above figures are estimates based on limited data, we can have some confidence in them for two reasons. One is that the people who compiled the lists were concerned to count the number of Iroquois fairly accurately and had reasonable means to do so.[6] The other is that the larger body of documentation used in this book, which provides numbers of people on campaign, in refugee camps, or elsewhere, does not conflict with these figures. It would have been unusual, for example, to see a community mobilize its entire force of warriors. Therefore, lists of men in the field at any particular time normally should be smaller, and never more than, the numbers indicated above. This is indeed the case, as revealed by a comparison of the figures from above, repeated under 'Number of warriors' in Table A.6, with the data in the last column of that table.

TABLE A.6   Number of Warriors in Action, 1812–1814

Action	Group	Total number of warriors	Number of warriors in action
1812			
Queenston	Grand River Cayugas	85	80
	All Grand River	400	240
Lacolle	Kahnawake	300	233[a]
1813			
Relief of Niagara	Akwesasne	250	60
Peninsula	Kahnawake	300	160
	Kanesatake	150–250	120[b]
Beaver Dams	Seven Nations	800	180
	Grand River Mohawks	90	72
	Grand River Oneidas	10	9
	Grand River Aughquagas	33	11
	Grand River Tuscaroras	30	15
	Grand River Cayugas	85	40
	Grand River Onondagas	47	20
	Grand River Senecas	8	5
	Grand River Delawares	63	25
	Grand River Tutelos	22	4
	Grand River Nanticokes	2	2[c]
Black Rock	Niagara Senecas	225	40[d]
Fort George Picket	NY Iroquois	776	400[e]
Crysler's Farm	Tyendinaga Mohawks	50	30[f]
Lewiston	NY Tuscaroras	53	30[g]
1814			
Various dates	NY Iroquois/Algonkians	932	600[h]
Sandy Creek	NY Oneidas	214	120[i]
Chippawa	NY Iroquois/Algonkians	932	350[j]

[a] John Norton, *The Journal of Major John Norton, 1816,* Carl F. Klinck and James Talmon, eds. (Toronto 1970), 308; Memorandum, 6 Nov. 1812, AO, John Strachan Papers; and C.M. Johnston, *Brant County* (Toronto 1967), 21

[b] E.A. Cruikshank, 'Blockade of Fort George,' Niagara Historical Society, *Transactions* 3 (1898), 28

[c] William Kerr to William Claus, 8 Dec. 1815, in E.A. Cruikshank, ed., in *Documentary History of the Campaigns on the Niagara Frontier, 1812–14,* 9 vols. (Welland and Lundy's Lane 1902–8), 6:122

[d] Erastus Granger to William Armstrong, 9 Aug. 1813, in Charles M. Snyder, ed., *Red and White on the New York Frontier* (Harrison 1978), 68–9

[e] Arthur C. Parker, 'The Senecas in the War of 1812,' *New York History* 15 (1916), 84

[f] Wade Hampton to Armstrong, 1 Nov. 1813, in Cruikshank, ed., *Documentary History of the*

(*continued*)

TABLE A.6 (*concluded*)

Campaigns, 8:119–20; and Eleazer Williams, *Life of Te-ho-ra-qwa-ne-gen, alias Thomas Williams* (Albany 1859), 71

[g] Elias Johnson, *Legends, Traditions and Laws of the Iroquois, or Six Nations, and History of the Tuscarora Indians* (Lockport 1881), 167–70

[h] Muster roll of the Indain warriors, 1814, Vassar College Library, Jasper Parrish Papers. The number 600 is derived from the largest number of warriors sent by the different villages who served at various times during 1814.

[i] J. Mackay Hitsman, *The Incredible War of 1812* (1965; Toronto 1972), 183–6

[j] A captain in Fenton's Regiment of Pennsylvania Volunteers to the *Boston Sentinel*, 7 July 1814, in Cruikshank, ed., *Documentary History of the Campaigns*, 1:49

Likewise, other figures for general Iroquois populations conform more or less to the numbers noted above. For example, at the Buffalo Council in July 1813, when the Iroquois in New York declared war on Upper Canada, Allegany (where pacifism was relatively strong) offered 7 of its estimated 92 warriors, whereas more militant communities offered more, such as Buffalo Creek, which pledged 162 of 168 warriors. After the American victory at Moraviantown, 1,398 Grand River residents fled to Burlington as refugees out of the roughly 1,925 people.[7] This last figure seems reasonable, given that not all of them would have left the Grand and that others would probably have sought refuge elsewhere or gone off on the traditional autumn hunt to avoid a possible American attack.

Notes

Abbreviations for Commonly Cited Sources

AO   Archives of Ontario

B&ECHS   Buffalo and Erie County Historical Society

BD   William Wood, ed., *Select British Documents of the Canadian War of 1812*, 4 vols. (Toronto 1920–8)

DCB   *Dictionary of Canadian Biography* (Toronto, various dates)

DH   Ernest A. Cruikshank, ed., *The Documentary History of the Campaigns on the Niagara Frontier, 1812–14*, 9 vols. (Welland and Lundy's Lane 1902–8)

Handbook Bruce G. Trigger, ed., *Handbook of North American Indians*, 15 ('Northeast') (Washington 1978)

JMJN   John Norton, *The Journal of Major John Norton, 1816*, Carl F. Klinck and James J. Talman, eds. (Toronto 1970)

NAC   National Archives of Canada

NARA   National Archives and Records Administration, Washington

NYH   *New York History*

OH   *Ontario History*

R&W   Charles M. Snyder, ed., *Red and White on the New York Frontier: A Struggle for Survival; Insights from the Papers of Erastus Granger, Indian Agent, 1807–1819* (Harrison 1978)

VSN   Charles M. Johnston, ed., *The Valley of the Six Nations: A Collection of Documents on the Indian Lands of the Grand River* (Toronto 1964)

WMQ   *William and Mary Quarterly*, 3rd series

Introduction

1 G.F.G. Stanley, 'The Significance of the Six Nations Participation in the War of 1812,' *OH* 55 (1963), 215–31; Arthur C. Parker, 'The Senecas in the War of 1812,' *NYH* 15 (1916), 78–90; Carl Benn, 'Iroquois Warfare, 1812–1814,' in R. Arthur Bowler, ed., *War Along the Niagara* (Youngstown 1991), 60–76; and C.M. Johnston, 'William Claus and John Norton,' *OH* 57 (1965), 101–8

2 *JMJN*; *VSN*; *R&W*; and John Norton, *Memoirs of a Mohawk War Chief*, Carl Benn, ed. (forthcoming)

3 Elias Johnson, *Legends, Traditions and Laws of the Iroquois, or Six Nations, and History of the Tuscarora Indians* (Lockport 1881). Johnson was a Tuscarora chief and his book is an interesting example of Iroquois tradition and thought in the late nineteenth century. A Seneca example is Governor Blacksnake's *Chainbreaker*, Thomas S. Abler, ed. (Lincoln, Neb. 1989), consisting of Blacksnake's Revolutionary War memoirs as dictated to another Seneca in the mid-nineteenth century. From the Grand River, two examples are 'The Battle between the Americans and the British during the War of 1812,' oral tradition as told by Roy Buck, MS 1986, Woodland Cultural Centre, Brantford; and George Loft, 'Indian Reminiscences of 1812,' *Saturday Night*, 11 Sept. 1909. For an analysis that incorporates material culture, see Chapter 3.

4 NARA, M15, Records of the Office of the Secretary of War, Letters Sent, Indian Affairs; and M271, Letters Received by the Office of the Secretary of War Related to Indian Affairs

5 Carl F. Klinck, 'Norton, John,' *DCB*, 6:552

6 John Norton to John B. Glegg, 4 Aug. 1812, AO, Alexander Fraser Papers; cf. *JMJN*, 298–9. Also, a preserved fragment of a diary he kept closely matches his journal; see *JMJN*, xviii–xxi, 5.

7 Norton completed the work during a visit to the United Kingdom in 1816 and entrusted it to friends to send to a publisher for editing and printing. His friends, however, thought he needed to revise it before it could go to final editing. The project died at that point and the manuscript sat unpublished (in the possession of the Duke of Northumberland) until 1970, when the Champlain Society brought out a scholarly edition. For the journal's history, see *JMJN*, xxiv–xcvii. My edition of Norton's experiences between 1812 and 1814, *Memoirs of a Mohawk War Chief*, will be a more accessible version which corrects his spelling and punctuation while leaving the order of his words untouched and which will include annotations to assist understanding among non-specialist readers.

8 *JMJN*, lxxvi–lxxvii; Klinck, 'Norton,' *DCB*, 6:550–3; and A. Irving Hallowell, 'American Indians, White and Black, the Phenomenon of Transculturalization,' *Current Anthropology* 4 (1963), 519–31

9 Francis Gore to Lord Bathurst, 15 Dec. 1815, NAC, CO 42, Colonial Office
   Papers (Canada), vol. 356, 159–63; and Carol M. Whitfield and Wesley B.
   Turner, 'Sheaffe, Sir Roger Hale,' *DCB*, 8:793–4
10 Barbara Graymont, 'Atiatoharongwen,' *DCB*, 5:39; and Timothy J. Shannon,
   'Dressing for Success on the Mohawk Frontier,' *WMQ* 53 (1996), 26
11 Nancy L. Hagedorn, 'A Friend to Go Between Them,' *Ethnohistory* 35 (1988),
   60–80; Henry Robie, 'Red Jacket's Reply,' *New York Folklore* 12 (1986), 99–117;
   Robert S. Allen, *His Majesty's Indian Allies* (Toronto 1992), 114; Francis Jennings, 'Iroquois Alliances in American History,' in Jennings, et al., *The History
   and Culture of Iroquois Diplomacy* (Syracuse 1985), 45; and A.F.C. Wallace, *The
   Death and Rebirth of the Seneca* (1969; New York 1972), 179–83

1: Survival

1 Little Abraham to the Iroquois at Fort Niagara, 1780, NAC, Claus Family
   Papers, F1, vol. 2, 165
2 Iroquoian society in the seventeenth century is discussed in Conrad E.
   Heidenreich, *Huronia* (Toronto 1971); Bruce G. Trigger, *The Children of
   Aataentsic* (1976; Kingston and Montreal 1987); Daniel K. Richter, *The Ordeal of
   the Longhouse* (Chapel Hill, NC 1992); and James W. Bradley, *Evolution of the
   Onondaga Iroquois* (Syracuse 1987).
3 Committee of Chiefs Appointed by the Six Nations Council of Grand River,
   'The Code of Dekanahwideh together with the Tradition of the Origin of the
   Five Nations' League,' 1900, in Arthur C. Parker, ed., 'The Constitution of the
   Five Nations,' *New York State Museum Bulletin* 184 (1916), 61–109. This committee dated the league's formation to about 1390, somewhat earlier than what is
   generally advocated by modern scholars. For academic views, see Bradley,
   Onondaga Iroquois, 43; Dean R. Snow, *The Iroquois* (Cambridge, Mass. 1994),
   33–76; and William N. Fenton, 'Structure, Continuity, and Change in the Process of Iroquois Treaty Making,' in Francis Jennings, et al., *The History and Culture of Iroquois Diplomacy* (Syracuse 1985), 16.
4 Bradley, *Onondaga Iroquois*, 181–6; Bruce G. Trigger, *Natives and Newcomers*
   (Kingston and Montreal 1985), 171; cf. Elisabeth Tooker, 'The United States
   Constitution and the Iroquois League,' *Ethnohistory* 35 (1988), 305–36; Richter, *Ordeal*, 6–7, 44–7; Jack Campisi, 'The Iroquois and the Euro-American
   Concept of Tribe,' *NYH* 63 (1982), 165, 181–2; and Fenton, 'Iroquois Treaty
   Making'
5 John Long, *Voyages and Travels of an Indian Interpreter and Trader* (1791; Toronto
   1974), 30; William N. Fenton, 'Northern Iroquoian Culture Patterns,' *Handbook*, 314–15; Richter, *Ordeal*, 42–9; and William N. Fenton, 'Leadership in the

Northeastern Woodlands of North America,' *American Indian Quarterly* 10 (1986), 23

6 See Claude Charles Le Roy Bacqueville de La Potherie's observations, 1722, in Trigger, *Natives and Newcomers*, 274–5; Richter, *Ordeal*, 190–254; and A.F.C. Wallace, *The Death and Rebirth of the Seneca* (1969; New York 1972).

7 Histories which explore these themes are: Bradley, *Onondaga Iroquois*; Richter, *Ordeal*; Francis Jennings, *The Ambiguous Iroquois Empire* (New York 1984); Barbara Graymont, *The Iroquois in the American Revolution* (Syracuse 1972); and Wallace, *Death and Rebirth*. For the importance of adopting prisoners, especially in warfare, see José Brandão, 'The Iroquois on the Warpath,' PhD II paper, Department of History, York University, 1986, discussed in Conrad E. Heidenreich, 'History of the St. Lawrence–Great Lakes Area to A.D. 1650,' in Chris J. Ellis and Neal Ferris, eds., *The Archaeology of Southern Ontario to A.D. 1650* (London, Ont. 1990), 488–9. For a history of the Iroquois written by Mohawk chief John Norton in c. 1812, see *JMJN*, 196–285. For a modern Mohawk understanding, see Gerald R. Alfred, *Heeding the Voices of Our Ancestors* (Toronto 1995), 24–51.

8 Richter, *Ordeal*, 238–40; Jennings, *Iroquois Empire*, 258–62; James Thomas Flexner, *Mohawk Baronet* (1959; 1979; Syracuse 1989), 266, 271; and Gregory Evans Dowd, *A Spirited Resistance* (Baltimore 1992), 1–46

9 Robert J. Surtees, *Indian Land Surrenders in Ontario, 1763–1867* (Ottawa 1983), 60; Robert A. Williams, Jr, *The American Indian in Western Legal Thought* (New York 1990), 233–86; and Flexner, *Mohawk Baronet*, 160, 294, and map on 325. The boundary is described in Isabel Thompson Kelsay, *Joseph Brant, 1743–1807* (Syracuse 1984), 127. The Iroquois seem to have been willing to sell major tracts of land to important cultural brokers such as Johnson, partly as a way of solidifying the boundary between them and the great mass of unsympathetic and uncontrollable whites who might otherwise penetrate their borders.

10 Helen Hornbeck Tanner, ed., *Atlas of Great Lakes Indian History* (Norman 1987), 66; Kelsay, *Joseph Brant*, 24; and A. Irving Hallowell, 'American Indians, White and Black, the Phenomenon of Transculturalization,' *Current Anthropology* 4 (1963), 519–31

11 Tanner, *Atlas*, 44, 65–6; Robert J. Surtees, 'The Iroquois in Canada,' in Jennings, et al. *Iroquois Diplomacy*, 70; Dowd, *Spirited Resistance*, 23–4, 29; Richard White, *The Middle Ground* (New York 1991), 188–9; Francis Jennings, *Empire of Fortune* (New York 1988), 31–2; Marian E. White et al., 'Cayuga,' and William C. Sturtevant, 'Oklahoma Seneca-Cayuga,' in *Handbook*, 502, 537

12 Flexner, *Mohawk Baronet*, 275, 293; and Kelsay, *Joseph Brant*, 115–21

13 George Washington to William Crawford, 21 Sept. 1767, in John C. Fitz-

patrick, ed., *Writings of George Washington from the Original Manuscript Sources, 1745–1799* (Washington 1931), 2:468–9

14 Wallace, *Death and Rebirth*, 123–5

15 Ibid., 125–48; Graymont, *Iroquois in the American Revolution*; Kelsay, *Joseph Brant*; and Fenton, 'Leadership,' 39

16 A.F.C. Wallace, 'Origins of the Longhouse Religion,' and Jack Campisi, 'Oneida,' in *Handbook*, 443, 483

17 For discussions of white–native relations in this period, see Robert S. Allen, *His Majesty's Indian Allies* (Toronto 1992); Reginald Horsman, *Expansion and American Indian Policy, 1783–1812* (1967; Norman 1992); and Colin G. Calloway, *Crown and Calumet* (Norman 1987).

18 Allen, *Indian Allies*, 57–86; and White, *Middle Ground*, 366–412

19 Charles Hamori-Torok, 'The Acculturation of the Mohawks of the Bay of Quinte,' PhD thesis, University of Toronto, 1966, 33–6; Allen, *Indian Allies*, 66; Sally M. Weaver, 'Six Nations of the Grand River, Ontario,' in *Handbook*, 525; and Donald B. Smith, 'Tekarihogen,' *DCB*, 6:759–60

20 Kelsay, *Joseph Brant*, 350, 639; Surtees, 'Iroquois in Canada,' 73; Smith, 'Tekarihogen,' *DCB*, 6:759–60; and Reg Good, 'Crown-Directed Colonization of Six Nations and Métis Land Reserves in Canada,' PhD thesis, University of Saskatchewan, 1994, 26–9

21 Surtees, *Land Surrenders*, 33–4

22 Carl Benn, 'The Iroquois Nadir of 1796,' in Brian Leigh Dunnigan, ed., *Niagara – 1796* (Youngstown 1996); Barbara Graymont, 'New York State Indian Policy after the Revolution,' *NYH* 57 (1976), 438–74; Wallace, 'Longhouse Religion,' 443; 'Descriptive Treaty Calendar,' in Jennings, et al., *Iroquois Diplomacy*, 200–1; and White, et al., 'Cayuga,' 502

23 *JMJN*, 282

24 For discussions on the frontier war, see Wiley Sword, *President Washington's Indian War* (Norman 1985); Wallace, *Death and Rebirth*, 159–68; and C.M. Johnston, 'Joseph Brant, the Grand River Lands and the Northwest Crisis,' *OH* 55 (1963).

25 Carl Benn, *Historic Fort York, 1793–1993* (Toronto 1993), 15–21, 29–32; and Allen, *Indian Allies*, 72–86

26 Benn, 'Iroquois Nadir,' 54–7

27 Benn, *Fort York*, 32–4

28 Elisabeth Tooker, 'League of the Iroquois' and 'Iroquois Since 1820,' in *Handbook*, 435, 450; Tooker, 'U.S. Constitution and the Iroquois League,' 332; and Wallace, *Death and Rebirth*, 159–236

29 John Logan, 1794, quoted in Wallace, *Death and Rebirth*, 197

30 Elisabeth Tooker, 'The Iroquois White Dog Sacrifice in the Latter Part of the

Eighteenth Century,' *Ethnohistory* 12 (1965), 129–40; Wallace, *Death and Rebirth*, 239–337; and Tanner, *Atlas*, 100–1

31 Wallace, 'Longhouse Religion,' 442–8; and Dowd, *Spirited Resistance*, 128

32 Wallace, *Death and Rebirth*, 199, 303–14; Kelsay, *Joseph Brant*, 561–647; and Henry H. Howland, 'The Seneca Mission at Buffalo Creek,' Buffalo Historical Society *Publications* 6 (1903), 125–61

33 Jeremy Belknap and Jedidiah Morse, 'Report on the Oneida, Stockbridge and Brotherton Indians, 1796,' *Indian Notes and Monographs* 54 (1955), 17

34 Elisabeth Tooker, 'Women in Iroquois Society,' in Michael K. Foster et al., eds., *Extending the Rafters* (Albany 1984)

35 *JMJN*, ciii

36 See Appendix.

37 Kelsay, *Joseph Brant*, 521–44, 614–15; Tanner, *Atlas*, 100–1; watercolour by Elizabeth Simcoe, *The Mohawk Village, Grand River, 1793*, at the AO; *Claypole's American Daily Advertiser*, 10 June 1799; Frank H. Severance, ed., 'Narratives of Early Mission Work on the Niagara Frontier and Buffalo Creek,' Buffalo Historical Society *Publications* 6 (1903), 165–380; Lewis H. Morgan, *Report on the Fabrics, Inventions, Implements and Utensils of the Iroquois*, 1851, republished in Elisabeth Tooker, *Lewis H. Morgan on Iroquois Material Culture* (Tucson 1994), 256; and Charles Hamori-Torok, 'The Iroquois of Akwesasne (St. Regis), Mohawks of the Bay of Quinte (Tyendinaga), Onyota'a:ka (the Oneida of the Thames), and Wahta Mohawk (Gibson), 1750–1945,' in Edward S. Rogers and Donald B. Smith, eds., *Aboriginal Ontario* (Toronto 1994), 260–1, 263

38 Marshall Smelser, *The Democratic Republic* (New York 1968), 285; and Richard Glover, *Britain at Bay* (London 1973), 68–72

39 J.C.A. Stagg, *Mr. Madison's War* (Princeton 1983), 3–119; Roger R. Brown, *Republic in Peril* (New York 1964); Bradford Perkins, *Causes of the War of 1812* (New York 1962); and G.F.G. Stanley, *The War of 1812* (Ottawa 1983), 3–43

2: The Crisis of Alliance

1 *JMJN*, 290

2 Communication to the House of Representatives, 13 June 1812, in *American State Papers, Indian Affairs* (Washington 1832), 4:797

3 *Public Speeches Delivered at the Village of Buffalo, on the 6th and 8th days of July, 1812, by Hon. Erastus Granger, Indian Agent, and Red Jacket, One of the Principal Chiefs and Speakers of the Seneca Nation* (Buffalo 1812), 13–14; cf. Little Billy's speech, June 1812, *JMJN*, 290

4 *Public Speeches*, 13–14

5 Erastus Granger to the Six Nations, Sept. 1808, *R&W*, 38

6 Colin G. Calloway, *Crown and Calumet* (Norman 1987), 58, 61; Frederick
   Houghton, *The History of the Buffalo Creek Reservation* (Buffalo 1920), 160;
   Arthur C. Parker, 'The Senecas in the War of 1812,' *NYH* 15 (1916), 81;
   Franklin B. Hough, *A History of St. Lawrence and Franklin Counties* (Albany 1853),
   195; and Allan S. Everest, *The War of 1812 in the Champlain Valley* (Syracuse
   1981), 72–3

7 *JMJN*, 285–6; Red Jacket's speech, 13 Feb. 1819, in *American State Papers*, 4:804;
   and A.F.C. Wallace, *The Death and Rebirth of the Seneca* (1969; New York 1972),
   287–8

8 *JMJN*, 286; The Iroquois to William Claus, 10 Oct. 1808, in Robert S. Allen,
   'The British Indian Department on the Frontier in North America, 1755–
   1830,' *Occasional Papers in Archaeology and History* 14 (1975), 70

9 Robert Hoops to — Van Campan, c. June 1812, in Benson J. Lossing, *Pictorial
   Field Book of the War of 1812* (New York 1869), 400

10 John Deseronto's speech, Sept. 1810, *VSN*, 54; Sir John Johnson to Lord
   Dorchester, 28 Jan. 1790, *VSN*, 54–5; George Martin's speech, 1 Dec. 1818,
   NAC, RG 10, Records of the Department of Indian Affairs, vol. 489, 29471–8;
   and *JMJN*, 285.

11 Upper Canada, Executive Council minutes, 29 June 1797, in E.A. Cruikshank,
   ed., *The Correspondence of the Honourable Peter Russell* (Toronto 1932–6), 1:199;
   Peter Russell to Joseph Brant, 3 and 15 July 1797, ibid., 1:204, 214; Brant to
   Russell, 10 July 1797, ibid., 1:211; Russell to the Duke of Portland, 29 July
   1797, ibid., 1:228; and C.M. Johnston, 'Joseph Brant, the Grand River Lands
   and the Northwest Crisis,' *OH* 55 (1963)

12 Carl F. Klinck, 'Norton, John,' *DCB*, 6:550–3; and *JMJN*, xiii–xcvii. His original
   Mohawk name was Dowwisdowwis, or 'the Snipe.' Teyoninhokarawen, or
   'Open Door,' signified 'frankness and an open heart' (*JMJN*, xxxvii–xxxviii).

13 Isabel Thompson Kelsay, *Joseph Brant, 1743–1807* (Syracuse 1984), 590; *JMJN*,
   cviii–cx, 285–370; Robert J. Surtees, 'The Iroquois in Canada,' in Francis Jennings et al., *The History and Culture of Iroquois Diplomacy* (Syracuse 1985), 76;
   and G.F.G. Stanley, 'The Indians in the War of 1812,' in Morris Zaslow, ed., *The
   Defended Border* (Toronto 1964), 175

14 Portland to Peter Hunter, 11 June 1799, NAC, CO 42, vol. 324

15 *JMJN*, lvi, 285–370

16 Ibid., cx, 287, *et passim*; and Stanley, 'Indians in the War of 1812,' 175

17 *JMJN*, xxxv–xxxvi, ciii–cxv; Kelsay, *Joseph Brant*, 614–48; Reg Good, 'Crown-
   Directed Colonization of Six Nations and Métis Land Reserves in Canada,'
   PhD thesis, University of Saskatchewan, 1994, 194, 198, 215, 239–40; and
   Robert S. Allen, 'Claus, William,' *DCB*, 6:151–3. The politicians were Robert
   Thorpe, Benejah Mallory, William Weekes, and William Willcocks.

18 Diary of an Officer in Indian Country, 14 June–2 July 1794, in E.A. Cruik-shank, ed., *Correspondence of Lieut. Governor John Graves Simcoe* (Toronto 1923–31), 5:93–4; Wiley Sword, *President Washington's Indian War* (Norman 1985), 272–9; and letter to the author from Wiley Sword, 7 June 1995. The diary states that on the day before the action near Fort Recovery, on the Wabash River, Norton disappeared and was suspected of having deserted to the enemy, and that on another day after the battle he reappeared, claiming to have been lost in the woods. However, the Americans only received a warning from one native, Jimmy Underwood, who did not speak English and therefore failed to stop the Americans from suffering the defeat of a supply column that left the fort and fell into an ambush. It is possible, however, that Norton had decided not to participate in the battle and had absented himself rather than got lost; see Lord Selkirk, *Lord Selkirk's Diary, 1803–1804*, P.C.T. White, ed. (Toronto 1958), 243–5. Norton's description of the campaign is silent on the matter (*JMJN*, 183).
19 Brant to the Duke of Northumberland, 24 Jan. 1806, in *JMJN*, lvii; cf. John Norton to Robert Barclay, 16 Oct. 1810, in *JMJN*, lxxv; *JMJN*, cviii–cxv; and Good, 'Crown-Directed Colonization,' 142–242
20 C.M. Johnston, 'William Claus and John Norton,' *OH* 57 (1965), 101–3; Stanley, 'Indians in the War of 1812,' 185–6; and Everest, *Champlain Valley*, 67. Claus had used government presents to fulfil personal objectives before, in 1804, in his opposition to Brant (Good, 'Crown-Directed Colonization,' 191).
21 Isaac Brock to Sir George Prevost, 25 Feb. 1812, *BD*, 1:170–1
22 *JMJN*, 288
23 Raweanarase's speech, 18 Apr. 1811, NAC, RG 10, vol. 27, 16288–91; and Good, 'Crown-Directed Colonization,' 234–7, 251
24 Anonymous Mohawk in 1811, quoted in Donald B. Smith, 'Tekarihogen,' *DCB*, 6:759
25 Brant's speech, Aug. 1803, NAC, RG 10, vol. 789, 6883–94; *JMJN*, 287, 290; Kelsay, *Joseph Brant*, 553–96, 643–6; Good, 'Crown-Directed Colonization,' 34–8, 60–1, 98–141, 192; 234–9; and Johnston, 'Northwest Crisis'
26 Tekarihogen's speech, 18 Apr. 1811, NAC, RG 10, vol. 27, 16288–91
27 *JMJN*, 287–8; cf. *VSN*, *passim*, especially Brock's proclamation on 1 Feb. 1812, 113
28 Martin's speech, 1 Dec. 1818, RG 10, vol. 489, 29471–8; and Good, 'Crown-Directed Colonization'
29 *JMJN*, 288
30 Ibid., 288–9
31 Blind-Warrior's speech, *JMJN*, 289
32 Brock to the Earl of Liverpool, 25 May 1812, NAC, RG 7, Governor-General's

Records, G12, vol. 4, 53–5; and Brock to Prevost, 2 Dec. 1811, in Allen, 'Indian Department,' 72

33 Jean-Baptiste Rousseau to Claus, 7 June 1812, *VSN*, 193–4

34 *JMJN*, 286

35 Ibid.

36 Captain Strong's speech, June 1812, *R&W*, 47

37 *JMJN*, 289–90

38 Ibid., 290–2

39 Claus to the Grand River Iroquois, June 1812, *R&W*, 47

40 *JMJN*, 291

41 Ibid., 290–1; and Robert S. Allen, *His Majesty's Indian Allies* (Toronto 1992), 58

42 *JMJN*, 290–2. The speaker may have been Norton because he sometimes switched from writing in the first person to the third, apparently out of a sense of modesty (*JMJN*, xxiii; cf. his speech at the battle of Queenston Heights, *JMJN*, 305).

43 Grand River Council memorandum, June 1812, *R&W*, 48

44 *JMJN*, 291–2, *et passim*

45 Ibid., 291–3; and *Public Speeches*, 24, 27, 29–30. See the discussion about the attack on Black Rock in Chapter 6 for an example of this lack of coordination.

46 *JMJN*, 294

47 *Public Speeches*, 17–18

48 Arosa's speech, 12 July 1812, AO, Alexander Fraser Papers

49 Council minutes, 12 July 1812, AO, Fraser Papers

50 *JMJN*, 294

51 Ibid., 294–5

52 Ibid., 297–301; and William Kerr to John B. Glegg, 7 Aug. 1812, AO, Fraser Papers

53 Brock to Lord Liverpool, 29 Aug. 1812, NAC, CO 42, vol. 352, 105; and William Hull to the Six Nations, 12 July 1812, *BD*, 1:359

54 *JMJN*, 295–7; Kerr to Glegg, 17 Aug. 1812, AO, Fraser Papers; and ? to ?, 15 Oct. 1812, Tupper Papers

55 *JMJN*, 297–8, 301

56 The son of Karhagohha (the Hawk), quoted in *JMJN*, 297

57 ? to ?, 15 Oct. 1812, AO, Tupper Papers

58 Brock to Prevost, 3 and 26 July 1812, *DH*, 3:94, 145; Brock to Liverpool, 29 Aug. 1812, NAC, CO 42, vol. 352, 105; Brock to Edward Baynes, 4 Aug. 1812, *BD*, 1:409; *JMJN*, 296; Charles Askin Journal, 24 July–12 Sept. 1812, *John Askin Papers*, Milo Quaife, ed. (Detroit 1928–31), 2:711; E.A. Cruikshank, 'The Employment of the Indians in the War of 1812,' *Annual Report of the American Historical Association, 1895*, 331; and Cruikshank, 'A Study of Disaffection in

Upper Canada, 1812–5,' *Proceedings and Transactions of the Royal Society of Canada*, 3rd ser., 6 (1912), 23, 48

59 John Strachan to William Wilberforce, 1 Nov. 1812, *John Strachan Letter Book, 1812–1834*, George W. Spragge, ed. (Toronto 1946), 21–2. Strachan was well positioned to know what was going on. He was in regular contact with Robert Addison, rector of Niagara, whose flock included the Grand River Anglicans. Logically, Addison knew more about the mood of the Iroquois than did most whites. Strachan also moved in senior government and military circles in York and acquired information from his acquaintances.

60 Brock to Baynes, 4 Aug. 1812, *BD*, 1:409; Brock to Prevost, 28 July 1812, *DH*, 3:148–9; and Cruikshank, 'Disaffection,' 21–2

61 Brock to Liverpool, 29 Aug. 1812, NAC, CO 42, vol. 352, 105

62 Hull to the inhabitants of Canada, 13 July 1812, *BD*, 1:357

63 Brock to Liverpool, 29 Aug. 1812, NAC, CO 42, vol. 352, 105

64 *JMJN*, 293

65 Brock to Prevost, 2 Dec. 1811, *DH*, 3:22; *JMJN*, 308; Kerr to Glegg, 17 Aug. 1812, AO, Fraser Papers; ? to ?, 15 Oct. 1812, AO, Tupper Papers; Cruikshank, 'Disaffection,' 22, 26–7; and J. Mackay Hitsman, *The Incredible War of 1812* (1965; Toronto 1972), 69

66 Brock to the people of Upper Canada, 22 July 1812, in Ferdinand Brock Tupper, *Life and Correspondence of Major-General Sir Isaac Brock, K.B.* (London 1845), 190–1. See Strachan to Wilberforce, 1 Nov. 1812, *Letter Book*, 21–4, for an Anglican priest's defence of employing native allies.

67 Joseph Willcocks to John Macdonell, 1 Sept. 1812, *VSN*, 197; *JMJN*, 287–9, 297–9, 301; Norton to Glegg, 11 Aug. 1812, AO, Fraser Papers; Brock to Prevost, 3 July 1812, *DH*, 3:94. *JMJN*, 128–9, provides Norton's definition of the differences between what he called 'partizan warfare ... carried on by war chiefs independently' and warfare where 'the Nation apprehends some approaching danger of magnitude, or meditates a weighty blow on the enemy.' See Leroy V. Eid, '"National" War among Indians of Northeastern North American,' *Canadian Review of American Studies* 16 (1985), 129.

68 For a description of the Detroit campaign with an aboriginal focus, see Allen, *Indian Allies*, 123–40. The Kahnawake people at Mackinac are mentioned in Eleazer Williams, *Life of Te-ho-ra-gwa-ne-gen, alias Thomas Williams* (Albany 1859), 61.

69 Brock to Hull, 15 Aug. 1812, in Hitsman, *Incredible War*, 73

70 Hitsman, *Incredible War*, 61–76; and Norton to Henry Goulburn, 29 Jan. 1816, in E.A. Cruikshank, ed., 'Campaigns of 1812–14,' *Niagara Historical Society Transactions* 9 (1902), 43

71 List of ... ordnance taken, 1 Apr. 1813, NAC, CO 42, vol. 123, 127; J.C.A. Stagg,

Mr. Madison's War (Princeton 1983), 205; Allen, *Indian Allies*, 123–40; and Hitsman, *Incredible War*, 74–6

72 *JMJN*, 301; State of the Indian tribes, Oct. 1812, NAC, RG 10, vol. 11, 16106–9; Brock to Liverpool, 29 Aug. 1812, NAC, CO 42, vol. 352, 105–7; and Helen Hornbeck Tanner, ed., *Atlas of Great Lakes Indian History* (Norman 1987), 118

73 Brock to Prevost, 7 Sept. 1812, *VSN*, 197; cf. Strachan to Wilberforce, 1 Nov. 1812, *Letter Book*, 21

74 Kerr to Glegg, 17 Aug. 1812, AO, Fraser Papers; *JMJN*, 301–2 (cf. 128–9); Willcocks to Macdonell, 1 Sept. 1812, *VSN*, 197; *Buffalo Gazette*, 4 Aug. 1812, *DH*, 3:165; and Eid, '"National" War,' 129–30

75 *JMJN*, 302

76 James Hall, 'A Reminiscence,' *Knickerbocker* 6 (1835), 15. This article records a meeting between the author (an American officer admitted to the British lines under a flag-of-truce) with Mohawk leader John Brant. It is a highly coloured reconstruction of the debate, written primarily to support the American government's policy of 'Indian Removal' in the 1830s. Despite its corruption, it refers to the Hull proclamation to the Upper Canadians, especially the two quoted sentences, and their impact on the thinking of the Six Nations. For example, in contemplating those sentences, the author of the article had Brant say, probably with some accuracy: 'I know General Hull made use of that expression [re not giving quarter], – and I know very well that if white people won't give quarter to each other, it's a bad chance for the Indian to get it.' Cf. *JMJN*, 288–9, 296.

77 Black Hawk, *Life of Black Hawk*, Antoine Leclair, trans., J.B. Patterson, ed. (1834); Milo Quaife, ed. (1916; reprinted New York 1994), 20

78 George Simon Snyderman, *Behind the Tree of Peace* (Philadelphia 1948), 30; Claude Charles Le Roy Bacqueville de la Potherie, n.d., in Cadwallader Colden, *History of the Five Indian Nations of Canada* (1747; Ithaca 1958), 5; Daniel K. Richter, 'War and Culture,' *WMQ* 40 (1983), 530–1; Richter, *The Ordeal of the Longhouse* (Chapel Hill 1992), 32–5; and Wallace, *Death and Rebirth*, 102. On this subject, Norton wrote: 'A man who had lost either his friend or his Cousin, in War, or by natural death, was required, by the Laws of Honor, to replace him with a prisoner or a scalp, or to cover him with wampum' (*JMJN*, 111).

79 Snyderman, *Tree of Peace*, 36; William N. Fenton, 'Answers to Governor Cass's Questions by Jacob Jameson, a Seneca [ca. 1821–1825],' *Ethnohistory* 16 (1969), 121–2; and Kelsay, *Joseph Brant*, 335. Some adoptions of white captives did take place in the War of 1812. One interesting account of a traditional adoption by some natives in the Detroit region of an American prisoner is

William Atherton, *Narrative of the Sufferings & Defeat of the North-Western Army* (Frankfort, Ky 1842), 82–3, *et passim.*

80 Wallace, *Death and Rebirth,* 44, 95–7, 101–2

81 I thank Dr Gregory Evans Dowd of the University of Notre Dame for his insights into spiritual interpretations of the situation in 1812.

82 John Enys, *American Journals of Lt. John Enys,* Elizabeth Cometti, ed. (Syracuse 1976), 30, 48

83 Askin Journal, 24 July–12 Sept. 1812, *Askin Papers,* 2:721–4

84 Patrick Campbell, *Travels in the Interior Inhabited Parts of North American* (1793), H.H. Langton, ed. (Toronto 1937), 165

85 J.G. Simcoe to Henry Dundas, 16 Sept. 1793, *Simcoe Papers,* 2:53. The relationship between this practice and the abolition of the importation of slaves into Upper Canada has yet to be studied.

86 George McFeely, Dec. 1813, quoted in John C. Fredriksen, ed., 'Chronicle of Valor,' *Western Pennsylvania Historical Magazine* 67 (1984), 254

87 Samuel White, *A History of the American Troops during the Late War under Colonel Fenton* (Baltimore 1829), 18, 23; cf. *JMJN,* 350

88 An inventory listing some of the goods given to natives allied to the British on the Niagara Peninsula dates from 1813. It includes muskets, ball and shot, gunpowder, flints, butchers' knives, pocket knives, blankets, buttons, baize cloth, cotton calico, coating flannel, shawls, silk handkerchiefs, hats, linen, needles, thread, pipes, brass kettles, soap, and tobacco (General abstract of Indian stores issued in the Indian Department serving with the Centre Army, between 25th June & 24th September 1813, NAC, RG 10, vol. 477, 171597). A British list of presents additional to normal allotments required in 1813 in Upper Canada because of the war included, among other vast quantities of goods, 5,000 common guns, 5,000 chiefs guns, 200 gun locks, 1,000 pistols, 16,400 kg of gunpowder, 460 kg of lead, 50 kg of shot, 1,000 'Indian lances' or pikes, 2,000 swords, 9,600 butchers' knives, 1,200 clasp knives, 200 pipe tomahawks, 1,000 pairs of shoes, 2,000 coats, 200 saddles, 600 medals, 300 silver gorgets, 24,000 ear bobs, and 550 kg of vermilion dye (Requisition for an extra quantity of goods to supply ... the Indians in ... U.C. ... for ... 1813, RG 10, vol. 476, 171540–2). In 1812 the estimated foodstuffs needed for the natives in Upper Canada amounted to 128,000 rations and 2,800 litres of rum (Requisition for provisions and rum ... for ... 1812,' 12 Aug. 1811, RG 10, vol. 476, 171486). Some Akwesasne people received cash in 1813 (Account for Indian supplies, AO, Military Records, 1813, no. 9) and Brock told Prevost he would have to 'sacrifice some money to gain ... [the Grand River Iroquois] over' (Brock to Prevost, 3 July 1812, *DH,* 3:94).

89 *JMJN,* 293

90 Richter, *Ordeal*, 262–3; and Kelsay, *Joseph Brant*, 115–17
91 James McNair to Peter B. Porter, 15 May 1814, B&ECHS, Peter B. Porter
    Papers; Porter to Daniel Tompkins, 26 May 1814, *DH*, 2:399–400; and
    Calloway, *Crown and Calumet*, 135
92 Chiefs of the Brothertown people to Porter, 14 May 1814, B&ECHS, Porter
    Papers
93 Calloway, *Crown and Calumet*, 62. This may have given rise to the belief that
    natives did not look after their weapons. However, the large number of late
    eighteenth- and early nineteenth-century native firearms in museums and pri-
    vate collections that survived to be converted to percussion ignition from flint
    in the 1840s or later suggests this was not the case. See De Witt Bailey, 'Those
    Board of Ordnance Indian Guns – Again!,' *Museum of the Fur Trade Quarterly* 21
    (1985), 16. Archaeological evidence indicates that natives from the seven-
    teenth century onwards not only looked after their weapons, but owned tools
    to maintain them and reused parts from older guns to make repairs; see T.M.
    Hamilton, *Colonial Frontier Guns* (Chadron 1980), 116–19.
94 Calloway, *Crown and Calumet*, 61; Richard White, *The Middle Ground* (New York
    1991), 128–35; Kelsay, *Joseph Brant*, 189; and Snyderman, *Tree of Peace*, 36
95 Brock to Prevost, 3 July 1812, *DH*, 3:94; and Dorchester to ?, 6 May 1790, NAC,
    RG 10, vol. 8, 8705–7
96 Brock to Prevost, 7 Sept. 1812, *VSN*, 198
97 Bruce G. Trigger, *Natives and Newcomers* (Kingston and Montreal 1985), 171
98 William N. Fenton, 'Leadership in the Northeastern Woodlands of North
    America,' *American Indian Quarterly* 10 (1986), 38, 42–3; Barbara Graymont,
    The Iroquois in the American Revolution (Syracuse 1972), 20–3; Lewis H. Morgan,
    League of the Iroquois (1851; Secaucas 1972), 72; Kelsay, *Joseph Brant*; and
    Snyderman, *Tree of Peace*, 21
99 Citations to the customs of going to war, here and in later chapters, come
    from a variety of sources that span a long period of time but that resonate well
    with seventeenth-century sources, suggesting cultural continuities. For exam-
    ple, a description of these customs close to the War of 1812 is found in George
    Heriot, *Travels through the Canadas* (London 1807). Heriot knew the Seven
    Nations and what he wrote had to conform to his experience. Yet much of his
    information came from an older work that was based largely on Seven Nations
    practice, Joseph François Lafitau's *Customs of the American Indians Compared
    with the Customs of Primitive Times* (1724), 2 vols. William N. Fenton and Eliza-
    beth L. Moore, eds. and trans. (Toronto 1974–7). This work, written by a mis-
    sionary to the Iroquois, itself contained material from seventeenth-century
    sources (*Customs*, 2:103, n.1), but the older material also had to ring true to
    Lafitau's experience. Furthermore, there are several documents from the

Iroquois world or from outside observers of the end of the eighteenth and early nineteenth centuries that confirm the 1812-era continuation of these practices (which also seem to have extended more or less consistently throughout the eastern woodlands as far south as the Iroquoian Cherokee people), such as *JMJN*, 128–9; MS on warfare, ascribed as late eighteenth century but probably early nineteenth century judging from internal evidence, *VSN*, 32; Joshua Marsden, *Narrative of a Mission to Nova Scotia, New Brunswick, and the Somers Islands; with a Tour to Lake Ontario* (Plymouth, Eng. 1816), 191–2; William N. Fenton, 'Answers to Governor Cass's Questions by Jacob Jameson, a Seneca [ca. 1821–1825],' *Ethnohistory* 16 (1969); and Douglas W. Boyce, 'A Glimpse of Iroquois Culture History through the Eyes of Joseph Brant and John Norton,' *Proceedings of the American Philosophical Society* 117 (1973), 286–94.

100 *JMJN*, 129, 293; and Heriot, *Travels*, 2:424

101 Martin's speech, 1 Dec. 1818, RG 10, vol. 489, 29471–8; Brant to Johnson, Nov. 1801, in William L. Stone, *Life of Joseph Brant – Thayendanegea* (New York 1838), 2:407–9; Granger to Jasper Parrish?, 24 Oct. 1812, Vassar College, Jasper Parrish Papers; Atotoarho's speech, 8–10 Mar. 1812, RG 10, vol. 27, 15872–82; Good, 'Crown-Directed Colonization,' 193, 213; and Kelsay, *Joseph Brant*, 636–7

102 *JMJN*, 177; Lafitau, *Customs*, 2:98–9; Anne Powell, 'A Journey from Montreal to Detroit' (1789), in William Renwick Riddell, ed., *Old Province Tales* (Toronto 1920), 84–5; *Lord Selkirk's Diary*, 20 Nov. 1803, 148, 161; Wallace, *Death and Rebirth*, 29–30, 101; and Dean R. Snow, *The Iroquois* (Cambridge, Mass. 1994), 60–5

103 Six Nations council minutes, 10 Mar. 1809, NAC, RG 10, vol. 27, 15873–9; cf. a similar record from Seneca society in the 1790s in Wallace, *Death and Rebirth*, 182

104 Kerr to Glegg, 17 Aug. 1812, AO, Fraser Papers; Willcocks to Macdonell, 1 Sept. 1812, *BD*, 1:417–18; Smith, 'Tekarihogen,' *DCB*, 6:760–1; Good, 'Crown-Directed Colonization,' 233; and Kelsay, *Joseph Brant*, 563–5

105 Heriot, *Travels*, 2:422–4; Fenton, 'Cass's Questions,' 120, 134; Claus quoting an unidentified native, Dec. 1813, in Calloway, *Crown and Calumet*, 61; Kelsay, *Joseph Brant*, 32; Graymont, *Iroquois in the American Revolution*, 21; C.M. Chadwick, *People of the Longhouse* (Toronto 1897), 61; and Wallace, *Death and Rebirth*, 116

106 Heriot, *Travels*, 2:467; and Snyderman, *Tree of Peace*, 24. Heriot wrote, perhaps with some exaggeration, that warriors younger than twenty-one or older than fifty only went on 'predatory expeditions, which are not the regular occupations of a warrior.'

107 John Caldwell to ?, 1774, in Paul Stevens, *A King's Colonel at Niagara, 1774–1776* (Youngstown 1987), 28
108 See Chapter 3.
109 John Long, *Voyages and Travels of an Indian Interpreter* (1791; Toronto 1974), 78; Lafitau, *Customs*, 2:110–11; Graymont, *Iroquois in the American Revolution*, 20–3; Morgan, *League*, 72–3; and Wallace, *Death and Rebirth*, 46. Lafitau suggests that in the seventeenth century desertion might have been punished severely, but that the early eighteenth century witnessed a growth in personal freedom to leave war parties without punishment.
110 See Appendix.
111 E.J. Devine, *Historic Caugnawaga* (Montreal 1922), 321–2
112 Henry Dearborn to Granger, 29 Sept. 1812, Vassar College, Parrish Papers; Lawrence Ostola, 'The Seven Nations of Canada and the American Revolution,' MA thesis, Université de Montréal, 1989; Everest, *Champlain Valley*, 68, 70–2; Barbara Graymont, 'Atiatoharongwen,' *DCB*, 5:39–41; Geoffrey Buerger, 'Williams, Thomas,' DCB, 7:911–12; and Philippe Sylvain, 'Williams, Eleazer,' *DCB*, 8:939–40
113 Joseph Marcoux, 'Mémoire pour la défense de la neutralité des Sauvages de S. Regis,' 1 Aug. 1818, *Le Bulletin des recherches historiques* 67 (1961), 20–30
114 Strachan to Wilberforce, 1 Nov. 1812, in Strachan, *Letter Book*, 21; St Regis chiefs to Prevost, 9 Mar. 1813, NAC, RG 8, British Military Records, vol. 257, 60–2; Marcoux, 'Mémoire,' 20–3; Hitsman, *Incredible War*, 99; Hough, *St. Lawrence and Franklin Counties*, 156; and E.A. Cruikshank, 'From Isle aux Noix to Chateauguay,' *Proceedings and Transactions of the Royal Society of Canada*, 3rd ser., 7 (1913), 147, 153. Blockhouses are defensible buildings with bullet-proof walls to protect their garrisons and are constructed with loopholes and other features to allow troops to fire out at attackers.
115 *New York Evening Post*, 13 Aug. 1812; Isaac LeClaire to Johnson, 26 Nov. 1813, NAC, RG 10, vol. 28, 16572–3; Marcoux, 'Mémoire,' 22–9; E.A. Cruikshank, *The Glengarry Light Infantry* (c. 1910; n.p., c. 1975), 13; Cruikshank, 'From Isle aux Noix,' 171; Hitsman, *Incredible War*, 99, 103; Allan J. Ferguson, 'New York's Captured British Flag, 1812,' *Military Collector and Historian* 36 (1984), 13–14; Hough, *St. Lawrence and Franklin Counties*, 156, 195–7; and Everest, *Champlain Valley*, 72–3
116 Chief Warrior to Granger, 19 Dec. 1811, *R&W*, 44; Chiefs and warriors of the Oneida, Onondaga, Stockbridge, Tuscarora, and Seneca tribes to James Madison, 29 Sept. 1812, *R&W*, 56; William Eustis to Ephriam Webster, 12 Oct. 1812, *R&W*, 57; Eustis to Dearborn, 23 Sept. 1812, *DH*, 3:291; and Parker, 'Senecas in the War of 1812,' 79
117 *R&W*, 40

118 *Buffalo Gazette*, 4 Aug. 1812, *DH*, 3:165
119 Buffalo council minutes, 8 Sept. 1812, *DH*, 4:20
120 Ibid.
121 Speech of the deputies of the Oneidas, Onondagas, Stockbridges, Tuscaroras, and Senecas, 29 Sept. 1812, *DH*, 3:303
122 Tanner, *Atlas*, 119; Wallace, *Death and Rebirth*, 294–6; and William N. Fenton, *The Iroquois Eagle Dance, an Offshoot of the Calumet Dance* (1953; Syracuse 1991), 104–11
123 For a discussion differentiating small scale and 'national' war among native peoples, see Eid, '"National" War.'

3: 'We Wish Not to Be Sold'

1 Black Hawk, *Life of Black Hawk*, Antoine Leclair, trans., J.B. Patterson, ed. (1834); Milo Quaife, ed. (1916; reprinted New York 1994), 20. It should be noted that the Iroquois tended to value the capture of enemies more highly than Black Hawk's people did.
2 *JMJN*, 183, 298–9, 313, 325; and Franklin B. Hough, *A History of St. Lawrence and Franklin Counties* (Albany 1853), 197. Norton provides a few rare references to natives fighting on horseback, one concerning the western tribes in 1794 (p. 183), another about some Wyandots at Frenchtown in 1813 (p. 313). For descriptions of Euroamerican warfare in the 1812 period, see Donald E. Graves, *Red Coats and Grey Jackets* (Toronto 1994), 47–64, 168–72; and Graves, *The Battle of Lundy's Lane* (Baltimore 1993), 19–40.
3 B.P. Hughes, *Firepower* (London 1974); Hew Strachan, *From Waterloo to Balaclava* (Cambridge 1985), 32; Jeffrey Kimball, 'The Battle of Chippawa,' *Military Affairs* 32 (1968), 184; and David Gates, *The British Light Infantry Arm, c.1790–1815* (London 1987), 47
4 Richard Glover, *Peninsular Preparation* (Cambridge 1963), 122–9; and Gates, *Light Infantry*
5 James Fitzgibbon, 'Hints to a Son on Receiving his first Commission in a Regiment Serving in the Canadas,' written in the 1820s, in Mary Agnes Fitzgibbon, *A Veteran of 1812* (Toronto 1894), appendix; William Dunlop, 'Recollections of the American War, 1812–1814' (1847), in *Tiger Dunlop's Upper Canada*; Carl F. Klinck, ed. (Toronto 1967), 44, 47–8; Capt. Barber, *Instructions for the Formation and Exercise of Volunteer Sharp-Shooters* (1804; Ottawa 1968), iii; Hughes, *Firepower*, 29; and John K. Mahon, 'Anglo-American Methods of Indian Warfare, 1676–1794,' *Mississippi Valley Historical Review* 14 (1958–9), 256; as well as author's personal experience as a curator in a military history museum, 1985–97

6 Personal curatorial experience, 1985–97

7 William Smith, *An Historical Account of the Expedition Against the Ohio Indians,* reprinted as *Expedition Against the Ohio Indians* (1765; Ann Arbor 1966), 38; John Long, *Voyages and Travels of an Indian Interpreter and Trader* (1791; Toronto 1974), 53; Barbara Graymont, *The Iroquois in the American Revolution* (Syracuse 1972), 17; and George S. Snyderman, *Behind the Tree of Peace* (Philadelphia 1948), 44–7. Another way of keeping fit for war was to engage in small-scale, low-grade raids against an enemy living far away, although by 1812 this way of getting combat training was no longer of real significance because of the loss of most opportunities for its practice; see Leroy V. Eid, '"National" War among Indians of Northeastern North America,' *Canadian Journal of American Studies* 16 (1985), 133–4.

8 Cornelius J. Jaenen, *Friend and Foe* (Toronto 1976), 134

9 Weapons associated with native use with carved-down shoulders appear on the antique market and in museums. It is also possible that the Iroquois, who first owned Dutch muskets which had low combs, preferred this design to later British and American patterns. Low combs on aboriginal arms were common over great chronological and geographical distances. There is, for example, a Métis firearm from the Northwest Rebellion of 1885 with a carved comb (Heritage Toronto). In addition to carving out the combs to improve aiming, aboriginal people, in the weapons they re-stocked in Canada (usually after the original stocks had broken), had them re-stocked with lower combs to improve aim (personal curatorial experience, 1985–97). Sometimes white authorities also criticized high combs as inhibiting aiming (T. Graham, Inspection return on the 1st Battalion of the 95th Regiment or Rifle Corps, 12 May 1809, Public Record Office (London), WO 27/94).

10 Long, *Travels,* 29. The expression 'half man high' was hyperbole: whites did not fire from the waist, but from the shoulder.

11 MS on hunting, ascribed as from the late eighteenth century but probably from the early nineteenth, judging from internal evidence, *VSN,* 28

12 John Howison, *Sketches of Upper Canada,* 1821, *VSN,* 28

13 Long, *Travels,* 19

14 Kimball, 'Chippawa,' 172; and Glover, *Peninsular Preparation,* 126, 141. Larger amounts of ammunition were used during periods of intensive training; see J.A. Houlding, *Fit For Service* (Oxford 1981), 335–7.

15 Dunlop, 'Recollections,' 48

16 Washington *National Intelligencer,* Jan. 1813, *DH,* 5:25; Michael Smith, *Geographical View of the Province of Upper Canada* (Philadelphia 1813), 40; and Leroy V. Eid, 'American Indian Military Leadership,' *Journal of Military History* 57

(1993), 82–3. I owe thanks to Dr Conrad Heidenreich of York University for the observation on deer hunting (cf. *JMJN*, 182).

17 Harry Holbert Turney-High, *Primitive Warfare* (Columbia, SC 1949), 55; William N. Fenton, 'Answers to Governor Cass's Questions by Jacob Jameson, a Seneca [ca. 1821–1825],' *Ethnohistory* 16 (1969), 122, 135; and personal curatorial experience, 1985–97

18 Keith F. Otterbein, 'Why the Iroquois Won,' *Ethnohistory* 11 (1964), 56–61; and Graves, *Chippawa*, 91–2

19 Peter B. Porter to William L. Stone, 26 May 1840, A. Conger Goodyear Collection, B&ECHS. See Chapter 7 for details on Chippawa.

20 Graymont, *Iroquois in the American Revolution*, 20–3; and Lewis H. Morgan, *League of the Iroquois* (1851; Secaucas 1972), 72

21 Articles sent up ... , 1814, NAC, RG 10, vol. 477, 172052–3; Requisition for the ... post of St Joseph for ... 1813, RG 10, vol. 476, 171490–1; Req. of goods to supply H.M. Indian stores, Amherstburg ... 1814, RG 10, vol. 477, 171772–4; Req. for stores for presents to Indians who resort to Michilimackinac ... for ... 1814, RG 10, vol. 476, 171438–44; and Req. made on behalf of the people of the River Thames, 24 June 1814, RG 10, vol. 3, 1446

22 Barber, *Instructions*, 1–3; De Witt Bailey, 'Those Board of Ordnance Indian Guns – Again,' *Museum of the Fur Trade Quarterly* 21 (1985); Lee Burke, 'Wilson Cypher Guns – Chief's Guns of the Revolution,' American Society of Arms Collectors *Bulletin*, 1996, 22–33; Ross Egles, 'Canadian Indian Treaty Guns,' *Canadian Journal of Arms Collecting* 14 (1976), 53; Glover, *Peninsular Preparation*, 54–5; and personal curatorial experience, 1985–97

23 Account of Indian presents forwarded to Burlington, 28 Oct. 1814, NAC, RG 10, vol. 477, 172069; and James Mann, *Medical Sketches of the Campaigns of 1812, 13, 14* (Dedham, Mass. 1816), 215. At Queenston Heights the British captured buck and ball and buckshot cartridges. It seems logical that they issued them to militia and natives along with the weapons captured there (Return of ordnance, &c. captured, 1 Dec. 1812, *DH*, 4:75). Archaeologists found buckshot within the skull of an American soldier excavated from the 1814 field hospital graveyard near Fort Erie in 1988 (communication from Dr Ron Williamson of Archaeological Services Inc., 21 Jan. 1990).

24 Bailey, 'Ordnance Indian Guns – Again,' 11. This article was modified by Bailey, 'Those Board of Ordnance Indian Guns – Again? – Supplement,' *Museum of the Fur Trade Quarterly* 2 (1985), 6

25 Smith, *Geographical View*, 43; Fitzgibbon, 'Hints'; Dunlop, 'Recollections,' 48; and MS on Hunting, *VSN*, 28

26 Gordon Drummond to Lord Bathurst, 31 Jan. 1814, NAC, CO 42, vol. 355, 12–16

27 *JMJN*, 298. A watercolour by Rudolph von Steiger showing a native with a bayonet on his musket, *Deputation of Indians from the Mississippi Tribes to the Governor-General*, dated 1814, is at NAC.

28 Porter to ?, 17 July 1813, B&ECHS, Peter B. Porter Papers; Porter to John Armstrong, 8 Apr. 1814, in Allan J. Ferguson, 'Notes on the Dress of Indian Allies, 1814,' *Military Collector and Historian* 33 (1981), 85; Robert M. Reilley, *United States Martial Flintlocks* (Lincoln 1986), 85–9, 126–9, 224–5; and René Chartrand, *Uniforms and Equipment of the United States Forces in the War of 1812* (Youngstown 1992), 99–100. One limited source lists the ratio of rifles to muskets among Iroquois allied to the United States as eleven to seven (Deputation of the Six Nations to the secretary of war, 20 Feb. 1815, American Philosophical Society, Philadelphia).

29 Matthew Elliott to Isaac Brock, 12 Jan. 1812, *BD*, 1:281; William Claus to Brock, 16 June 1812, *BD*, 1:311; *JMJN*, 298; Porter to Jacob Brown, 26 May 1814, *DH*, 2:398; Snyderman, *Tree of Peace*, 47, 72; Arthur C. Parker, 'The Senecas in the War of 1812,' *NYH* 15 (1916), 86; and Lewis H. Morgan, *Report to the Regents of the University upon the Articles Furnished the Indian Collection* (1849), in Elisabeth Tooker, ed., *Lewis H. Morgan on Iroquois Material Culture* (Tucson 1994), 183. *The Seneca Schoolhouse*, a watercolour painted in 1821 by a Tuscarora named Dennis Cusick (private collection, New York), shows Iroquois using bows and arrows.

30 'Articles sent up ... 1814,' NAC, RG 10, vol. 477, 172052–3; Requisition for the ... post of St Joseph for ... 1813, RG 10, vol. 476, 171490–1; Req. of goods to supply H.M. Indian stores, Amherstburg ... 1814, RG 10, vol. 477, 171772–4; Req. for stores for presents to Indians who resort to Michilimackinac ... for ... 1814, RG 10, 476, 171438–44; Req. made on behalf of the people of the River Thames, 24 June 1814, RG 10, vol. 3, 1446; Dunlop, 'Recollections,' 48; *JMJN*, 69; *Peter of Buffalo*, watercolour by the Baroness Hyde de Neuville (1807; New-York Historical Society); Lewis H. Morgan, *Report on the Fabrics, Inventions, Implements and Utensils of the Iroquois, made to the Regents of the University*, 22 Jan. 1851, in Tooker, *Material Culture*, 249; Morgan, *League*, 364; Snyderman, *Tree of Peace*, 73; George C. Neumann, *History of Weapons of the American Revolution* (New York 1967), 342–3; and Paul W. Sciulli and Richard M. Gramly, 'Analysis of the Fort Laurens, Ohio Skeletal Sample,' *American Journal of Physical Anthropology* 80 (1989), 15

31 Unidentified witness, c. 1777, cited in E.A. Cruikshank, *Butler's Rangers* (1893; Niagara Falls 1988), 50; and Smith, *Geographical View*, 43. Snyderman, *Tree of Peace*, 57, quotes a source from the 1750s describing spears being thrown, but in the American Revolution they seem to have been used principally as thrusting weapons (Patrick Campbell, *Travels in the Interior Inhabited Parts of North*

220 Notes to pages 76–7

America, 1793, cited in *VSN*, 63). There is also an account of an American-allied Iroquois thrusting his spear into a Canadian in 1813 (Livingston petition, after 1815, *DH*, 7:39). A spear point survives in the collection of Heritage Toronto. Although pikes had fallen into general disuse among professional troops long before 1812, they still saw limited service among poorly armed militia, in naval situations, among some infantry, such as British army sergeants, and as revived experimental weapons in parts of the U.S. Army.

32 Lewis H. Morgan, Tonawanda field notes, 1849, in Tooker, *Material Culture*, 120; Ruth B. Phillips, *Patterns of Power* (Kleinburg, Ont. 1984); William L. Stone, *Life and Times of Sa-go-ye-wat-ha, or Red Jacket* (Albany 1866), 349; Morgan, *League*, 362–3; and Sciulli and Gramly, 'Analysis of the Fort Laurens, Ohio Skeletal Sample,' 15

33 Inventory of goods supplied to British-allied natives, c. 1813, NAC, RG 10, vol. 477, 171833; Porter to Armstrong, 27 Mar. 1814, in Ferguson, 'Dress of Indian Allies,' 85; Smith, *Ohio Indians*, 39; Anon., 'First Campaign of an A.D.C.,' *Military and Naval Magazine of the United States* 2 (1834), 334–5; Snyderman, *Tree of Peace*, 79; and Timothy J. Shannon, 'Dressing for Success on the Mohawk Frontier,' *WMQ* 53 (1996), 13–42

34 Ruth B. Phillips, 'Like a Star I Shine,' in Julia D. Harrison et al., eds., *The Spirit Sings* (Calgary 1987), 83; Phillips, *Patterns of Power*, 26; and Stone, *Red Jacket*, 333. Prisoners were tied by the neck (Anon., 'First Campaign,' 260–1); cf. a French copy (c. 1666) and adaptation of an Iroquois pictograph showing this practice, from the Archives nationales (Paris), illustrated in *Handbook*, 299. A pre-1822 Iroquois (probably Mohawk) belt is in the Royal Ontario Museum. For a discussion on these belts, see Gary S. Zaboly, 'The Use of Tumplines in the French and Indian War,' *Military Collector and Historian* 46 (1994), 109–13.

35 Laurence M. Hauptman, 'Samuel George (1795–1873),' *NYH* 70 (1989), 10–11; cf. Anne Powell, 'A Journey from Montreal to Detroit,' 1789, in William Renwick Riddell, ed., *Old Province Tales* (Toronto 1920), 82–8

36 Phillips, 'Like a Star,' 81

37 François Alexandre Frédéric La Rochefoucault-Liancourt, *Travels in Canada, 1795*, Henry Neuman, trans., William Renwick Riddell, ed., in *Thirteenth Report of the Bureau of Archives for the Province of Ontario, 1916* (Toronto 1917), 45–6

38 Note on goods remaining in H.M. Indian storehouses, Upper Canada, 1812, NAC, RG 10, vol. 3, 1232; George Heriot, *Travels through the Canadas* (London 1807), 2:292; Snyderman, *Tree of Peace*, 57; and Phillips, 'Like a Star,' 83

39 Samuel Holmes, 'A Pedestrian Tour to the Falls of Niagara in Upper Canada,' MS c. 1815, Public Record Office of Northern Ireland, 156, 198. I thank Ian Vincent for bringing this document to my attention.

40 La Rochefoucault-Liancourt, *Travels*, 45–6

41 Heriot, *Travels*, 2:292–3; William N. Fenton, 'Northern Iroquois Culture Patterns,' in *Handbook*, 303; and, Phillips, 'Like a Star,' 83. A painting of an Oneida with tattooing is *Good Peter* by John Trumbull, 1792 (Yale University Art Gallery). The most famous image of an Iroquois with tattoos is Benjamin West's *Death of Wolfe*, 1770 (National Gallery of Canada).

42 Illustrations of scalp locks include: William Berczy's 1807 portrait of Joseph Brant (National Gallery of Canada); West's *Death of Wolfe*, and in the depiction of an Iroquois school house at Grand River by James Peachy, in *A Primer for the Use of the Mohawk Children* (London 1786), reproduced in *VSN*, pl. 1.

43 John Heckewelder, *History, Manners, and Customs of the Indian Nations*, 1824, in James Axtell, 'The Unkindest Cut, or Who Invented Scalping,' in Axtell, *The European and the Indian* (New York 1981), 214; George Catlin, *North American Indians* (1841; New York 1989), 213–14, 220, 231–3; and Phillips, 'Like a Star,' 81

44 Pierre Pouchot, *Memoirs on the Late War in North America between France and England* (1782), Michael Cardy, trans., Brian Leigh Dunnigan, ed. (Youngstown 1994), 444. A watercolour of this practice is *Peter of Buffalo*, by the Baroness Hyde de Neuville (1807; New-York Historical Society).

45 Phillips, 'Like a Star,' 80. A late example of a shell gorget is shown in Gilbert Stuart's 1786 portrait of Joseph Brant (New York Historical Association, Cooperstown). The Royal Ontario Museum has a shell gorget with silver decorations that is said to have been Brant's (illustrated in *Handbook*, 435). For silver ornamentation, including gorgets, see N. Jaye Fredrickson, *The Covenant Chain* (Ottawa 1980); and Martha Wilson Hamilton, *Silver of the Fur Trade, 1680–1820* (Chelmsford, Mass. 1995).

46 *JMJN*, 126–7, 129

47 Ibid., 129; Heriot, *Travels*, 2:431; Alexander McMullen narrative, n.d., *DH*, 2:373; Fenton, 'Cass's Questions,' 121; Mahon, 'Indian Warfare,' 259; Wiley Sword, *President Washington's Indian War* (Norman 1985), 195; Morgan, *League*, 340; and Snyderman, *Tree of Peace*, 56

48 MS on warfare, *VSN*, 33

49 Ibid., and *JMJN*, 129–30

50 Jacques Viger diary, 28 May 1813, NAC, MG 24; Fitzgibbon, 'Hints'; and David Wingfield, 'Four Years on the Lakes of Canada,' MS, n.d., NAC, MG 24

51 Dunlop, 'Recollections,' 48

52 Fitzgibbon, 'Hints'; *JMJN*, 127–8; William Atherton, *Narrative of the Suffering & Defeat of the North-Western Army* (Frankfort, Ky 1842), 38–9; Snyderman, *Tree of Peace*, 62; and Fenton, 'Cass's Questions,' 123

53 John Sugden, *Tecumseh's Last Stand* (Norman 1985), 16–17; Mahon, 'Indian Warfare,' 257; Fenton, 'Cass's Questions,' 121; Eid, 'Indian Leadership,' 85;

Douglas W. Boyce, 'A Glimpse of Iroquois Culture History through the Eyes of
Joseph Brant and John Norton,' *Proceedings of the American Philosophical Society*
117 (1973), 290; and Graymont, *Iroquois in the American Revolution*, 21–2.
Norton (*JMJN*, 129), in his description of Iroquoian Cherokee warfare, notes:
'One rencounter is all that is sought for in an expedition, and when it is met
with, they say, "This is the fortune, the Great Spirit has prepared for us."' Presumably this attitude was common to a great many different native peoples as
the historical record is full of examples of war parties leaving for home after
an engagement when tactical and strategic considerations suggest that
remaining in the field was more desirable. Furthermore, the rest of Norton's
description of Cherokee warfare conforms to practices that were common
among the Six Nations and other aboriginal people of the lower Great Lakes
region. Cf. D. Peter MacLeod, *The Canadian Iroquois and the Seven Years' War*
(Ottawa 1996), 30. The ability of people to come and go from campaign can
be seen throughout the 1813 and 1814 campaigns described in subsequent
chapters of this book.

54 MS on warfare, *VSN*, 33–4; Peter E. Russell, 'Redcoats in the Wilderness,'
   WMQ 35 (1978), 629–52; Sword, *Washington's Indian War*, 299–311; and
   Mahon, 'Indian Warfare'

55 *JMJN*, 305–7, 323. For an interpretation of Iroquois stoicism and its psychological strains, see A.F.C. Wallace, *The Death and Rebirth of the Seneca* (1969; New
   York 1972), 59–93.

56 *JMJN*, 323

57 Richard Holmes, *Firing Line* (Harmondsworth 1987), 206–8

58 *JMJN*, 315, 321; cf. Atherton, *Suffering and Defeat of the North-Western Army*,
   51–71. Anecdotal evidence suggests that the guilt for atrocities committed by
   combatants falls disproportionately at the feet of those who shirk their
   combat responsibilities. I thank Dr J.L. Granatstein for this observation.

59 Governor Blacksnake, *Chainbreaker*, Thomas S. Abler, ed. (Lincoln 1989), 109

60 James E. Seaver, *A Narrative of the Life of Mrs. Mary Jemison* (1824; Syracuse
   1990), 92; Porter to Stone, 26 May 1840, Goodyear Collection, B&ECHS; John
   Smoke Johnson comment to Lyman C. Draper, 11 Oct. 1877, Brant Papers,
   Draper MSS, State Historical Society of Wisconsin, ser. F, vol. 15, 192; Gregory
   Evans Dowd, *A Spirited Resistance* (Baltimore 1992), 87–9; Wallace, *Death and
   Rebirth*, 137; Isabel Thompson Kelsay, *Joseph Brant, 1743–1807* (Syracuse 1984),
   288; and Graymont, *Iroquois in the American Revolution*, 174, 217

61 Long, *Travels*, 22; Seaver, *Mary Jemison*, 92; Kelsay, *Joseph Brant*, 21; and Sword,
   Washington's Indian War, 186

62 John Richardson, 1826, quoted in Sugden, *Tecumseh's Last Stand*, 131

63 Wingfield, 'Four Years on the Lakes,' NAC

64 Kelsay, *Joseph Brant*, 22; G.F.G. Stanley, *The War of 1812* (Ottawa 1983), 153; and Sword, *Washington's Indian War*, 191

65 Alexander Smyth to the ... Army of the Centre, 17 Nov. 1812, *DH*, 4:216; Porter to Stone, 26 May 1840, Goodyear Collection, B&ECHS; E.A. Cruikshank, ed., 'Reminiscences of Colonel Claus,' *Canadiana* 1 (1889), 182; and Cruikshank, 'Blockade of Fort George,' Niagara Historical Society, *Transactions* 3 (1898), 59, 64

66 Smith, *Ohio Indians*, 38; Heriot, *Travels*, 2:429; and Kelsay, *Joseph Brant*, 216

67 George McFeely, Dec. 1813, quoted in John C. Fredriksen, ed., 'Chronicle of Valor,' *Western Pennsylvania Historical Magazine* 67 (1984), 256; cf. Long, *Travels*, 22; Porter to Stone, 26 May 1840, Goodyear Collection, B&ECHS; and Seaver, *Mary Jemison*, 14

68 Smyth to the ... Army of the Centre, 17 Nov. 1812, *DH*, 4:216

69 Peter L. Chambers to William Smelt, 9 Nov. 1814, *DH*, 2:300

70 Black Bird's speech, 15 July 1813, *DH*, 6:242

71 An exception occurred in the United States Army in 1814. See Chapter 7.

72 Buffalo council minutes, 8 Nov. 1812, *DH*, 4:20–1

4: The Niagara Campaign

1 Quoted in George Heriot, *Travels through the Canadas* (London 1807), 2:428; cf. Joseph François Lafitau, *Customs of the American Indians Compared with the Customs of Primitive Times* (1724): William N. Fenton and Elizabeth L. Moore, eds. and trans. (Toronto 1974–7), 2:112

2 Isaac Brock to Lord Liverpool, 29 Aug. 1812, NAC, CO 42, vol. 352, 105–7; and *JMJN*, 302

3 Brock to Sir George Prevost, 28 Sept. 1812, *VSN*, 197–8

4 *JMJN*, 302

5 MS on warfare, ascribed as late eighteenth century but probably early nineteenth, judging from internal evidence, *VSN*, 32; Heriot, *Travels*, 2:427–8, 476; Lafitau, *Customs*, 2:110; William N. Fenton, 'Northern Iroquoian Cultural Patterns,' in *Handbook*, 316; Ives Goddard, 'Agreskwe, A Northern Iroquoian Deity,' in Michael Foster et al., eds., *Extending the Rafters* (Albany 1984); Gregory Evans Dowd, *A Spirited Resistance* (Baltimore 1992), 11–12; and William N. Fenton, *The Iroquois Eagle Dance, an Offshoot of the Calumet Dance* (1953; Syracuse 1991), 107

6 MS on warfare, *VSN*, 32; cf. Heriot, *Travels*, 2:477–8; Lafitau, *Customs*, 2:112–13; Joshua Marsden, *Narrative of a Mission to Nova Scotia, New Brunswick, and the Somers Islands; with a Tour to Lake Ontario* (Plymouth, Eng. 1816), 191–2; and Fenton, *Eagle Dance*, 104–11, 173

7 Jeremy Belknap and Jedidiah Morse, 'Report on The Oneida, Stockbridge and
   Brothertown Indians, 1796,' *Indian Notes and Monographs*, 54 (1955), 10; and
   Isabel Thompson Kelsay, *Joseph Brant, 1743–1807* (Syracuse 1984), 98

8 *JMJN*, 302; Heriot, *Travels*, 2:430–1; Lafitau, *Customs*, 2:114–15; William N.
   Fenton, 'Answers to Governor Cass's Questions by Jacob Jameson, a Seneca
   [ca. 1821–1825],' *Ethnohistory* 16 (1969), 122; Douglas W. Boyce, 'A Glimpse of
   Iroquois Culture History through the Eyes of Joseph Brant and John Norton,'
   Proceedings of the American Philosophical Society 117 (1973), 290

9 *JMJN*, 302; and various documents, *DH*, 4

10 Brock to Prevost, 7 Sept. 1812, *VSN*, 197

11 Brock to the Earl of Liverpool, 29 Aug. 1812, NAC, CO 42, vol. 352, 105–7

12 *JMJN*, 302–3; and John Norton to Henry Goulburn, 29 Jan. 1816, in E.A.
   Cruikshank, ed., 'Campaigns of 1812–14,' *Niagara Historical Society Transactions* 9 (1902), 43

13 Brock to Prevost, 9 Oct. 1812, *DH*, 4:44

14 List of troops under Stephen Van Rensselaer, 12 Oct. 1812, *DH*, 4:68; and *DH*,
   4:*passim* (e.g., Report of the state of the Twelfth Infantry, 5 Oct. 1812, 243;
   Report on the state of the Fourteenth Infantry, 5 Oct. 1812, 241–2; and Report
   on the militia [New York *Evening Post*], 25 Nov. 1812, 219)

15 Van Rensselaer to Henry Dearborn, 8 and 9 Oct. 1812, *DH*, 4:41–2; and
   Theodore J. Crackel, 'The Battle of Queenston Heights,' in Charles E. Heller
   and William A. Stofft, eds., *America's First Battles* (Lawrence 1986), 44

16 Crackel, 'Queenston Heights,' 44

17 Thomas Evans to ?, 15 Oct. 1812, *DH*, 4:111–13; Letter of 16 Oct. 1812 to the
   Philadelphia *Aurora*, 4 Nov. 1812, *DH*, 4:128

18 John Wool to William L. Stone, 13 Sept. 1838, reprinted in *New York Public
   Library Bulletin* 9 (1905), 120–2; Wool, 'General Wool on General Scott's Auto-
   biography,' *Historical Magazine and Notes and Queries*, 2nd ser., 2 (1867), 263–5;
   Archibald McLean to the editor of the *Quebec Mercury*, 27 Oct. 1812, *DH*,
   4:114–6; G.S. Jarvis Narrative, n.d., *DH*, 4:116–17; and J. Mackay Hitsman, *The
   Incredible War of 1812* (1965; Toronto 1972), 87–9

19 *JMJN*, 304–5; and C.M. Johnston, *Brant County* (Toronto 1967), 21

20 John Chrystie to Thomas H. Cushing, 22 Feb. 1813, *DH*, 4:100; Thomas
   Mead's statement, 18 Nov. 1812, *DH*, 4:91; and Jared Willson to a friend, 9
   Nov. 1812, in 'A Rifleman of Queenston,' Buffalo Historical Society *Publica-
   tions* 9 (1906), 374

21 *JMJN*, 305–6

22 Ibid., 306; Willson to a friend, 9 Nov. 1812, 'A Rifleman of Queenston,' 374;
   and Chrystie to Cushing, 22 Feb. 1813, *DH*, 4:101

23 John Lovett to Joseph Alexander, 14 Oct. 1812, in Carol Whitfield, 'The Battle

of Queenston Heights,' *Occasional Papers in Archaeology and History* 11 (1974), 16

24 *JMJN*, 306

25 Ibid., 306–7. Shrapnel were hollow round shells filled with small balls and gunpowder. When fired, a fuse on the shell ignited so that the shell would explode close to the target and rain iron fragments and balls down upon the enemy.

26 Mead statement, 18 Nov. 1812, *DH*, 4:92

27 Willson to a friend, 9 Nov. 1812, in 'A Rifleman of Queenston,' 374

28 Chrystie to Cushing, 22 Feb. 1813, *DH*, 4:101; cf. *JMJN*, 308

29 Norton to Goulburn, 29 Jan. 1816, in Cruikshank, 'Campaigns,' 44

30 Roger Sheaffe to Prevost, 13 Oct. 1812, in Robert S. Allen, 'The British Indian Department on the Frontier in North America, 1755–1830,' *Occasional Papers in Archaeology and History* 14 (1975), 80

31 *JMJN*, 308

32 Chrystie to Cushing, 22 Feb. 1813, *DH*, 4:102

33 Van Rensselaer to William Eustis, 14 Nov. 1812, *DH*, 4:81; Chrystie to Cushing, 22 Feb. 1813, *DH*, 4:101–2; and Whitfield, 'Queenston Heights,' 15

34 A member of Captain Cameron's Company of York Militia to the editor of the *Kingston Gazette*, 14 Oct. 1812, *DH*, 5:14

35 *JMJN*, 308–9; the New York *War*, 31 Oct. 1812, *DH*, 4:120; and Letter of 14 Oct. 1812 to the *Quebec Mercury*, 27 Oct. 1812, *DH*, 4:117

36 John Smith to Henry Procter, 18 Oct. 1812, NARA, War of 1812 Papers of the Department of State, Misc. Intercepted Correspondence, 1789–1814

37 *JMJN*, 309

38 Return of killed, wounded, and prisoners, n.d., *DH*, 4:74; Alexander Smyth to Dearborn, 24 Oct. 1812, *DH*, 4:159–60; T.G. Ridout to his brother, 21 Oct. 1812, *DH*, 4:146; and Hitsman, *Incredible War*, 90

39 Sheaffe–Van Rensselaer–Smyth correspondence, Oct. 1812, in 'The Letterbook of Gen. Sir Roger Sheaffe,' Buffalo Historical Society *Publications* 17 (1914), 277–311; Sheaffe to Prevost, 13 Oct. 1812, *DH*, 4:73; Casualty list, n.d., *DH*, 4:76; *Buffalo Gazette*, 20 Oct. 1812, *DH*, 4:122; Hitsman, *Incredible War*, 90; Daniel J. Glenney, 'An Ethnohistory of the Grand River Iroquois and the War of 1812,' MA thesis, University of Guelph, 1973, 79; and E.A. Cruikshank, 'The Employment of the Indians in the War of 1812,' in *Annual Report of the American Historical Association for the Year 1895*, 333. Another source said six Iroquois were killed (letter of 14 Oct. 1812 to the *Quebec Mercury*, 27 Oct. 1812, *DH*, 4:118).

40 General order, 21 Oct. 1812, *DH*, 4:151

41 *JMJN*, 308

42 Examples from 1813 include ibid., 334; George McFeely, May 1813, in John C.

Fredriksen, ed., 'Chronicle of Valor,' *Western Pennsylvania Historical Magazine* 67 (1984), 263. For a discussion of the limitations of riflemen versus musketmen in terms of volume of fire, see David Gates, *The British Light Infantry Arm, c.1790–1815* (London 1987), 82–4

43 Patrick McDonogh to ?, 13 Nov. 1812, *DH*, 5:16–17

44 Lovett to Alexander, 14 Oct. 1812, *DH*, 4:86

45 Carl F. Klinck, 'Norton, John,' *DCB*, 6:551; and *JMJN*, cxvii

46 *JMJN*, lxxviii, cxc

47 This Mohawk tradition is preserved in a letter from Albert Johnson to Lyman C. Draper, 11 Feb. 1878, State Historical Society of Wisconsin, Draper MSS, ser. F, Brant Papers, vol. 14, 23–4. Writing from the Six Nations Reserve, Johnson noted that the assessment came from his grandfather, John Smoke Johnson, who 'fought under ... [Norton] at the Battles of Queenston, Chippewa, Lundy's Lane, & Fort Erie.'

48 Ridout to his brother, 21 Oct. 1812, *DH*, 4:147

49 Fort George council minutes, 6 Nov. 1812, *DH*, 4:198–9

50 *JMJN*, 310; and Dearborn to Smyth, 28 Oct. 1812, *DH*, 4:168

51 *JMJN*, 310–11; Cecil Bisshopp to Sheaffe, 1 Dec. 1812, NAC, CO 42, vol. 354, 11–15; and Hitsman, *Incredible War*, 91–3. Total native strength at this event was ninety; see John Strachan, 'Life of Col. Bishoppe,' Dec. 1813, in *John Strachan Letter Book*, George W. Spragge, ed. (Toronto 1946), 7.

52 William H. Winder to Smyth, 3 Nov. 1812, *DH*, 4:177; and Abstract of provisions issued to Indians at ... Cattaraugus Creek, 31 Oct. 1812, *R&W*, 68

53 Norton to Goulburn, 29 Jan. 1816, in 'Campaigns,' 45; and *JMJN*, 312. The presence of women on campaign had also been a reason during the American Revolution in preventing the Iroquois from harvesting their crops; see Barbara Graymont, *The Iroquois in the American Revolution* (Syracuse 1972), 203. In 1812 this seems to have continued to be a factor, while the move of many men into agricultural labour exacerbated the problem (see Chapter 1).

54 Memorandum, 6 Nov. 1812, AO, John Strachan Papers; Hitsman, *Incredible War*, 102–3; E.A. Cruikshank, 'From Isle aux Noix to Châteauguay,' *Proceedings and Transactions of the Royal Society of Canada*, 3rd ser., 7 (1913), 169–70; and E.J. Devine, *Historic Caugnawaga* (Montreal 1922), 322

55 See Chapter 2.

56 Carl Benn, *The Battle of York* (Belleville 1984), 18–22

5: The Twisted Road to Beaver Dams

1 *JMJN*, 327. See *JMJN*, xxv–xxvii re his cousin.

2 J. Mackay Hitsman, *The Incredible War of 1812* (1965; Toronto 1972), 103–12,

115–16; corrections and notations on troop strength are based on research shared with me by Stuart Sutherland, to whom I am grateful.

3 *JMJN*, 312–14; George Macdonnell to Edward Baynes, 22 Feb. 1813, *DH*, 5:76; Hitsman, *Incredible War*, 113–14, 117–20; and Franklin B. Hough, *A History of St. Lawrence and Franklin Counties* (Albany 1853), 156

4 *JMJN*, 315–17; and John Vincent to Sir Roger Sheaffe, 25 Mar. 1813, NAC, CO 42, vol. 354, 78–9

5 *JMJN*, 318–20; Sheaffe to Henry Procter, 13 Apr. 1813, in 'The Letterbook of Gen. Sir Roger Hale Sheaffe,' *Buffalo Historical Society Publications* 17 (1914), 377; and Sheaffe to Gordon Drummond, 19 Apr. 1813, quoted in J. McE. Murray, 'John Norton,' *OH* 37 (1945), 12

6 Carl Benn, *Historic Fort York, 1793–1993* (Toronto 1993), 48–9

7 Ibid., 49–66

8 Ibid., 62; *JMJN*, 318–19; and Vincent to Sir George Prevost, 19 May 1813, NAC, RG 8, vol. 678, 301

9 *JMJN*, 322–7; and E.A. Cruikshank, 'Blockade of Fort George,' *Niagara Historical Society Transactions* 3 (1898), 5

10 Jacques Viger diary, 28 May 1813, NAC, MG 24; Hitsman, *Incredible War*, 127–8, 131–2; and Patrick A. Wilder, *The Battle of Sackett's Harbour* (Baltimore 1994), 73

11 John B. Glegg to William Claus, 24 June 1813 (copy), AO, Kirby Collection; and Hitsman, *Incredible War*, 127–8

12 Notes by W.H. Merritt, n.d., *DH*, 5:262; *JMJN*, 327; and *VSN*, lxxiv. Among other reasons why Vincent did not retreat are that Burlington was the strongest defensible position west of Kingston, that the roads were in very bad condition that spring, and that the American squadron might have been able to intercept him if he tried to march east (John Harvey, Journal of a staff officer, c. 1815, AO, MS 842).

13 Harvey, Journal, AO

14 William Claus's military report, 4 Dec. 1813, *VSN*, 209

15 Henry Dearborn to John Armstrong, 8 June 1813, 'Blockade,' 23. See. Chapter 2 re Sullivan.

16 *JMJN*, cxviii

17 *VSN*, lxxiii

18 Vincent's speech to the Six Nations, 22 Oct. 1813, *VSN*, 207; *JMJN*, 327–8; William Claus report, 4 Dec. 1812, *VSN*, 213–14; John C. Fredriksen, ed., 'Memoirs of Captain Ephraim Shaler,' *New England Quarterly* 57 (1984), 416; Fredriksen, 'Lawyer, Soldier, Judge: Incidents in the Life of Joseph Lee Smith of New Britain, Connecticut,' *Connecticut Historical Society Bulletin* 51 (1986), 111–12; and Hitsman, *Incredible War*, 133–4

19 Anon., 'First Campaign of an A.D.C.,' *Military and Naval Magazine of the United States* 2 (1834), 207–9; *JMJN*, 328–9; and Hitsman, *Incredible War,* 134–5

20 *JMJN*, 329

21 Petition of fifteen chiefs, 9 Jan. 1814, *VSN*, 219

22 *JMJN*, 329

23 Cruikshank, 'Blockade,' 9

24 The memory of the Iroquois-American skirmish that followed this crisis (described in the next paragraph) is preserved in 'The Battle between the Americans and the British during the War of 1812,' as told by Ray Buck, MS, 1986. I thank Tom Hill of the Woodland Cultural Centre for sharing a printed copy with me.

25 *JMJN*, 327

26 Cf. similar threats made in 1812: *JMJN*, 297; and William Kerr to Glegg, 17 Aug. 1812, AO, Alexander Fraser Papers

27 *JMJN*, 329–30; Anon, 'First Campaign,' 282–4; Buck 'The Battle between the Americans and the British,' Woodland Cultural Centre; and Hitsman, *Incredible War,* 135. The anonymous American account, 'First Campaign,' agrees well with the Buck oral tradition.

28 Anon., 'First Campaign,' 210, 280–8; Charles Askin to John Askin, 8 July 1813, *DH*, 6:204; and Cruikshank, 'Blockade,' 18–20

29 Vincent to ?, n.d., Hitsman, *Incredible War,* 135; cf. *JMJN*, 330

30 James B. Dennis to ?, 8 June 1813, *DH*, 6:59; Claus report, 4 Dec. 1813, *VSN*, 209; George McFeely, June 1813, in John C. Fredriksen, ed., 'Chronicle of Valor,' *Western Pennsylvania Historical Magazine* 67 (1984), 266; Thomas Evans to John Harvey, 10 June 1813, *DH*, 6:62; and G.F.G. Stanley, 'The Indians in the War of 1812,' in Morris Zaslow, ed., *The Defended Border* (Toronto 1964), 182

31 *JMJN*, 330; Cruikshank, 'Blockade,' 28; and Stanley, 'Indians,' 182

32 Claus report, 4 Dec. 1813, *VSN*, 209; Cruikshank, 'Blockade,' 29; and Cruikshank, *The Fight in the Beechwoods* (Niagara 1889), 12

33 Cyrenius Chapin, *Chapin's Review of Armstrong's Notices of the War of 1812* (Black Rock, NY 1836), 10; Cruikshank, *Beechwoods*, 11, 14; Ruth McKenzie, 'Ingersoll, Laura,' *DCB*, 9:406; cf. Norton's brief notation about Secord, *JMJN*, 330–1. I am grateful to Robert Malcomson for letting me read his forthcoming book, *The Battle of Beaver Dams*, to be published by the Canadian War Museum.

34 *JMJN*, 332; Dominique Ducharme's account, 5 June 1826, *VSN*, 201–2; Journal of Major Isaac Roach, 1812–24, in *Pennsylvania Magazine of History and Biography* 17 (1893), 148–9; Charles G. Boerstler's narrative, n.d., *DH*, 6:131; Kerr to Claus, 8 Dec. 1815, *DH*, 6:122; C. Askin to J. Askin, 8 July 1813, *DH*, 6:203; Return of the Six Nations tribesmen at Beaver Dams, 24 June 1813, *VSN*,

203–5 (which lists all their names); and Cruikshank, *Beechwoods*, 16. Askin placed 454 men on the Iroquois side. The Return and Kerr's list are slightly different. Kerr designated them: 12 from Thames River; 70 from Rice Lake; 180 Seven Nations; and 72 Mohawks, 9 Oneidas, 11 Aughquagas, 15 Tuscaroras, 40 Cayugas, 20 Onondagas, 5 Senecas, 25 Delawares, 4 Tutelos, and 2 Nanticokes from the Grand River. Norton's account agrees in terms of the total number of men involved, although he seems to have made mistakes in enumerating the sub-units. His account is useful, however, in noting that the Seven Nations contingent included people from Kahnawake, Kanesatake, and Akwesasne.

35 Boerstler narrative, n.d., *DH*, 5:131; and Roach journal, 1812–24, 148

36 Roach journal, 1812–24, 148–9; and Ducharme account, 5 June 1826, *VSN*, 201

37 Boerstler narrative, n.d., *DH*, 6:132; Ducharme account, 5 June 1826, *VSN*, 201; Roach journal, 1812–24, 149; and Cruikshank, *Beechwoods*, 17. Canister was a tin filled with iron balls which, when fired, fell apart so that the balls could spray out at their target, like an enormous shotgun blast.

38 Roach journal, 1812–24, 149; Report of a court of enquiry on the conduct of Lieutenant-Colonel Boerstler, 17 Feb. 1815, *DH*, 6:152; and Cyrenius Chapin's story in the *Buffalo Gazette*, 29 July 1813, *DH*, 6:142

39 Boerstler narrative, n.d., *DH*, 6:132

40 Roach journal, 1812–24, 149

41 Boerstler narrative, n.d., *DH*, 6:132; and Ducharme account, 5 June 1826, *VSN*, 201

42 Report of a court of enquiry, 17 Feb. 1815, *DH*, 6:152; Boerstler narrative, n.d., *DH*, 6:133; and Roach journal, 1812–24, 150. A column of platoons consisted of small groups of ten or so men standing in two-deep linear formations, with a space of a few metres between them and the groups in front and behind. If necessary while on a march, these little lines could all wheel to the right or left in unison to form one long line and open fire or otherwise deploy as required.

43 Boerstler narrative, n.d., *DH*, 6:133; and Cruikshank, *Beechwoods*, 17

44 Ducharme account, 5 June 1826, *VSN*, 201

45 Boerstler narrative, n.d., *DH*, 6:134; cf. Report of a court of enquiry, 17 Feb. 1815, *DH*, 6:152

46 Ducharme account, 5 June 1826, *VSN*, 201

47 C. Askin to J. Askin, 8 July 1813, *DH*, 6:203; and Mary Agnes Fitzgibbon, *A Veteran of 1812* (Toronto 1894), 86. See Chapter 3 re weapons issues.

48 Ducharme account, 5 June 1826, *VSN*, 201. French was the primary European language among Seven Nations people at that time, unlike today when English dominates; see Elizabeth Simcoe, 7 July 1793, *Diary of Mrs. John Graves Simcoe*, John Ross Robertson, ed. (Toronto 1911), 175.

49 *Montreal Gazette*, 6 July 1813, *DH*, 6:118; Boerstler narrative, n.d., *DH*, 6:133–4; and Cruikshank, *Beechwoods*, 18

50 Roach journal, 1812–24, 150; Chapin's story, 29 July 1813, *DH*, 6:143; and Ducharme account, 5 June 1826, *VSN*, 201

51 Roach journal, 1812–24, 151

52 Chapin's story, 29 July 1813, *DH*, 6:144. Allowing troops to loot captured enemies often was preferable to ordering them not to do so because soldiers otherwise might murder prisoners and rob the bodies; see J.G. Simcoe, *Journal of Operations of the Queen's Rangers*, reprinted as *Simcoe's Military Journal* (1787); John Gellner, ed. (Toronto 1962), 6–7.

53 John Le Couteur, 24 June 1813, *Merry Hearts Make Light Days*, Donald E. Graves, ed. (Ottawa 1993), 127

54 Anon., 'First Campaign,' 201–2, 204

55 Roach journal, 1812–24, 151; Baynes memorandum, 28 June 1813, AO, Tupper Papers; Claus to Cecil Bisshopp, 25 June 1813, in E.A. Cruikshank, 'Reminiscences of Colonel Claus,' *Canadiana* 1 (1889), 178; and Le Couteur, *Merry Hearts*, 24 June 1813, 126–7

56 Ducharme account, 5 June 1826, *VSN*, 201–2; *VSN*, lxxv; Cruikshank, 'Colonel Claus,' 178; 'From the Soldier's Companion,' c. 1826, AO, Tupper Papers; and Cruikshank, *Beechwoods*, 20

57 Le Couteur, *Merry Hearts*, 24 June 1813, 127–9, 28n. 60

58 John Norton (who missed the action) joked, 'The *Cognawaga Indians* fought the *battle*, the *Mohawks* or Six Nations got the *plunder*, and *Fitzgibbon* got the *credit*'; see Merritt notes, n.d., *DH*, 6:123. For his part, Fitzgibbon wrote that it was the natives who 'beat the American detachment into a state of terror' and that he claimed credit only for 'taking advantage of a favorable moment to offer ... [the Americans] protection from the tomahawk and scalping knife'; see James Fitzgibbon to Kerr, 30 Mar. 1818, *DH*, 6:120–1.

59 *JMJN*, 332

60 Baron de Rottenburg to Baynes, 14 July 1813, *DH*, 6:233. See Chapter 2 re presents.

61 Anonymous speech, 26? June 1813, *DH*, 6:155–6. However, cash was distributed to cover expenses; see e.g., the receipt signed by John Brant, 14 July 1813, NAC, RG 10, vol. 477, 171628.

62 Ten Mile Creek council minutes, 8 July 1813, *DH*, 6:202; and Cross Roads council report, 5 July 1813, *DH*, 6:274

63 Baynes to Prevost, 1 July 1813, *BD*, 2:168; General Order, 30 Dec. 1813, in L. Homfray Irving, *Officers of the British Forces in Canada during the War of 1812–15* (Welland 1908); *Report of the Loyal and Patriotic Society of Upper Canada* (Montreal 1817); David Wingfield, 'Four Years on the Lakes of Canada,' n.d.,

NAC, MG 24; Claus to Sir John Johnson, 11 July 1813, *DH* 6:215–16; General Order, 6 July 1813, *DH*, 6:192; and Cruikshank, 'Colonel Claus,' *Canadiana* 1 (1889), 182. Claus said it was very difficult to obtain supplies for more than fifty men since the 'country was so stript of everything' because of the war. In contrast to Norton's claims, Claus said 'there was little discontent on that Head [among the natives attached to him] except by worthless fellows'; see Claus report, 4 Dec. 1813, *VSN*, 217. The gifts sent from Britain for the natives in 1813 did not arrive at Quebec until August; see John Sugden, *Tecumseh's Last Stand* (Norman 1985), 28. Some Seven Nations men still fought with the British in August (*JMJN*, 338).

6: Iroquois versus Iroquois

1 Quoted in Louis L. Babcock, *The War of 1812 on the Niagara Frontier* (Buffalo 1927), 108
2 John Armstrong to John Boyd, 7 July 1813, NARA, RG 107, Records of the Secretary of War, vol. 7, 7–8; and G.F.G. Stanley, *The War of 1812* (Ottawa 1983), 197–8
3 *JMJN*, 333
4 George Heriot, *Travels Through the Canadas* (London 1807), 2:432; Joseph François Lafitau, *Customs of the American Indians Compared with the Customs of Primitive Times* (1724); William N. Fenton and Elizabeth L. Moore, eds. and trans. (Toronto 1974–7), 2:149–50; Sir William Johnson to Arthur Lee, 28 Feb. 1771, in *Documentary History of the State of New York*, E.B. O'Callaghan, ed. (Albany 1849–51), 4:273; and William N. Fenton, 'Answers to Governor Cass's Questions by Jacob Jameson, a Seneca [ca. 1821–1825],' *Ethnohistory* 16 (1969), 121, 134
5 Quoted in E.A. Cruikshank, 'Blockade of Fort George,' Niagara Historical Society *Transactions* 3 (1898), 35–6. For information on de Rottenburg, see David Gates, *The British Light Infantry Arm, c.1790–1815* (London 1987).
6 Baron de Rottenburg to Sir George Prevost, 20 July 1813, *DH*, 6:243–4
7 Cruikshank, 'Blockade,' 34; and J. Mackay Hitsman, *The Incredible War of 1812* (1965; Toronto 1972), 147
8 *JMJN*, 333–4, 336; de Rottenburg to Prevost, 9 July 1813, *DH*, 6:207; and Cruikshank, 'Blockade,' 34. There also may have been some Seven Nations people present because one of their interpreters, Louis Langlade, participated; see William Claus report, 4 Dec. 1813, *VSN*, 211.
9 W.H. Merritt account, n.d., in E.A. Cruikshank, 'Reminiscences of Colonel Claus,' *Canadiana* 1 (1889), 185–6
10 *JMJN*, 334–5

11 Ibid., 335–6; Merritt account, n.d., in Cruikshank, 'Reminiscences,' 187; Claus report, 4 Dec. 1813, *VSN*, 210; and John Harvey to William Claus, 16 July 1813, *DH*, 6:213

12 *JMJN*, 335–6

13 Merritt account, n.d., in Cruikshank, 'Reminiscences,' 186–7

14 Claus to Sir John Johnson, 11 July 1813, *DH*, 6:216; and Cruikshank, 'Blockade,' 37

15 Black Bird's speech, 18 July 1813, in William Kirby, *Annals of Niagara* (Niagara Falls 1896), 197–8. For a U.S. officer's experience of being taken prisoner in 1814 by natives (probably by either Norton's war party or men operating close to Norton), see Samuel White, *A History of the American Troops during the Late War Under Colonel Fenton* (Baltimore 1829), 17–24; cf. *JMJN*, 350.

16 Anon., 'First Campaign of an A.D.C.,' *Military and Naval Magazine of the United States* 2 (1834), 336

17 Cruikshank, 'Blockade,' 45

18 *JMJN*, 336–7; and ibid., 42, 52

19 Peter B. Porter to ?, 27 July 1813, in G.F.G. Stanley, 'The Indians in the War of 1812,' in Morris Zaslow, ed., *The Defended Border* (Toronto 1964), 183

20 Erastus Granger to Armstrong, 9 Aug. 1813, *R&W*, 68–9; Claus report, 4 Dec. 1813, *VSN*, 212; and Cruikshank, 'Blockade,' 29, 36

21 Council with the Tuscaroras at Queenston, 5 July 1813, *DH*, 6:187

22 Cruikshank, 'Blockade,' 36

23 Porter MS on the Black Rock Raid, n.d., A. Conger Goodyear Collection, B&ECHS; and Granger to Armstrong, 9 Aug. 1813, *R&W*, 68–9

24 Thomas Clark to Harvey, 12 July 1813, *DH*, 6:217; de Rottenburg to Edward Baynes, 14 July 1813, *DH*, 6:233; Granger to Armstrong, 9 Aug. 1813, *R&W*, 69; Porter MS on the Black Rock Raid, Goodyear Collection, B&ECHS; Porter to Henry Dearborn, 13 July 1813, *DH*, 6:225; Hitsman, *Incredible War*, 147; and Babcock, *Niagara Frontier*, 185–6. This was not the first time that American military officers and Indian agents did not communicate with each other. In the autumn of 1812 the army and the secretary of war directed the Indian agent for New York State to invite Six Nations and Stockbridge people to take up arms without telling the local federal Indian agents who felt they had to affirm to the Iroquois that the United States in fact had not made such an invitation (Secretary of War William Eustis to New York State agent Ephriam Webster, 12 Oct. 1812, *R&W*, 57; and Eustis to American army commander Dearborn, 23 Sept. 1812, *DH*, 3:29; cf. United States Indian agent Granger to Jasper Parrish, 24 Oct. 1812, Vassar College, Jasper Parrish Papers).

25 Porter MS on the Black Rock Raid, n.d., Goodyear Collection, B&ECHS

26 Ibid.; Granger to Armstrong, 9 Aug. 1813, *R&W*, 70; Porter to Henry Dear-

born, 13 July 1813, *DH*, 6:224; Buffalo *Gazette*, 13 July 1813, *DH*, 6:226; Clark to Harvey, 12 July 1813, *DH*, 6:217–18; and Babcock, *Niagara Frontier*, 105–7

27 Babcock, *Niagara Frontier*, 107–8; and Arthur C. Parker, 'The Senecas in the War of 1812,' *NYH* 15 (1916), 84. A brigade consisted of three or four battalions, each commanded by a lieutenant-colonel who reported to the brigade's senior officer, usually a brigadier-general. Thus, within the Iroquois battalion command was exercised by the Iroquois themselves, although the decision of where to deploy them in the field was made by senior white officers.

28 Boyd to Granger, June 1813, *R&W*, 64

29 Granger to Armstrong, 9 Aug. 1813, *DH*, 6:326; Granger to the Six Nations, 6–8 July 1812, in William L. Stone, *Life and Times of Sa-go-ye-wat-ha, or Red Jacket* (Albany 1866), 308; Armstrong to the Six Nations, 7 Apr. 1813, NARA, M15, Records of the Office of the Secretary of War, Letters Sent, Indian Affairs

30 Johnston Silverheels, Big John, Black Snake, and Henry O'Bail to Granger, 30 June 1813, *R&W*, 65; and Stone, *Red Jacket*, 316

31 Chiefs of the Six Nations at Allegany to Granger, 30 June 1813, *DH*, 6:167

32 Cruikshank, 'Blockade,' 30

33 Red Jacket's speech, 25 July 1813, *DH*, 6:275

34 Council minutes, 25 July 1813, *R&W*, 66

35 Henry O'Bail's speech, 25 July 1813, *R&W*, 67. See A.F.C. Wallace, *The Death and Rebirth of the Seneca* (New York 1972), 303–10, for a discussion of temperance among the Senecas.

36 Council notes by Granger, 25 July 1813, *R&W*, 66–7; Red Jacket's speeches, 25 July 1813 and 25 May 1812, *R&W*, 67, 47

37 Porter to Boyd, 22 July 1813, *DH*, 6:263; George McClure to the people of Canada, 16 Oct. 1813, in Allen J. Ferguson, 'George McClure and the Indians at Fort George, 1813,' *Military Collector and Historian* 35 (1983), 86

38 Alexander Smyth to the men of New York, 10 Nov. 1812, *DH*, 4:194

39 Letter of 30 May 1813 to the editor of the Baltimore *Whig*, *DH*, 5:275

40 Granger to Boyd, 6 Aug. 1813, *DH*, 6:316

41 Winfield Scott, *Memoirs of Lieut.-General Scott, LL.D.* (New York 1864), 1:95

42 Ibid.; Donald E. Graves, 'Joseph Willcocks and the Canadian Volunteers' MA thesis, Carleton University, Ottawa, 1982, 56; and E.A. Cruikshank, 'A Study of Disaffection in Upper Canada, 1812–15,' *Proceedings and Transactions of the Royal Society of Canada*, 3rd ser., 6 (1912), 48

43 Boyd to Porter, 5 Aug. 1813, B&ECHS, Peter B. Porter Papers; Hitsman, *Incredible War*, 147; Carl Benn, *Historic Fort York, 1793–1993* (Toronto 1993), 66–8; and Cruikshank, 'Blockade,' 53–8

44 *JMJN*, 337; Hitsman, *Incredible War*, 147; and Margaret Coleman, 'The Ameri-

can Capture of Fort George, Ontario,' *Parks Canada History and Archaeology Reports* 13 (1977), 44–5

45 Boyd to Armstrong, 31 July 1813, *DH*, 6:295

46 Claus to ?, n.d., Cruikshank, 'Blockade,' 34; de Rottenburg to Baynes, 14 July 1813, *DH*, 6:233; and Samuel Holmes, 'A Pedestrian Tour to the Falls of Niagara in Upper Canada,' MS (c. 1815), Public Record Office of Northern Ireland, 155

47 Among the claimants was Catharine Brant, widow of Joseph, who lost over £250 in property when natives damaged her house, burned her fence rails, destroyed her wheat and meadows, and killed her sheep. Claims ranged from £4 to £3,715, with most falling between £25 and £75. See War of 1812 Losses Claims, various post-1815 dates, NAC, RG 19, Department of Finance, Upper Canada, vol. 3732, file 8.

48 General Order, 29 July 1813, *DH*, 6:291

49 Province of Canada, *Appendix GGG to the Fourth Volume of the Journals of the Legislative Assembly of the Province of Canada, 1844–1845* (n.p., c. 1846) lists each person and the amount owing in the third of three more or less equal payments. Both men and women received awards. The lowest was thirteen shillings, the highest was seventy pounds. Most fell between two and eighteen pounds. In summary form, the payments to the different Grand River groups were as follows:

Group	No. of people affected	Group award	Average award
Akwesasne	4	£ 39	£ 10
Aughquagas	28	242	9
Cayugas	62	771	12
Delawares	34	488	14
Mohawks	77	672	9
Onondagas	27	324	12
Senecas	7	84	12
Tuscaroras	19	124	7
Tutelos	10	42	4
Total	268	£2,786	£ 10

50 Holmes, 'Pedestrian Tour,' 155; *JMJN*, 367–9; Edward McMahon to John Small, 6 Dec. 1814, NAC, RG 1, Upper Canada State Papers, E3, vol. 37, 17–18; and AO, Minute Books of the Court of King's Bench and the General Quarter

Sessions, ser. 134/4 and 94/2. A search in court records by archival staff at the Law Society of Upper Canada provided no evidence that anyone was tried for the crime. I thank Dr Carolyn Strange and her staff for their assistance. A number of men by the name of Green, such as Elisha (who is known to have joined the American forces), Samuel, and Wheeler, all from Ancaster, disappeared from Upper Canada with the law after them; see High Treason Register, AO; War of 1812 Losses Claims, NAC, RG 19, vol. 3732, file 8; and Cruikshank, 'Disaffection,' 62.

51 Brendan O'Brien, *Speedy Justice* (Toronto 1992), 29–67

52 I thank Bill Gray for the information about the militia.

53 'Philalethes,' 'The Last War in Canada,' *United Service Magazine* (1848), 427, 431

54 John Carroll, 'Reminiscences of the American Occupation of Niagara from 27th May to 19th Dec. 1813,' Niagara Historical Society *Transactions* 11 (1904), 26. The only natives at the battle of Fort George were Grand River people. Cf. Michael Smith, *Geographical View of the Province of Upper Canada* (Philadelphia 1813), 95–6.

55 James Commins, quoted in Norman C. Lord, ed., 'The War on the Canadian Frontier, 1812–1814,' *Journal of the Society for Army Historical Research* 18 (1939), 209

56 An anonymous Canadian dragoon captain in October or November 1813, quoted in Sandy Antal, 'Myths and Facts Concerning General Procter,' *OH* 79 (1987), 258

57 John Le Couteur to Philip Bouton, 24 Oct. 1813, in Donald E. Graves, ed., *Merry Hearts Make Light Days*, (Ottawa 1993), 146

58 C. Winton-Clare, 'A Shipbuilder's War,' *Defended Border*, 165–73

59 Porter to Boyd, 5 Aug. 1812, *DH*, 6:311–12; Granger to Boyd, 6 Aug. 1813, *DH*, 6:315–16; Red Jacket to Granger, 21 Oct. 1813, *R&W*, 71–2; List of Indians who delivered up horses taken of the inhabitants in Canada, n.d., *R&W*, 70; and Cruikshank, 'Blockade,' 46

60 Porter to Boyd, 22 July 1813, *DH*, 6:263; Boyd to Porter, 13 Aug. 1813, B&ECHS, Porter Papers; Parker, 'Senecas in the War of 1812,' 84; and Cruikshank, 'Blockade,' 59

61 Boyd to Armstrong, 13 Aug. 1813, *DH*, 7:36

62 G.F.G. Stanley, 'The Significance of the Six Nations Participation in the War of 1812,' *OH* 55 (1963), 227

63 Claus report, 4 Dec. 1813, *VSN*, 44; *JMJN*, 337; Thomas G. Ridout to his brother, 20 July 1813, *DH*, 6:255; and Cruikshank, 'Blockade,' 59

64 *JMJN*, 337–8; and Claus report, 4 Dec. 1813, *VSN*, 214

65 *JMJN*, 338

66 Ibid.; and Claus report, 4 Dec. 1813, *VSN*, 214

67 *National Advocate* (New York), 28 Aug. 1813, *DH*, 7:37

68 Charles Askin to John Askin, 17 Aug. 1813, *DH*, 7:33; Claus report, 4 Dec. 1813, *VSN*, 214–15; and Cruikshank, 'Blockade,' 59–60

69 *JMJN*, 338–9; T. Ridout to his brother, 20 Aug. 1813, *DH*, 6:255; Boyd to Armstrong, 17 Aug. 1813, *DH*, 7:30; and Cruikshank, 'Blockade,' 60, 66

70 Scott, *Memoirs*, 1:97

71 Claus report, 4 Dec. 1813, *VSN*, 215

72 *JMJN*, 338–9. For Ojibway tradition on Iroquois–Ojibway warfare, see William W. Warren, *History of the Ojibway People* (1885; St Paul, Minn. 1984), 146–8

73 *Ontario Repository of Canadaigua*, 3 Sept. 1813, *DH*, 7:94; *JMJN*, 339; Cruikshank, 'Blockade,' 60–1; and *Buffalo Gazette*, 24 Aug. 1813, *DH*, 7:60

74 Claus report, 4 Dec. 1813, *VSN*, 215–16; and Prevost to ?, n.d., in Hitsman, *Incredible War*, 147–8

75 Norton to either Prevost or de Rottenburg, 23 June 1813, NAC, RG 8, vol. 257, 93–5; cf. *JMJN*, 340. *JMJN*, 337, records Norton's delicately phrased view of the Indian Department's failings during a lull in the fighting near Fort George in 1813: 'Subsequent to this Skirmish, the Enemy remained tranquil within their Lines, & we never made any serious attempt upon them. All that passed among us was the Bustle of the Indian Department, this, & the sickness caused by the badness of the water, continued to diminish our numbers every day, for whoever became either sick or discontented, generally went home.'

76 Quoted in *JMJN*, cxx

77 De Rottenburg to ?, 15 Aug. 1813, *JMJN*, cxxi

78 See Chapter 2.

79 Report of a Board of Officers, 26 July 1813, NAC, RG 10, vol. 28, 16491–2; *JMJN*, lxxviii, cxviii, cxx; and Stanley, 'Indians,' 186; cf. Chapter 5

80 General order, 27 Aug. 1813, *VSN*, 206

81 Claus report, 4 Dec. 1813, *VSN*, 209; and Norton to Prevost, 1 June 1813, NAC, RG 8, vol. 257, 84–5

82 Claus report, 4 Dec. 1813; and E.A. Cruikshank, ed., 'Campaigns of 1812–14,' Niagara Historical Society *Transactions* 9 (1902), 31–3

83 Cruikshank, 'Blockade,' 48; and *JMJN*, lxxvii. She was his second wife; his first was a Mohawk. Norton was about fifty years old, Karighwaycagh probably was a teenager. Mohawk oral tradition, via John Smoke Johnson, holds that she was a full-blooded Delaware; see Albert Johnson to Lyman C. Draper, 11 Feb. 1878, State Historical Society of Wisconsin, Draper MSS, ser. F, Brant Papers, vol. 14, 24. According to a copy of the marriage notation in the records for St Mark's Anglican Church in Niagara, Karighwaycagh was baptized the day of her marriage: see Draper MSS, Brant Papers, vol. 15, 30.

84 W.H. Merritt, *Journal of Events Principally on the Detroit and Niagara Frontiers, During the War of 1812* (St Catharines 1863), 68. Cf. John Lang diary, 19th Light Dragoons, 2 June 1812, Perkins Library, Duke University, which describes her as the prettiest native woman Lang had ever seen.

85 General Order, 9 Sept. 1813, NAC, RG 10, vol. 28, 16542; and Cruikshank, 'Blockade,' 69

86 Claus report, 4 Dec. 1812, *VSN*, 217

87 Cruikshank, 'Blockade,' 79

88 Letter of 2 Oct. 1813 to the *Albany Argus*, *DH*, 7:188; James Wilkinson to Armstrong, 11 Sept. 1813, *DH*, 7:119; McClure to Porter, 3 Oct. 1813, *DH*, 7:190; John F. Bacon to Daniel Tompkins, 31 Oct. 1812, *DH*, 8:111; Coleman, 'Fort George,' 56; and ibid., 70–3

89 Wade Hampton to Armstrong, 22 Sept. 1813, *DH*, 7:159; George Izard, 21 Oct. 1813, in John C. Fredriksen, ed., 'The War of 1812 in Northern New York,' *NYH* 76 (1995), 187; Tyendinaga Mohawks to Prevost, 4 July 1814, NAC, RG 10, vol. 3, 1451; Hampton to Armstrong, 1 Nov. 1813, *DH*, 8:119–20; Eleazer Williams, *Life of Te-ho-ra-gwa-ne-gen, alias Thomas Williams* (Albany 1859), 71; and Isaac LeClaire to Sir John Johnson, 26 Nov. 1813, NAC, RG 10, vol. 28, 16572–3

90 Helen Hornbeck Tanner, ed., *Atlas of Great Lakes Indian History* (Norman 1987), 118; Marian E. White, et al., 'Cayuga,' in *Handbook*, 502; and Robert S. Allen, 'The British Indian Department on the Frontier in North America, 1755–1830,' *Occasional Papers in Archaeology and History* 14 (1975), 77–8

91 *JMJN*, 342–3; and Claus report, 4 Dec. 1813, *VSN*, 218. Return of the Six Nations and other Indians from the Grand River, 26 Oct. 1813, *DH*, 8:97, lists the number of Grand River refugees at Burlington at 420 men and 978 women and children from the Mohawk, Oneida, Aughquaga, Onondaga, Cayuga, Tutelo, Nanticoke, and Delaware nations.

92 R.C. Muir, 'Burford's First Settler, Politician and Military Man – Benajah Mallory,' *OH* 26 (1930), 495

93 *JMJN*, 343

94 De Rottenburg to John Vincent, 23 Oct. 1813, *DH*, 8:88; Vincent to de Rottenburg, 18 Oct. 1813, *DH*, 8:78

95 Vincent to de Rottenburg, 18 Oct. 1813, *DH*, 8:78; de Rottenburg to Prevost, 23 Oct. 1813, with marginalia by Prevost, n.d., *DH*, 8:90; and de Rottenburg to Vincent, 1 Nov. 1813, *DH*, 8:117. The quote is by Robert Nichol in a letter to Vincent of Nov. 1813; see E.A. Cruikshank, 'Public Life and Service of Robert Nichol,' *OH* 19 (1922), 31.

96 Vincent's speech to the Six Nations, 22 Oct. 1813, *VSN*, 207

97 Reginald Horsman, *Matthew Elliott, British Indian Agent* (Detroit 1964), 214; and Donald E. Graves, *Red Coats and Grey Jackets* (Toronto 1994), 6

98 De Rottenburg to Vincent, 1 Nov. 1813, *DH*, 8:118; and McClure to Tompkins, 21 Nov., before 26 Nov., and 6 Dec. 1813, *DH*, 8:222, 253

99 Armstrong to the Six Nations, 7 Apr. 1813, NARA, M15, Records of the … Secretary of War, Letters Sent, Indian Affairs; Red Jacket's speech, 21 Oct. 1813, *R&W*, 71; Jeremiah Bronaugh to Granger, 2 Sept. 1813, *R&W*, 76; *R&W*, 16, 73–6; Notes by Dorothy May Fairbank accompanying, 'Letters and documents relating to the government service of Jasper Parrish among the Indians of New York State, 1790 to 1831,' 1940, Vassar College Library, Parrish Papers, 151–2; and C.M. Johnston, 'William Claus and John Norton,' *OH* 57 (1965), 10

100 McClure to Tompkins, 10 Dec. 1813, *DH*, 8:253; McClure to Armstrong, 10 and 12 Dec. 1813, *DH*, 8:262–3, 271

101 George McClure, *Causes of the Destruction of the American Towns on the Niagara Frontier* (Bath, NY 1817), 17–18; Sir Gordon Drummond to Prevost, 19 and 22 Dec. 1813, *DH*, 9:11, 33; Drummond to Lord Bathurst, 18 Jan. 1814, NAC, CO 42, vol. 355, 4–11; Shadrach Byfield, 'A Common Soldier's Account,' 1839, in John Gellner, ed., *Recollections of the War of 1812* (Toronto 1964), 31–2; E.A. Cruikshank, *Drummond's Winter Campaign*, 2nd ed. (Lundy's Lane, n.d.), 14–16; Babcock, *Niagara Frontier*, 125. Hot shot consisted of heated solid iron cannon balls that not only smashed their targets but set them on fire.

102 *JMJN*, 346; Drummond to Prevost, 22 Dec. 1813, *DH*, 9:38; Elias Johnson, *Legends, Traditions and Laws of the Iroquois, or Six Nations, and History of the Tuscarora Indians* (Lockport 1881), 167–70; O. Turner, *Pioneer History of the Holland Purchase* (Buffalo 1850), 590–1; and letter to the author from Dennis Farmer, 29 Mar. 1997

103 James Monroe to the Six Nations, 11 Mar. 1815, *R&W*, 81; Deputation of the Six Nations to the secretary of war, 20 Feb. 1815, American Philosophical Society, Philadelphia; and Johnson, *Legends*, 170

104 McClure to the Iroquois, 21 Dec. 1813, *DH*, 9:34

105 Sources generally claim that the Iroquois offered no resistance (e.g., Amos Hall to Tompkins, 6 Jan. 1814, *DH*, 9:95; and *Ontario Repository*, 14 Jan. 1814, *DH*, 9:78–80) but there were Iroquois casualties, such as Red Jacket who was wounded, which suggests that they put up at least something of a fight (*R&W*, 28).

106 *JMJN*, 347

107 C. Askin diary, 14 Dec. 1813, *John Askin Papers*, Milo Quaife, ed. (Detroit 1931), 2:775–6; Hall to McClure, 29 Dec. 1813, *DH*, 9:64; *New York Evening Post*, 19 Jan. 1814, *DH*, 9:84; Red Jacket's speech, 27 Nov. 1815, *R&W*, 83; Turner, *Pioneer History*, 580–1; George R. Harris, 'Life of Horatio Jones,' Buffalo Historical Society *Publications* 6 (1903), 504; and Lewis H. Morgan, *Report on the Fabrics,*

Inventions, Implements and Utensils of the Iroquois, 1851, reprinted in Elisabeth
Tooker, ed., *Lewis H. Morgan on Iroquois Material Culture* (Tucson 1994), 251
108 Drummond to Prevost, 19 Feb. 1814, in Hitsman, *Incredible War,* 178

7: The Last War Dance

1 *JMJN,* 351
2 J. Mackay Hitsman, *The Incredible War of 1812* (1965; Toronto 1972), 249–51
3 Ibid., 190–1; Jeffrey Kimball, 'Strategy on the Northern Frontier, 1814,' PhD
    thesis, Louisiana State University, 1969, 99–122; and John D. Morris, 'General
    Jacob Brown and the Problems of Command in 1814,' in R. Arthur Bowler,
    ed., *War along the Niagara* (Youngstown 1991), 29–42
4 List of killed and wounded and missing ... at La Cole Mill on the 30 Mar. 1814,
    n.d., *BD,* 3:17; Helen Hornbeck Tanner, ed., *Atlas of Great Lakes Indian History*
    (Norman 1987), 113; and Hitsman, *Incredible War,* 183–6
5 *JMJN,* 347; William Kerr to William Claus, 21 Apr. 1814, NAC, RG 10, vol. 3,
    1352–3; Return of the Grand River Indians, 1 May 1814, NAC, RG 10, vol. 28,
    16819; Gordon Drummond to Sir George Prevost, 25 Mar. 1814, *DH,* 1:11;
    Matthew Elliott to Claus, 25 Mar. 1814, NAC, RG 10, vol. 28, 16753; Donald E.
    Graves, *The Battle of Lundy's Lane* (Baltimore 1993), 44; G.F.G. Stanley, *The
    War of 1812* (Ottawa 1983), 275–86; Kimball, 'Northern Frontier,' 103–4; and
    Franklin B. Hough, *A History of St. Lawrence and Franklin Counties* (Albany
    1853), 158
6 Carl F. Klinck, 'Norton, John,' *DCB,* 6:552; and Noah Freer to Drummond,
    1 Mar. 1814, *VSN,* 219–20
7 Claus to Kerr, 31 Mar. 1814, NAC, RG 10, vol. 3, 1351; John Norton to William
    Jervois, 30 May 1814, *VSN,* 221; Petition from fifteen Grand River chiefs to
    Claus, 9 Jan. 1814, *VSN,* 219; and *JMJN,* lxxix
8 Drummond to Prevost, 9 Apr. 1814, *JMJN,* cxxii
9 Norton to Jervois, 30 May 1814, *VSN,* 221; and *JMJN,* cxxi–cxxii
10 Claus to his son, 11 May 1814, *DH,* 8:168; Six Nations to Prevost, June 1814,
    JMJN, 348; Freer to Robert Loring, 9 July 1814, *VSN,* 222; Freer to Drummond,
    1 Mar. 1814, *VSN,* 220; Drummond to Prevost, 11 July 1814, *DH,* 1:55; *JMJN,*
    cxxii; and John Sugden, *Tecumseh's Last Stand* (Norman 1985), 198
11 Neywash to William Caldwell, 14 June 1814, *VSN,* 221–2
12 Klinck, 'Norton,' 552
13 *JMJN,* 348; John Harvey to Phineas Riall, 23 Mar. 1814, *VSN,* 220–1; and Hits-
    man, *Incredible War,* 194
14 Peter B. Porter to Jacob Brown, 25 May and 23 June 1814, *DH,* 2:398, 406;
    Winfield Scott to Porter, 29 May 1814, B&ECHS, Peter B. Porter Papers;

Joseph Whitehorne, *While Washington Burned* (Baltimore 1992), 116; Louis L. Babcock, *The War of 1812 on the Niagara Frontier* (Buffalo 1927), 609; Arthur C. Parker, 'The Senecas in the War of 1812,' *NYH* 15 (1916), 86–7; and Graves, *Lundy's Lane*, 20–3, 31–7

15 Porter to John Armstrong, 27 Mar. 1814, *DH*, 2:382

16 J. Hubbard, *An Account of Sa-Go-Ye-Wat-Ha, or Red Jacket* (Albany 1886), 267

17 Porter to Armstrong, 8 Apr. 1814, *DH*, 2:387

18 William Carpenter to Porter, 5 June 1814, B&ECHS, Porter Papers; and White-horne, *While Washington Burned*, 143–4. The company commands were divided: Seneca Main Village; Allegany and Cattaraugus; Onondagas; Tuscaro-ras and Delawares; Tonawandas; and Stockbridges. An additional force of about twenty Brothertown natives also joined the Americans.

19 John Strachan, 'Life of Col. Bishoppe,' Dec. 1813, in George W. Spragge, ed., *John Strachan Letter Book* (Toronto 1946), 7

20 Isabel Kelsay, 'Tekarihogen (John Brant),' *DCB*, 6:760

21 Porter to the Six Nations, before 1 June 1814, *DH*, 2:392–3

22 Porter to Daniel Tompkins, 3 July 1814, *DH*, 1:26; and Parker, 'Senecas in the War of 1812,' 85. Parker thought they fought with the men, but Iroquois soci-ety, with its strong division of gender roles, does not seem to have made such an occurrence the most likely interpretation. Perhaps Parker did not know armies carried women on pay lists to fill support roles. A Seneca from New York of the War of 1812 generation noted that the 'women *sometimes* follow the men to war, but never to battle'; see William N. Fenton, 'Answers to Governor Cass's Questions by Jacob Jameson, a Seneca [ca. 1821–1825],' *Ethnohistory* 16 (1969), 122. For Iroquois women in previous conflicts, see Barbara Graymont, 'The Six Nations Indians in the Revolutionary War,' in J.R. Miller, ed., *Sweet Promises* (Toronto 1992), 100–3; and D. Peter MacLeod, *The Canadian Iroquois and the Seven Years' War* (Ottawa 1996), 7.

23 *JMJN*, 348–9; and Jeffrey Kimball, 'The Battle of Chippewa,' *Military Affairs* 32 (1969), 178

24 *JMJN*, 349; Riall to Drummond, 6 July 1814, *BD*, 3:115; A captain in Fenton's Regiment of Pennsylvania Volunteers to the *Boston Sentinel*, 7 July 1814, *DH*, 1:49; and Kimball, 'Chippewa,' 179

25 *JMJN*, 349; Kimball, 'Chippewa,' 178; and Donald E. Graves, *Red Coats and Grey Jackets: The Battle of Chippawa* (Toronto 1994), 82

26 *JMJN*, 349–50; and Graves, *Chippawa*, 82, 105

27 Drummond to Prevost, 11 July 1814, *BD*, 3:123–4; and Riall to Drummond, 6 July 1814, *VSN*, 223

28 Porter to Brown, after 5 July 1814, *DH*, 2:410; Porter to William L. Stone, 26 May 1840, A. Conger Goodyear Collection, B&ECHS; Kimball, 'Chippewa;' and Graves, *Chippawa*, 91–2

29 Porter to Stone, 26 May 1840, Goodyear Collection, B&ECHS
30 Ibid.; and *JMJN*, 350–1; cf. Drummond to Prevost, 10 July 1814, *DH*, 1:35–6; Porter to Brown, after 5 July 1814, *DH*, 2:410; Riall to Drummond, 6 July 1814, *DH*, 1:31; and Graves, *Chippawa*, 93–4
31 *JMJN*, 350. Grapeshot was a bag full of iron balls which, when fired from a cannon, sprayed out towards the target like a large shotgun blast, much like canister shot.
32 Porter to Brown, after 5 July 1814, *DH*, 2:410; Kimball, 'Chippewa,' 182, 184; and Graves, *Chippawa*, 101–10, 117–26
33 Return of killed, wounded, and missing, 13 July 1814, *DH*, 1:50; Report of the killed and wounded of the Left Division, 7 July 1814, *DH*, 1:43; Six Nations to the secretary of war, 20 Feb. 1815, American Philosophical Society, Philadelphia; *JMJN*, 350–1; and G.F.G. Stanley, 'The Significance of the Six Nations Participation in the War of 1812,' *OH* 55 (1963), 228
34 Drummond to Prevost, 10 July 1814, *DH*, 1:35; and Kimball, 'Chippewa,' 185
35 Brown to Armstrong, 7 July 1814, *DH*, 1:39; and Drummond to Prevost, 10 July 1814, *DH*, 1:35–6
36 Porter to Stone, 26 May 1840, Goodyear Collection, B&ECHS; cf. Alexander Smyth to the Army of the Centre, 17 Nov. 1812, *DH*, 4:216
37 Porter to Stone, 26 May 1840, Goodyear Collection, B&ECHS; see chapters 2 and 3 re scalps
38 *JMJN*, 352
39 Ibid., 353; Riall to Drummond, 8 July 1814, *DH*, 1:54; Porter to Stone, 26 May 1840, Goodyear Collection, B&ECHS; and Daniel MacFarland to his wife, before 25 July 1814, *DH*, 1:73
40 *JMJN*, 353
41 Ibid.; Riall to Drummond, 17 July 1814, *DH*, 1:70; Porter to Farmer's Brother, et al., 25 July 1814, *R&W*, 77–8; Porter to Stone, 25 May 1840, Goodyear Collection, B&ECHS; Tanner, *Atlas*, 119; Stanley, 'Six Nations,' 229; and Hubbard, *Red Jacket*, 267
42 *JMJN*, 353–4
43 Ibid.
44 Riall to Drummond, 17 July 1814, *DH*, 1:70–2; Drummond to Prevost, 15 July 1814, *DH*, 1:59; and Drummond to Prevost, 22 July 1814, in Hitsman, *Incredible War*, 197
45 Riall to Drummond, 17 July 1814, *DH*, 1:70; and *JMJN*, 354–5
46 Drummond to Prevost, 10 July 1814, *DH*, 1:35–6
47 *JMJN*, 340, lxxix; Freer to Loring, 9 July 1814, *VSN*, 222–3; Robert S. Allen, 'The British Indian Department on the Frontier in North America, 1755–1830,' *Occasional Papers in Archaeology and History* 14 (1975), 80–1; and C.M. Johnston, 'William Claus and John Norton,' *OH* 57 (1965), 104–6

48 Porter to Farmer's Brother, et al., 25 July 1814, *R&W,* 77–8

49 Jacob Brown's diary, 1814, *DH,* 2:466; Jasper Parrish to Porter, 27 July and 15 Aug. 1814, *DH,* 2:419, 433; Porter to Parrish, 31 July 1814, *DH,* 2:426–7; and Farmer's Brother's speech, 7 Aug. 1814, *DH,* 2:430

50 Porter to Stone, 25 May 1840, Goodyear Collection, B&ECHS

51 Ibid.; and Whitehorne, *While Washington Burned,* 33

52 Fleming to Porter, 6 Aug. 1814, B&ECHS, Porter Papers

53 J.B. Varnum Jr to Joseph B. Varnum 24 July 1814, Goodyear Collection, B&ECHS; Isaac Chauncey to Brown, 10 Aug. 1814, in Donald R. Hickey, *The War of 1812* (Urbana 1989), 187; and Graves, *Lundy's Lane*

54 *JMJN,* 359–66; *Niles' Weekly Register,* 30 July 1814, *DH,* 1:64; Drummond to Prevost, 4 Aug. 1814, *BD,* 3:168; — Miller to ?, 19 Sept. 1814, *DH* 2:223; Drummond to Prevost, 12 Aug. 1814, in Babcock, *Niagara Frontier,* 191; Drummond to Prevost, 21 Aug. 1814, *DH,* 2:183; and Stanley, *War of 1812,* 325–6

55 *JMJN,* 366. Interestingly, Norton seems not to have told the truth at this point. He claimed that only one hundred men assembled because the rest had gone hunting and could not be reached. However, the fact that a much larger number mustered to defend the Grand shortly afterwards (see below) suggests that was not true but that the summertime treaty was still in effect.

56 Drummond to Prevost, 18 Oct. 1814, *BD,* 3:219; and Graves, *Lundy's Lane,* 202–3

57 *JMJN,* 367; Drummond to Prevost, 26 Oct. 1814, *DH,* 2:277; William Smelt to the officer commanding in York, 26 Oct. 1814, *DH,* 2:278; Drummond to Sir James Lucas Yeo, 13 Nov. 1814, *BD,* 3:290; Smelt to Harvey, 6 Nov. 1814, *DH,* 2:296; Smelt to Louis de Watteville, 8 Nov. 1814, *BD,* 3:288; Duncan McArthur to George Izard, 18 Nov. 1814, *VSN,* 234; *VSN,* lxxvii; David Owen, *Fort Erie* (Fort Erie 1986), 53–4; and E.A. Cruikshank, 'The County of Norfolk in the War of 1812,' *OH* 20 (1923), 37–8

58 *JMJN,* 370

59 Tanner, *Atlas,* 115; Allan S. Everest, *The War of 1812 in the Champlain Valley* (Syracuse 1981), 161–87; and Marshall Smelser, *The Democratic Republic, 1801–1815* (New York 1968), 285

60 One historian has written this about the Iroquois role in preventing the American conquest of British North America: 'Canadians ... cannot fail to recognize that it was during the critical years of this war, 1812 and 1813, when British troops were few in number and Britain was still heavily engaged upon the continent of Europe, that Iroquois Indians, both from Grand River and Caughnawaga, helped preserve their country's independence'; see Stanley, 'Significance,' 231.

61 After the war, when American officers analysed their mistakes, some realized

how effective natives had been as light infantry and how their aboriginal allies' skills had been wasted; see e.g., 'Remarks of Major General E.P. Gaines relative to the civilization of the [Indians],' n.d., in *American State Papers*, Documents Legislative and Executive, of the Congress of the U.S. ... from 1828 ... [to] 1832, Class 5, Military Affairs, (Washington 1860), 130

62 Despite his praises, G.F.G. Stanley, one of Canada's leading military historians, wrote of natives in general: 'The Indians, however useful their services may have been at Michilimackinac, Brownstown, and Detroit, were at best, unsatisfactory soldiers. They were devoid of discipline. They lacked tenacity and were easily discouraged by failure. They were restless, dissatisfied during periods of enforced inactivity, and yet inclined to fight for only brief periods of time'; see Stanley, 'The Indians in the War of 1812,' in Morris Zaslow, ed., *The Defended Border* (Toronto 1964), 178.

8: 'Gives Us Hopes of Finding Some Relief'

1 Five Nations' speech, 19 Mar. 1815, NAC, RG 10, vol. 4, 1701–2
2 J.C.A. Stagg, *Mr. Madison's War* (Princeton 1983), 419–500; J. Mackay Hitsman, *The Incredible War of 1812* (1965; Toronto 1972), 232–42; and Donald R. Hickey, *The War of 1812* (Urbana 1989), 287–97
3 The figure for whites comes from Hickey, *War of 1812*, 290 (who estimated natives at 20,000); the figure for natives comes from State of the Indian tribes, Oct. 1812, NAC, RG 10, vol. 11, 16106–9, based on a figure of 8,850 warriors and a warrior-to-population ratio of 1:4.82 (see Appendix).
4 John Adams to Henry Goulburn, 1 Sept. 1814, in Hickey, *War of 1812*, 290–1
5 Goulburn to Lord Bathurst, 26 Nov. 1814, in Hickey, *War of 1812*, 291
6 Lord Liverpool to Lord Castlereagh, November 1814, in Hitsman, *Incredible War*, 235
7 Treaty of Ghent, 24 Dec. 1814, *BD*, 3:524; and A.L. Burt, *The United States, Great Britain, and British North America* (New Haven 1940), 351–60
8 John K. Mahon, 'Indian-United States Military Situation, 1775–1848,' in Wilcomb E. Washburn, ed., *Handbook of North American Indians* 4, 'History of Indian–White Relations' (Washington 1988), 156
9 Colin G. Calloway, *Crown and Calumet* (Norman 1987), 241; Robert S. Allen, *His Majesty's Indian Allies* (Toronto 1992), 168–94; and G.F.G. Stanley, *The War of 1812* (Ottawa 1983), 396–7
10 Council of the Iroquois in New York, 27 Nov. 1815, *R&W*, 83; Barbara Graymont, 'New York State Indian Policy after the Revolution,' *NYH* 57 (1976), 468; and Marian E. White, et al., 'Cayuga,' in *Handbook*, 502
11 Arthur C. Parker, 'The Senecas in the War of 1812,' *NYH* 15 (1916), 88; and

Elisabeth Tooker, 'League of the Iroquois' and 'Iroquois Since 1820,' in *Handbook*, 436, 449

12 Peter Gillis et al., *Records Relating to Indian Affairs (RG 10)* (Ottawa 1975)

13 Noah Freer to Gordon Drummond, 4 Mar. 1815, NAC, RG 10, vol. 4, 1667–8

14 Five Nations' speech, 19 Mar. 1815, NAC, RG 10, vol. 4, 1701–2; List of presents, Mar. 1815, RG 10, vol. 4, 1704–5; and Statement of provisions, Mar.–Apr. 1815, RG 10, vol. 4, 1706

15 Council minutes, Apr. 1815, National Library of Scotland, Adv. MS 46.6.5; cf. Model speech from Sir George Prevost, n.d., NAC, RG 10, vol. 4, 1669–71

16 Council minutes, Apr. 1815, National Library of Scotland, Adv. MS 46.6.5

17 Ibid.; Council memorandum, Apr. 1815, NAC, RG 10, vol. 12, 10560–6; and Hickey, *War of 1812*, 290

18 Council minutes, 26–8 Mar. 1819, NAC, RG 8, vol. 716; Council memorandum, Apr. 1815, NAC, RG 10, vol. 12, 10566–9; Lists of presents, Mar. 1815, RG 10, vol. 4, 1705–5; and Statement of provisions required, Mar.–Apr. 1815, RG 10, vol. 4, 1701. John Le Couteur, the young lieutenant who got a horse at Beaver Dams (see Chapter 5), for example, had to wait thirty years for a fifty shilling bounty payment for his participation in the capture of an American ship earlier in the war; see Le Couteur, *Merry Hearts Make Light Days*, Donald E. Graves, ed. (Ottawa 1993), 68–70.

19 Proceedings of a meeting between the Grand River and American Indians from Buffalo, held 31 Aug. and 1 Sept. 1815, NAC, RG 8, vol. 258, 204–8; cf. William N. Fenton, 'Answers to Governor Cass's Questions by Jacob Jameson, a Seneca [ca. 1821–1825],' *Ethnohistory* 16 (1969), 122, 134–5

20 Parker, 'Senecas in the War of 1812,' 88–90. Alternatively, it is possible that swearing allegiance was somehow akin to the traditional Iroquois way of integrating themselves and other peoples into a friendly relationship by establishing some sort of fictive consanguinity; see Matthew Dennis, *Cultivating a Landscape of Peace* (Ithaca 1993), 4.

21 *R&W*, 18

22 James Monroe to the Six Nations, 11 Mar. 1815, *R&W*, 80–1; cf. Red Jacket's speech, 27 Nov. 1815 *R&W*, 83

23 Abner W. Hendrick to Erastus Granger, 6 Jan. 1816 and 15 June 1816, *R&W*, 84; and *R&W*, 18

24 Granger to George Graham, 20 Jan. 1817, *R&W*, 85

25 Saccarissa, William Prentiss, Solomon Long Board, and Nicholas Cusick to Graham, 24 Feb. 1817, *R&W*, 85–6; *R&W*, 18; and notes by Dorothy May Fairbank accompanying, 'Letters and documents relating to the government service of Jasper Parrish among the Indians of New York State, 1790 to 1831,' 1940, Vassar College, Jasper Parrish Papers, 156

26 A.F.C. Wallace, *The Death and Rebirth of the Seneca* (1969; New York 1972), 323–4; Frank H. Severance, 'Our Neighbours the Tuscaroras,' Buffalo Historical Society *Publications* 22 (1918), 324–9; Parker, 'Senecas in the War of 1812,' 90; Helen Hornbeck Tanner, ed., *Atlas of Great Lakes Indian History* (Norman 1987), map 31; *R&W*, 18–22; Dean R. Snow, *The Iroquois* (Cambridge, Mass. 1994), 162–7; and Elisabeth Tooker, 'League of the Iroquois,' 436

27 George Ironside to William Claus, 22 Apr. 1817, *VSN*, 284–5; Tooker, 'League,' 437; Jack Campisi, 'Oneida,' in *Handbook*, 485, 487; Tanner, *Atlas*, 178; Tony Hall, 'Native Limited Identities and Newcomer Metropolitanism in Upper Canada,' in David Keane and Colin Read, eds., *Old Ontario* (Toronto 1990), 151; and William C. Sturtevant, 'Oklahoma Seneca-Cayuga,' in *Handbook*, 537–9

28 Elisabeth Tooker, 'Iroquois Since 1820,' 449–53

29 Wallace, *Death and Rebirth*, 327–9

30 Little Billy's speech, June 1812, in *JMJN*, 289. See Chapter 2.

31 Thomas S. Abler, 'Factional Dispute and Party Conflict in the Political System of the Seneca Nation, 1845–1898,' PhD thesis, University of Toronto, 1969

32 John Norton to C. Foster, 25 May 1815, NAC, RG 8, vol. 695, 80–1; Norton to — Wilson, 16 Nov. 1816, RG 8, vol. 260, 471–4; Memorandum, 1 July 1816, RG 8, vol. 260, 266; Requisition, 15 June 1816, RG 8, vol. 260, 267; Louis de Watteville to — Hall, 25 June 1816, RG 8, vol. 260, 288; J.F. Addison to Claus, 7 Jan. 1817, RG 8, vol. 1241, 44–5; and Addison to Sir John Johnson, 22 Apr. and 25 Jan. 1817, RG, vol. 1241, 81, 49–50

33 Gore to Bathurst, 2 Sept. 1816, NAC, CO 42, vol. 357, pt 1, 308–13

34 Gore to Bathurst, 27 Dec. 1815, NAC, RG 7, Governor-General's Records, G12, vol. 9

35 Drummond to Prevost, 11 Mar. 1815, NAC, CO 42, vol. 356, 165–6

36 Ibid.; Gore to Bathurst, 2 Sept. 1816, CO 42, vol. 357, pt 1, 308–13; and Kenneth Bourne, *Britain and the Balance of Power in North America, 1815–1908* (London 1967), 9

37 Gore to Bathurst, 15 Dec. 1815, NAC, CO 42, vol. 356, 159–63

38 Foster to Claus, 24 Apr. 1815, NAC, CO 42, vol. 356, 167; Foster to Norton, 18 Apr. 1815, NAC, CO 42, vol. 356, 169–70; and C.M. Johnston, 'William Claus and John Norton,' *OH* 57 (1965), 106

39 Order-in-council of the Privy Council of Great Britain, 27 June 1816, appointing William Claus to the Upper Canada Executive Council, NAC, CO 42, vol. 358, pt 2, 89; Gore to the Bathurst, 27 Jan. 1817, CO 42, vol. 359, 13; William Dickson to Claus, 5 Apr. 1816, NAC, Claus Papers, vol. 17, 262–4; Sir John Colborne to Sir George Murray, 20 Oct. 1829, NAC, CO 42, vol. 389, 234; E.G. Stanley to R.W. Hay, 18 Apr. 1828, NAC, CO 42, vol. 387, 379–94; *JMJN*, 323–4;

and Reg Good, 'Crown-Directed Colonization of Six Nations and Métis Land Reserves in Canada,' PhD thesis, University of Saskatchewan, 1994, 261–7

40 *JMJN*, lxxx–lxxxiii

41 *Niles Register*, 11 May 1816

42 Addison to Johnson, 30 Nov. 1816, NAC, RG 8, vol. 1241, 35–6; Norton to Addison, 7 Nov. 1816, RG 8, vol. 260, 450–1; Addison to Norton, 30 Nov. 1816, RG 8, vol. 1241, 36–7; George Bowles to Claus, 8 Jan. 1819, RG 8, vol. 1253, 9–12; J. McE. Murray, 'John Norton,' *OH* 37 (1945), 7–16; and *JMJN*, lxxx–lxxxii, lxxxvi–lxxxvii

43 *JMJN*, xci–xciii; and *Niagara Gleaner*, 20 Sept. 1823, which wrote: 'The King vs. Col. Norton. Tried for murder – found guilty of manslaughter only, and fined £25, which was instantly paid, and he discharged. His conduct in the affair (a duel with another Chief,) was truly honourable, and he would no doubt have been acquitted altogether, if he had not from feelings of delicacy withheld his best defence.'

44 Norton to John Harvey, n.d., *JMJN*, xci–xcii

45 John Norton Jr to John Norton Sr, n.d., *JMJN*, xcii–xciii; Karighwaycagh to J. Norton Sr, after 3 Aug. 1823, *JMJN*, xciii–xciv; J. Norton Sr to John Harvey, n.d., *JMJN*, xcii; and J. Norton Jr to J. Norton Sr, n.d., *JMJN*, xcii–xciii

46 Robert S. Allen, 'Claus, William,' *DCB*, 6:153; Carl F. Klinck, 'Norton, John,' *DCB*, 6:551–3; and *JMJN*, xcv–xcvii. Mohawk oral tradition is preserved in a letter from Albert Johnson to Lyman C. Draper, 11 Feb. 1878, State Historical Society of Wisconsin, Draper MSS, ser. F, Brant Papers, vol. 14, 23–4.

47 Tyendinaga Mohawks to Prevost, 4 July 1814, NAC, RG 10, vol. 3, 1451

48 Louis de Salaberry, memorandum on a Seven Nations council, 1 Oct. 1816, NAC, RG 8, vol. 260, 430–2; Addison to Johnson, 24 Jan. and 24 Mar. 1817, RG 8, vol. 1241, 56, 72

49 Robert J. Surtees, 'The Iroquois in Canada,' in Francis Jennings, ed., *The History and Culture of Iroquois Diplomacy* (Syracuse 1985), 71; Tanner, *Atlas*, 123; Jack A. Frisch, 'Iroquois in the West,' in *Handbook*, 544–6; and Hall, 'Native Limited Identities,' 151

50 Addison to Johnson, 30 July 1817, NAC, RG 8, vol. 1241, 97–8; and Franklin B. Hough, *A History of St. Lawrence and Franklin Counties* (Albany 1853), 159–62

51 Akwesasne people to ?, 26 May 1815, in E.J. Devine, *Historic Caugnawaga* (Montreal 1922), 326

52 Addison to Johnson, 9 Sept. 1816, 25 May and 13 June 1818, NAC, RG 8, vol. 1241, 19, 115, 117; William N. Fenton and Elisabeth Tooker, 'Mohawk,' in *Handbook*, 477; Surtees, 'Iroquois in Canada,' 72; and Hough, *St. Lawrence and Franklin Counties*, 177

53 Good, 'Crown-Directed Colonization,' 253–86

54 Gore to Bathurst, 2 Sept. 1816, NAC, RG 7, G12, vol. 9; and Sir Peregrine
   Maitland to Bathurst, 1 Nov. 1823, RG 7, G12, vol. 12
55 W.W. Baldwin, 'Thoughts on the Civilization of the Chippewa and Mississauga
   Tribes,' 1819, W.W. Baldwin Papers, Metropolitan Toronto Library; R.J. Routh
   to James Stewart, 7 Mar. 1834, Metropolitan Toronto Library, S.P. Jarvis
   Papers; Sir Francis Bond Head, *The Emigrant* (London 1846), 122; *Canadian
   Emigrant*, 20 June 1835; S.P. Jarvis to the Commissioners on Indian Affairs, 20
   Jan. 1843, Legislative Assembly of the Province of Canada, *Journals*, Appendix
   T (c. 1844); Province of Canada, 'Report of the Affairs of the Indians of
   Canada,' *Journals of the Legislative Assembly*, 1844–5, Appendix EEE (c. 1846);
   Norton to John Owen, 10 Aug. 1808, NAC, RG 10, vol. 2, 900–12; Norton to
   William Wilberforce, 1 Sept. 1808, RG 10, vol. 27, 15823–9; Robert S. Surtees,
   'The Development of an Indian Reserve Policy in Canada,' *OH* 61 (1969),
   87–98; Allen, *His Majesty's Indian Allies*, 177–83; Good, 'Crown-Directed
   Colonization,' xi–xiii; Surtees, *Indian Land Surrenders in Ontario, 1763–1867*
   (Ottawa 1983), 113, 118–19; Surtees, 'Iroquois in Canada,' 75; and C.M.
   Johnston, 'The Six Nations in the Grand River Valley, 1784–1847,' and Sally M.
   Weaver, 'The Iroquois,' both in Edward S. Rogers and Donald B. Smith, eds.,
   Aboriginal Ontario (Toronto 1994), 178–9, 183–7
56 Bruce Emerson Hill, *The Grand River Navigation Company* (Brantford 1994);
   and Good, 'Crown-Directed Colonization,' 287, 300, 307–41
57 George Phillpotts to Sir John Colborne, 17 Nov. 1837, NAC, Colborne Papers,
   vol. 2, 2952–5; Sir George Arthur to Lord Glenelg, 27 June 1838, CO 42, vol.
   448, 315; Mary Beacock Fryer, *Volunteers and Redcoats, Rebels and Raiders*
   (Ottawa 1987); and Elinor Kyte Senior, *Redcoats and Patriotes* (Ottawa 1985)
58 T.R. Preston, *Three Years' Residence in Canada* (London 1840), 1:144
59 E.g., photograph of Jimmy Johnson, 1849, Rochester Museum and Science
   Center, illustrated in *Handbook*, 452. An interesting archaeological analysis of
   the material culture of a Mohawk community during this period is Ian Kenyon
   and Neal Ferris, 'Investigations at Mohawk Village, 1983,' *Arch Notes* (Ontario
   Archaeological Society), Jan.–Feb. 1984.
60 Receipts, 1841, AO, Brock Monument Papers
61 Tyendinaga Mohawks to Jarvis, 26 Dec. 1840, AO, Brock Monument Papers
62 Preston, *Three Years' Residence in Canada*, 1:144
63 Six Nations of the Grand River to Arthur, 1840, AO, Brock Monument Papers
64 Quoted in *Touch the Earth*, T.C. McLuhan, comp. (New York 1971), 100
65 Fenton, 'Cass's Questions,' 118; Louis Jackson, *Our Caughnawagas in Egypt*
   (Montreal 1885); photograph in the collection of the Woodland Cultural Centre, Brantford, illustrated in Sheila Staats, *Warriors* (Brantford 1986), 16; and
   Laurence M. Hauptman, *The Iroquois in the Civil War* (Syracuse 1993)

66 Surtees, *Land Surrenders*, 67; and Douglas McCalla, *Planting the Province* (Toronto 1993), 86

67 E.g., 'The Battle between the Americans and the British during the War of 1812,' oral tradition as told by Roy Buck, MS, 1986, Woodland Cultural Centre; and George Loft, 'Indian Reminiscences of 1812,' *Saturday Night*, 11 Sept. 1909

68 Collection of the Woodland Cultural Centre

Appendix

1 Number of different nations of Indians living at the Grand River, 1810–11, *VSN*, 281; and State of the Indian tribes, Oct. 1812, NAC, RG 10, vol. 11, 16106–9

2 State of the Indian tribes, Oct. 1812, NAC, RG 10, vol. 11, 16106–9; Geoffrey York and Loreen Pindera, *People of the Pines*, rev. ed. (Toronto 1992), 90–2; and Jack A. Frisch, 'Iroquois in the West,' in *Handbook*, 544

3 Erastus Granger's statistical report, 1816, *R&W*, 30; David Landy, 'Tuscarora,' Harold Blau et al., 'Onondaga,' Marion E. White et al., 'Cayuga,' and Thomas S. Abler and Elisabeth Tooker, 'Seneca,' in *Handbook*, 521–2, 495–6, 501–2, 509. The figure of five thousand was the estimate of Indian agent Horatio Jones; see James E. Seaver, *A Narrative of the Life of Mrs. Mary Jemison* (1824; Syracuse 1990), 156.

4 William C. Sturtevant, 'Oklahoma Seneca-Cayuga,' in *Handbook*, 537–9

5 Seaver, *Mary Jemison*, 156

6 The British list of warriors in 1812 enumerated 8,850 warriors in the Old Northwest which presumably is a coarser estimate than those made with the Canadas and New York, where it was easier to count people. That figure suggests a population of 42,657.

7 Granger's council notes, 25 July 1813, *R&W*, 66; and Return of the Six Nations ... from the Grand, 26 Oct. 1813, *DH*, 8:97

Selected Bibliography

Because so much of the story relating to the Iroquois in the War of 1812 is spread thinly throughout many works and collections, I have restricted this bibliography to sources that include a concentrated body of information and that were particularly useful in preparing this study, either directly or in providing contextual data and analysis. Other primary and secondary sources may be found in the notes.

Primary Sources

Manuscripts

Archives of Ontario
    Brock Monument Papers
    Alexander Fraser Papers
    John Norton Papers
Buffalo and Erie County Historical Society
    A. Conger Goodyear War of 1812 Manuscripts
    Peter B. Porter Papers
National Archives of Canada
    Claus Papers
    Colonial Office Papers, CO 42 (Canada). Originals held at the Public Record Office, London
    Record Group 8, British Military Records
    Record Group 10, Indian Affairs
National Library of Scotland, Adv. MS. 46.6.5, Minutes of a council held at Burlington, April 1815
State Historical Society of Wisconsin, Draper MSS, Brant Papers

Vassar College Library, Jasper Parrish Papers in the Lucy Maynard Salmon Collection of Historical Manuscripts

Printed

Belknap, Jeremy, and Jedidiah Morse. 'Report on the Oneida, Stockbridge and Brotherton Indians, 1796.' *Indian Notes and Monographs* 54. New York: Museum of the American Indian 1955.

Black Hawk. *Life of Black Hawk.* 1834. Antoine Leclair, trans., J.B. Patterson, ed. Rev. ed., 1916, Milo Quaife, ed. Reprinted New York: Dover 1994.

Boyce, Douglas W., ed. 'A Glimpse of Iroquois Culture History through the Eyes of Joseph Brant and John Norton.' *Proceedings of the American Philosophical Society* 117 (1973).

Canada, Province of. *Appendix GGG to the Fourth Volume of the Journals of the Legislative Assembly of the Province of Canada, 1844–1845.* N.p. c. 1846.

Cruikshank, Ernest A., ed. 'Campaigns of 1812–14: Contemporary Narratives by Captain W.H. Merritt, Colonel William Claus, Lieut.-Colonel Matthew Elliott and Captain John Norton.' Niagara Historical Society *Transactions* 9 (1902).

– *The Documentary History of the Campaigns on the Niagara Frontier, 1812–14,* 9 vols. Welland and Lundy's Lane: Lundy's Lane Historical Society 1902–8.

Fenton, William N., ed. 'Answers to Governor Cass's Questions by Jacob Jemison, a Seneca [ca. 1821–1825].' *Ethnohistory* 16 (1969).

Gaines, E.P. 'Remarks of Major General E.P. Gaines Relative to the Civilization of the [Indians].' *American State Papers.* (Class V, Military Affairs.) Washington: Gales and Seaton 1860.

Governor Blacksnake. *Chainbreaker: The Revolutionary War Memoirs of Governor Blacksnake as told to Benjamin Williams.* Thomas S. Abler, ed. Lincoln: University of Nebraska Press 1989.

Johnston, Charles Murray, ed. *The Valley of the Six Nations: A Collection of Documents on the Indian Lands of the Grand River.* Toronto: Champlain Society 1964.

Lafitau, Joseph François. *Customs of the American Indians Compared with the Customs of Primitive Times.* 1724. William N. Fenton and Elizabeth L. Moore, eds., and trans. 2 vols. Toronto: Champlain Society 1974–7.

Le Couteur, John. *Merry Hearts Make Light Days: The War of 1812 Journal of Lieutenant John Le Couteur, 104th Foot.* Donald E. Graves, ed. Ottawa: Carleton University Press 1993.

Long, John. *Voyages and Travels of an Indian Interpreter and Trader.* 1791. Toronto: Coles 1974.

Lowrie, Walter, and Matthew St Clair Clarke, eds. *American State Papers.* (Class II, Indian Affairs, 4.) Washington: United States Government 1932.

Marcoux, Joseph. 'Mémoire pour la défense de la neutralité des Sauvages de S. Regis dans la dernière guerre avec les Américans.' *Le Bulletin des recherches historiques* 67 (1961).

McFeely, George. 'Chronicle of Valor: The Journal of a Pennsylvania Officer in the War of 1812.' John C. Fredriksen, ed. *Western Pennsylvania Historical Magazine* 67 (1984).

Norton, John. *The Journal of Major John Norton, 1816.* Carl F. Klinck and James J. Talman, eds. Toronto: Champlain Society 1970.

– *Memoirs of a Mohawk War Chief: John Norton/Teyoninhokarawen, 1812–1814.* Carl Benn, ed. Forthcoming.

Public Speeches Delivered at the Village of Buffalo, on the 6th and 8th days of July, 1812, by Hon. Erastus Granger, Indian Agent, and Red Jacket, One of the Principal Chiefs and Speakers of the Seneca Nation, Respecting the Part the Six Nations Would Take in the Present War Against Great Britain. Buffalo: S.H. and H.A. Salisbury 1812.

Seaver, James E. *A Narrative of the Life of Mrs. Mary Jemison.* 1824. Syracuse: Syracuse University Press 1990.

Severance, Frank H. 'Narratives of Early Mission Work on the Niagara Frontier and Buffalo Creek.' Buffalo Historical Society *Publications* 6 (1903).

Smith, Michael. *Geographical View of the Province of Upper Canada; and Promiscuous Remarks on the Government.* Philadelphia: John Bioren 1813.

Snyder, Charles M., ed. *Red and White on the New York Frontier: A Struggle for Survival; Insights from the Papers of Erastus Granger, Indian Agent.* Harrison, NY: Harbor Hill Books, 1978.

Wood, William, ed. *Select British Documents of the Canadian War of 1812.* 4 vols. Toronto: Champlain Society 1920–8.

Secondary Sources

Books and Monographs

Alfred, Gerald. *Heeding the Voices of Our Ancestors: Kahnawake Mohawk Politics and the Rise of Native Nationalism.* Toronto: Oxford University Press 1995.

Allen, Robert S. *His Majesty's Indian Allies: British Indian Policy and the Defence of Canada, 1774–1815.* Toronto: Dundurn 1992.

Babcock, Louis L. *The War of 1812 on the Niagara Frontier.* Buffalo: Buffalo Historical Society 1927.

Bradley, James W. *Evolution of the Onondaga Iroquois: Accommodating Change, 1500–1650.* Syracuse: Syracuse University Press 1987.

Calloway, Colin G. *Crown and Calumet: British–Indian Relations, 1783–1815.* Norman: University of Oklahoma Press 1987.

Cruikshank, Ernest A. *The Fight in the Beechwoods*. Niagara: Niagara Historical Society 1889.

Dennis, Matthew. *Cultivating a Landscape of Peace: Iroquois–European Encounters in Seventeenth-Century America*. Ithaca: Cornell University Press 1993.

Devine, E.J. *Historic Caugnawaga*. Montreal: Messenger Press 1922.

Dickason, Olive Patricia. *Canada's First Nations: A History of Founding Peoples from Earliest Times*. Toronto: McClelland and Stewart 1992.

Dowd, Gregory Evans. *A Spirited Resistance: The North American Indian Struggle for Unity, 1745–1815*. Baltimore: Johns Hopkins University Press 1992.

Everest, Allan S. *The War of 1812 in the Champlain Valley*. Syracuse: Syracuse University Press 1981.

Fitzgibbon, Mary Agnes. *A Veteran of 1812: The Life of James Fitzgibbon*. Toronto: William Briggs 1894.

Flexner, James Thomas. *Mohawk Baronet: A Biography of Sir William Johnson*. 1959. Rev. ed. 1979. Syracuse: Syracuse University Press 1989.

Foster, Michael K., et al., eds. *Extending the Rafters: Interdisciplinary Approaches to Iroquoian Studies*. Albany: State University of New York 1984.

Fredrickson, N. Jaye. *The Covenant Chain: Indian Ceremonial and Trade Silver*. Ottawa: National Museums of Canada 1980.

Gilman, Carolyn. *Where Two Worlds Meet: The Great Lakes Fur Trade*. St Paul: Minnesota Historical Society 1982.

Graves, Donald E. *The Battle of Lundy's Lane on the Niagara in 1814*. Baltimore: Nautical and Aviation Publishing 1993.

– *Red Coats and Grey Jackets: The Battle of Chippawa, 5 July 1814*. Toronto: Dundurn 1994.

Graymont, Barbara. *The Iroquois in the American Revolution*. Syracuse: Syracuse University Press 1972.

Hamilton, T.M. *Colonial Frontier Guns*. Chadron, Neb.: Fur Trade Press 1980.

Heidenreich, Conrad E. *Huronia: A History and Geography of the Huron Indians, 1600–1650*. Toronto: McClelland and Stewart 1971.

Hitsman, J. Mackay. *The Incredible War of 1812*. 1965. Toronto: University of Toronto Press 1972.

Horsman, Reginald. *Expansion and American Indian Policy, 1783–1812*. 1967. Norman: University of Oklahoma Press 1992.

Houghton, Frederick. *The History of the Buffalo Creek Reservation*. Buffalo: Buffalo Historical Society 1920.

Jaenen, Cornelius J. *Friend and Foe: Aspects of French–Amerindian Cultural Contact in the Sixteenth and Seventeenth Centuries*. Toronto: McClelland and Stewart 1976.

Jennings, Francis. *The Ambiguous Iroquois Empire: The Covenant Chain Confederation of Indian Tribes with the English Colonies from Its Beginnings to the Lancaster Treaty of 1744.* New York: W.W. Norton 1984.

– *Empire of Fortune: Crowns, Colonies and Tribes in the Seven Years War in America.* New York: W.W. Norton 1988.

Jennings, Francis, et al. *The History and Culture of Iroquois Diplomacy.* Syracuse: Syracuse University Press 1985.

Johnson, Elias. *Legends, Traditions and Laws of the Iroquois, or Six Nations, and History of the Tuscarora Indians.* Lockport: Union Printing and Publishing, 1881.

Kelsay, Isabel Thompson. *Joseph Brant, 1743–1807: Man of Two Worlds.* Syracuse: Syracuse University Press 1984.

Malone, Patrick M. *The Skulking Way of War: Technology and Tactics among the New England Indians.* Lanham: Madison Books 1991.

Morgan, Lewis Henry. *League of the Iroquois.* 1851. Secaucas: Citadel 1972.

Phillips, Ruth B. *Patterns of Power: The Jasper Grant Collection and Great Lakes Indian Art of the Early Nineteenth Century.* Kleinburg, Ont.: McMichael Canadian Collection 1984.

Richter, Daniel K. *Ordeal of the Longhouse: The Peoples of the Iroquois League in the Era of European Colonization.* Chapel Hill: University of North Carolina Press 1992.

Rogers, Edward S., and Donald B. Smith, eds. *Aboriginal Ontario: Historical Perspectives on the First Nations.* Toronto: Dundurn 1994.

Snow, Dean R. *The Iroquois.* Cambridge, Mass.: Blackwell 1994.

Staats, Sheila. *Warriors: A Resource Guide.* Brantford: Woodland Cultural Centre 1986.

Stagg, J.C.A. *Mr. Madison's War: Politics, Diplomacy, and Warfare in the Early American Republic, 1783–1830.* Princeton: Princeton University Press 1983.

Stanley, George F.G. *The War of 1812: Land Operations.* Ottawa: Canadian War Museum 1983.

Stevens, Paul L. *A King's Colonel at Niagara, 1774–1776.* Youngstown: Old Fort Niagara Association 1987.

Stone, William L. *Life of Joseph Brant – Thayendanegea.* 1838. Secaucas: Corinth 1972.

– *The Life and Times of Sa-go-ye-wat-ha, or Red Jacket.* Albany: J. Munsell, 1866.

Sugden, John. *Tecumseh's Last Stand.* Norman: University of Oklahoma Press 1985.

Surtees, Robert J. *Indian Land Surrenders in Ontario, 1763–1867.* Ottawa: Department of Indian and Northern Affairs 1983.

Sword, Wiley. *President Washington's Indian War: The Struggle for the Old Northwest, 1790–1795.* Norman: University of Oklahoma Press 1985.

Tanner, Helen Hornbeck, ed. *Atlas of Great Lakes Indian History.* Norman: University of Oklahoma Press 1987.

Tooker, Elisabeth, ed. *Lewis H. Morgan on Iroquois Material Culture*. Tucson: University of Arizona Press 1994.

Trigger, Bruce, ed. *Handbook of North American Indians* 15 (Northeast). Washington: Smithsonian Institution 1978.

– *The Children of Aataentsic: A History of the Huron People to 1660*. 1976. Kingston and Montreal: McGill-Queen's University Press 1987.

– *Natives and Newcomers: Canada's 'Heroic Age' Reconsidered*. Kingston and Montreal: McGill-Queen's University Press 1985.

United States Department of the Interior. *Biographical and Historical Index of American Indians and Persons Involved in Indian Affairs*. Boston: G.K. Hall and Company 1966.

Wallace, Anthony F.C. *The Death and Rebirth of the Seneca*. 1969. New York: Vintage 1972.

Washburn, Wilcomb E., ed. *Handbook of North American Indians* 4 (History of Indian–White Relations). Washington: Smithsonian Institution 1988.

White, Richard. *The Middle Ground: Indians, Empires, and Republics in the Great Lakes Region, 1650–1815*. New York: Cambridge University Press 1991.

Articles

Allen, Robert S. 'The British Indian Department on the Frontier in North America, 1755–1830.' *Occasional Papers in Archaeology and History* 14. Ottawa: Parks Canada 1975.

Bailey, De Witt. 'Those Board of Ordnance Indian Guns – Again!' *Museum of the Fur Trade Quarterly* 21 (1985).

– 'Those Board of Ordnance Indian Guns – Again! – Supplement.' *Museum of the Fur Trade Quarterly* 21 (1985).

Benn, Carl. 'Iroquois Warfare, 1812–1814,' *War along the Niagara: Essays on the War of 1812 and Its Legacy*. R. Arthur Bowler, ed. Youngstown: Old Fort Niagara Association 1991.

– 'The Iroquois Nadir of 1796.' *Niagara – 1796: The Fortress Possessed*. Brian Leigh Dunnigan, ed. Youngstown: Old Fort Niagara Association 1996.

Burke, Lee. 'Wilson Cypher Guns – Chief's Guns of the Revolution.' American Society of Arms Collectors *Bulletin* 1996.

Cruikshank, Ernest A. 'Reminiscences of Colonel Claus.' *Canadiana* 1 (1889).

– 'The Employment of the Indians in the War of 1812.' *Annual Report of the American Historical Association for the Year 1895* (1895).

– 'Blockade of Fort George.' Niagara Historical Society *Transactions* 3 (1898).

– 'From Isle aux Noix to Châteauguay: A Study of the Military Operations on the

Frontier of Lower Canada in 1812 and 1813.' *Proceedings and Transactions of the Royal Society of Canada* 3rd ser., 7 (1913).

Egles, Ross. 'Canadian Indian Treaty Guns.' *Canadian Journal of Arms Collecting* 14 (1976).

Eid, Leroy V. '"National" War among Indians of Northeastern North America.' *Canadian Review of American Studies* 16 (1985).

– 'American Indian Military Leadership: St. Clair's 1791 Defeat.' *Journal of Military History* 57 (1993).

Evans, Jack. 'A Forgotten Battle of the War of 1812 [Sandy Creek].' *Magazine of American History* 29 (1893).

Fenton, William N. 'The Hyde de Neuville Portraits of New York Savages in 1807–1808.' *New-York Historical Society Quarterly* 38 (1954).

– 'Leadership in the Northeastern Woodlands of North America.' *American Indian Quarterly* 10 (1986).

Graymont, Barbara. 'New York State Indian Policy after the Revolution.' *New York History* 57 (1976).

Guthman, William H. 'Frontiersmen's Tomahawks of the Colonial and Federal Periods.' *Antiques* 119 (1981).

Hadlock, Wendell S. 'War among the Northeastern Woodland Indians.' *American Anthropologist* 44 (1947).

Hagedorn, Nancy L. 'A Friend to Go Between Them: The Interpreter as Cultural Broker during Anglo–Iroquois Councils, 1740–1770.' *Ethnohistory* 35 (1988).

Hall, Anthony. 'Native Limited Identities and Newcomer Metropolitanism in Upper Canada, 1814–1867.' *Old Ontario: Essays in Honour of J.M.S. Careless.* David Keane and Colin Read, eds. Toronto: Dundurn 1990.

Johnston, Charles Murray. 'William Claus and John Norton: A Struggle for Power in Old Ontario.' *Ontario History* 57 (1965).

Kimball, Jeffrey. 'The Battle of Chippawa: Infantry Tactics of the War of 1812.' *Military Affairs* 32 (1968).

King, J.C.H. 'Woodland Artifacts from the Studio of Benjamin West, 1738–1820.' *American Indian Art* 17 (1991).

Klinck, Carl F. 'New Light on John Norton.' *Transactions of the Royal Society of Canada* 4th ser., 4 (1966).

– 'Norton, John (Snipe, Teyoninhokarawen).' *Dictionary of Canadian Biography* 6. Toronto: University of Toronto Press 1987.

Mahon, John K. 'Anglo-American Methods of Indian Warfare, 1676–1794.' *Mississippi Valley Historical Review* 45 (1958–9).

Murray, J. McE. 'John Norton.' *Ontario History* 37 (1945).

Nadeau, Gabriel. 'Techniques of Indian Scalping.' *Bulletin of the History of Medicine* 10 (1941).

Otterbein, Keith F. 'Why the Iroquois Won: An Analysis of Iroquois Military Tactics.' *Ethnohistory* 11 (1964).

Parker, Arthur C. 'The Senecas in the War of 1812.' *New York History* 15 (1916).

Phillips, Ruth B. 'Like a Star I Shine: Northern Woodlands Artistic Traditions.' *The Spirit Sings: Artistic Traditions of Canada's First Peoples.* Julia D. Harrison, et al., eds. Toronto: McClelland and Stewart 1987.

Richter, Daniel. 'War and Culture: The Iroquois Experience.' *William and Mary Quarterly* 40 (1983).

Robie, Henry. 'Red Jacket's Reply: Problems in the Verification of a Native American Speech Text.' *New York Folklore* 12 (1986).

Sciulli, Paul W. and Richard M. Gramly. 'Analysis of the Fort Laurens, Ohio Skeletal Sample.' *American Journal of Physical Anthropology* 80 (1989).

Shannon, Timothy J. 'Dressing for Success on the Mohawk Frontier: Hendrick, William Johnson, and the Indian Fashion.' *William and Mary Quarterly* 53 (1996).

Smith, Donald B. 'Tekarihogen.' *Dictionary of Canadian Biography* 6. Toronto: University of Toronto Press 1987.

Stanley, George F.G. 'The Significance of the Six Nations Participation in the War of 1812.' *Ontario History* 55 (1963).

– 'The Indians in the War of 1812.' *The Defended Border: Upper Canada and the War of 1812*, Morris Zaslow, ed. Toronto: Macmillan 1964.

Surtees, Robert J. 'The Development of an Indian Reserve Policy in Canada.' *Ontario History* 61 (1969).

Whitfield, Carol. 'The Battle of Queenston Heights.' *Occasional Papers in Archaeology and History* 11. Ottawa: Parks Canada 1974.

Theses

Benn, Carl. 'The Iroquois in the War of 1812.' PhD, York University 1995.

Cooper, Virginia. 'A Political History of the Grand River Iroquois, 1784–1880.' MA, Carleton University 1975.

Glenney, Daniel J. 'An Ethnohistory of the Grand River Iroquois and the War of 1812.' MA, University of Guelph 1973.

Good, Reg. 'Crown-Directed Colonization of Six Nations and Métis Land Reserves in Canada.' PhD, University of Saskatchewan 1994.

Green, Andrea Elizabeth. 'Land, Leadership, and Conflict: The Six Nations' Early Years on the Grand River.' MA, University of Western Ontario 1984.

Hall, Anthony J. 'The Red Man's Burden: Land, Law, and the Lord in the Indian Affairs of Upper Canada, 1791–1858.' PhD, University of Toronto 1984.

Ostola, Lawrence. 'The Seven Nations of Canada and the American Revolution 1774–1783.' MA, Université de Montréal 1989.

Index

Abenakis, 15
Adams, John Quincy, 175
Addison, Robert, 143, 210n. 59
adoption of outsiders, 13–14, 53, 120, 211n. 79
Akwesasne: founded, 15; divided by international border, 19; New Yorkers' fears of, 30–1; crises and skirmishes at, 62–3, 152; warriors at Ogdensburg, 104; at blockade of Fort George, 114; in 1813 Montreal campaign, 144–5; smuggling, 155; post-war problems, 188. *See also* Seven Nations of Canada
alcohol: abuse, 23; drinking after battle, 149, 150, 165, 168; native comments on Euroamerican practices, 67, 132; in recruiting warriors, 63, 88; temperance, 24, 25, 131–2
Algonkians, 10, 15, 158. *See also individual tribal names*; western tribes
Algonkins at Kanesatake, 195
Allegeny Reservation, 40, 65, 131, 132, 184. *See also* Iroquois in New York and Pennsylvania
American Revolution, 16–18, 54, 60;

in American thought, 20–1, 27; and the decline of torture, 53, 83; in Iroquois memory, 32, 38, 40, 44, 52, 61, 63, 87, 109, 110, 146
Amherstburg: in 1812, 45, 48, 49; in 1813, 104, 105, 145, 147; in 1814, 155, 170
Armstrong, John, 106–7, 124, 130–1
Arosa (or Silver Heels) (Seneca), 42, 43–4
Article IX, Treaty of Ghent, 176–8, 179
assassination, 60, 113
assimilation and acculturation: before 1763, 14, 16; views of William Johnson and George Washington, 15–16; during early reservation period, 20–1; reformers, 24–6, 38; conservatives, 25–6, 36; impact of legal systems, 53, 135–6; changing allegiances, 181, 244n. 20; post-war acceleration, 183–4, 188–9, 192–3. *See also* land issues; subsistence and economy; torture, terror, and desecration; warfare, aboriginal
avenging deaths, concepts of, 53–4, 59, 181, 186–7; 211n. 78